MODERN APPLIED
PSYCHOLOGY
(PGPS-145)

Pergamon Titles of Related Interest

Related Journals

PERGAMON GENERAL PSYCHOLOGY SERIES
EDITORS
Arnold P. Goldstein, Syracuse University
Leonard Krasner, Stanford University & SUNY at Stony Brook

MODERN APPLIED PSYCHOLOGY

ARNOLD P. GOLDSTEIN
Syracuse University
LEONARD KRASNER
Stanford University & State University of
New York at Stony Brook

PERGAMON PRESS
New York   Oxford   Beijing   Frankfurt   São Paulo   Sydney   Tokyo   Toronto

U.S.A.	Pergamon Press, Inc., Maxwell House, Fairview Park, Elmsford, New York 10523, U.S.A.
U.K.	Pergamon Press plc, Headington Hill Hall, Oxford OX3 0BW, England
PEOPLE'S REPUBLIC OF CHINA	Pergamon Press, Room 4037, Qianmen Hotel, Beijing, People's Republic of China
FEDERAL REPUBLIC OF GERMANY	Pergamon Press GmbH, Hammerweg 6, D-6242 Kronberg, Federal Republic of Germany
BRAZIL	Pergamon Editora Ltda, Rua Eça de Queiros, 346, CEP 04011, Paraiso, São Paulo, Brazil
AUSTRALIA	Pergamon Press Australia Pty Ltd., P.O. Box 544, Potts Point, N.S.W. 2011, Australia
JAPAN	Pergamon Press, 5th Floor, Matsuoka Central Building, 1-7-1 Nishishinjuku, Shinjuku-ku, Tokyo 160, Japan
CANADA	Pergamon Press Canada Ltd., Suite No. 271, 253 College Street, Toronto, Ontario, Canada M5T 1R5

Copyright © 1987 Pergamon Press, Inc.

First printing 1987
Reprinted 1988

Library of Congress Cataloging in Publication Data

Goldstein, Arnold P.
    Modern applied psychology.

    (Pergamon general psychology series ; 145)
    Bibliography: p.
    1. Psychology, Applied. I. Krasner, Leonard,
1924-   . II. Title. III. Series. [DNLM:
1. Psychology, Applied. BF 636 G624m]
BF636.G56   1987   158   86-22493
ISBN 0-08-034501-8
ISBN 0-08-034500-X (soft)

Printed in Great Britain by A. Wheaton & Co. Ltd., Exeter

Dedicated with love and admiration to

— Susan and Cindy Goldstein,
my daughters and very special friends

A. P. G.

— All the Krasner family

L. K.

Contents

1 History of Applied Psychology

Modern applied psychology begins with the tale of a psychologist, John B. Watson, and the application of his behavioral brand of psychology, particularly via advertising, to the personal, social, and community life of American society.

Our major point throughout this book is that applied psychology is not the simple procedure of *applying* a basic science called *psychology*. Rather, there is a complex interrelationship between psychological theory, application, historical context, social influence, and the individual behavior of the applier and the recipient of application (which includes all of us). Watson, with his application to advertising, is a prototype of and, in itself, a major influence on, all of our lives and as such, sets the stage for the other illustrations of applications to be described. ·

John B. Watson was born in 1878 on a farm outside the small town of Greenville, South Carolina. This simple piece of information is usually used to emphasize the fact that the roots of the founder of behaviorism were in 19th-century rural America. Such a setting was to affect his subsequent career. Growing up on a farm was to train him in tinkering with his environment, particularly machinery, and in getting things done. During his college training, at the University of Chicago, he was initially uncertain as to what field to go into. However, he was attracted to working with rats in the laboratory, which at that period meant entering the emerging field called *psychology*. After completion of his doctorate in 1903, his research and writings very quickly established a national reputation for him, resulting in his appointment as professor at Johns Hopkins University at, even then, the remarkably young age of 29. His rise to fame, including his presidency of the American Psychologial Association, was rapid. However, in 1920 he was abruptly dismissed from his professorship because of a juicy divorce scandal that received national publicity. It was at this point that his impact on applied psychology, particularly in advertising, was to begin in earnest. One of the first national advertising agencies, J. Walter Thompson in New York, was attracted to Watson and to the potential in the application of psychological techniques to the business of *selling* commodities.

Watson soon became quite happy with this new, wider, latitude for research and application than had ever been possible within a university. In fact, he later commented that he "began to learn that it can be just as thrilling to watch the growth of a sales curve of a new product as to watch the learning curve of animals or men" (Buckley, 1982, p. 212). The New Yorker magazine, in a profile on Watson, nicely captured and simply expressed the significance of his being hired by the Thompson agency: It was done so that "the doctor could apply his scientific knowledge to the sale of commercial products" (Macgowan, 1928, p. 31).

Watson was to be a fundamental influence on the direction and development of advertising from the 1920s on. By the 1980s the application of psychology had become an integral part of the field, and psychologists functioning in applied areas are no less respected than their academic colleagues and are far more numerous. This was not so in the 1920s for two reasons. Applications of psychology were considered undignified and were identified with Watson, "that Behaviorist."

The shift from the laboratory to the marketplace was particularly noted and encouraged by Watson. Market research became a basic part of advertising campaigns. Actually, advertisers instituted their "objective" research to test consumer reactions to aspects of their own products.

As part of the training process, Watson worked for several months as a clerk in Macy's, to learn about the atmosphere of store selling. For example, he noticed that items would sell better if they were close to the cash register on the shoppers' way out. When you go to the supermarket this week you will probably notice on your way out the candy and popular magazines, material you were unlikely to seek out in the store, near the cash register. All this is due to early environmental design originated by Watson.

An interesting example of Watson's approach to the advertising of specific products were the plans for Johnson and Johnson's Baby Powder (a product likely to have been sprinkled on most of us, reader and writers alike). Watson incorporated demographic data, in that he intended the advertising campaign to appeal to young, white, upwardly mobile, middle-class mothers expecting their first children. The ad campaign emphasized the cleanliness of the baby powder as a means of avoiding infection in the infants. The aim of this applied psychology was to arouse the fear response on the part of the mother that she might be incompetent in safeguarding the health of her child.

Another psychological technique used with the baby powder was the endorsements by "experts." For this particular product, Watson offered the testimony of scientific experts, individuals who were qualified to speak on any topic with scientific authority. Thus, the baby powder was endorsed by a Dr. Holt, apparently the Dr. Spock of the day. Other kinds of experts were prominent public figures or entertainers who would praise a particular product. Watson's greatest coup could well have been persuading the current queens of Romania and of Spain (for $5,000 each) to endorse the then new product, Pond's Cold Cream. As we all know, the use of testimonial endorsements has continued to this day.

Watson's role in the application of psychology, Watsonian brand, extended beyond advertising into the business and industrial worlds. He contended that tests could be developed to measure the performance of office workers. Such tests could both measure and control the activity of individual employees. Beyond such testing, the psychologist could develop managerial techniques that would enhance the work efficiency of offices and industries (D. Cohen, 1979).

Watson was also the premier pop psychologist of his day, as manifested by articles in newspapers and popular magazines of the day (*McCall's, Harper's, Parents Magazine, Cosmopolitan*, etc.) (Buckley, 1982). In effect, he was advising the great masses on how to live and raise children. Watson was, therefore, the exemplar and prototype of the psychologist who tells the public *how to* live their lives by applying psychology for better living, health, happiness, wealth, sexual satisfaction, and all the good things of life.

Watson became involved in the development of private consulting firms (such as the Scott Company and the Psychological Corporation) in order to extend the influence of the psychologist from the laboratory to the market-place. He also felt that such organizations would strengthen the position of the applied psychologist within the field of psychology. He thought that emphasis on practical techniques would attract students and therefore expand the field.

Watson's major contribution to advertising was that, in effect, he made it *applied* psychology. He argued (in his 1919 *Psychology from the Standpoint of a Behaviorist*) that society and business should apply psychology, so that it could more effectively *control* people in the belief (hope?) that it was for the betterment of society. This is a belief that has characterized applied psychology throughout its history. In a sense, this is a justification and a rationale that the professional applier is doing a socially accepted, even desirable, thing.

The concepts of the laboratory itself were applied to the real-life situation in that the consumer became the experimental subject in the "laboratory" of the marketplace. The Watsonian version of behaviorist principles could then be applied to predict and influence the behavior of the consumer, or subject. The emotional responses of the individual consumer could be conditioned to affect his or her buying behavior in the "correct" direction. Watson did not preclude, in fact, he actually encouraged, the use of laboratory testing of procedures before application in the broader world. This was not an absolute necessity but an enhancement of the eventual effectiveness of the techniques used.

Thus, in the broadest sense, Watson believed that *social control* was the major result of applying psychology. Psychologists had to go beyond merely predicting human behavior; they had to formulate laws to enable society to control that behavior. In effect, the psychologist was replacing the clergyman and the politician in the maintenance of social order. Behaviorism would replace the traditional trial-and-error methods of the political and social process with the new and efficient scientifically based technology. A basic element in the belief system of behavioral psychologists, led by Watson, was that behavioral and psychological theory were as applicable in industry and the marketplace as in the laboratory. Psychology as behaviorists viewed it was, from its very inception, a psychology of *application*. Watson was not the only applied psychologist of the era but was part of a generation of professionals functioning in the early part of the century. The focus of this group was on applying their talents and training to the solution of problems created by an expanding industrial economy.

The introduction to a book on modern applied psychology should be quite simple—define the three terms in the title and then proceed with illustrations of the application of psychology to modern life. But it is not that easy, because the meanings of these terms have been in a continual state of change. Our goal in this book is to communicate an understanding of this process, because, perhaps more than any other field of human endeavor, modern applied psychology affects all of our lives virtually everyday. Throughout, even though our aim is to be quite comprehensive in our coverage, we can only discuss a portion of the applications of psychology that have so thoroughly permeated our society. In many instances the application is not even recognized as an application but is seen as a natural or commonsense thing.

Of the three title terms, *modern* is probably the easiest to define because it means "just now," "of or characteristic of the present or recent times" (Webster, 1977, p. 739). But when does modern start? We will concentrate on illustrations from the past decade, but they can be understood and appreciated only in the context of the historical development of applied psychology, going back at least to the early part of the 20th century.

The term *applied psychology* itself implies that there are two separate elements involved. First, there is a basic *science* of psychology involving rigorous laboratory research, often with animal subjects, from which theoretical models and principles of human behavior are developed. These basic principles are then *applied* to real-life situations outside the laboratory to bring about desired changes in human behavior. This view implies two virtually distinct entities, a basic and an applied psychology. However, our own view is to agree with those who argue that theory and practice are an integral whole. Psychologists (e.g., Dewey, 1899) have been stressing the view that theory and practice, basic and applied, are interwoven and are a social, cultural product of a given period of time. "Psychological methods, in short, derive from a time and place based conception of what people are or can be" (Sarason, 1981b, p. 143).

Within the field of psychology itself, the basic–applied issue has been expressed in terms of professional organization. Prior to 1945 there were two separate organizations: The American Association for Applied Psychology for practitioners and the American Psychological Association, in which scientifically oriented psychologists were members. In 1946 the two organizations united into the present-day American Psychological Association. The significance of this reorganization for the application of psychology is perhaps captured in the description of the goals of the new organization.

> The constitution had formerly stated that the object of the APA was the advancement of psychology as a science. The corresponding statement in the new constitution reads: "The object of the American Psychological Association shall be to advance psychology as a science, as a profession, and as a means of promoting human welfare." (Wolfe, 1946, p. 3)

It is the phrase "promoting human welfare" that has important implications for the direction of psychology and its applications. Implicit in this phrase are the questions of what is best for human welfare and *who decides?*

These issues shall be with us for the remainder of this text and, of course, are ever present in our daily lives.

HISTORICAL CONTEXT

Although we are emphasizing throughout the extent of the "modern" (1980s) applications of psychology, it is ironic, and perhaps exhilarating, to note that our path was laid out for us in the early part of the century. The first issue of the *Journal of Applied Psychology* in March 1917 (yes, 1917, in the midst of World War I), edited by G. Stanley Hall, one of the most reknowned psychologists of the day, defined the scope of the journal as including the following:

1. The application of psychology to vocational activities, such as law, art, public speaking, industrial and commercial work, and problems of business appeal
2. Studies of individual mentalities, such as types of character, special talents, genius, and individual differences, including the problems of mental diagnosis and vocational prognosis
3. The influence of general environmental conditions, such as climate, weather, humidity, temperature; also such conditions as nutrition and fatigue
4. The psychology of everyday activities, such as reading, writing, speaking, singing, playing games or musical instruments, sports, and the like

In effect, this list embraces much of the material included in this very *modern text* we are presenting. The extent of the field is further emphasized in the Foreword to the journal, in which the editors (G. S. Hall, Baird, & Geissler, 1917) very nicely summarized the then (and still current) scope of this all-encompassing field.

> The past few years have witnessed an unprecedented interest in the extension of the application of psychology to various fields of human activity. Teachers and administrators of educational affairs were among the first to realize that the findings of the psychologist may be of value in the solving of practical problems; and the voluminous and growing literature of educational psychology testifies to a widespread belief that psychology is a valuable asset to the educator. Within the past decade one finds increasing evidence, in various quarters, of an equally widespread but more recent conviction that a knowledge of psychology is no less serviceable in the practice of medicine, in the administration of justice, and in various other pursuits. And attempts are now being made to apply the principles of psychology to the solving of problems in such widely divergent disciplines as history, religion, sociology, art, politics, and language.
>
> But perhaps the most strikingly original endeavor to utilize the methods and the results of psychological investigation has been in the realm of business.

This movement began with the psychology of advertising, — where at a relatively early date investigators attacked the analytic problems of determining what psychological factors are concerned in the "appeal of the advertisement," and the practical problem of utilizing and controlling these factors more judiciously and effectively, — but it soon spread to the adjacent field of salesmanship. (p. 5)

Finally, on the issue of the goals of application and the relationship between *basic* and *applied*, the editors took a position with which we agree and to which we will repeatedly return.

Yet the problem which is here concerned is one which must appeal to the interest of every psychologist who besides being a "pure scientist" also cherishes the hope that in addition to throwing light upon the theoretical problems of his science, his findings may also contribute their quota to the sum-total of human happiness; . . . The problem, therefore, is one which touches the psychologist not only as a scientist but in his relations to his fellowmen and to the practical concerns of life; . . . The psychologist finds that the only distinction between pure and applied science is already obscured in his domain; and he is beginning to realize that applied psychology can no longer be relegated to a distinctly inferior plane. (p. 6)

Early Appliers of Psychology

The attempt to apply the findings and insights of psychological research conducted in laboratory and field settings to diverse real-world contexts has a long and varied history in American psychology. Such efforts began in the 1890s, under the energetic leadership of Hugo Munsterberg at Harvard (Moskowitz, 1977). He was born in Germany and spent the last 25 years of his life in the United States.

In his 1915 book, *Psychology: General and Applied*, Munsterberg sought to bring psychology's collective knowledge at that early stage of its development to bear upon a host of functional concerns. In this manner, he examined laboratory research on psychophysics, vision, audition, central nervous system functioning, perception, and much more for its applied implications in education, economics, the law, medical practice, leisure, "psychotechnics," the arts, and other areas of real-world, human concern. Between 1907 and 1916, while at the Harvard Psychological Laboratory, Munsterberg wrote a series of papers and books that founded and defined the field of applied psychology, although clearly he was not the first to *apply* psychology.

Currently, applications of psychology are routinely accepted in virtually every aspect of our society. Munsterberg advocated, suggested, and illustrated these extensions at a time when psychology was still in its infancy. He argued that:

If experimental psychology is to enter a period of practical service, it can not be a question of simply using the ready-made results for ends which were not in view during the experiments. What is needed is to adjust research to the practical problems themselves . . . Applied Psychology will then become an independent experimental science which stands related to the ordinary experimental psychology as engineering to physics . . . those fields of practical life which come first may be said to be education, medicine, art, economics and law. (1908, pp. 8–9)

He was offering a prototype of what applied psychology was to become in American society within the next half century. It was his influence that helped shift psychology "from a totally academic discipline . . . into a broad field with strong professional and applied aspects" (Moskowitz, 1977, p. 833).

Among the very earliest books to apply psychology were two treatises by a noted and respected psychologist of the day, Walter Dill Scott (*The Theory of Advertising*, 1903, and *Psychology of Advertising*, 1908). Here, indeed, were applications of the then emerging science of psychology to a very specific domain, that of *advertising*. Scott, director of the School of Salesmanship at the University of Pittsburgh, was applying the ideas of William James to advertising. He emphasized the application of the "law of suggestion" to influencing the buying behavior of what was considered to be a nonrational consuming public.

In fact, Scott was actually the first psychologist to hold the title of Professor of Applied Psychology at an American university when he received that appointment from Carnegie Institute of Technology in 1915. Along with other psychologists, including John Watson, he founded in 1919 the first consulting company in the United States (appropriately called the Scott Company) to be devoted to applications of psychology to industrial settings. What was to develop into the major company in the industrial application of psychology was the Psychological Corporation, headed by James McKeen Cattell and other influential psychologists of the era.

American involvement in World War I stimulated the development of a new role for applying psychology to a wide range of human problems. Psychologists emerged from the war with a wide reputation for being experts in all aspects of personnel management. The use of intelligence tests in the armed services during the war had been widely publicized. Thus the career of the psychologist as expert in nearly everything was well under way.

There are a number of other events in the history of applied psychology that are worth noting, primarily because of being firsts and forerunners of things to come. We mention them to emphasize the scope of applications and the fact that we are dealing with issues that have a long tradition. All of these were events in the development and progression of an applied psychology and will be brought up to date in the chapters to follow. The roots of modern applied psychology can be traced to these events (Fryer & Henry, 1950).

In the latter part of the 19th century and the early part of the 20th century there developed the first laboratory to study psychology, founded by Wilhelm Wundt in Germany, initiating the "science" of psychology; the first psychology laboratory in America, at Johns Hopkins University, founded by G. Stanley Hall, bringing this new science to the new world; and the first psychological clinic, developed by Lightner Witmer in 1896 at the University of Pennsylvania, applying that science to real-life problems. Chapter 3 continues the clinical story to current days.

In this early period, there also developed the research and statistical procedures that were to be the basis for the subsequent research underlying applications: Galton introduced the field of *psychometrics* and invented the concept and methodology of *correlation*; Fechner introduced *psychophysical* methodology; J. McKeen Cattell introduced *psychological tests* of individual differences; Spearman introduced *factor analysis*; and Kraepelin described the concept of *learning curves*. Specific aspects of human behavior began to be investigated. The concept of *intelligence* and its testing was created by Binet. The first "objective" test of *educational achievement*; the first study of a specific skill, typewriting; the study of specific occupations, such as telegrapher and streetcar operator; and even the "scientific" study of the behavior of children came into existence.

In 1887 the first psychological journal appeared in the United States, the *American Journal of Psychology*, with G. Stanley Hall as editor. Hall also developed the first journal whose purpose was to present papers on the application of psychology, *Pedagogical Seminary* in 1891. Another early journal that focused on the practice of psychology appeared in 1907, *The Psychological Clinic*, edited by Lightner Witmer. Books began to appear on specific applications of psychology. Munsterberg (1908) applied psychology to law in *On the Witness Stand*. Thorndike (1903) published the first application of psychology to education, *Educational Psychology*.

In a study that preceded, by many years, the applications of psychology to issues of health (chapter 4), Hollingsworth in 1912 reported a study on the "Influence of Caffeine on Mental and Motor Efficiency." Thus appeared the first studies of the effects of motor and mental performance on metabolism from what was to become a wide and still growing range of addictive substances.

Growth of Publications and Organizations

The hallmark of a field of human endeavor having really arrived is the emergence of organizations and publications that push (sell?) the products of the field. In the 1920s and 1930s, there were several books in the applied field. We describe them in order to illustrate the growing diversity of the concept of *applied* even in that period. Bush, in his 1922 *Applied Psychology and Scientific Living*, melded psychology with a measure of religion and philosophy and dealt with the role of the "subconscious mind," suggestion, and related phenomena for such applied concerns as love, fear, poverty, and thinking. Laboratory psychology progressed, and applied psychology marched right along.

Dresser, in *Psychology in Theory and Application* (1924), drew upon many of the same domains as had Munsterberg but broadened the range of applications to clinical matters (e.g., habits and conflicts, abnormal behavior, psychotherapy), vocational and industrial realms (e.g., human engineering, mental testing, vocational guidance), and social psychology (e.g., group phenomena, propaganda and public opinion, prejudice).

Husband's *Applied Psychology* (1934) was devoted strictly to industrial and vocational applications. At that time as for a minority of psychologists even now, applied psychology meant industrial psychology. For most recent and contemporary psychologists, however, applied psychology remains within the scope of the broad sweep of Munsterberg's artful brush: using psychological research from many domains and seeking its relevance and value for a wide host of areas of human functioning.

Then Gray (*Psychology in Use: A Textbook in Applied Psychology*, 1941) focused upon applications in the vocations, in the home, in education, in industry, in warfare, in medicine, and in clinical practice. Berrien's chapters in his 1948 *Practical Psychology* dealt with education, mental health, industry, consumer behavior, advertising, crime, and personal problems.

By emphasizing the enormous amount of applications of psychology in the modern era, we could run the danger of giving the impression that what is involved is a sudden burst of such work (beyond the World War II period) in the last decade or so. It should be clear by now that such an impression would be erroneous, in that applied psychology was already a burgeoning field by the end of World War II. This scope is further exemplified by the publication of a two-volume *Handbook of Applied Psychology* (Fryer & Henry, 1950) of over 800 pages and approximately 100 authors, each of whom was in a setting in which there was the application of psychology. Some of the major headings in this handbook give us some indication of the scope of the applied field at midcentury: group living, individual efficiency, personnel psychology, industrial psychology, transportation, business psychology, educational psychology, clinical psychology, and penology. Yet all of these areas were already booming in the early part of the century, as we have seen in the Forword to the 1917 issue of the *Journal of Applied Psychology*.

A quarter of a century after the Fryer and Henry handbook, much of the specific content was new, but the broad application areas weren't terribly different—education, politics, the marketplace, religion, the law, aesthetics, athletics (Ehrlich, 1972). The depth, range, and applied implications of psychological knowledge have continued to grow, and grow rapidly, especially in recent years.

It is important to note that, as this sustained growth of applied psychology has both continued and expanded, its expression in the publication of relevant books has been paradoxical. On the one hand, many dozens of books have been published addressing one or another applied psychological domain. These are examinations of a single assessment or intervention method or set of methods or other applied techniques in industry, or in education, or in clinical practice, or in another area. In recent years, only one noteworthy exception, Anastasi's *Fields of Applied Psychology* (1979), has ventured beyond a single applied domain and sought to present a comprehensive statement of the full span of applied psychology, with some slant toward industrial, vocational, and consumer applications.

Anastasi's approach to applied psychology is to put it in the context of the fields of psychology itself: "Applied psychology does not differ in any fundamental way from the rest of psychology. In terms of training and orientation, every applied psychologist is a psychologist first and applied specialist secondarily" (p. 6). Thus the areas covered in her text, in terms of section or chapter headings, are industrial and organizational psychology; engineering and environmental psychology; consumer psychology; clinical, counseling and community psychology; psychology and education; psychology and medicine; and psychology and law.

As another illustration of the growth and diversity of psychological applications, we merely cite the names of those current divisions of the American Psychological Association that clearly involve application: Developmental; Evaluation and Measurement; Personality and Social; Society for Psychological Study of Social Issues; Psychology and the Arts; Industrial and Organizational; the Experimental Analysis of Behavior; School Psychology; Psychologists in Public Service; Military Psychology; Adult Development and Aging; Society of Engineering Psychologists; Consumer Psychology; Community Psychology; Mental Retardation; Population and Environmental Psychology; Psychology of Women; Psychologists Interested in Religious Issues; Child, Youth and Family Services; Health Psychology; Psychology and Law; and Society for the Psychological Study of Lesbian and Gay Issues. Thus there is virtually no aspect of modern life for which there is not a sizable number of psychologists ready, willing, and able to apply their version of psychology.

It might seem as though we are overdoing the emphasis on the broad span of the field, but we cannot resist one further statistic. The American Psychological Association publishes a journal of abstracts of various fields. The January 1984 issue of *PsychSCAN: Applied Psychology* contained abstracts from the various journals that publish articles on materials considered to be within the scope of applied psychology. The number of such journals published in 1983 or 1984 totaled 56! The field has indeed grown since that first *Journal of Applied Psychology* appeared in 1917.

In the 1980s, almost 100 years since its initiation by Munsterberg, the field of applied psychology is an exceedingly diverse, productive, and healthy dimension of American psychology. In school, home, community, clinic, industry, hospital, prison, and virtually anywhere else in the real world where people behave, meet, strive, plan, and interact, applied psychology has something constructive to offer. Childrearing, education, marital relationships, psychotherapy, business management, sports, leisure, energy use, transportation, military efficiency, communication, the criminal justice system are collectively but a sampling of the interests of the applied psychologist.

Sometimes this interest takes the form of better *understanding*, sometimes increased *effectiveness*, sometimes more *control* of a specific issue or problem. Much of the work that constitutes applied psychology involves utilizing laboratory research results to help improve understanding of, or more readily solve, real-world problems and challenges. Other applied psychology knowledge grows from the hands-on work of the applied psychology practitioner—in industry, in clinics, in schools, in the community. Whether this knowledge is research-based, practiced-based, or both, these 100 years have yielded a broad, fertile, and useful range of theories, methods, and insights. It is this substance that is the content of our version of *modern* applied psychology.

LEARNING THEORY APPLIED

Thus far we have described the development of applied psychology very broadly, particularly in terms of the activities of specific psychologists and the growth of publications of all sorts about the research in and applications of psychology in general. At this point we discuss the topic from a somewhat different approach. In describing the various aspects of applied psychology, we must emphasize that psychology itself is not a unified, single concept. In fact, there are many psychologies, that is, sets of theories or models of behaviors. We will take one of these models, *learning theory*, and trace its development from early formulation and research to application in the real world outside of the psychology laboratories (L. Krasner, 1985). It is learning theory, in its various forms, that is the basis of the applications to be described in subsequent chapters (e.g., N. E. Miller, 1984 illustrates an application to health). When we say *learning theory*, it implies a single, unified concept. Yet, even here, we are dealing with a variety of theories that have in common a focus on human behavior as primarily a function of experience (nurture) rather than biology (nature). To a large extent, learning theories of some sort have been the basis of many, if not most, applications of psychology.

In a historical context, the application of a theory of learning did not start with Watson. Like most approaches to human behavior, it probably could be traced back to the ancient Greeks, and even perhaps to the Bible. Our historical context begins with the 18th-century philosophical and intellectual *Zeitgeist*. At that time John Locke's (1632–1704) doctrine of the child's mind as a tabula rasa was widely accepted. Locke had developed his views in opposition to the then prevailing doctrine that man's ideas and, therefore, the sources of his behavior, were *innate*. Locke argued that ideas were not inborn but came from interaction with the external environment, that is, from experience. Locke expressed his view of learning in this classic observation:

> Let us suppose the mind to be, as we say, white paper, void of all characters, without any ideas; How comes it to be furnished? Whence comes it by the vast store, which the busy and boundless fancy of man has painted on it with almost endless variety? Whence has it all the materials of reason and knowledge? To this I answer, in one word, *experience*. In that all knowledge is founded, and from that it ultimately derives itself. (Locke's *Essay Concerning Human Understanding*, 1690, cited in Boring, 1929, p. 172)

Although other philosophers, such as Aristotle, also believed that experience determines behavior, it was Locke who was most influential in making this concept central to philosophy and to psychology. The implications of this view were basic to the eventual application of various learning theories that developed in psychology.

Another important philosophical stepping-stone toward current theories of learning was David Hartley's (1705–1757) concept of *associationism*. Association of thought through temporal contiguity could be found in Aristotle. Hobbes, in fact, even had a chapter entitled "The Association of Ideas" in his classic, *Leviathan*, published in 1651. Hartley observed what he felt to be a fundamental law of behavior and labeled it *association*. He then expanded it into a psychological system, created a formal doctrine, and founded a new "school." At that point the only thing missing was systematic application to social behavior.

Jeremy Bentham (1748–1832), a philosopher, economist, and lawyer, broadened and amplified Hartley's theory of associationism and made it the central mechanism of the psychology of the period. Bentham's theory was deterministic and automatic and did not involve any of the mentalistic concepts then in vogue. Pavlov's later development of the conditioned reflex, and even Skinner's operant conditioning principles, are frequently viewed as being based on the same general associationistic concepts.

Another of Bentham's principles, that men try to attain the greatest possible happiness and pleasure for themselves, also foreshadows concepts of *positive reinforcement*, a basic principle in later applications. Bentham, as might be expected of one who believed learning to be based on experience, was very concerned with education and had supreme confidence in its limitless power to modify and remedy behavior in all situations (chapter 6) continues the educational application). Skinner's (1948) Utopian society of *Walden Two* is, in part, a modern-day application of Bentham's theories of associationism and utilitarianism, refined by later findings in experimental psychology. Chapter 2 describes the extension of the broad social views into the community.

Locke's views had particular influence on the Russian physiologist, L. M. Sechenov, who argued that all animal and human behavior, physical or psychic, conscious or unconscious, voluntary or involuntary, simple or complex was *reflexive* in origin and nature. In effect, the basic unit of behavior was the reflex and, as such, was learned. The mechanism of learning was association, which in itself is reflexive. Association, and not the innate nature of reflexes, determines "psychic content." Sechenov argued that psychic activity can only be initiated by stimulation of one or more of the senses and that the real cause of every human activity lies outside man, in external sensory stimulation. Sechnov tried to account for all the psychic phenomena such as thought, sensation, perception, will, wish, desire, memory, imagination within the framework of the reflex arc. Here indeed was the basis of a theory of learning that would have useful implications for applications.

Association and the reflex as basic concepts were added to by several Russian investigators of the late 19th century. It was particularly the research of the physiologist Ivan Petrovich Pavlov (1849–1936) that emphasized the connection between a person's behavior and environmental stimuli. His work came to be accepted outside Russia as symbolic of what was to become a scientifically based *behavioristic movement*. Pavlov's early research dealt with circulation and the heart, and he won the Nobel Prize in 1904 for investigations of the physiology of digestion. His work on conditioned reflexes began in 1899 and continued until his death. His basic and now classic experimental procedure was simple. He sounded a tuning fork simultaneously with the application of a given quantity of powdered meat to a dog's tongue, and he repeated this procedure at intervals until the tuning fork alone, without the meat, produced a reasonably constant flow of saliva. Thus appeared on the scene the *conditioned reflex method*, which was the basis, in theory at least, for many applications, particularly in advertising.

Although many investigators argue that learning and Pavlovian conditioning are synonymous, most psychologists studying learning distinguish between at least two types of conditioning (Bower & Hilgard, 1981; Hilgard,

1948). Pavlovian conditioning is now usually labeled *classical conditioning* to distinguish it from the *instrumental*, or the *operant*, conditioning of Skinner and the behavior analysts influenced by his research.

Behavior Modification

We use the concept of *behavior modification* as one illustration of the application of psychology for a number of cogent reasons. Many of the procedures to be described in subsequent chapters are based upon the basic learning theory principles of behavior modification. Further, this approach has had enormous impact on the field of psychology and, more generally, American society. In fact, the expression *behavior modification* has become part of the language, appearing both in comic strips (e.g., in Gary Trudeau's, "Doonesbury," *San Francisco Chronicle*, January 26, 1985) and from the lips of political figures.

Psychological theories are generally focused on one of two explanatory theories of human behavior. There is the focus on *inner* concepts (e.g., genes, personality, cognitions, the unconscious, the ego) or outer explanations (e.g., environmental and social influences). In effect, we are referring to the perennial nature-versus-nurture controversy. Behavior modification is clearly within the outer (nurture) category.

Kazdin (1978) defined behavior modification as "the application of basic research and theory from experimental psychology to influence behavior for purposes of resolving personal and social problems and enhancing human functioning" (p. ix). Actually, it could be argued that behavior modification is the modern, up-dated version of Watson's efforts to apply the behavioral psychology of his day.

This approach to influencing human behavior labeled *behavior modification* exemplifies most of the ways in which basic psychology becomes an applied psychology, but applied to what kinds of behavior? In their introduction to an early text on behavior modification, Ullmann and Krasner (1965) defined the emerging field within the framework of applied learning theory, "but learning with a particular intent, namely, clinical treatment and change" (p. 1). The important aspect of this approach is the contention that the focus of application (treatment) was to change undesirable personal behavior. Subsequently, the focus of behavior modification was to expand to dealing with the relationship between changes in the environment and changes in the individual's behavior in a wide range of categories such as social, familial, economic, and political (Krasner & Ullmann, 1965).

Thus, initially, behavior modification was the application of the results of learning theory and experimental psychology to the problem of altering maladaptive behavior. However, because the focus of attention was on overt behavior, in terms of both the development and change of behavior, it soon became clear that no distinction could really be made between adaptive and maladaptive responses.

In the clinical setting, early behavior modification started with the question, What do we wish to accomplish through our application of learning theory? If, for example, the objective were to increase the number of emotional words an individual verbalized, the question would be put thus: What would be the social consequences of such an increase in verbalization? Perhaps others would consider the individual to be a more expressive, warm person, hence more likable.

This focus on applying learning theory to the changing of specific behavior was succinctly stated by Eysenck (1959) in an early version of the approach that, at that point, was considered an alternative to psychoanalysis: "Learning theory does not postulate any such 'unconscious causes,' but regards neurotic symptoms as simple learned habits; there is no neurosis underlying the symptom, but merely the symptom itself. *Get rid of the symptom and you have eliminated the neurosis*" (p. 62).

Thus it seemed that applications of learning theory offered clear-cut implications and that here was a nice, simple concept, *applied*, and everyone knew what it meant. But, alas, nothing is simple in life or in psychology. It has been pointed out by some investigators, particularly those with a behavioral approach, such as Deitz and Baer (1982), that the term *applied* has sometimes been used to describe the seeking by scientific inquiry of the causes of not just any behavior but of socially important behavior. Applied behavior analysis then becomes a form of research linked with a socially important problem. Ah, but who is to determine what is of social importance?

Thus, for many of the investigators within the learning-theory and behavioral framework, the concept of *application* denoted an investigator's behavior that had *social consequences*. Further, the emphasis in much of applied behavior analysis was on improving social problems, not finding the causes of those problems.

The issues of application were extended further by D. M. Baer (1984), who offered an analysis of the development of *applied behavior analysis* that can be a prototype of, and model for, the application of learning theory. Baer wrote that "The roots of behavior analysis always meant to do more than describe the acquisition and maintenance of new behaviors. Indeed, all of them meant to understand the control of behavior in general by the environment in general" (p. 2). Baer noted that, in their application of reinforcement, punishment, and extinction contingencies, behavior analysts were quite similar to other appliers of environmental-control techniques. However, the behavior analysts differed in ways that were to make theirs a separate discipline, and they maintained the conceptual imperialism of the early learning theories: that they would eventually explain everything and, implicitly, control everything. As we shall see in later chapters, they attempted to really bring about social and utopian changes with their applications of operant psychology.

BASIC VERSUS APPLIED RESEARCH

We have been describing the historical context and early developments in the field of applied psychology. We have also been describing the diversity of the science of psychology and the wide range of applications. At this point we will discuss the concept of *basic research* as contrasted with *applied research*. It is an aspect of the broader issue between theory and practice that pervades psychology. A most useful delineation in the context of a basic-versus-applied research categorization was offered by Baer:

> A common stereotype of basic and applied research suggests that basic research discovers new knowledge, clarifies principles, and accomplishes carefully quantified statements of how much A results in how much B. Applied research then takes this knowledge and puts it to work in the service of society, solving practical problems and thereby maximizing happiness. . . . Another, less common stereotype asserts the opposite dependency: Applied research finds out what is possible and prevalent in the real world by solving problems that exist there. Basic research, thus informed of where the truth must lie, then proceeds to clarify it in laboratories, unconfounding whatever variables may have been packaged together in the real-life solutions, quantifying whatever functions may exist, and finally emerging with a language system that should explain why happiness is so maximal. (1979, p. 11)

Baer was, of course, not satisfied with these stereotypes. Rather, he went to the core of the behaviorist application of theory to real life, in contrast with the laboratory. He pointed out that, as a clinical researcher, he had had two guiding principles. The first was to adhere to the notion of an objective scientific research methodology, which for him was operant conditioning. As do most psychologists, he strongly believed in the "objectivity" of scientific research. The second principle was to develop an effective method of changing behavior. At first, his plan was to take the principles of operant conditioning as developed in the laboratory and apply them to real-life, practical problems in the community. Baer compared his orientation with that of other practitioners of what is believed to be *basic* psychology, such as behavior modification and behavior therapy. Working in the real world changed his initial preconceptions that applied research was a *simpleminded* application of basic research principles. The complexities of life forced him to move away from concern about strict research design and toward meeting the needs of the individual client, be it an individual or an organization.

Most investigators argue that applied research has different requirements from basic research. Azrin (1977) cogently argued that these differences involve:

. . . outcome versus conceptual analysis; clinical significance versus response simplicity; situational complexity versus stimulus and laboratory simplicity; population heterogeneity versus subject homogeneity; a systems approach versus single variables; subject preferences versus objective apparatus measures; practicality and cost benefits versus statistical significance; and side effects versus central tendency. (p. 141)

Thus, clinical researchers tend to use correlational rather than real clinical situations, college sophomore volunteers rather than real patients, studies that have implications rather than applications, and problem-oriented strategy rather than method-oriented.

Implicit in the application of learning theory research from the laboratory to the environment are three basic assumptions. *First*, human behavior is, at least to some extent, learned, and there is at least general agreement on this assumption. *Second*, it is assumed that experiments performed in laboratory settings can have relevance to real life. This assumption has been much criticized with the argument that an organism's natural behavior can be studied only in a "natural" environment. *Third*, animal laboratory experiments can be generalized. Of course, there has been much criticism of this assumption in that it has been accurately observed that rats are very different from humans, and there is little or no relevance of animal learning experiments to human behavior. All three of these issues will be lurking in the background throughout this volume (and beyond to real-life applications).

ETHICAL AND VALUE ISSUES

It should be clear at this point that ethical and value issues are now an integral aspect of applied psychology and have been since its inception. This section will present a brief overview of the major issues involved. There has been a growing awareness of the complexities, paradoxes, and myths involved and the need to deal with these issues rather than ignore and deny their existence.

As we have seen, applied psychology grew out of a more basic experimental psychology that its practitioners tried to base on the science of the time. Learning theory itself derived from, and was an integral part of, experimental psychology, and psychology was indeed considered to be a science, and science was, of course, value free. This brings us to one of the most important issues of our times: the relationship between the value and ethical views of the psychologist as scientist, and the application of psychological principles and techniques. L. Krasner and Houts (1984), in exploring this issue, placed their study of the value system of behavioral scientists within the context of the controversy of science as *value free* or *value laden*. They noted that the traditional value-free conceptualization of science is captured in the phrase "science is about facts not values." The argument for the value neutrality of science was founded on pivotal assumptions about epistemology and ethics developed in the logical positivist philosophy of science.

The history of science was conceived of as a story of progress toward unbiased, objective knowledge. Currently, however, the traditional view of the history of science as a story of gradual progress toward "objective truth" has been seriously challenged. On the basis of his examination of the history of science, Kuhn (1970) argued that major scientific change was due to changes in the assumptive framework (belief systems, values) of investigators and not to the deliberate logical evaluations of new factual discoveries. Thus, if the basic science is value laden, then, of course, its application is even more so.

Virtually all the early investigators in the applications of learning theory, particularly in behavior modification, considered that there was a very close linkage between their research investigations and social and ethical applications and implications. This view was clearly influenced and led by Skinner's own writings, particularly *Walden Two*. This novel, from a scientist whose basic research had not yet had a major impact on the field of psychology, raised issues about ethics and morality in social systems. Published in 1948, *Walden Two* anticipated social and ethical issues arising from the applications of behavior modification that have become a focus of social concern from the 1960s to the current time. Other early behavioral investigators were to point out the relationship between their laboratory research and broader social implications (Goldiamond, 1974; Kanfer, 1965; L. Krasner, 1965).

Ethical and value issues involve decisions on the part of the individual who is applying learning theory as to what is "good" or "bad" behavior for a specific individual. Ideally, a more "open" behavior modifier would view the goals as helping the individual make these decisions for one's self. Some behavior modifiers would argue that their major contribution is to reinterpret or operationalize this decision-making process as involving the assessment of the consequences of a given behavior: that which leads to positive reinforcement for the individual is good, and that which leads to aversive consequences is bad. Some would argue for the criterion of *survival* as an alternative or as a supplement to these goals.

Bandura (1969), in a most influential book that placed the principles of behavior modification within the conceptual framework of social learning, devoted an entire chapter to the discussion of value issues in the modification of behavior. He identified the specification of goals as the major value feature of behavior modification.

> The selection of goals involves value choices. To the extent that people assume major responsibility for deciding the direction in which their behavior ought to be modified, the frequently voiced concerns about human manipulation be-

come essentially pseudo issues. The change agent's role in the decision process should be primarily to explore alternative courses of action available, and their probable consequences, on the basis of which clients can make informed choices. However, a change agent's value commitments will inevitably intrude to some degree on the goal selection process. These biases are not necessarily detrimental, provided clients and change agents subscribe to similar values and the change agent identifies his judgments as personal preferences rather than purported scientific prescriptions. (p. 112)

These problems were also discussed by Kanfer (1965), who argued that the ethical dilemma of the then emerging behavior modification procedures consisted of:

. . . justifying use of subtle influencing techniques in clinical procedures in the face of the popular assumption of integrity, dignity and rights to freedom of the patient. The first step in the resolution of this dilemma is the recognition that a therapeutic effort *by necessity* influences the patient's value system as well as his specific symptoms. (p. 188)

These early statements clearly and unequivocally linked the behavior of those identifying their professional efforts within behavior modification with a deep concern for the ethical implications of their work and their social and value systems, and they set a precedent for current behavior modifiers and all groups of applied psychologists.

Problems of ethics and values are, of course, not unique to or caused by behavior modification, but it was believed by friends and foes alike that the development of behavior modification brought with it certain issues and concerns that did not exist before. The theme was expressed that, because behavior modification had arrived on the scene, psychologists must hurry before it was too late.

Does this mean that we, as psychologists, researchers, or even therapists, *at this point* could modify somebody's behavior in any way we want? The answer is no, primarily because research into the techniques of control thus far is at the elementary stage. Science moves at a very rapid pace, however, and now is the time to concern ourselves with this problem before basic knowledge about techniques overwhelms us. (Krasner, 1962, p. 201)

The decision as to whether this concern was justified we will leave to the reader to decide after reading this volume.

Others have, of course, expressed the same notion that at long last the complete manipulation of behavior was a possibility, and the application of behavior modification received the credit (blame). There might even be some who still believe that we are close to the state of nirvana. Yet the usage of any set of procedures, even behavior modification, in the ultimate control of our society (even for our own "good") is still, fortunately, a thing of the indefinite future. These ethical and value concerns are involved with the applications of all psychological approaches to human behavior, not only the behavioral. For a while, the concentration of concern (both in and out of psychology) was on the behavioral, because it looked as if here, at last, was an approach that really worked when applied to human behavior in virtually any setting. This leads us to a note of caution about what works and under what circumstances.

In a book on applied psychology, particularly on its history, there are cautions and dangers that we must point out. In describing the growth of this field from the early days of Munsterberg to the world of the 1980s, we might be giving the impression of great progress and of a growing contribution to society by a scientifically oriented and socially concerned profession. Enlightenment is being spread throughout society from the psychology laboratory to education, industry, the community, and every aspect of American life. Yet this optimism could be a carefully nurtured myth. Thus, we must talk about evidence for the effectiveness of the applied procedures and ethical and value and legal issues of who is doing what to whom.

We will return to these themes of values and what works in each chapter. There is no way in which a book on applied psychology can, or should, avoid ethical value implications of social applications.

2 Community Applications

In this chapter we focus on psychology applied in the community. At first this sounds as if we are about to offer a new area separate from previous ones. Yet, as we have been emphasizing, the thrust of application is virtually always into the community. As we have seen in the historical description of chapter 1, all applications of psychology, from its early stages in the first part of the century (particularly with Munsterberg), involved community applications. Our chapters on business, sports, and the judicial system deal *ipso facto* with community affairs. The chapters on education, mental health, and health psychology emphasize the thrust of recent developments away from focus on the individual to focus on the broader social systems, hence *community*.

As with all the topics of application, the volume of publications and the scope of reported research applications is overwhelming, and our approach is to focus on the behavior of psychologists who identify their work within this general area. This involves separate but overlapping fields of psychology with labels such as *environmental psychology*, *ecological psychology*, *consumer psychology*, *environmental design*, and, of course, *community psychology*. These are all areas that go beyond a mere label, but each has arrived at the point where it involves some organizational structure and, of course, journals, the ingredients of having arrived on the professional scene. There is certainly overlap in territory and function, but all are community oriented. Then we will concentrate on specific prototypical applications such as littering, energy consumption, and social planning. Thus, we note that in this chapter we are not including such topics as education, business, medicine and health, mental health, criminal justice, and sports, which are covered in other chapters but are still community.

We have touched upon various ramifications of the concept of *application* in a variety of contexts. But what does the concept *community* mean? In one sense it could be used to cover everything outside the psychology laboratory. However, as we have seen, this is a distinction that readily breaks down. We could turn to a straightforward dictionary definition (Webster, 1977, p.

229) of *community*, which gives us selections such as "a group of people living together and having interests, work, etc. in common: as a college *community*," or "society; the public," or "people living in the same district, city, etc., under the same laws." Certainly the concept of *community* is broad enough to include the locus of the applications described in every chapter of this book.

FIELDS OF PSYCHOLOGY IN THE COMMUNITY

Community Psychology

As an applied field, community psychology has "come of age" (O'Connor & Lubin, 1984). The concept of *community psychology* is, as with most other labels in psychology, an "amorphous entity, difficult to specify" (G. L. Martin & Osborne, 1980, p. 1). Most of the definitions of the term emphasize the interaction between environmental forces, which to some extent are controllable, and individual behavior. Rappaport (1977), one of the major contributors to this field, noted that:

> Community psychology is concerned with the right of all people to obtain the material, educational, and psychological resources available to their society. In this regard community psychology is a kind of reform movement within the larger field of applied psychology, and its adherents have advocated more equitable distribution of resources than psychology and the "helping professionals" control. (p. 2)

The application of psychology in the community was to a large extent influenced by and a creature of major developments in American society in the 1960s, particularly of the community mental health movement. This was an approach to working with individuals who had major problems in living. Prior to the 1960s if an individual had serious problems, he or she would be likely to wind up in a mental hospital in, at least, individual, one-on-one psychotherapy. In the early 1960s, the U.S. Congress passed legislation establishing 300 community mental health centers throughout the country. Thus, the shift took place from emphasis on isolation of the individual from family, job, and social environment to emphasis on remaining in the community and working on problems within a social context. Suddenly and quickly the community became a viable focus for applying psychology of every sort.

Inevitably, the goal of community psychologists shifted from the *treatment* of individual and social problems, after they had developed, to the *prevention* of such problems. In many ways community psychology of the 1960s and 1970s set the model of approach emulated by the health psychologists of the 1970s and 1980s (chapter 4). The idea was to bring about environmental changes in social conditions and individual changes in behavior that would prevent the eventual development of mental, social, and health disorders.

To carry out their objectives, community psychologists would actually shift the locus of professional activity from the office, laboratory, or classroom into the community itself, the real world, by becoming involved in a variety of community settings such as schools, community centers, stores, and homes. Related to such involvement was the training of nonprofessionals (peers, parents, teachers, friends, colleagues) as agents of social change.

The focus of intervention procedures shifted from the individual to small groups, organizations, and the community itself. Thus, such group procedures as family therapy, group therapy, and sensitivity groups flourished. At the organizational level, such as in schools, hospitals, and businesses, the issue became one of examining the specific organization and the methods and processes by which it was attempting to influence the behavior of its people. For example, teachers, mental hospital staff, and corporate managers would attend sensitivity sessions, weekend marathons, and special pop courses given by psychologists, of course, which were intended to sensitize them to and maximize positive, personal relationships in their setting. A major element in all of these activities was the development of an enhanced heightened awareness of the basic values, philosophy, and goals of the particular institution and of the broader society itself.

To convey the scope of applications and potential implications of the work of those individuals identified as community psychologists, we will cite examples from a typical newsletter (Fall 1984) of the Division of Community Psychology of the American Psychological Association. It should be noted that this newsletter was Volume 18; so the origins of this division go back to 1966, a period in which, as noted in chapter 1, there was another enormous outburst and growth of applied psychology.

Annette Rickel, in her presidental column, noted the new directions being undertaken by the division membership, self-identified as community psychologists. She observed that there was an emergence of a "fresh perspective on our involvement in public policy and advocacy issues" (p. 1). She emphasized current attempts to produce "relevant research":

> . . . research that will provide guidance to public policy decision makers, and research that will in the long run benefit those most affected by the policy decisions. The role of the researcher, the practitioner, and the professional organization in influencing and advocating policy is a complex issue requiring interface with governmental decision makers at multiple levels. (p. 1)

This observation aptly captures the relationship between research and public policy. Thus, in still another area, the old, and apparently clear-cut, distinction between basic and applied research no longer has the meaning it once had. Further, Rickel's comments reflected an awareness of the value implications of any research, a linkage to which psychologists are increasingly sensitive.

Other topics involving psychological applications touched upon in this issue of the newsletter included prevention programs, the victimization process and victim assistance, intrafamily abuse, unemployment, latchkey children, a hazardous waste disposal facility as a community stressor, alternatives to mental hospitals, program planning and evaluation in community service organizations, and countless others. We would also include studies of consumer behavior (Sternthal & Craig, 1982) and the interface between psychology and public health (Singer & Krantz, 1982) within the community psychology framework. Each of these is an area of social concerns involving a broad spectrum of the community. In a later section we will expand upon one of the most important of these topics, that of prevention.

Behavioral Community Psychology

A new subfield within psychology is in the process of developing the very title that epitomizes the theme of this chapter, behavioral community psychology. The label itself represents the combination of a theoretical approach, a behavioral approach, and the locus and focus of that approach, the community. Glenwick (1982) described the scope of the applications of this orientation.

> The term "behavioral community psychology" incorporates behavioral approaches which interact with both community mental health (e.g., characterized by an active intervention stance, use of paraprofessionals and natural change agents, consultation by professionals) and community psychology strategies (e.g., prevention orientation; competency and strength building; modification of environmental factors predisposing to behavioral difficulties; interventions aimed at groups; organizations, and communities). (p. 13)

Interventions in the community are, of course, very complex and sometimes, not surprisingly, contraproductive. Interventions to improve the "mental health" and well-being of the community should be well structured, systematic, generally educational in focus, and participatory. Intervention planners and evaluators should be sensitive to possible negative effects. The focus in many applications is to deemphasize individual skill training and instead emphasize changing the environments in which people interact. Interventions mainly occur within a natural living context or series of contexts (neighborhood, family, school, workplace) to enhance a psychological sense of community.

Although there were many hints in its history foreshadowing this development, it was in the early 1970s that the self-identified behaviorists, the progenitors of the appliers of the 1980s, emerged from the laboratory, the clinic, and the mental hospital to a broader world. Influenced to some extent by earlier applications of behavioral principles in schoolrooms and hospitals and affected by the national concerns and debates of the 1960s, a new generation of behaviorists began to take on the total natural and man-made environment as the focus for investigation and social change with a purpose, namely a better environment for all members of society.

For example, Nietzel, Winett, McDonald, and Davidson (1977), in a chapter on environmental problems in a volume descriptively entitled, *Behavioral Approaches to Community Psychology*, covered the topics of litter control, recycling, energy conservation, transportation, architectural design, and population change. Of immediate interest here is not so much the specifics of research in these areas as the context in which Nietzel and his cohorts placed this material. They started their chapter with a quote from Fairweather (1972), who, in part, stated that:

> . . . population growth . . . environmental degradation . . . and human relations crises face man today. He must solve these problems if he is to survive in a liveable environment. He must also find ways of aiding society to adopt the solutions found. Such problem-solving action requires basic social change. (p. 1)

The Fairweather comments were used to emphasize "the urgency of finding solutions to these problems" and to accentuate the view that "the amelioration of conditions which degrade the environment may have more to do with maintaining and improving the quality of our life and 'mental health' than much of the current work conducted under the rubric of mental health" (Neitzel et al., 1977, p. 310).

Thus, a new theme was emerging from the behaviorists, namely, the urgency of the solution of the environmental problems of our society and the belief that the behaviorists, as applied psychologists, might have the skill to contribute to the solution.

As noted, a major element in many behavioral community psychology applications is the training and use of *mediators*. A supervisor, a clinical or consulting psychologist, or an environmental designer trains a student, teacher, peer, parent, spouse, or paraprofessional to work with and influence a client, patient, family member, or fellow worker. In effect, the mediator is trained in the general principles of behavioral psychology and its applications. Standard techniques such as modeling and role playing are used. What such training does is literally move the theory, philosophy, and techniques of applied behaviorism into the community as the mediator's own behavior is influenced and, in turn, the target individual is affected (Acker, 1980). When one considers that the settings in which mediators function include family, school, workplace, and, indeed, community, then these procedures have been extended well into the community.

The goals of the practitioners of the new behavioral community psychology are expressed in a variety of ways, all, of course, very positive. For example, Iscoe (1980) emphasized an

> affirmation to devoting attention to genuine preventive measures, to tailoring interventions at the community level to fit the problem, and to moving away from traditional one-to-one clinical services and into the broad arena of social systems, public policy, and innovative use of behavioral science findings. (p. vi)

Given the kinds of visionary goals the practitioners of community psychology have, there is the issue of acceptability to consumers and to policymakers. This issue is always a major element in the influence process. In effect, how does the professional influence people to "want to change"? This, of course, is the key issue in all applications by professionals who "know" what is best for the individual and the society.

Larger-scale applications also require focusing on delivery systems or organizational structures. To solve many community problems, the intervention procedures probably should be directly incorporated into the system in which the behavior normally occurs rather than be superimposed on the existing system as an afterthought. A related issue is that of implementation. Contact between those who design programs and those who implement them can decrease over time, thus influencing their effectiveness. This links with the training of implementers, who are the presumed targets of behavior change, in designing their own programs with an understanding of the principles involved, thus putting them in a position to see to it that the program is carried out by the designers, the subjects themselves (Jeger & Slotnick, 1981).

Environmental Psychology

Environmental psychology and ecological psychology (Barker, 1968) represent major streams of investigation illustrating psychological applications in the community. Although not synonymous, both of these fields are concerned with the influence of physical and social settings on behavior. Some investigators in these fields focus on the physical, others on the society, many on both. The systematic planning of architectural space to affect behavior also falls in these areas. The roots of environmental psychology lie in social, experimental, and clinical psychology, and the major early influencers, with quite diverse backgrounds, are psychologists such as Altman (1975), Craik (1970), Moos (1973), Proshansky (1976), Sommer (1969), and Wohlwill (1970).

As with other fields, environmental psychology can be conceptualized in three aspects: theoretical (as represented by the book that first labeled the field, *Environmental Psychology*, edited by Proshansky, Ittelson, and Rivlin in 1970); research (on a wide range of issues involving interaction between the individual and the environment); and organizational/training (e.g., graduate training programs in environmental/ecological psychology at such institutions as City University, University of California at Irvine, Pennsylvania State University, and Michigan State University).

Ittelson, Proshansky, Rivlin, and Winkel (1974) offered a reasonable viewpoint on how environmental psychologists view their field and their role in it.

> It should be clear that environmental psychology is not a theory of determinism. It sees man not as a passive product of his environment, but as a goal directed being who acts upon his environment and who, in turn, is influenced by it. In changing his world, man changes himself, a dynamic interchange between man and his milieu. The traditional conception of a fixed environment to which organisms must adapt or perish is replaced by the ecological view that emphasizes the organism's role in creating its own environment. (p. 5)

Perhaps the major recent development in the field of environmental psychology has been the shift away from the individual orientation so characteristic of most of psychology to an individual-in-a-physical-and-social-environment approach. This is, of course, consistent with the focus on the individual-in-a-social-context model that we are describing throughout the book.

Proshansky (1980) traced the origins of this approach in environmental psychology to developments in American urban life in the two decades following World War II. During this time there was a very major increase in the need for a variety of new environmental settings in virtually every American community, especially new housing and accompanying facilities such as shopping areas, settings for primary health care, and settings for mental health problems, which abounded. The postwar baby boom resulted in the growth of primary schools, secondary schools, and college facilities.

> All of this was taking place in a context of urban living in which suburban living was on the increase while there was a simultaneous decay of large urban centers. The result of this almost runaway growth and decay was a persistent and continuing demand for answers to questions that directly touched on person/physical environment relationships. These questions came from government officials, industry leaders, community constituents, and most directly from socially concerned architects, planners, interior designers, and landscape architects. Indeed the design professions at that period were going through a soul searching evaluation about their own gullibility in design decisions, largely because of a failure to examine a host of implicit assumptions about human behavior and experience underlying these decisions. Turning to psychology and other behavioral sciences was a logical consequence of this evaluation process. (Feimer & Geller, 1983, p. 9)

Professionals involved in the design of environments turned with a sense of urgency to psychology to ask basic questions about applications. Ways of studying the individual in an environmental context include studies of crowding, privacy, and territoriality. For example, the perception of feeling crowded while living in a small apartment can be changed by dividing up space in different ways, such as rearranging doorways, walls, and pictures. The concept of personal space (Sommer, 1969) was a major contribution to conceptualizing the individual in a social setting. Such simple things as arranging seating and distance between individuals leads to changes of comfortableness in conversation. It has become quite clear that psychologists are not dealing with carefully structured laboratory situations, but rather with very real-life social situations that have major social and economic implications (even of life or death) for a community.

The future growth of environmental psychology could be difficult because of several societal and intrapsychological developments that actually pertain to virtually all fields of applied psychology. These include the reduction in government support for research and graduate programs, particularly in new areas, and the generally anti-intellectual and antiscience sociopolitical climate of the 1980s (Proshansky, 1980). Within the field itself, the point is made that environmental psychology, to be really effective, must employ research studies that take full consideration of the individual–environment interaction. Thus, carefully controlled laboratory studies are generally inappropriate. The individual researcher therefore must develop strategies that are less controlled, more unique, and therefore less likely to receive institutional rewards for publications. Further, development of a unifying theory and unique research has not yet really occurred.

Ecological Psychology

Ecological psychology can be viewed as an area of psychology that relates to and interacts with environmental and community psychology. The early investigators in this area were Roger Barker and Herbert Wright, who virtually created this field with their 1955 examination of the "psychological ecology" of an Amerian Midwest town (Barker & Wright, 1955). Their emphasis was on the study of human behavior and experience in their natural context.

They stressed the study of the human environment at a molar level at a time (in the mid 1950s) when psychology was focusing on stimulus-response in the laboratory. The basic unit in the ecological approach is the *behavior setting*, which is a miniature social system that could develop in any situation (Wicker, 1979). Barker emphasized the long-term physical and social context of human behavior. He argued that there were regularized forms of behavior elicited by such institutional settings as schoolrooms, churches, sports stadia, and even hotel lobbies. An individual's behavior is influenced by the physical arrangements of the furniture as well as by what the individual knows of the intended purpose of the setting, the types of people who use it, and its social traditions. For example, a public lecture can be a behavior setting, and it includes a variety of human behavior and a variety of arrangements of physical objects within a set boundary.

Ecological psychologists have applied their theoretical approach to the systematic study of community and organizational behavior settings and the impact of stress in work settings. Their focus has been on developing a technology to improve human environments.

Environmental Design

Environmental design is an approach to applying psychology in its very broadest sense to the changing of human behavior that, itself, derives from several streams of investigations. It applies empirically derived principles of behavior that offer both a database and a philosophy for intervention to the modification and design of environments (L. Krasner, 1980). The behavioral (environmental, social learning) model of man has evolved to the point where it now represents a comprehensive approach to human behavior, with major social and political ramifications. This expanded version of the behavioral model can be labeled *environmental design*, a term that is both eloquently simple and sufficiently broad to convey the complexities of the approach.

Use of a term such as *environmental design* can be viewed as a kind of territorial growth for the behavioral model in that there are few fields indeed that do not encompass the individual's involvement with the environment. Heimstra and McFarling (1974) wrote that "The relationship between man and his environment is of interest to individuals in many areas, including architecture, urban and regional planning, civil and sanitary engineering, forest and parks management, geography, biology, sociology, and psychology, to name only a few" (p. 3).

Colman (1975) offered a useful description of environmental design that incorporates most of the elements in this orientation:

A more useful definition of environmental design would relate the planning of a coherent program and set of procedures to effect the total human and nonhuman environment in ways that increase the probability that certain goals or "needs" will be achieved. The goal of environmental design would relate to social behavior, such as planning an educational or therapeutic system, as much as to aesthetics such as constructing an awe-inspiring church. Input into environmental design problems must then include knowledge related to modifying human behavior and social systems as well as structural information from engineering and perceptual psychology. The field would expand toward a new view of man, always powerfully effected by his physical and social environment, now actively developing an environmental design model and methodology that would place the effect of the total environment on his behavior more in his own control, and the responsibility for the design and control of the environment of his behavior, in himself. (p. 411)

Thus the environmental-design approach represents a conceptual and applied linking of behavior modification with environmental, ecological, and community psychology.

The environmental-design approach demonstrates a very important element in the application of psychology, which we allude to in various other places. This is the training of professional individuals to apply the principles of the specific approach. All too often the focus in training is on the application of techniques, and this results in the professional applier's becoming a technician; whereas an understanding of the general principles, theory, and philosophy of an approach opens the door to wider, more meaningful, and more helpful applications and interventions. The environmental-design approach trains people to conceptualize the environment in which they are working in such a way that they can apply the general principles of environmental design. Succinctly stated, these principles, as formulated by L. Krasner, 1980, are:

1. A hypothesized model of human behavior conceptualizes the locus of influence, as in the *interaction* between an individual's behavior and the environment.
2. An individual learns by observing and doing.
3. Behavior followed by a rewarding event is likely to be repeated.
4. Any situation can be analyzed so that the designer can set up specific behavioral goals that are socially desirable, taking into consideration both social and individual needs and desires.
5. Techniques should not be developed in isolation but only in the context of learning environments with which the individual designer is dealing. The broader influences on behavior such as social roles and the impact of institutional rituals and restraints must be considered.
6. The professional influencer is part of the influence process itself; in effect, a *participant-observer*. As such, she or he must be aware, and in control, of the influence on her or him.
7. There is a symbiotic relationship between therapist and patient, influencer and influencee, designer and designee. Both need each other.
8. Research and application, theory and practice are mutually interactive and inseparable.
9. Social and personal change are continuous processes.
10. The variables of influence lie in the environment (man-built, natural, and social), but they can differentially influence as a function of the history of the individual.
11. Meaning and truth are not intrinsic but are imposed currently and repeatedly by the observer, investigator, or designer.

Perhaps the most fundamental issue in environmental design is design for what and by whom? Of course, this is not a new issue, in that it was expressed early in the behavioral movement in terms of modification for what and by whom, and it is implicitly and explicitly with us in virtually all applications of psychology from any or all theoretical models. A major point deriving from this viewpoint is that the goal of helping individuals is to enable them to learn how to control, influence, or design their own environments. Implicit in this is a value judgment that individual freedom is a desirable goal, and the more an individual is able to affect his or her environment the greater his or her freedom. Of course, there is no absolute freedom in this sense. In this context, *environment* is both the people and the physical objects in one's life. The goals of environmental design may be explicated by noting that:

> The best way to increase freedom is not merely to say people *may* choose but to work so that people *can* choose. Just as humans have gone far in changing their physical environments, we hope that the next decade will see humans controlling and changing their psychological environments. The how is being developed rapidly in schools, clinics, families, and formal organizations. An attempt is being made to reduce the gap between decision makers and the populations they affect, especially in the areas of education and consumer affairs and to a lesser extent in political and industrial settings. (L. Krasner & Ullmann, 1973, p. 502)

Consumer Psychology

Yes, we are all consumers! And consumer psychology has become one of the common fields of application by psychologists. To give a sense of what is happening in this field, we will briefly cite some of the topics of the papers presented within the framework of the Consumer Psychology Division (23) at the 1984 annual meeting of the American Psychological Association. One major topic covered from a variety of viewpoints was that of advertising (the legacy of John B. Watson and Walter Dill Scott; see chapter 1). Included were studies on affective responses to advertising, content and repetition of advertising, cognitive–response approaches to persuasion, consumer nutrition behavior; influences on decision making, stimulus control of consumer behavior, and the impact of attitude and values on consumer behavior. A term that appears repeatedly in various forms is *persuasion*. Clearly, psychologists of all persuasions are applying their theories and principles to influence the behavior of all of us as consumers of the necessities and luxuries of life.

Behavioral Economics

The systematic application of psychology to the economic environment has been labeled *behavioral economics*, an approach that developed in part from the early token-economy programs of the applied behavior analysts (Atthowe & Krasner, 1968; Ayllon & Azrin, 1965, 1968). These programs emerged from the early operant conditioning studies that used tokens in place of primary reinforcers (see chapter 3).

Staats, Staats, Schutz, and Wolf (1962) were the first to utilize a backup reinforcement system (tokens) in a program training children to read. The tokens were exchangeable for a variety of edibles and toys. This meant that the therapist or experimenter was no longer dependent upon the momentary desirability of an object such as candy. The major breakthrough in the development of the technique of token economy was the program of Ayllon and Azrin (1965), who used tokens to influence, shape, or reinforce the desired social and self-care behavior (such as making beds, working, attending therapy sessions, feeding oneself) of patients in a state mental hospital. The individuals would perform the behavior, which was desirable for them and for the hospitals, and they would receive tokens for it (reinforcement) that could later be exchanged for the "good" things in life such as food, clothing, shelter and leisure activities.

Tokens opened up an almost limitless economic world of rewards. Developments in token-economy programs in mental hospitals, in institutions for the mentally retarded, with delinquents, and in the schoolroom have been exciting, controversial, hopeful, and depressing. In effect, token economy represents a broad model of an intervention/theoretical orientation/field of psychology/interdisciplinary approach/applied technique. We are using this concept to link the various *fields* of community psychology and some specific areas of community intervention and application. Behavioral economics, indeed, is both a field of endeavor and a set of applied techniques.

Winkler (1971) reported a series of studies on token-economy programs that extended this concept, or technique, into an important new dimension, that of testing predictions from economic theory and thus systematically investigating the core of token programs and of society itself. He investigated the complex relationships among the variables of prices, wages, and savings and the ways in which these influence individual behavior in the community.

Token economies were found to operate according to principles similar to those economists have identified in national, money-based economies. Token economies not only look like real economies, they function like them, and research in the new field has enhanced the linkage of the behavioral movement with social planning.

Winkler and Winett (1982) have extended the application of psychology considerably in their report on behavioral interventions in resource conservation, which they call a *systems approach* based on behavioral economics. They put their work in the context of the growing awareness of the need for interdisciplinary conceptualization (P. C. Stern & Gardner, 1981) and examples of interdisciplinary groups of psychologists, engineers, architects, economists, human factors experts, and media consultants who are working on such socially relevant problems as energy and water conservation (Rohles, 1981; Socolow, 1978; Winett, Neale, & Grier, 1981). Winkler and Winett concluded by optimistically (perhaps one may even say grandiosely) noting that:

> As the energy and resource situation in the 1980's becomes progressively more critical, decisions not only affecting resource conservation policy but, without exaggeration, affecting the course of civilization will have to be made. To date energy policy has been formulated with little input from psychologists and, hence, with minimal awareness or focus on effectively modifying human behavior. . . . We have noted the potential contributions of a psychologically based information technology for influencing consumer choice behaviors and have discussed the role of experimental methodology for policy development. On a theoretical and practical level, it is our hope that it may be possible to integrate economic and psychological conceptualizations to develop more effective approaches to resource conservation. (1982, pp. 433–434)

COMMUNITY APPLICATIONS

Thus far in this chapter we have viewed applications in the community in the broad framework of psychological fields of endeavor. Having presented the broad picture, we now focus on some specific illustrations of community applications, starting with an important concept that has increasingly influenced the focus of applications, prevention.

Prevention

In recent years there has developed another new movement in the application of psychology, *prevention* (or its derivatives) manifested in conferences, papers, and books (e.g., Joffe & Albee, 1981). Felner, Jason, Moritsugu, and Farber (1983) have even delimited a field, preventive psychology. The immediate question is: Prevention of what? In what was probably the first conference on this topic (1975 at the University of Vermont) it was *psychopathology* that was to be prevented. Implicit in such terminology is the prevention of mental disorders, and early writings in this area focused on environmental influences on behavior, social competence in children, and competence and coping in adulthood. Thus, the emphasis was on affecting the environments of children and adults so that emotional problems could be "prevented."

However, the shift in the focus of studies of prevention is indicated by the title of the book on the fifth of the Vermont conferences, edited by Joffe and Albee (1981), *Prevention Through Political Action and Social Change.* Here, indeed, it was clearly put that psychologists were now involved in social change and political action, which again brings in the whole question of values. The theme of this conference was expressed by Albee's belief that most of our social problems are the result of the arbitrary use and misuse of power. Thus, the shift in emphasis from changing the individual to changing the society was clearly expressed.

The concept of *prevention* itself has grown very rapidly. For example, there is now an Office of Prevention (established in 1979) in the National Institute of Mental Health. Goldston (1984), in giving a report on the development and current status of the "networks for prevention," noted that the interest in prevention developed in the mid-1970s, fostered by a small group of individuals who were interested in applying community mental health principles to primary prevention of mental disorders. Goldston then explained:

> Today, there is a complex network, of often interlocking directorates, composed of national organizations, as well as State and local agencies. The linkages are so multiple in nature that, in many instances, any effort to categorize by national, State, or local network is quite artificial. . . . the efforts of the NIMH Office of Prevention to develop, consolidate, and advance a constituency for prevention, not for the self-serving purpose of having political allies, but predominantly to have access to the very best thinking about prevention available, and to advance the democratic principle of participatory involvement in major decision-making by those groups and forces most knowledgeable and most likely to be affected by decisions made at the Federal level. (p. 339)

He then described numerous committee councils and conferences enhancing the prevention network. Even three journals have been established to facilitate communication (*Journal of Primary Prevention, Journal of Preventive Psychiatry, Journal of Prevention and Human Services*). In a 1-year period there were over 30 national workshops on prevention.

A survey of prevention programs (Lorion, 1983) indicated that prevention promotion efforts focus on a very wide range of target problems including developmental, learning, and behavioral difficulties, substance abuse, and coping with stressful life events such as divorce and illness. Nearly half of all programs identified children, adolescents, or both as their primary target populations. The group of the population that seems least served is the elderly. Demographically, program recipients are primarily minority and low socioeconomic groups. The goals of these many programs included improvements in educational functioning, in effective parenting, and in the living of health-promotive life-styles. Thus, it is quite clear that the prevention area represents a major development, virtually instantaneous, in the application of psychology in the community, with considerable social, political, economic, and value implications.

An illustration of specific preventative endeavors would be the focus on *stress*. At first the reader's reaction might well be, "Stress. So what's new? Everybody knows that life is stressful and that stress is bad for you." Yet it has only been in recent years that the details and complexities of the individual–environment interactions that elicit and enhance stress have become clearer (Lazarus & Folkman, 1984).

J. E. Singer and Baum (1980) focused on the development of the three Cs of environmental stress—crowding, commuting, and cacophony. They emphasized cognitive mediation and appraisal of environmental stress factors, which have a major impact on the physiological and psychological responses to environmental threat.

For example, fairly recent research on commuting, simply going to work from home and returning, has indicated that several aspects of commuting engender higher physiological stress reactions: driving on urban streets with low-access control, as against driving on freeways; using more complex commuting routes, such as curved roadways; and driving in high heat and humidity or polluted air. Once again the reaction might be that this is not really news. However, what is new is that the physiological and psychological effects of such environmental stress have been demonstrated by psychologists applying their skill in appraising physiological measures of heart rate and blood pressure taken following actual or simulated driving (Stokols, Novaco, Stokols, & Campbell, 1978).

Community Issues

Littering

We now focus on several community issues: littering, energy, safety, and social planning. Whereas littering is a major problem, it is certainly not crucial to our lives or our survival. The multitude of issues involved in the energy area, however, are crucial to our well-being and survival. Needless to say, the application of psychology to broad social issues and to new and alternative forms of social structure subsumed under social planning ("Utopias") is vital to ourselves and to future generations.

The littering problem was the first major environmental problem psychologists tackled, and the procedures applied are prototypical of approaches to all other environmental problems. Although it might sound like a simple problem, it becomes very complex because it affects our daily lives and interrelates with other aspects of society such as community attitudes and legislation.

As with virtually every other area in which psychology is applied, the literature on litter control is vast (e.g., Geller, 1980; Geller, Winett, & Everett, 1982; Osborne & Powers, 1980). A simple definition of litter would be that it is misplaced solid waste ranging from a discarded cigarette butt to hulks of abandoned vehicles. Of course, the particular environmental setting is an element in the determination of what is litter. A rusting auto hulk in front of one's house is clearly litter, whereas that same hulk in one of the automobile graveyards one finds around the country is not.

Why is littering a problem on which so much effort has been focused? So what if a few cigarette butts are lying about? Various reports of governmental agencies indicate that the nationwide cost of removing litter is as much as a billion dollars! Litter involves fire, safety, and health hazards. Litter represents a danger to wildlife and to domestic animals. One study reported that in California alone it costs $1.5 million a year to pay for medical attention for people involved in litter-related accidents (Purcell, 1981).

The psychologist would initially focus on the characteristics of the litterer. Is there a litterer personality type? Geller, Winett, and Everett (1982) concluded that:

> . . . there is really insufficient evidence for making any conclusions regarding individual characteristics of the "litterbug." Verbal reports are very apt to be inconsistent with actual behaviors, and the behavioral data is [sic] likely to be unreliable or limited by environmental constraints. At this point it may be safest to say that everyone is a potential litterer in certain situations, and that it is presently most cost effective to alter situations so as to decrease littering by the most frequent user of the environment. (p. 53)

This is a clear statement of the view that the problem lies not in the individual but in the environment, and, to bring about changes, environmental events and influences should be altered.

Most of the research investigating ways of affecting the behavior of littering derives from the behavioral model. Thus the strategies used involve two major approaches. The investigator works with either *antecedents* (events that occur before the target behavior) or *consequences* (events that occur after the behavior).

Examples of antecedent instructions include one-page flyers distributed to incoming store customers urging the purchase of drinks in returnable bottles (Geller, Farris, & Post, 1973), promotion posters, car bumper stickers, information pamphlets, window displays, and newspaper articles on antilitter campaigns (including photographs of badly littered areas). A favorite technique is to place such antilitter "prompts" on drink cans (Coke, beer, etc.) as "Please Don't Litter." The various flyers used in these campaigns vary in terms of the kinds of information provided. One finding in such studies is that specifying places to put litter increased the likelihood of their usage, as against more general admonitions not to litter. In a series of studies, Geller, Witmer, and Orebuth (1976) found, with specific nonlittering instructions, a 20% to 35% reduction in littering behavior from a baseline of observed littering, as against 5% to 10% reductions for general instructions. Consequent strategies included "thank you" signs on trash cans and specific reinforcers for using trash cans such as offering coupons that are exchangeable for drinks, movie tickets, lottery tickets, badges, trinkets, and toys.

A sample analysis of the problem involves pointing out that littering in public places is a matter of concern because of the unsightly pollution it creates and the financial cost it necessitates to remove the litter. Some studies have demonstrated that prompts in the form of written messages or instructions (posters, small signs, conspicuously marked trash cans with antilitter messages) can decrease littering (Geller, 1973, 1975). For example, Geller (1973) used written messages to remind individuals to use trash cans in separate studies in six settings: a college classroom, the lobby of a university building, a college snack bar, a grocery store, and two movie theaters.

Incentives to control littering have been used in various settings: movie theaters, forest grounds, schools, football stadia, and zoos. In most of the littering studies, individuals received incentives for collecting trash. In most of these programs, someone was required to carefully monitor behavior and to administer the reinforcing consequences. The supervision required to administer the program raises the question of the feasibility of conducting large-scale antilitter programs.

A major alternative behavior to littering (and the behaviorists' focus on developing alternatives) is the concept of *recycling*. If waste products (e.g., cans, paper, returnable bottles) could be recycled they would become a resource rather than waste. Thus, reinforcement techniques were used to alter consumer purchasing to materials that can be recycled, such as returnable rather than nonreturnable containers and bottles. Using such incentives, investigators (Geller, Chaffee, & Ingram, 1975) were able to increase the percentage of grocery store customers who bought returnable containers. Extrinsic incentives are not always necessary to increase recycling. Some investigators (Luyben & Bailey, 1976) merely informed the residents of three apartment complexes of the location of recycling containers to be used to collect newspapers. Other studies have demonstrated the effects of providing both prompts and convenient collection containers on the recycling of newspapers in places such as mobile home parks. Incentive systems have effectively reduced littering or increased the removal of existing litter in a wide range of environmental settings such as national forests, schools, movie theaters, university campuses, and athletic stadia (Geller, 1980; Osborne & Powers, 1980).

As with virtually all of the applications of psychological principles and techniques that we have been describing, the evidence for successful behavior change is far from conclusive. For example, the evidence seems to show that, when the reinforcements are removed, litter disposal behavior tends to stop. "In addition, there is evidence that the effectiveness of anti-litter instructions is a direct function of the specificity of the request and the convenience of the requested behavior" (Geller, Winett, & Everett, 1982, p. 97). Sometimes the antilitter message becomes so specific that the individual feels a threat to her or his freedom. Thus psychological resistance sets in, and there is an increase in behaviors contrary to the request.

Although a variety of reinforcers, as listed earlier, successfully work to enhance litter pickup, even they have disadvantages. The number of people needed to run such programs is out of proportion to the effects produced. It is interesting to note that there seems to be evidence of individuals who deliberately produce litter in order to get a reward for getting rid of it. Who would believe that such things can happen?

The caution that surrounds the present status of the littering situation is nicely expressed by Martin and Osborne (1980):

> No current approach to litter control can be considered the entire answer to the problem. A total solution cannot be expected from the sole manipulation of antecedent variables, consequent variables, the legal system, or the educational system. It is more than likely that well-researched combinations of these variables will provide some answers. The community and statewide attempts to control litter, while having the greatest emotional and psychological impact on the problem, are typically the most poorly documented and, therefore, the most difficult from which to draw strong inferences about litter control. Clearly, these are cases where the implementation of large systems precedes the scientific data base necessary to predict their outcomes. . . . In most of these studies the data are well analyzed and the procedures are adequately documented. The major difficulty is that these studies are so small-scale that extrapolation to the region or national level is unwarranted. (pp. 164–165)

Energy

In recent years there has been a growing societal concern about the use and misuse of energy resources, including fuel, electricity, natural gas, and oil, all of which are limited resources. Reinforcement techniques have been applied in several studies to control energy consumption in the home. For example, in one study, contingent points reduced the number of minutes that electrical appliances were used. However, as with many such studies, a follow-up only 1 week after the program was withdrawn indicated that energy consumption had returned to baseline levels (Geller, Winett, & Everett, 1982).

By applying the technique of reinforcement, M. H. Palmer, Lloyd, and Lloyd (1976) reduced the consumption of electricity of four families, using variations of feedback or prompting techniques. Hayes and Cone (1977) decreased use of electricity in four units of a housing complex for married university students. Feedback was effective but not as effective as monetary incentives for reduction of energy consumption. Winett and Neale (1979) compared the effects of information on how to reduce energy consumption with information, feedback, and monetary incentives for reduction in a study of 31 homes.

A major source of energy consumption is, of course, the use of automobiles. Many people drive to work when mass transportation is available. The benefits of mass transportation have been stressed to reduce fuel consumption and pollutants in the air. For example, token reinforcement was extended on a large university campus to promote use of mass transit (Everett, Hayward, & Meyers, 1974). Ridership on the bus increased when the contingency was in effect and returned to baseline levels when the contingency was withdrawn. Ridership did not increase on a control bus that never received the token system.

Safety

An important element in the community's quality of life is that of enhancing safety in various aspects of the environment. The aim would be to prevent injury and death in a wide variety of situations. Accidents are the fourth leading cause of death in adults (after heart disease, cancer, and stroke). The major areas in which accidents occur are in motor vehicles, in the workplace, and in the home (G. Sulzer-Azaroff, 1982).

In the area of highway safety, Parsons (1979) remarked that:

> Psychologists and other behavioral scientists have analyzed the behavior of driving a vehicle from a number of perspectives—cognitive, information processing, perceptual–motor, human factors, task analysis, personality, social interactions, emotion—but interestingly the operant or behavioral analysis world seems to have neglected this important segment of human behavior. (p. 5)

A major element in the quality of life is highway safety, which would involve the use of seat belts (Winett, 1984). Recent attempts to increase safety restraint use have included psychologically based incentive intervention to increase seat belt usage (Geller, Paterson, & Talbott, 1982) and the passage of laws (of different scope and contingencies) to promote increased use of appropriate child restraints and fines for nonuse. Such laws put constraints on individual behavior for the collective good and raise ethical issues that will be discussed in a later section.

Social Planning and Quality of Life

A general term applied to community living is *quality of life*. Increasingly, psychologists, particularly those with a behavioral orientation, have been applying their techniques to the improvement of general living conditions in society. Broadly conceived, what we are dealing with is a process of social planning for "better living."

The concept of *environment* encompasses the total surroundings of an individual's life and its relationship to the person's behavior. We all live surrounded by air, which can be clean, smoggy, or full of sulphur and carbon monoxide. We all drink water, which can be pure or contaminated. We are all affected by radiation. We all live in neighborhoods that are safe or too dangerous to walk in. All of these factors are a consequence of some human behavior.

We must all use some form of transportation—bicycle, auto, train, bus.

We all make use of energy. We are all affected by the intangible "quality of life." We must all live and work in a setting, be it a room, an office, a store, or a factory. We all shop for food, be it in a small store or a large supermarket. All of these settings and areas have become the focus of systematic attempts to change environments to affect behavior.

As we have seen, some of the specific areas of community-relevant problems have included pollution control, fuel consumption, waste material recycling, energy conservation, and mass transit use. These are very specific aspects of the environment, but subtler and perhaps more pervasive issues of community living have also been affected by psychological intervention (Kazdin, 1977). These include increasing the *involvement* of people in decisions affecting their own welfare. With increased *self-help skills* in the community and developed *problem-solving skills* in individuals, more effective self-government follows. There have been attempts to increase the involvement of lower socioeconomic individuals in community affairs. For example, Miller and Miller (1970) increased the attendance of welfare recipients in a monthly *self-help group* discussing such problems as receipt of welfare checks, medical allotments, and community issues such as urban renewal, school board policy, police problems, and city government.

SOCIAL PLANNING AND PLANNED SOCIETIES

We are making the point in this chapter that within the disciplines that focus on studying human behavior there is emerging a new development that emphasizes interpretation of basic research and its application to social values, beliefs, life-styles, and social policy and is appropriate to every segment of society, including industry, the military, sports, and religion. In effect, the goal of change is a better society, a goal often labeled *utopian*, once a positive label but now more likely to be used to denigrate.

Related to this are two phenomena involving the application of psychology. First, there is an uneasiness about where psychology is going as a science and as a profession (Phillips, 1982). At the same time, and often expressed by the same individuals, there is a clarion call for change and for psychology to explicitly take the leadership in applications of the basic science to broader social and policy issues, in effect, to develop a better world. Sarason (1981a, 1981b) cogently argued that psychology as a science and a profession has become "misdirected" because of its focus on the individual (personality dynamics) as an entity without consideration of the social context that influences the individual. Sarason's critique sharply rebuked the direction of postwar mainstream psychology because of its avoidance of social issues and its concentration on the individual.

This malaise is nicely expressed in the headlines of the *New York Times* (Section B) of April 7, 1981, "B. F. Skinner Now Sees Little Hope for the

World's Salvation." The high hopes and optimism of the post-World War II period, in part generated by the victorious war over an "evil" enemy and in part generated by the ever optimistic view of an environmental–behaviorist model of human nature, appear to have faded in frustration.

Skinner, staying within the utopian framework, boldly asks the question "Why Are We Not Acting to Save the World?" in the title of his invited 1982 APA address.

> . . . to change the behavior of those, mainly in governments, religion, or industry and trade, who control the contingencies under which people live. . . . a promising strategy would be to induce people to act to promote a better world. The Utopian literature approaches the problem of the future in that way. But Utopianism which merely portrays a better way of life with no indication of how it is to be achieved is no help. (pp. 22–23)

Although Skinner built Walden Two as an extrapolation of his earlier animal studies to human behavior, a number of other Utopia builders have either deliberately or inadvertently incorporated specific procedures based on the experimental laboratory. Perhaps the best example of this comes from Huxley's *Brave New World* (1932), in which he satirically applied his version of Pavlovian conditioning to a society that had a *value* system holding that certain individuals destined to be workers should not be distracted by literature. To be sure that this occurred, Huxley's planners would put a child on the laboratory floor near a few attractive books. As the child moved to the books or touched them, he was frightened by loud noises or electrically shocked. This was repeated as necessary, and books remained an aversive object for the rest of his life. This is, of course, *not* a desirable application of psychology in the community.

Morawski (1982) enhanced the notion of a utopian application for psychologists by reporting that several prominent psychologists in the early part of the century were also utopiasts.

> . . . four utopias published between 1915 and 1930 by the hardly obscure psychologists G. Stanley Hall, William McDougall, Hugo Munsterberg, and John B. Watson. These utopias clearly reflect Baconian thinking. . . . in their dedication to explaining how psychology, as a science, is instrumental to human welfare. . . . These men were psychologists themselves . . . they were unique in their tendentious belief that their own profession was absolutely essential to improving society. The seriousness of this belief is evidenced in the correspondence between their utopian visions and many of their scientific and professional writings. (pp. 1083, 1090)

There are several major streams of theory, research, and applications of psychology emerging and coalescing into what can be labeled a broad *utopian movement*. Those areas are subsumed under the more generic labels, which we have been describing, of applied behavior analysis, community psychology, social ecology, health psychology, preventive psychology, and social policy. These streams of research and application seem to have as their goal a better life for individuals in our society.

Related to this development was the interaction between psychology and the social reform and social activism movements of the 1960s. Some psychologists applied their skills in the community to bringing about social change and to helping create a better society. The issues of the 1960s, the urban crisis and racial and sexual inequality, became targets for intervention.

The social planning–utopian application of psychology in the community is typified by Fred Keller's vision of community development (Keller, 1980). Keller was a classmate of Skinner and a major influence in applying behavioral procedures in community settings. His vision involved conversion of an old house in a southern city into a community learning center in which there would be taught many things not in the curriculum of the local school such as bicycle repair, picture framing, bookbinding, income tax filing, and esoteric courses in history and nature. The faculty and students of the center are now drawn from all segments of the community. The courses are taught by personalized systems of instructions (PSI). There is a constantly changing curriculum at the center as new people move into the community. An intimate relationship develops among teachers, students, proctors, and administrators. The purpose of the center goes beyond supplying interest, excitement, and friendship to its members to that of binding the members of a community together and thus "prolong its life" (p. 404). Keller used a term that has almost disappeared from the American way of life, *community spirit*, as the major goal of the center. He ended his vision with a plea to the reader to "help to make the dream come true" (p. 404).

Values: Change for What and by Whom?

It should be clear at this point that the most fundamental issue in applying psychology in the community is application *for what* and *by whom*? We emphasize in each chapter of this book an awareness of and concern about values and ethical issues in the particular application of psychology. It is in the area of community that these issues are of particular concern and urgency. The psychologist is now going beyond fostering change in individuals to attempting changes in the society itself. This involves questions of philosophy, politics, social mores, religion, and law.

It is important to note that the application of psychology to the community goes beyond the earlier applications research of the laboratory to life outside the laboratory. Now we are describing the application of values, most of which have not been "validated" in laboratory settings but involve ideas about social change. There has been an outburst of empirically based efforts involving community change and organizational intervention and applications to promote environmental and conservation-related behaviors. However, the intention of these projects goes beyond demonstrating the potential of psychological behaviors. Rather, these projects actually involve change in organizational, community, and even national policies.

Thus, the applier of psychology finds that there is very little room to maneuver except behind the rationale that individuals in the community are being trained so that everyone in sight can control his or her own environment. But there might be a paradox here. If I plan the situation, be it a classroom, clinic, home, or industry, so that an individual learns the procedures to control his or her own environment, then who is the prime mover, the Grand Designer?

A major point that derives from an applied psychology (or social learning) model is that the goal of helping individuals is to enable them to learn how to control, influence, or design their own environments. Implicit in this is a *value judgment* that individual freedom is a desirable goal and that the more an individual is able to affect her or his environment the greater her or his freedom. Of course, there is no absolute freedom in this sense. In this context, *environment* is both the people and the physical objects in one's life.

In dealing with people, we are involved in an influence process that is ubiquitous, not a process of curing or helping unfortunate "sick" people. In this model, everyone is involved in designing and controlling environments: the individual who seeks help, the therapist, the researcher, the schoolteacher, the parent, the student, the warden, the reader of books on applied psychology.

The traditional focus of change in psychology has developed from the one-on-one therapy situation in which the therapist attempts to influence the behavior or internal dynamics (depending on his or her orientation) of the patient or client by interpersonal or environmental manipulations. An extension of that situation is group therapy, in which a therapist works with a group of "people with problems," either for economy over individual therapy or because the group process aids change (or both). The next logical extension has been to go into the community to change "faulty environments" that are causing behavior problems for an individual or a group. In these situations there apply the same principles of influence to achieve behavioral goals as in any situation, without the sometimes intermediate step of labeling nondesired behavior *sick*, *deviant*, or *undesirable*.

Two important elements of the approach we have been describing are relevant to this issue. In eschewing a "disease" model, we can no longer justify changes in the behavior of an individual as a restoration of health, a return to equilibrium. Second, the concept of participant-observer implicitly shifts professionals away from an elitist concept of *expertise*.

The first necessary step in systematic, planned behavior change is to specify the desired behaviors. The fact that value judgments have to be made in choosing desirable behaviors should become very clear. In some models of behavior it has always seemed possible to escape making value judgments. For instance, in traditional psychotherapy, there was no need to question whether a "mentally ill" person's behavior should be changed: The individual was to be "healed." In education, there was no hesitation about forcing children to sit quietly in their seats: How could they learn what they *had to learn* if they did not sit still and pay attention?

But when any behavioral-change program is planned, especially in a community setting, target behaviors have to be laid out for everyone to view, discuss, and criticize; and the decision process brings questions of values into open debate. It can be a very difficult and painful process, but bringing the issues and choices into the open results in a much higher degree of self-control. Bandura (1986) recognized the social issues involved by placing the development of his version of self-control, self-efficacy, in the context of "social foundations."

Although effective behavior influence–control technology presents the possibility of malevolent controllers, the necessity for this decision-making process at least suggests the direction in which to move — toward "controlling the controllers." The professional must "face the hard problems of *what* procedures may be used by *whom* to attain *what* permissible ends" (L. Krasner & Ullmann, 1973, p. 502). The best way to increase freedom is not merely to say people *may* choose but to work so that people *can* choose. Just as humans have gone far in changing their physical environments, we hope the next decade will see humans controlling and changing their psychological environments. The "how" is being developed rapidly in schools, clinics, families, and formal and informal community organizations. An attempt is being made to reduce the gap between decision makers and the populations they affect, especially in the areas of education and consumer affairs and, to a lesser extent, in political and industrial settings. Communicaton among students, parents, and teachers, for example, not only increases the efficiency of the teacher but becomes increasingly the best way to help the teacher decide what ends will best serve all concerned. We need to foster greater communication and awareness between influencers (all of us) and influencees (all of us). We are residents of the same community!

At first it seemed so reasonable and exciting. The whole idea of psychology was to understand and help people. Generally, through the years, applying psychology meant working with individuals, people with problems. Eric's training had been in clinical psychology, and he was quite skilled in treating mentally sick individuals. He was proud of his psychotherapeutic skills. Eric's own background in psychology consisted of the training as a clinical psychologist typical of the post–World War II period, which meant heavy emphasis on working in a one-on-one psychotherapeutic relationship with people who had all kinds of emotional problems.

Then, in effect, Eric has what could be called a *conversion experience*, based on reading Orwell's novel *1984*. This occurs in the early 1960s, and Eric is also influenced by the *Zeitgeist* of the period. He suddenly realizes that his mission in life as a professional psychologist is to prevent the disasters envisioned by Orwell, which would occur in American society in about 2 decades. But what can Eric as one person do about it? Eric does some digging into the influences on Orwell when he wrote this book. To his surprise, he finds that *1984* is really a reversal of the numbers of the year—1948—in which Orwell wrote. This was the post–World War II period, in which there was both great optimism about the future of American society and great concern about the implications of entering the Nuclear Age.

Eric recalls that 1948 was also the year that Skinner published *Walden Two*. Eric had never been keen on Skinner because he represented a viewpoint on the human being that Eric felt was wrong and dangerous. In fact, it seemed to Eric that *1984* represented the end state of the kind of psychology that Skinner advocated.

Eric reads *Walden Two* and becomes interested enough to look further into behavioral methods. What begins to excite him are the broad possibilities of *changing society* that the Skinnerian approach offers. Eric visits communes influenced by *Walden Two*, such as Twin Oaks. He also visits the first token-economy program in a state mental hospital in southern Illinois. He meets with a few of the psychologists beginning to apply Skinner's ideas in community settings. He becomes quite enthused and determined to get involved in the application of this new kind of psychology to bring about a better society and prevent the events of *1984*.

Eric decides to set up a center for training professionals, paraprofessionals, and members of the community in ways of changing society and building a better world. Eric's *resource center*, which he calls Santa Cassandra, becomes the focus of training and planning for applications in the home, school, business, and community in general.

The technique on which Eric's center focuses is that of token economy, because it seems to be so basic to understanding and changing society. Just develop an award system in which a person performs a behavior considered desirable or good. A token (a piece of paper, cardboard, or something called "money") is given. The token can then be exchanged for the good things in life. A new world is opened.

It looks to Eric as if here indeed is the answer to building a better society. He gathers about him a half dozen psychologists who agree with him about the importance of using behavioral principles to create a better society. Support for all these highly charged individuals comes from a nice foundation Eric had persuaded to back these activities. Enthusiasm abounds as special groups are set up for members of the community, including teachers, parents, businesspeople, physicians, political figures, officers from local military bases, and, of course, lawyers. They even set up groups for some special health problems that members of the community have, such as being overweight or fearing to fly or drive a car.

All of these group and community efforts seem to be useful and helpful to the individuals involved, including the professionals. Then a series of new elements enters the situation: From various university settings what appears to be objective research, carried out by investigators with a strong need to publish, begins to raise questions as to whether any community interventions really work; financial problems and issues arise involving "third-party payments'' for treatments; legal suits from several clients charge ''malpractice'' with the result that there are large increases in the cost of malpractice insurance; squabbling among the members of the organization develops as to goals and directions of the various community interventions; and, finally, political intervention, subtle and not so subtle, tries to achieve the goals of the particular party or organization, whatever it may be. Yet, in all, there are some real and positive changes in the community, making it a better place in which to live.

Eric; the members of Santa Cassandra, both professionals and clientele; and you, the reader, are faced with the question, now that 1984 has actually come and gone, Was it worth it?

3 Clinical Applications

The work of the clinical psychologist, varied in both content and setting, is an especially important application of psychological knowledge to real-world concerns. Who are the clinical psychologists, where do they work, and what do they do? In 1985, 5,418 of the 60,120 psychologists of the American Psychological Association were also members of its Clinical Psychology Division. Approximately one third of all graduate students enrolled in psychology programs in American and Canadian universities are clinical psychology students. Employed in clinics, hospitals, service agencies, universities, industry, schools, the military, and private practice, the clinical psychologist provides psychotherapy for a wide variety of clients (40%),* conducts psychological testing (15%), teaches (15%), plans and carries out clinical research (10%), provides a variety of consultation services (10%), or functions as a unit or facility administrator 10 (%).

As these figures indicate, the clinical psychologist engages in a variety of applied activities, but psychotherapy as a direct service—its teaching, its supervision, its investigation—is now a major focus (as such, psychotherapy will also be the major focus of the present chapter). But this was not always the case, for in its formative and early years, psychological testing was the prime concern of the clinical psychologist. In fact, when the first psychological clinic was established (at the University of Pennsylvania) in 1896 by Lightner Witmer (who also coined the term *clinical psychology*), its major function was "mental testing" of children experiencing learning or related problems in school settings. As we described in chapter 1, the goal of most psychological testing was at first the measurement of mental abilities, that is, "intelligence." Used for this purpose, testing proved to be of very considerable applied value, especially for selection and classification purposes in America's world wars. As the early years of the century unfolded, use of psychological testing, in increasingly diverse forms, became widespread.

---

*Approximate percentage of time allocated to activity is based on surveys conducted by Cuca (1975); Garfield and Kurtz (1976), and Goldschmid, Stein, Weissman, and Sorrells (1969).

Twenty psychological clinics existed by 1914; hundreds exist today. In such settings, as well as in the context of private practice, industry, the schools, and elsewhere, the modern clinical psychologist develops, administers, and interprets a wide variety of intelligence, personality, vocational aptitude and interest, neuropsychological, and other specialty psychological tests.

But much more often, most of his or her professional time is spent as a psychotherapist, working with a wide variety of clients and seeking to relieve their distress, to encourage relearning, and to stimulate personal growth. At almost precisely the same time that Witmer's clinic and the role of the psychologist as psychological tester were first established, the roots of modern psychotherapy first developed. Josef Breuer and Sigmund Freud published *Studies in Hysteria* in 1895, a book in which they put forth the then revolutionary idea:

> . . . that many symptoms of their patients seemed to be symbolic attempts to express and resolve chronic conflicts that had their roots in upsetting experiences of early life. This led Freud to develop a form of treatment based on minute exploration of patients' personal histories, with emotional reliving of childhood experiences in the treatment setting. From the information thus gained he formed a theory of human nature and mental illness known as psychoanalysis, which supplied a rationale for his psychotherapy. (Frank, 1961, p. 80)

We will examine the contemporary nature of psychoanalytic psychotherapy in detail later in this chapter. For now, we simply wish to note that Freud's half-century of seminal thinking influenced the character of clinical psychology greatly, and, though such influence has waned in recent years, it is nevertheless still strongly felt. Korchin (1976) accurately captured the psychological testing and historical psychoanalytic basis of modern clinical psychology.

> Clinical psychology has roots in both the psychometric and dynamic [psychoanalytic] traditions of psychology. The psychometric tradition, emphasizing measurement and individual differences mainly in intellectual processes, was of greater prominence in the early history of the field. . . . The dynamic tradition, with concern focused on motivation, adaptation, and personality change, had its greatest impact at a later date and is represented in the concern of clinicians with personality dynamics, development, and psychotherapy. However, the two trends coexisted over the short history of psychology and intertwine in the development of clinical psychology. (pp. 41–42)

The Child Guidance Movement of the 1920s and 1930s, which led to the establishment of many new facilities for the treatment of childhood emotional disorders; the Veterans Administration's widespread employment of clinical psychologists to work in therapeutic capacities with emotionally impaired veterans, which began in the 1940s; and the major financial support provided to clinical psychology training programs beginning in the

1950s by the National Institute of Mental Health each contributed in very important ways to the growth of clinical psychology in general and to the present-day role of the clinical psychologist as a skilled and effective psychotherapist.

PSYCHOTHERAPY: DEFINITIONS, DIFFERENCES, AND COMMONALITIES

What is psychotherapy? Kazdin (1978) has usefully defined psychotherapy as " . . . any intentional application of psychological techniques by a clinician to the end of effecting sought-after personality or behavioral changes" (p. 281). Beyond such broad and general definitions, the originators of most of the 130 different forms of psychotherapy said to exist (Parloff, 1976) have emphasized, in defining their own brands of psychotherapy, the one or two ingredients or procedures that, on the surface at least, make their psychotherapy different from (and purportedly better than) most or all other brands. Thus, we find highlighted in various definitions of psychotherapy such techniques as examination and interpretation of repressed material made available by free association, dreams, slips, or analysis of the transference relationship (psychoanalytic psychotherapy); counterconditioning via reciprocal inhibition of progressive relaxation and imagined approach to feared objects (systematic desensitization therapy); disputation of irrational beliefs (rational–emotive therapy); correction of parataxic distortions (interpersonal psychotherapy); assignment of real-life roles and scripts for enactment (fixed-role therapy); paradoxical intervention and reframing (strategic family therapy); imagined presentation of feared stimuli to maximize anxiety (flooding); demonstration plus guided approach to feared stimuli (participant modeling); modeling, role playing and performance feedback (psychological skills training); and even the use of dance, art, massage, screaming, or other procedures, rituals, or activities. A number of these unique features of various psychotherapies will be examined in detail later in this chapter as we describe several of the more popular approaches to psychotherapy in current use in the United States.

In contrast with this considerable emphasis upon the diverse procedures that make psychotherapies *look* different, many recent writers have sought to better understand and better utilize the psychotherapies by emphasizing what these differences mask, that is, the qualities that *all* psychotherapies essentially share. This stress on *commonalities* is evident in the writings of Frank (1961, 1978), for example. He enumerated as central, common factors (a) an intense confiding *relationship* with a culturally sanctioned therapist; (b) a *rationale* or myth that both therapist and client believe in and that explains both the causes and the nature of the client's difficulties, as well as a method for their remediation; (c) a strengthening of the client's *expectation* that psychotherapy will be helpful; (d) the encouragement of *corrective experiences*; and (e) the facilitation of *emotional arousal*.

Much of Frank's viewpoint, interestingly, was anticipated many years earlier by Rosenzweig who, in 1936, pointed out that all psychotherapies of that era shared an emphasis upon the therapist–patient relationship, catharsis, inspiration, and a systematic ideology. In recent years, belief in the importance of shared features for better understanding and utilizing of psychotherapies has appeared in the writings of many other psychotherapists including especially Goldfried (1982), A. P. Goldstein and Stein (1976), Lambert (1982), and Strupp (1982). It is a viewpoint that has been supported and encouraged by the outcomes of a number of studies examining the effectiveness of diverse psychotherapies. If the qualities upon which therapies differ are more important than the qualities they share, then research comparing the effectiveness of different therapies should more or less consistently show some therapies to be better than others. If it is the qualities they share that are responsible for whatever effectiveness emerges, therapies should generally be approximately equivalent in their successfulness. Although some approaches appear to be somewhat more useful than others in particular instances, the general result of outcome research strongly leans toward viewing therapies as approximately equivalent in effectiveness. Garske and Lynn (1984) summarized in this regard:

> Using this statistical method to compile and evaluate therapy effects, Luborsky et al. (1975) found that many techniques and forms of psychotherapy were effective but not much different relative to each other. . . . Smith et al. (1980) completed an exhaustive meta-analysis in which they reviewed 475 psychotherapy outcome studies. . . . In general, various forms of psychotherapy produced positive outcomes. . . . the average recipient of psychotherapy is more improved than 80 percent of those who go untreated. Therapies tended to be most effective, regardless of orientation or modality, with depressives, simple phobics, and analogue clients solicited for treatment. Other comparative effects were also difficult to demonstrate. Brief versus long-term interventions, individual versus group therapies, and experienced versus novice therapists produced similar effect sizes. (pp. 502–503)

Clearly, therapies appear to be largely equivalent in their effectiveness and, equally clearly, one highly plausible explanation of this result is that their shared effectiveness depends in very large measure on the common qualities we have begun to describe. We thus concur with Garske and Lynn (1984), who conclude:

> Specific factors give a therapy character and definition, albeit innocuous; common factors give a therapy clout. Second, it is assumed that many apparently specific factors are really common factors in disguise. Therapies do similar things in seemingly unique ways. For example, the process of interpretation in psychoanalysis and the exposure to increasing levels of fear-inducing stimuli

while relaxed during systematic desensitization are both effective because they expose a client to an anxiety-evoking thought that he or she was avoiding. (p. 505)

Given this considerable theoretical and experimental evidence in support of the importance of common features for better understanding and employing psychotherapies, we may now return to our earlier question, What is psychotherapy? and answer it more fully by describing in greater detail what we view as the core commonalities constituting much of the essence of all psychotherapies.

CORE COMMONALITIES

Expectancies

Clients come to psychotherapies of all types bringing with them *pretherapy expectations* about what will happen and how well it will work. For each client, such expectations grow from many cultural and personal sources including mass media portrayals of psychotherapy (in soap operas, magazines, etc.); heresay about psychotherapy in general as well as about particular therapies and therapists from friends, relatives, and others; information from their own past experiences, such as relevant books they have read, psychology courses they have taken, or previous counseling or psychotherapy they've undergone; and specific details from the person or agency who referred them to the psychotherapist they are about to meet. Once this meeting takes place, *early psychotherapy expectations* begin to form. These first impressions stem mostly from the manner, appearance, and apparent competence of the psychotherapist. As the therapy sessions unfold—three, four, five—these early bases for forming expectations give way to *results-based expectations*. Is it working? Am I feeling better? Am I less fearful, less anxious, more assertive, more self-confident, better able to eat, less depressed, or improved on some other dimension? Positive or negative answers to such crucial questions, therefore, come to be the primary shapers of patient expectations. Thirty years of research has convincingly demonstrated that pretherapy, early therapy, and results-based patient expectancies can each be an important influence on therapeutic outcome, and it is clearly appropriate to include patient expectancies among the core commonalities being considered here.

Beginning with D. Rosenthal and Frank's article in 1956, "Psychotherapy and the Placebo Effect," applied psychologists have been actively studying the nature, role, and influence of this core commonality across several different approaches to psychotherapy. Two major classifications of patient expectations have been examined: prognostic and role. Prognostic expectancies concern outcome. Is psychotherapy going to be, or anticipated to be, helpful, effective, successful? Role expectancies are relevant to the therapy process itself. What will I be expected to do, how will my therapist behave, what are my rights and responsibilities as a patient? For both types of expectancies, a number of important research findings have emerged. For prognostic expectancies, that is, how successful the patient expects his or her therapy to be, clearly the most important research result is that of several investigations that have shown that such prognostic expectations of change influence the degree of change that actually takes place (Friedman, 1963; A. P. Goldstein, 1959, 1960; Lipkin, 1954; Marcia, Rubin, & Effran, 1969; Tollinton, 1973). It has also been shown that patient prognostic expectancies are influenced by both the referral source (Heine & Trosman, 1960) that helped steer the patient to the particular therapist and the degree of distress the patient experiences (Frank, 1978). Prognostic expectancies, in turn, influence not only degree of change as noted previously, but also the duration of therapy (A. P. Goldstein, 1962; Overall & Aronson, 1962) and the patient's willingness to be open to and influenced by the psychotherapist (A. P. Goldstein, 1971; Wilson & Evans, 1977). Positive prognostic expectancies, in all psychotherapies, could well be an especially central ingredient in establishing and carrying forward a positive therapeutic outcome. As Lambert (1982) remarked in this regard:

> . . . expectations may play a role in determining therapy success in the following sequence: The client's faith in the therapist that is fostered by the relationship leads to an increase in the client's expectations for a positive outcome from therapy. These increased expectations, in turn, persuade the client to follow the therapist's lead in trying out new behaviors. Bandura found empirical support for his hypothesis that such behavior change increases self-efficacy expectation,—that is, the expectations of personal capability. . . . Increased self-efficacy expectations, in turn help maintain the behavior change. (p. 92)

Role expectations in psychotherapy—what you expect to do and what you believe will be expected of you—have also been shown to be an important aspect of diverse psychotherapies. Some role-expectation research has sought to identify different types of expectations and to examine how they develop and what they lead to. Thus, Apfelbaum (1958) and A. P. Goldstein and Heller (1960) have investigated the place of Nurturant, Critic, and Model role expectations. Guidance (i.e., tell me what to do) versus Participation (i.e., let's figure it out together) patient role expectations are a second useful breakdown (Schofield, 1964). Several research findings have been reported using role-expectation categories such as these, but the most useful are those several studies showing the crucial importance of congruence or mutuality of the role expectations held by the patient and those held by the psychotherapist for the successful course of the treatment (Appel, 1960; Chance, 1959; Lennard & Bernstein, 1960). As the last authors observed:

When both members of a dyad are in general agreement regarding their reciprocal obligations and returns, there is a consensus or similarity of expectations, and harmony or stability occurs in their interpersonal relations. . . .
But when there is any degree of discrepancy or lack of consensus between the
participants, and their expectations are dissimilar . . . manifestations of strain
appear in their interpersonal relations. If expectations are too dissimilar, the
system disintegrates unless the differences can be reconciled. (p. 153)

If the patient expects to make rapid progress within a few sessions and does
not learn that this expectation is unrealistic, he may become so discouraged that
he terminates treatment. . . . If he expects the therapist to be a parent figure
toward him . . . he may terminate treatment when the disappointment reaction sets in, or he may enter a stage of resistance until his misconceptions are
exposed and corrected. If a patient expects to tell the therapist only those
things of which he is proud and hides those things of which he is ashamed, the
patient will make little progress until he learns to do otherwise. Thus, unrealistic role expectations tend to increase strain and destroy equilibrium. (p. 118)

Finally, with regard to role expectations, note should also be made of the
important work of Jerome Frank and his research group (Hoehn-Saric et al.,
1964) on developing and evaluating the Role Induction Interview. This is a
set of pretherapy interview and instructional procedures, used successfully
with a number of different types of patients to correct erroneous role expectations and effectively socialize them into accurate sets of beliefs and antici-
pations about what occurs in psychotherapy and what is expected of them
for positive outcomes to be more likely.

These several investigations, examining the impact on both the therapy
process and the outcome of patient prognostic and role expectations, clearly
demonstrate such expectations to be a significant core commonality in defining what psychotherapy is and in utilizing it most effectively.

Therapist–Patient Relationship

Essentially all descriptions of psychotherapeutic approaches, of whatever
theoretical orientation, place considerable emphasis upon the potency of the
therapist–patient relationship for both the enhancement of the process of
therapy itself and the bringing about of patient change. As we have noted
elsewhere:

. . . perhaps the major responsible ingredient in determining whether such
change occurs is the quality of the helper-client relationship. The same conclusion emerges if one examines descriptions of almost all of the many different approaches to formal psychotherapy. These several approaches vary in
many respects—therapist activity and directiveness, how much focus is upon
behavior versus the patient's inner world of feelings and attitudes, whether
emphasis is placed upon the patient's present life or his childhood history,
which aspects of his current difficulty are examined, and in a host of procedural ways. Yet, almost every approach to psychotherapy emphasizes the impor-

tance of the therapist-patient relationship for patient change. The better the relationship: (1) the more open is the patient about his feelings, (2) the more likely he is to explore these feelings deeply with the helper, (3) the more likely he is to listen fully to and act upon any advice offered him by the helper. (A. P. Goldstein, 1971, p. 19)

This is a widely held view. Much of the clout in diverse psychotherapies lies in the relationship, whether the therapy is psychoanalytic (Ferreira & Rosen, 1982), client-centered (Rice, 1982), cognitive (Arnkoff, 1982), behavioral (R. J. Morris & Magrath, 1982), gestalt (Greenberg, 1982), family (Stahmann & Harper, 1982), or group (Fuhriman & Barlow, 1982). What is the patient–therapist relationship? Several key ingredients are frequently mentioned, one cluster of which could be described as attraction, liking, and warmth, experienced reciprocally patient to therapist, therapist to patient. In addition to these emotional components, a good therapist–patient relationship also captures and responds to the role of the helper as a competent expert. Thus, one often finds mentioned such key relationship ingredients as patient perception of the therapist as trustworthy, credible, and skilled in the task. It appears, therefore, that a good therapist–patient relationship can best be defined as a relationship fully characterized by attitudes and behaviors reflecting both warmth and respect (A. P. Goldstein, 1971; Lambert, 1982).

In their continuing effort to better understand how psychotherapy works, and to make it work better, applied psychologists have conducted many investigations of the therapist–patient relationship, focusing in particular on its association with patient improvement. Does a good therapist–patient relationship actually lead to a better outcome for the patient, as so many psychotherapists claim? The answer appears to be a confident yes. The scientific study of psychotherapy began in 1950, and, throughout its approximately 35-year history, there have been many research demonstrations of the relationship–outcome association (Bown, 1954; Goldstein, 1971; J. Hunt, Ewing, LaForge, & Gilbert, 1959; Lambert, 1982; Parloff, 1961; Vander Veen, 1965).

The potency of the therapeutic relationship for patient change can be demonstrated not alone by research such as that just cited showing that a good relationship leads to positive patient change. The relationship–outcome connection can be further demonstrated by showing that a poor relationship results not in patient improvement but in deterioration. Lambert (1982) disclosed that:

. . . the recognition that some patients are actually made worse by the therapy that was intended to help them has proved even more informative about the active ingredients in psychotherapy. Empirical research has helped us to identify several specific ways in which people are made worse by or hurt in therapy. Reviews of this phenomenon . . . suggest that, although some negative outcomes may be the result of a misapplication of specific techniques, by and large they are more clearly associated with the quality of the therapeutic relationship. (p. 17)

Concretely, patient deterioration has been found to result from such relationship deficiencies as a therapist who is rejecting, manipulative, or low in her or his own interpersonal skills (Lambert, 1982), is intrusive or aggressively confronting (Yalom & Lieberman, 1971), displays low energy levels or low interest in the patient (Ricks, 1974), or makes serious errors of technique (Sandell, 1981). Indeed, psychotherapy can be for better or for worse, and a crucial determiner of which occurs is the therapist–patient relationship.

How does a good psychotherapeutic relationship develop, and can concrete steps actually be taken to improve it in situations where its quality is threatened? Observations offered by Korchin (1976) are helpful in these regards.

What does the therapist do? Above all, he listens with unswerving attention, sympathetic concern, and continuous effort to understand the patient's personal meanings. The capacity to listen without responding in terms of one's own needs and feelings or the demands of social convention is . . . the fundamental requisite of effective psychotherapy. At appropriate moments, the therapist communicates his understanding to the patient or otherwise acts to relieve the patient's suffering. The clinician values the patient's integrity as a person and his striving for self-betterment, nor does he fault the patient for his inadequacies. At the same time, he maintains necessary objectivity and detachment. The therapist is simultaneously compassionate and dispassionate. . . . The blend of these characteristics gives the psychotherapeutic relationship its special character as a setting within which emotional relearning can take place. (pp. 284–285)

But what of the situation in which such positive relationship attitudes and behaviors by the psychotherapist are insufficient? What can be done to optimize the therapist–patient relationship when the patient is resistive to psychotherapy and feels neither warmly nor respectfully toward the psychotherapist? Means for improving the quality of the therapeutic relationship do exist and include those examined in our own research program on the enhancement of "psychotherapeutic attraction" (A. P. Goldstein, 1971, 1980). As Figure 3.1 summarizes, several interventions derived originally from social psychological laboratory studies of interpersonal attraction were used by us with resistive or low-relatability patients. In this extended research program, we were able to show that, with certain major types of patients, most of the relationship enhancers employed did increase patient liking, respect, or trust of the therapist, with positive consequences for both the therapy process (e.g., communication, openness, persuasability) and the therapy outcome.

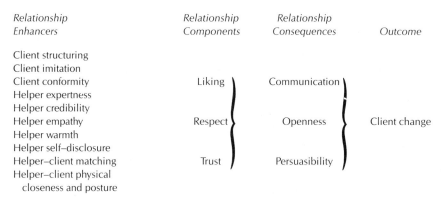

Relationship Enhancers	Relationship Components	Relationship Consequences	Outcome
Client structuring			
Client imitation			
Client conformity	Liking	Communication	
Helper expertness			
Helper credibility			
Helper empathy	Respect	Openness	Client change
Helper warmth			
Helper self–disclosure			
Helper–client matching	Trust	Persuasibility	
Helper–client physical closeness and posture			

FIGURE 3.1. Progression from relationship enhancement to client change. (*Note.* From "Relationship-Enhancement Methods" by A. P. Goldstein in *Helping People Change* (3rd ed., p. 20) edited by F. H. Kanfer and A. P. Goldstein, 1986, Elmsford, NY: Pergamon. Copyright 1986 by Pergamon)

In 1959, Bordin stated:

> The key to the influence of psychotherapy on the patient is in his relationship with the therapist. Wherever psychotherapy is accepted as a significant enterprise, this statement is so widely subscribed to as to become trite. Virtually all efforts to theorize about psychotherapy are intended to describe and explain what attributes of the interactions between the therapist and the patient will account for whatever behavior change results. (p. 235)

As this section has made clear, research on both therapeutic gain and deterioration amply supports Bordin's (1959) assertion. Further, as the work of Korchin (1976) and A. P. Goldstein (1971) noted earlier suggests, the ways in which good therapeutic relationships naturally develop, or can be promoted to develop, are also largely known today. In combination, these various theoretical and research advances make it unequivocally clear that the therapist–patient relationship is indeed a most central core commonality.

New Learning: By Rationale, Modeling, and Exposure

In our view, psychotherapy is in its essence a relearning experience. The "lesson plans" can vary greatly, as can the modes of teaching and what is taught, but, nonetheless, all psychotherapies share a major focus upon the patient's learning new attitudes and behaviors. Such new learning begins with the given therapy's *rationale*, as communicated by the therapist to the patient.

> The conceptual framework of the psychotherapy facilitates this [positive] outcome by providing both an explanation of the behavioral anomaly and a prescription for change. All therapies also provide for ample success experiences in understanding those thoughts and actions that had been confusing, and in coping with stresses and anxieties that had been avoided and dealt with

maladaptively. The patient is provided with new opportunities to learn different ways of thinking, feeling, and behaving. This is accomplished in his or her interaction with the therapist by means of interpretations, confrontations, role playing exercises, and so forth. Such novel learning opportunities are also provided outside of the therapeutic setting as homework assignments, behavioral recording, and self-monitoring. Therapeutic learning experiences, guided within a theoretical perspective by an expert practitioner solidify the patient's sense of mastery. (Garske & Lynn, 1984, p. 507)

Frank (1978) has similarly emphasized the relationship-enhancing and other positive consequences of providing the patient with a rationale, a belief system, or a "myth" about the therapy process, especially to the degree that *both* therapist and patient believe in, or come to believe in, this shared rationale.

A second shared avenue of new learning, common to all psychotherapies, is the therapist's role as a *model.* His or her attitudes, beliefs, problem-solving behaviors, language, and mannerisms may each be explicitly or implicitly modeled by the therapist and observed and imitated by the patient. Such modeling might be intentional, as in the psychological-skills-training therapies (A. P. Goldstein, 1981) or unintentional (but nonetheless as potent), as in the psychodynamic therapies (Strupp, 1982). Writing about therapist modeling as a commonality that cognitive–behavior therapy shares with other approaches, Arnkoff (1982) observed:

> In all therapies, the therapist becomes a model for the client of adaptive behavior, whether or not such modeling is planned by the therapist. . . . In the client's demoralized state, he or she may lack adequate role models, as Space and Cromwell found for depression. As the therapist persuades the client of the therapeutic rationale, the client may adopt not only the therapist's rationale and therapeutic procedures but also other aspects of the therapist's behavior, such as how the therapist responds to problems that came up in therapy. In an active therapy like cognitive therapy, the therapist displays problem-solving behavior that the client would adopt. When such problem-solving by the therapist is adaptive, cognitive therapy may be particularly strong in this factor. (p. 105)

Perry and Furukawa's (1986) extensive review of theory and research on modeling in diverse psychotherapies appropriately concluded that not only is its direct or implicit implementation widespread, but also, based on empirical evidence, it appears to play a particularly potent role in contributing to patient change.

Learning of new attitudes and behaviors by the patient can also be accomplished in many psychotherapies by a process of *exposure.* Exposure as a core commonality has been promoted most actively by Marks (1978), who explained, with regard to its potency in diverse behavioral therapies:

> The principle of exposure involves relief from phobias and compulsions by the individual's continued contact with those situations that evoke discomfort (the

MAP—C

evoking stimuli, ES) until it subsides. . . . Most behavioral approaches to the treatment of anxiety syndromes like phobic and obsessive–compulsive disorders employ the common principle of exposure to the ES. What at first sight seem to be widely different forms of fear reduction—for example, desensitization in fantasy, flooding in vivo, cognitive rehearsal, modeling, and operant conditioning—all appear to be ways of exposing the patient to the frightening situation until he or she gets used to it. This process could also be called adaptation, extinction, or habituation. (p. 498)

Marks (1978) has marshalled considerable evidence in support of his assertion of exposure as a broadly potent commonality. We agree that it appears to play such a central role in several behavioral therapies and would even extend its probable importance to a less obvious but perhaps equally important significance in a number of primarily nonbehavioral therapies. Exposure is a core commonality that influences outcome, we propose, in psychodynamic therapy when interpretation, free association, and lowering of defenses permit previously warded-off contents into the patient's awareness. Exposure appears to be salient in those several cognitively oriented therapies that train and encourage patients to engage in making self-statements or self-instructions, for example, rational emotive therapy, stress innoculation, and cognitive restructuring. And exposure is perhaps most clearly evident in those instigation therapies that by script or other real-world homework assignments strongly encourage direct patient exposure to and mastery of real-life evoking stimuli. Thus it appears clear that by means of an understandable rationale for both the patient's distress and the treatment process, by the modeling of constructive behaviors by the therapist, and by exposing the patient to typically avoided sources of distress, considerable opportunity for learning new attitudes and behaviors occurs. These three common avenues for new learning do not exhaust the possibilities. The core commonality of new learning can also be implemented in many other ways such as by persuasion (Frank, 1961), suggestion (Frank, 1978), skills training (Goldstein, 1981), and problem solving (D'Zurilla & Goldfried, 1971).

Reinforcement

A final core commonality characteristic of all psychotherapies is reward, or reinforcement, provided to the patient by the psychotherapist. Some therapies, especially the contingency-management approaches, consist of procedures explicitly concerned with optimizing the effectiveness of the provision or withdrawal of reinforcement. Reinforcement scheduling, shaping, extinction, fading, response cost, and token economies are all contingency-management procedures specifying the amount, rate, scheduling, timing, or other aspects of reinforcement delivery. A great deal of evidence supports the conclusion that contingency management can be a rapid and effective means of altering a wide variety of patient behaviors (Agras, 1967; Bandura, 1969; Kazdin, 1977; S. G. O'Leary, 1976; J. A. Sherman, 1965). Reinforcement by the therapist operates just as powerfully in psychodynamic, client-centered or other approaches, almost all of which tend to deny such a prominent influencing role to reinforcement. Even in the absence of tangible rewards for changed behavior, all therapists have been shown to provide the very powerful social reinforcement of attention to those therapy topics they wish explored further and to those patient behaviors they aspire to alter. As early as 1948, M. G. Gill and Brennan (1948) noticed that the

> . . . raw data in psychotherapeutic research is inevitably influenced by the therapist's views . . . the subtleties of showing interest in certain kinds of material, often not consciously detected either by therapist or patient, are manifold. This may include . . . a shifting of visual focus, a well-timed "mm-hmm," a scarcely perceptible nod, or even a clearing of the throat. (Krasner, 1962, p. 63)

Krasner (1955) pointed out that such subtle use of therapist reinforcement was common to all psychotherapies and, in a 1962 paper titled "The Therapist as a Social Reinforcement Machine" reviewed a wealth of evidence in support of the reinforcing potency of therapist attention and related behaviors. Evidence corroborating this conclusion has continued to accumulate in subsequent years (D. W. Johnson & Matross, 1977; Strupp, 1977). It is indeed a well-substantiated conclusion that therapist reinforcement of patient behavior is a core commonality across psychotherapies.

We have focused in this section on four core commonalities: enhanced and clarified expectations, a good therapist–patient relationship, the learning of new attitudes and behaviors, and reinforcement provided the patient by the psychotherapist. Although other possible common features across diverse therapies could eventually prove just as central — such as therapist communication skills (A. P. Goldstein & Stein, 1976; Schofield, 1964), therapist power or status (A. P. Goldstein & Stein, 1976; Schofield, 1964), the "asocial and unengaged" stance of the therapist (Beier, 1966), patient dependency and suggestibility (Frank, 1978), and the emotional arousal of the patient (Frank, 1961) — we believe the four we have emphasized constitute a very major part of the answer to What is psychotherapy?

MAJOR PSYCHOTHERAPIES

It is certainly the case that different approaches to psychotherapy look quite different from one another. Therapists of different orientations seem to be doing very different things to, with, and for their patients. It is not known at the present whether these considerable between-therapies differences in technique are merely equivalent (and in a sense interchangeable) ways of express-

MAP—C*

ing the same core commonalities, or whether they are differences that have at least some effect by, in fact, adding therapeutic clout to that provided by the core commonalities themselves. This latter view—that the core commonalities are the main factors bringing about patient change, but that technique differences between therapies add somewhat to this effectiveness—does not seem to be an unreasonable stance to take. This is especially true in light of evidence that has begun to slowly grow in recent years that some psychotherapies could be prescriptively more effective with some types of patients, and not with others (A. P. Goldstein & Stein, 1976; Magaro, 1969). If psychotherapies were in fact completely equivalent or transitive, if *only* what they shared were responsible for patient change, there would be little or no support for the prescriptive conclusion now emerging that, at least for some types of patients, one type of therapy actually is more effective than another type. In the remainder of this chapter, by means of both factual text and constructed case histories, we will describe in detail a number of the major psychotherapies in current use today, in conjunction with the type of patient problem for which each appears most prescriptive. In doing so, we will highlight both the manner in which each therapy expresses the core commonalities described earlier and the particular technique differences that give each approach its unique character.

Cognitive–Behavior Therapy

The Golner Center for Psychotherapy

The Golner Center for Psychotherapy was established in 1954 as a clinic whose purpose was to provide psychotherapy for large numbers of patients, regardless of their ability to pay. Both its founders and its staff of 13 full-time psychotherapists were clinical psychologists. Anticipating the research evidence on the value of conducting psychotherapy prescriptively that began to appear in the 1970s, the staff of psychotherapists were diverse in their preferred approaches to psychotherapy, unlike in most other clinics, then and now, which are mostly psychoanalytic, or mostly behavioral, or mostly some other particular orientation. More and more as years passed, which patient was assigned to which therapist for which psychotherapy was an intake and diagnostic decision that the Golner staff sought to make as prescriptively as possible.

On May 2, Verna Hill, age 28, white, single, and obviously very unhappy, presented herself at Golner for psychotherapy, accompanied (really escorted) by her sister. The intake interview and psychological testing revealed all the classic signs of a serious depression. Verna had been sleeping and eating poorly and had lost almost 15 pounds in the last 3 months. She tended to move around slowly, seemingly using great effort for even minor chores. She had little interest in many of the events going on around her and, when she did communicate with others, as often as not it was to express her feelings of worthlessness and guilt for behaviors most other people would not find troublesome. Her sister reported that on two occasions Verna had spoken with a sense of determination of trying to injure herself and, in fact, had been increasingly careless in the past month when using their kitchen stove and, before her sister had prohibited all driving, when driving their automobile.

Cognitive–behavior therapy currently appears to be the prescriptive psychotherapy of choice for adults experiencing depressive disorders. Growing out of rational–emotive therapy (Ellis, 1977), as well as the mainstream of the behavioral approaches, cognitive–behavior therapy was developed primarily by Beck (1976) and his co-workers. Much of what causes and maintains depression, according to Beck, is distorted thinking by the individual, especially in his or her underlying assumptions and information processing. The kinds of thinking that are held to characterize depression include:

1. *Arbitrary inference*, which is drawing conclusions when the evidence for the conclusion is actually contrary or absent. A frown on the face of a passerby results in the thought "He is upset with me or disgusted by me."

2. *Overgeneralization*, which is reaching broad conclusions based on very little data. In the example of the misunderstood frown just given, overgeneralization would involve adding the thought, "Just like most people are disgusted by me."

3. *Magnification and minimization*, which are the tendencies to distort by, respectively, exaggerating or catastrophizing the importance of a (possibly negative) event or downplaying or denying the importance of a (possibly positive) event. The depressed college student magnifies the negative implications of her C grade in biology, and denies or minimizes the perhaps counterbalancing implications of her A grades in chemistry and physics.

4. *Dichotomous reasoning*, which is the tendency to think in extremes or absolutes, in a polarized, all-or-none manner. The person must be perfect or totally good; the future is all black, with no hope; failure is seen as total, with no redeeming features.

It is this pattern of assumptions and thinking errors, therefore, that leads to the characteristic focus of depressed individuals on loss, a sense of inadequacy, expectation of negative outcomes and, consequently, leads to depressed emotions. As Hollon and Beck (1979), described it:

> . . . they regard themselves as deprived, defeated or diseased; their worlds as full of roadblocks to their obtaining even minimal satisfaction; and their futures as devoid of any hope of gratification and promising only pain and frustration. (p. 154)

Cognitive–behavior therapy consists of procedures that seek to alter these fundamental, erroneous assumptions and patterns of thinking. First, the individual is encouraged to monitor and record his or her negative automatic thoughts. This is a data-collection phase for the therapist (How much? Of what type?) and an increasing-awareness phase for the patient. The second phase, best labeled *rationale-expectancies relationship*, to reflect the core commonalities it seeks to establish, is captured well by Meichenbaum (1985):

> Over the course of treatment the therapist begins to impart to the client a conceptual framework for understanding the client's maladaptive behaviors. The translation process fosters a sense of positive anticipation and hope in · clients, and replaces the sense of helplessness and hopelessness. . . . A useful way to accomplish this translation process is to establish a collaborative working relationship between the client and the therapist. (p. 270)

Given this base of self-monitored information about disordered assumptions and thoughts, the provision of a rationale for change, and the beginnings of both positive prognostic expectancies and a positive therapist–patient relationship, the more didactic, instructional phases of cognitive–behavior therapy can proceed. Here, the therapist actively seeks to alter the patient's guiding assumptions, negative self-statements, and self-defeating behaviors. A variety of procedures is used to accomplish these goals. The therapist "arranges, encourages, challenges, cajoles, and persuades" (Meichenbaum, 1985, p. 270) the client to try out new positive behaviors under circumstances in which the outcomes are likely to refute negative assumptions. These are, in a sense, real-world "experiments" (exposures) the patient has typically not attempted on her or his own. By means of *reattribution* and *decentering* techniques, faulty assumptions are further challenged. Alternative, more balanced, and optimistic assumptions are proposed, and they are tested in both role play and real-life contexts. To increase the likelihood that these more balanced ways of thinking and more optimistic prognostications about the outcome of events prove accurate, the client might also be provided with new learning via interpersonal skills training to improve effectiveness and satisfaction in interactions with others. Research evidence available regarding the effectiveness of cognitive–behavior therapy for aiding depressed individuals is quite positive (Beck, 1976; R. Miller & Berman, 1981).

Psychodynamic Psychotherapy

Phil Beyer received the Junior Executive of the Year Award from his company last year, and it was clear that both his bosses and his co-workers saw him as a man on the way up. Phil was bright, very hard working, full of good ideas, and he had scores of friends. It looked more and more as if he'd someday become the first black vice president Bellweather Corporation ever had.

In the last half year, however, there had been a number of occasions on which Phil's efficient, friendly, and thoroughly competent exterior masked things going on inside him that were very troublesome. He'd had four or five periods in which he trembled for no apparent reason, feeling tense and jittery and easily startled. Just before and during these times, and also on a few other occasions, he had felt very anxious and apprehensive. He didn't know of what. There was nothing in particular he was fearful of; it was more a feeling of being worried about everything in particular. At those times he tried to check off, or check upon, the important things in his life—work, family, friends—but the fact that each was OK didn't seem to help. He still felt very apprehensive in kind of a free-floating way. Phil also noticed that, in the last 6 weeks, he'd begun to develop a few persistant physical symptoms—dry mouth, sweatiness, light-headedness, and a pounding heart. He'd always been in perfect health, and these symptoms of he-didn't-know-what made him more anxious than ever. On Monday Phil applied to the Golner Center for psychotherapy. Based on his intake interview and psychological testing, the staff decision was reached to offer to treat his Generalized Anxiety Disorder with psychodynamic psychotherapy.

Psychodynamic psychotherapy has its roots in the writings of Sigmund Freud and the psychoanalytic theory of personality that was the cornerstone of his work. As we shall see, the specific procedures and techniques constituting this therapeutic approach grow quite directly from psychoanalytic beliefs about how personality develops and about how it can become disordered. As Korchin (1976) wrote:

> The foundations for behavior and its problems are set down in childhood through satisfaction or frustration of basic needs and impulses. Because of their potentially central role in regard to these needs, the nature and quality of early relationships with parents, siblings, grandparents, peers, and authority figures . . . are given special emphasis and attention. There is thus a distinct historical flavor to the psychodynamic model and a concomitant focus upon the importance of past rather than present events. (p. 324)

In psychoanalytic thinking, neurotic symptoms were often seen as growing from such conflicted, early childhood experiences and frequently involving the child's sexual needs and feelings. Of special importance in this connection, and of special importance for the key techniques of psychodynamic psychotherapy, Freud proposed that there existed processes (e.g., repression) that kept such conflicted needs and feelings from the individual's awareness. These unconscious needs and feelings resulted in emotions and anxieties the individual might actively seek to avoid recognizing (by use of *defense mechanisms*) or dealing with (by use of *resistance* in the psychotherapy itself). The central goal of psychodynamic psychotherapy thus became the uncovering of these unconscious, childhood-based conflicts ("Making the unconscious conscious") and using the cause-and-effect insights thus gained to both relieve symptoms and reconstruct the individual's personality. How does the psychodynamic psychotherapist proceed? According to Korchin (1976):

> A central task of psychoanalysis is to bring out the hidden, unconscious wishes and conflicts which underlie present symptoms and behavior. An important tool toward this end is *free association*. The patient has to accept the *basic rule*, that he will minimize conscious control and without selection or censor-

ship he will tell everything that comes to mind. To facilitate free association, distracting stimuli are minimized and relaxation is encouraged. . . . Under these conditions, the patient's communications are more likely to follow the dictates of emotional and unconscious logic rather that that of more conventional rational thought. (p. 327)

In psychodynamic therapy, free association is the main, but not the only route to revealing and understanding unconscious material. Hypnosis was tried early by Freud (Breuer & Freud, 1895) but found to be too unreliable. The analysis of dreams is a second such path, one that Freud described as a "royal road to the unconscious." Both dreams and unintentional slips of the tongue were held to often reflect unconscious material whose expressions was relatively undefended against.

In addition to these means of eliciting unconscious antecedents of contemporary problems, equally central to the psychodynamic psychotherapy process is the development and analysis of the transference relationship. As Freud experienced the very strong positive or negative feelings his patients seemed to hold toward him, feelings he felt were highly out of proportion to what had actually occurred in the therapy itself, he reasoned that:

. . . such feelings were not generated by the present, but rather were brought forward (transferred) from childhood experiences with key persons, notably the parents. The patient was now acting *as if* the analyst were his father or mother, on his part acting out feelings, wishes, and fantasies of his childhood. (p. 329)

These transference reactions (or, in their most intense form, *transference neuroses*); the patient's free associations, dreams, and slips; and, equally important, the patient's resistances to the therapist's explanations of these materials; are all dealt with by the psychodynamic psychotherapist through interpretation. In a real sense, interpretation is the main active procedure in which the therapist engages. Interpretation means providing the patient with new learning by explaining the unconscious sources of current behavior and, by this means, trying to bring into awareness and better understanding the causes, connections, and meanings.

As can be seen, psychodynamic psychotherapy requires certain cognitive, introspective, and verbal skills of its recipients and, thus, is held by some to have only a narrow range of prescriptive applicability. This is especially true for the more intensive form of psychodynamic psychotherapy, psychoanalysis. For many years, psychodynamic psychotherapy was broadly used for a full range of disorders throughout the United States. Although it continues to be used relatively widely, the emergence of a number of other potent psychotherapies in the last 2 decades; the general absence of supportive research, especially for the psychoanalytic form of psychodynamic psychotherapy; and the restricted range of patients for whom it is applicable, as noted, have combined to result in a progressive decline in the use of the approach, a decline we expect will continue.

Behavior Therapies

Mary couldn't understand what was happening to her. All she knew was that it was getting worse and worse. Then Tuesday morning the answer came. She was straightening up her husband's desk and came across a book he seemed to have been looking at, buried under some papers. The book was *A Guide to Common Emotional Problems*, and a corner of one of the pages was turned down. With both curiosity and a bit of apprehension, Mary opened to the earmarked page and saw a paragraph her husband had bracketed in red:

> *Agoraphobia*. The essential feature is a marked fear of being alone or being in public places from which escape might be difficult or help not available in case of sudden incapacitation. Normal activities are increasingly constricted as the fears or avoidance behavior dominate the individual's life. The most common situations avoided involve being in crowds, such as on a busy street or in crowded stores, or being in tunnels, or bridges, on elevators, or on public transportation. Often these individuals insist that a family member accompany them whenever they leave home.

"Agoraphobia, agoraphobia," Mary repeated to herself "so that's what it's called."

Somehow knowing that the way she'd been acting and feeling the past 8 months had a name made her feel worse. She had become a virtual hermit, and the few times she went anywhere it was always with Carl, sometimes clinging to him for dear life.

On a Monday, after three cancellations, and holding on tightly to Carl's arm, a very anxious Mary Price arrived at Golner for her appointment.

The behavior therapies are a variety of procedures that originated in the laboratory research of the experimental or social psychologist, were shown to effectively change behavior in such research contexts, and have since been applied to the real-world concerns of unhappy, ineffective, or emotionally disturbed individuals. Unlike the psychodynamic therapies, they focus on the present, not the patient's long-term history. Because their fundamental assumption is that *all* behaviors, desirable and undesirable, effective and ineffective, are learned, they emphasize unlearning (the undesirable) and new learning (of the desirable) and not insight regarding unconscious or other historical causes of behavior. The person's current interpersonal and physical environment — what behaviors it stimulates, what behaviors it controls, what behaviors it rewards — is seen as the major cause of the behaviors of concern and, hence, is the major target of change efforts.

Several different behavior therapies have emerged in the past 2 decades, each present oriented, learning based, goal specific, and empirically evaluated. In 1958, Joseph Wolpe published his book *Psychotherapy by Reciprocal Inhibition*, a description of *systematic desensitization* therapy. Designed for phobic patients, it grows from the position that such persons have learned to associate high levels of anxiety with certain stimuli, for example flying in an airplane, handling a snake, seeing a dog approach, being in the dark. This is the original learning to be substituted for by new learning. Such new learning is accomplished in systematic desensitization by teaching the patient how to deeply relax and, in that relaxed state, because one cannot be both relaxed and anxious at the same time, to imagine ever-closer approach to and involvement with the feared stimulus. Systematic desensitization researchers have frequently found that when the patient can, in a relaxed manner, imagine such contact with an airplane, a snake, a dog, the dark, or whatever, she or he can actually, not in imagination, fly in an airplane, handle a snake, pet a dog, be in the dark, or whatever.

Skinner's experimental laboratory research on operant conditioning began to be utilized in a behavior therapy context in 1959 (Ayllon & Michael, 1959) and has had particularly widespread application with a variety of child and adult institutionalized and community patients. Operant conditioning, also known in its therapeutic application as *contingency management*, involves the provision or withdrawal, respectively, of rewards or reinforcements following those behaviors whose occurrence or frequency one seeks to increase or decrease. By systematic provision of material rewards (food, money, stars, check marks, tokens) or social rewards (praise, attention, approval) following behaviors the therapist or the client wants to increase, the probability that the behavior will recur does in fact increase. The withholding of reinforcement successfully decreases the likelihood any given behavior will occur, and thus an important part of contingency management is to withhold reinforcement following the occurrence of undesirable or inappropriate behaviors. This is typically done by means of ignoring the behavior (extinction), temporarily removing the person from possible sources of reward (time out), or taking away or withholding rewards expected by or already in the person's possession (response cost). With contingency management, the combination of rewarding desirable behaviors and removing rewards following undesirable behaviors (sometimes in combination with such other contingency-management procedures as shaping, fading, and prompting) has proven to be an especially powerful and successful behavior-therapy approach (Agras, 1967; A. P. Goldstein, 1983; Kazdin, 1977).

A particularly important quality of the behavior therapies is the willingness of many persons committed to this approach to submit their interventions to rigorous experimental evaluation and to change the intervention, if appropriate, on the basis of the evaluation's results. In spite of its early wide popularity, in recent years the systematic desensitization approach to alleviating phobias has been increasingly replaced by a different intervention, one which research findings show could be even more potent for such patients. Reflecting quite fully the core commonality of new learning described earlier, in this instance via both modeling and exposure, the behavior therapy called *participant modeling* involves procedures in which:

Initially, the therapist serves as a model in demonstrating safe interaction with the feared objects or situations, and then guides the client in performing the same sequence of graded activities. As treatment continues, the amount of demonstration, protection and guidance is gradually decreased until the client can confront the feared situations comfortably and effectively. (A. R. Sherman, 1979, p. 43)

According to Bandura (1977b), the developer of this approach, its reliable success grows from several sources. The fear or phobia could be reduced in part by a process called vicarious extinction, when the client sees the therapist directly involved with the feared object with no negative consequences. Also during this demonstration phase of participant modeling, the client could learn both fear-reducing information (about flying, snakes, etc) and skills (how to handle, how to approach). Following demonstration, the therapist could approach the feared object *with* the client (side by side, client's arm on therapist's arm as they reach for the snake, etc.), thus capitalizing on the core commonalities of expectancies and relationship. When the client does actually fly in the airplane or hold the snake and nothing terrible actually happens, a process of direct extinction of fear might occur. With these several factors for change operating, it is not surprising that several investigations have reported clearly positive results for participant modeling as a means of altering phobic behavior (Bandura, Jeffery, & Wright, 1974; Ritter, 1969; Thelen & Fry, 1981).

In addition to systematic desensitization, contingency management, and participant modeling, a number of other behavior therapies have been developed since 1960 and are being widely applied. These include assertiveness training, self-control training, flooding, contingency contracting, stress inoculation, and the several intervention approaches described in our examination of health psychology (chapter 4). Though over its history behavior therapy has at times been misunderstood and suffered from a bad image among both the professional community and the general public, much of that has changed, and the behavior therapies have increasingly come to be seen for what they truly are: effective, reliable, cost-efficient sets of procedures for altering in positive ways a broad array of unhappy, ineffective, or undesirable behaviors.

Client-Centered Psychotherapy

Benny Perez was now well into his third semester after transferring to Drumlin State University, and things seemed to be getting worse and worse. The year he had spent at Colston College hadn't been so hot either, but he thought it had been mostly a problem there of not fitting in with a tight little clique. Now here he was, in a place with over 30,000 other students, and he felt even more isolated and alone. "If I can't make a friend or two here, or get a date, or have some fun, or feel I fit in somehow . . . '' his thoughts ran, and sort of trailed off with no solutions in sight.

Partly, he had transferred to Drumlin in the first place because he'd heard it was a bit of a party school. It had plenty of fraternities, clubs, organizations, and partying, but Benny's attempts during these three semesters to join, or to join in, were one disaster after another. Either he didn't know what to say, and said nothing at all, or he tried to say something—anything—and it came out sounding stupid. The last date he'd had was almost 3 months ago, and, after about an hour and a half, the girl had said she felt sick and asked to be taken back to the dorm. Some success story!

At least for the first two semesters here his grades had held at more or less Benny's B-minus average, but, at midterm this semester, exam grades were running mostly Cs and Ds. Benny really felt like he was going down the tube.

On March 23, Benny called Golner and made an appointment for later that very week.

In clear contrast with the central place given unconscious material and its elicitation in psychodynamic psychotherapy, and with faulty learning and its relearning in the behavioral therapies, client-centered therapy rests on the fundamental belief that individuals experiencing psychological difficulty possess within themselves the resources necessary for dealing with these difficulties and growing beyond them into a more fully functioning, actualized self. It is the therapist's prime responsibility in this approach to provide the conditions, the therapeutic environment, most facilitative of such growth.

Developed by psychologist Carl Rogers, this approach was originally called *nondirective counseling* (Rogers, 1942) to emphasize the client's, rather than the therapist's role in selecting topics for discussion, setting the sessions' tone, and otherwise directing the flow of the therapy. This focus recieved even greater emphasis when Rogers (1951) changed the name of the approach to *client-centered therapy* in 1951. Korchin (1976) captured its tone and substance well:

> The proper therapeutic relation is seen as egalitarian, requiring permissiveness and nondirectiveness, unlike the more formal and authoritarian relation between doctor and patient. Diagnosis is specifically avoided. for it casts the therapist in the role of expert who could discover and tell the patient, conceived as a sick and inadequate person, what was wrong and what to do. . . . Similarly, interpretation just as reassurance, advice, or manipulation, is seen as a directive technique and to be avoided. Such acts all imply that the therapist knows, better than the client, why the client acts as he does and what is good for him. (p. 357)

It is clear from Korchin's comment what the client-centered therapist avoids doing, but what does he or she do? How does client-centered therapy proceed? As early as 1940, Rogers began to make clear that his answer to this question lay in a growth-facilitating, therapist–client relationship. He commented at that time:

> In the rapport situation, where he is accepted rather than criticized, the individual is free to see himself without defensiveness, and gradually to recognize and admit his real self with its childish patterns, its aggressive feelings, and its ambivalences, as well as its mature impulses, and rationalized exterior. (C. R. Rogers, 1942, p. 162)

Much of the theorizing and wealth of research on client-centered therapy in the subsequent decades of its growth and development has focused on identifying and understanding therapist attitudes that, in actuality, are facilitative of such client growth. Although several such conditions were proposed, three in particular came to be viewed as immensely potent in facilitating client change, so much so that at one point C. R. Rogers described them as the "necessary and sufficient conditions of therapeutic change" (1957, p. 96). This triad of purportedly highly potent therapist attitudes is composed of empathy, unconditional positive regard, and genuineness. Empathy is the experiencing of an accurate understanding of the client's private world, especially his or her emotional world, as if it were the therapist's own. It is taking the client's perspective, fully understanding it, experiencing it in an "as if" manner, and communicating this accurate understanding back to the client. Unconditional positive regard, also called *nonpossessive warmth*, is caring, prizing, or valuing the client in a manner not contingent on the diagnosis, difficulties, or statements during the therapy itself. Genuineness, or congruence, is a purported facilitative condition concerned with the therapist's realness. For the triad of conditions to be facilitative to client growth, the therapist's attitudes of empathy and nonpossessive warmth and the overt behaviors reflective of these attitudes in the therapy sessions themselves had to be genuine, not put on or a facade.

It is to the great credit of Carl Rogers and his students that the now healthy and widespread applied psychological activity of rigorously and scientifically studying the psychotherapeutic process and its outcome was originated by them in the 1940s and early 1950s (Butler, 1958; Covner, 1942; Haigh, 1949; Halkides, 1958; Snyder, 1945). As part of this broad and continuing research program, it has now become clear that, although Rogers (1957) was overly optimistic in his early view that psychotherapy for all types of clients would be greatly facilitated by therapist empathy, unconditional positive regard, and genuineness, it is nevertheless true that, for many psychotherapy patients of several types, such therapist attitudes indeed function to facilitate client openness, disclosure, growth, and, ultimately, movement toward the very type of self-actualization C. R. Rogers envisioned (Barrett-Lennard, 1962; A. P. Goldstein & Michaels, 1985; Parloff, Waskow, & Wolfe, 1978; Rogers, Gendlin, Kiesler, & Traux, 1967).

Family Therapy

Home sweet home for Russ and Helen Gibbons and their 13-year-old son Les was as often as not a war zone. The fighting was fierce and frequent. The alliances—Russ and Helen against Les, Russ and Les against Helen, Helen and Les against Russ, or everyone against everyone else—were shifting, confusing, and often without clear reason. The undeclared cease-fires weren't much better, sort of sullen periods of smoldering silence that seemed to flare up into open hostility for little or no apparent reason—some laundry not put in the clothes hamper, interruption of someone else's mealtime chatter, a minor disagreement about something in the morning paper. Clearly, the Gibbonses had real issues to deal with, and, just as clearly, they were doing all they could to avoid doing so.

One Friday evening the more-or-less usual mealtime battle escalated to a level new even for the Gibbonses. It started simply enough, with Russ and Helen disagreeing about the apparent motives of one of Russ's co-workers who had recently started dressing and acting differently at work. Sharp words and sharp tones grew to yelling. Les got up to leave in the middle of the meal and became the target of Russ's screaming himself. Helen defended Les, Russ got angrier and angrier, Helen tried to leave the room with Les, and Russ jumped up and slapped her hard on the face.

Four hours later, the tears having started to dry, the apologies still flowing, but the red marks from Russ's hand still on Helen's cheek, the Gibbonses decided to go ahead with an idea they had flirted with for months—to seek family therapy for all of them at the Golner Center for Prescriptive Psychotherapies.

Family therapy is therapy for the whole family. For decades, psychotherapists, particularly those seeking to aid disturbed children, involved family members, in addition to the "designated patient," in the patient's treatment. But, beginning in force in the early 1970s, the family itself, as a unit and as a system, became the patient. As Jacobson and Bussod (1983) noted:

> The fundamental tenet of a system-theory perspective is that traditional problems in living and other psychiatric disorders such as schizophrenia, depression, drug abuse, and anxiety are best understood as manifestations of disturbances in the family. . . . The family member with "symptoms" is little more than the messenger or family scapegoat; his or her symptoms serve to cover up the generalized family disturbance. (p. 613)

Five major approaches to family therapy have emerged: strategic, psychodynamic, multigenerational, structural, and behavioral. All, however, share certain basic principles. The first, viewing the family as a system, holds that the experience and behavior of one family member cannot be either understood or altered apart from the experience and behavior of all other family members. As Foster and Gurman (1985) succinctly put it, "The family is a highly interdependent social unit" (p. 380). This interdependence results in great pressure within the family to maintain the status quo, to resist change, often even if change means better mental health for the family's designated patient. Thus, all approaches to family therapy, in diverse ways, strive with energy to reduce such resistance to change and to thus become more able to alter family interaction and communication patterns. To do so, these several approaches, with the exception of the more historically oriented psychodynamic family therapy, focus on current determinants of family dysfunction and seek to intervene in an active, highly directive manner. In strategic family therapy (Haley, 1973), for example, the therapist often seeks to deal with tension-maintaining triangles, boundary confusion, role rigidity, double-binding and other dysfunctional communications, and other manifestations of family disorder and resistance to change. The therapist does this by "joining" the family or setting interactional tasks for himself or herself to observe directly, and by use of such active techniques as paradoxical interventions and reframing.

> Paradoxical interventions involve tasks prescribed by the therapist that appear to run counter to the goals of therapy. Usually these prescriptions consist of variations on the directive, Don't change! . . . At times, discouragement or hopelessness regarding the possibility of change. . . . Or, at the other extreme of explicitness, the therapist might instruct the patient to exaggerate their symptoms. Paradoxical directives are based on the belief that family members will resist the therapist's attempts at direct influence. . . . When the therapist instructs them to continue or increase the intensity of pathological behavior, the only way to resist the influence attempt is by changing for the better. (Jacobson & Bussod, 1983, p. 616)

Reframing (also called *ascribing noble intention*, Stanton and Todd, 1979, and *positive connotation*, Palazzoli-Selvini, Boscolo, Cecchin, and Prata, 1978) is a second example of an active intervention technique frequently used by the strategic family therapist. It involves recasting or redefining behaviors that family members interpret as negative or hostile by emphasizing their well-intentioned if inadequate qualities. As Jacobson and Bussod (1983) provided by way of example, "an uninvolved father and husband might be described by the therapist as 'feeling too inadequate and caring too much about the family to step in and mess things up'" (p. 379). Such accentuating of the positive, according to strategic family therapists, tends to reduce the level of family communication of blame and criticism and to release family members' time and energy to pursue constructive alternative interaction patterns.

At present, family therapy in its several diverse forms is quite popular in the United States. With the exception of the behavioral approach to family therapy, this growing level of prominence and widespread use does not rest on a foundation of experimental support for its effectiveness. Such evaluation research is very much needed, and it is hoped that the creative traditions of the family-therapy movement in the United States will soon expand to include energetic efforts at its experimental scrutiny and verification.

Psychological Skills Training

> *The Parenting Group* is what the seven of them had come to call their weekly meetings at Golner, and no one except they themselves and their two group trainers knew that each of them had been referred to Golner by the county's Child Protective Services agency for child abuse. Mary Edwards, Tom Gaston, Beth Lazlo each had caused a broken bone, or a burn with a cigarette or, as bad, done nothing at all in chronically neglecting her or his child. Being "sentenced" to psychotherapy seemed a lot better than jail, but the psycho-therapy they were getting was more like being back in school, rather than anything they'd ever seen or heard of a "shrink" doing on TV or elsewhere. What had Dr. Goldstein called it . . . *psychological skills training.*

Each major approach to psychotherapy described in this chapter grew from the beliefs of its originators regarding the primary sources of disordered behavior or emotional disturbance, be it irrational beliefs (cognitive–behavior therapy), unconscious processes (psychodynamic therapy), faulty learning (behavioral therapies), thwarted growth toward self-actualization (client-centered therapy), or dysfunctional family systems (family therapy). The final major approach to psychotherapy we wish to examine, psychological skills training, grows from yet another perspective on disordered human behavior, the behavior-deficit perspective. Called by various names—*interpersonal skills training, social skills training, psychological skills training*—and reflected in a number of specific programs, including Filial Therapy (Guerney, 1977), Directive Teaching (Stephens, 1976), Life Skills Education (Adkins, 1974), Personal Effectiveness Training (Liberman, King, DeRisi, & McCann, 1975) and our own Structured Learning Training (A. P. Goldstein, 1973, 1981), this approach rests squarely on a behavior-deficit notion of human dysfunction.

> Viewing the client more in educational terms, rather than as a patient in need of therapy, the psychological skills trainer assumed he or she was dealing with an individual lacking, deficient, or at best weak in the skills necessary for effective interpersonal relationships and satisfying daily living. The task of the skills trainer became, therefore, not interpretation, reflection or reinforcement, but the active and deliberate teaching of desirable behaviors. (A. P. Goldstein, Keller, & Erne, 1985, p. 41)

Thus, psychological skills training is explicitly a psychoeducational, psychotherapeutic approach to correcting disordered behavior by teaching clients its constructive alternatives. Child-abusive parents are taught a series of self-control, parenting, marital, and interpersonal skills (A. P. Goldstein et al., 1985). Chronic schizophrenic individuals about to reenter community living after long hospital stays are taught conversational, interpersonal, and planning skills (A. P. Goldstein, Sprafkin, & Gershaw, 1976). Aggressive adolescents incarcerated in facilities for juvenile offenders are taught aggression management, feeling awareness, and problem-solving skills (A. P. Goldstein, Sprafkin, Gershaw, & Klein, 1980). In its several applications since its appearance in the early 1970s, psychological skills training has been employed widely and successfully with very diverse populations of skill-deficient individuals.

Although psychological skills training usually takes place in groups, it is not group psychotherapy in the exploration of feelings or uncovering of past traumatic materials in the fashion of, respectively, experiential or psychodynamic psychotherapy groups. Instead, adhering to a psychoeducational perspective, psychological skills training groups typically proceed, as in our Structured Learning Training groups, by a sequence of instructional procedures: modeling, role playing, performance feedback, and transfer training. Small groups of clients ("trainees"), selected for their shared psychological skill deficits, are (a) shown by means of videotaped or live portrayals by the group's leaders ("trainers"), a person (the model) expertly performing the skill behaviors we wish the trainees to learn (*modeling*); (b) given considerable opportunity and encouragement to rehearse or practice the behaviors that have been modeled, in a manner relevant to each trainee's real-life need for the skill (*role playing*); (c) provided with positive feedback, approval, or reward as the role-playing behavior becomes more and more like the behavior of the model (*performance feedback*); and (d) exposed to these three processes in such a way that there is an increased likelihood that what the trainee learns in the training setting will be available to him or her to use in a reliable manner at home, at school, at work, or elsewhere in his or her real-life environment (*transfer training*).

In contrast with the psychodynamic and family therapies, and in a manner quite similar to the history of client-centered and behavior therapies, the psychological skill training approaches rest on a firm and continuing foundation of evaluation research. Clearly, such research is among the more important contributions of the applied clinical psychologist.

In her or his theorizing, research, and work as a practitioner, the clinical psychologist is first and foremost an applied psychologist. In this chapter we have examined the primary applied activity of the clinical psychologist, psychotherapy. We have sought to suggest and demonstrate that psychotherapy is optimally defined in terms of a small set of core commonalities, optimally practiced in terms of a prescriptive strategy, and optimally advanced by an energetic and continuing research effort.

4 Health Applications

Prologue

You are sitting peacefully before the TV as you do every night, watching the news. Tonight the big story is about implanting an artificial heart, with vivid details of the operation itself. As You watch, You think You are feeling some slight chest pains. Of course, it must be psychological. You had Your annual physical a few weeks ago, and You are in great shape, almost. The blood pressure is getting to be a little high. Your physician, who did not look in too great shape himself, went through the usual litany about cutting down on salt and cholesterol, exercising, and, of course, cutting out smoking.

You are more careful now, trying the best You can to avoid salt in the food You buy, but it is pretty rough when You go out to dinner at the homes of friends who have not gotten the word yet. You have tried to walk more, but You are quite busy. There are so many things that have to be done at work and You have so much responsibility, and stopping smoking is easy. You have already done it several times.

During the following week the news is filled almost every hour with intimate details about this chap with the artificial heart—about the variety of cardiac conditions that could lead to heart transplant, about valves, about surgery, even details about electocardiograms and the meaning of those squiggles.

The more You watch and read, the more it hits You that "I don't want this happening to me." Maybe the doc is right when he said that You really have control over what happens to You in many disorders, especially those dealing with the cardiovascular area, like blood pressure and heart rate. Damn it, it is time to do something to prevent these horrors.

All right, You are determined to change. So what to do? In fact, what is new? You have gone through this before, this determination to change. Fortunately, it soon goes away. But not this time. The item that your doctor bugs You about most is smoking. You decide to get some information about how to finally stop smoking. You call the American Cancer Society, and they tell You that there is a group just starting in your community.

You approach your first meeting of the group with great caution and great hope. From the beginning You are unimpressed, because the therapist is focusing on all kinds of unpleasant activities such as deliberate rapid smoking, mild shocks, holding the smoke until it becomes uncomfortable, and even having smoke blown in your face. You are convinced that these procedures are what's been called *behavior modification*, those techniques that make You do what you don't want to do, and You don't like it. Nobody is going to make You do what you don't want to do.

But You don't give up. You hear from a friend about another "smoke-watcher" group, and you decide to try again. This one is far pleasanter, and it's clear that the therapist is using the group to influence and support each other. You're impressed with the therapist, especially when she relates how she, herself, gave up smoking. You try the techniques she calls *self-control, self-efficacy*, and *expectancy*, and they really work. And one day You finally, actually, stop smoking. It is so nice to talk about it in the group, and to share that terrible aching feeling with the other members of the group who have, by now, become friends.

You do notice that now that You have stopped smoking (and never again will light up one of those "death warrants") You are beginning to gain weight, because you've been eating like mad, especially rich desserts and almost anything with chocolate in it. Well, that's easy enough to deal with. You go to the local Weight Watchers group. In this group, which really isn't very much different from the smoking group, you once again learn ways of self-control of eating. You even begin to exercise and to jog a bit.

Then one day you read a newspaper ad (full page, no less) by the Reynolds Tobacco Company that clearly indicates that the connection between smoking and all those physical diseases has *not been* conclusively *proven*. Come to think of it, if the scientists haven't really demonstrated that smoking does cause lung cancer and all those terrible things, then what is all the fuss about? So You finally decide to light up just *one* cigarette!

INTRODUCTION

Perhaps more than any other chapter in this book, this chapter involves all readers (and the authors, of course), both professionally and personally. In fact, because of this, we have selected as chief prologue character, *you*, the reader, rather than a fictional character. The reason for this involvement is the nature of the subject matter and the target of psychological focus, *health*.

The field of health psychology is now a prototype of the way in which the theories and research of psychology are applied to various human behaviors. Every field of behavior described in this book has gone through the same process, with some variations that we are describing herein. The only difference is the speed with which health psychology is developing. There are several reasons for this. Most importantly, as we keep noting, the field of health involves *all of us*. The second is the growth in the sheer number of psychologists, particularly in this applied area. And, there has been a sharp increase of grant funds for psychological research on health.

A major element in the growth of the field, both reflecting and enhancing growth, is the development of journals; publication outlets; professional organizations; communication networks; meetings at local, national, and international levels; individual mobility, and easy transportation (often reimbursed).

One of the issues we must touch upon in order to understand this field is that of *territoriality*. What profession is to predominate in the application of its research techniques and virtues to the particular human behavior involved? Because this is a book on applications of psychology to various fields and human problems, we start with the origins of health psychology rather than the label that has become predominant in this field, *behavioral medicine*. To use that term, however, would imply medical hegemony, and that, of course, would never do. At least not for a card-carrying psychologist.

HISTORICAL CONTEXT

As in every field we are describing, putting the applications of psychology in historical context is of major significance to understanding current developments. This is of even greater importance in the health psychology area. The origins of this field in most of the current literature are usually traced to the Yale Conference on Behavioral Medicine held in February 1977 at New Haven, Connecticut, to which the leading investigators in the health fields were invited and from which derived the major influences on the directions of research and application in this field (including the definition of behavioral medicine we will discuss in the next section).

Yet, what has been virtually lost, except for occasional footnotes, is the earlier applications of psychological principles to problems of physical disease and health, the field of *psychosomatic medicine*. In effect, this was of another era, in which the dominant psychological model of human behavior, then psychoanalytic/psychodynamic, was applied to problems of disease.

The term *psychosomatic medicine* was introduced in the early part of the 20th century. The psychosomatic movement was brought to the United States by Franz Alexander (1939, 1950). At first, psychoanalysts sought to interpret various bodily symptoms in terms of psychic conflicts (the development of ulcers was held to reflect repressed anger; constipation indicated an anal-retentive personality). During the ensuing years a wide range of physical problems was placed within this psychoanalytic/psychiatric framework. Flanders Dunbar's publications (1935, 1947, 1954) reviewed psychosomatic medicine from 1900 to the 1950s and unified the field of psychosomatic medicine. Between the 1930s and 1960s, there were two basic trends. Personality theorists, led by Alexander and his colleagues, attempted to determine the relationship between personality and disease. Wolf and colleagues studied the relationship between laboratory stresses and the development of physiological processes. The basic assumption behind psychosomatic medicine was that individual personality, or specific, conflicts are related to specific diseases (e.g., ulcerative colitis patients are "anal personalities").

The psychosomatic medicine movement in the post–World War II period created great enthusiasm, particularly among psychologists, psychiatrists, and physicians. Organizations were founded (e.g., Society for Study of Psychosomatic Medicine), new journals were published, and training programs were established. However, a sobering, recent view noted that, "Over the years the basic assumption of the personality theorists that personality or specific conflicts are related to specific diseases was rarely substantiated and, more important, the therapy was not effective" (Ferguson & Taylor, 1980, p. iii).

At this point, many of the investigators involved in the health psychology and behavioral medicine movement are also issuing similar notes of caution, which we will discuss in the section on the future.

Definitions

In the opening chapter of a large volume (over 700 page) entitled *Health Psychology* (Stone, Cohen, & Adler, 1979), the senior author, George Stone, noted that "the term *health psychology* is a new one. No book before this has borne that name" (p. 1). He was claiming, justifiably, that a new field of applied psychology was in the process of being born. It was accompanied by all of the accoutrements of such a development including the birth of new professional organizations, specialized journals, new training programs, controversy, and cautious optimism.

The meaning of the term *health* can be expressed in a straightforward dictionary definition of "health": "physical and mental well-being; soundness; freedom from defect, pain, or disease" (*Webster*, 1977, p. 668). Succinctly stated, "health is the state of being hale or whole" (Stone et al., 1979, p. 3). We particularly like the approach of Joseph Matarazzo (1980), who has been most influential in developing the health psychology field. He has offered the following definition of terms, which is useful in clarifying terminology:

> It is proposed here, however, that henceforth we use the term *behavioral medicine* for that broad interdisciplinary field of scientific inquiry, education, and practice which concerns itself with health and illness or related dysfunction (e.g., essential hypertension, cholesterolemia, stress disorders, addictive smoking, obesity, etc.); the term *behavioral health* for a new interdisciplinary subspecialty within behavioral medicine specifically concerned with the maintenance of health and the prevention of illness and dysfunction in currently healthy persons; and the term *health psychology* as a more discipline-specific term encompassing psychology's role as a science and profession in both of these domains. (p. 807)

Further, Matarazzo (1980) noted that, in the broad field of medicine, "physicians have recently echoed the earlier plea that medicine give up its traditional biomedical model and substitute instead a biopsychosocial model" (p. 808). He and others have argued against a narrow *biomedical* model, in both medicine and psychiatry and for a *biopsychosocial* model that considers the patient's, the physician's, and the society's belief systems about health and social and environmental influences. Thus, a major element in the health psychology field is a broad model of human behavior that conceptualizes health-related activity in overt behavioral terms in much the same way as any other human behavior.

One approach to health psychology is to trace its origins to three threads of investigation that came together in the 1970s (Agras, 1982; Blanchard, 1982; Feuerstein, Labbé, & Kuczmierczyk, 1986; Matarazzo et al., 1984). The first was the applications of a very impressive technology that seemed to be doing wonders in the mental health field, *behavior therapy*. This technology was being applied to more medically related problems such as obesity and smoking. In the same period the procedure called *biofeedback* was developed, which became a technology for reliably changing physiological responses. The third can be traced to the fact that infectious diseases were essentially conquered, and cardiovascular disease and cancer emerged as the major killers. In both of these it was recognized that certain behaviors, such as cigarette smoking, were a major factor in the etiology and maintenance of these diseases. Thus, there emerged a set of medical problems for which there was a technology, behavior therapy and biofeedback, which could be applied with some success.

The actual definition of the term *behavioral medicine*, which is a key to the development of the field, has varied in subtle but important ways. The first definition, developed from the Yale Conference noted earlier and thus carrying a note of authority to it, contains most of the key elements.

> Behavioral medicine is the field concerned with the development of behavioral science knowledge and techniques relevant to the understanding of physical health and the application of this knowledge and these techniques to prevention, diagnosis, treatment and rehabilitation. Psychosis, neurosis, and substance abuse are included only insofar as they contribute to physical disorders as the endpoint. (Schwartz & Weiss, 1978a, p. 6)

Of particular note is the exclusion of mental disorders from this field. Schwartz and Weiss (1978b), having rendered the official definition deriving from the conference, offered an amended definition that broadened the previous one by adding the term *biomedical* to behavioral science and dropping the exclusion of mental disorders. Thus, in effect, all research, behavioral and biological, and all aspects of health, physical and mental, were included. Indeed, this is the ultimate claim of territoriality for behavioral medicine. Other definitions of behavioral medicine (Blanchard, 1982; Ferguson & Taylor, 1980; Pomerleau & Brady, 1979; Weiss, 1981) more narrowly define the field as involving the application of techniques and procedures derived from the experimental analysis of behavior, behavior modification, and behavior therapy (L. Krasner, 1971). The importance of definition, particularly in terms of the theoretical model of behavior being utilized, is that, as we have been emphasizing in every chapter, the specifics of the applications are determined by the model from which they derive.

Psychologists as Health Professionals

Stone et al., (1979) made the major point that psychologists have, until very recently, been part contributors to the health system in the context of "psychology *in* medicine" and not "psychology *of* medicine": "being participants, they found it difficult to be observers" (p. 74). Thus, although psychologists were part of the medical scene and worked within the medical model from the beginning, study of the health system itself did not emerge until very recently. This can be contrasted with, for example, education, in which the study of the psychology of education, educational psychology, developed at a very early date.

One major impact of psychologists on the health field is in the area of appointments in medical schools, because the medical school is, of course, the major source of influence and training on approaches to the disease process. The number of psychologists with medical school appointments grew from approximately 250 in the early 1950s to over 3,000 by the late 1970s (Schofield, 1979). Until the 1970s, most of the research and application efforts of psychologists were directed toward mental disorders. In the 1970s, growing numbers of psychologists began to bring their skills to bear on behavioral and emotional problems associated with physical diseases and on programs to reduce susceptibility to certain physical diseases. The growth of psychologists' involvement in the health field accelerated in the late 1970s and the 1980s, as evidenced by research publications, organizations, and other factors (Belar, Deardorff, & Kelly, in press).

PSYCHOLOGY APPLIED TO HEALTH

At this point we offer a broad overview of the areas encompassed by the application of psychology to health. In effect, it is a list of human ailments and human hope. If we were to make a comprehensive catalog of human ailments to which there have developed some alleviating psychological approaches, it would include pain, enuresis, migraine headaches, sexual dysfunction, insomnia, hypertension, alcohol abuse, obesity, apprehension about surgery and postsurgical recovery, coronary artery disease, epileptic seizures, muscle spasms, cancer, sleep disorders, and premenstrual syndrome. Our aim in this chapter is to touch upon, albeit lightly, the major aspects of health psychology:

1. Role of psychologists as health professionals
2. Approaches to the major systems of bodily disorder such as cardiovascular, gastrointestinal, neurological, and respiratory
3. Use of specific techniques such as biofeedback, relaxation, self-help, self-management, desensitization, and social support systems
4. Fostering of adherence to medical regimes, such as exercise, special diets, and the taking of medication
5. Enhancement of disease-preventative behaviors and elimination of unhealthy behaviors such as smoking, overeating, and using high amounts of salt and cholesterol
6. Fostering of behaviors likely to prevent poor health such as better nutrition, exercise, early medical checkups, and safer environmental conditions in the home and workplace
7. Development of techniques for coping with serious diseases and physical handicaps
8. Evaluation of the outcome in health care
9. Recognition and handling of social, value, and ethical issues.

The elderly, such as nursing-home residents and geriatric patients especially, have been recipients of psychological applications, particularly behavioral. Programs based on social or token reinforcement have been used to increase social interaction, physical activity, and recovery from physical injury. The emphasis has been on development of self-care skills (e.g., self-bathing), enhancement of the desire to eat nutritious meals, and encouragement to engage in productive leisure-time activities.

Before we begin examining several of these specific application topics, however, we would make at least brief mention of the broad perspectives on health-related behavior that offer a theoretical framework from which the specific techniques emerge in a logical manner. The two models we are exploring are labeled *ecobehavioral* and *epidemiological*.

Ecobehavioral Approach

The ecobehavioral approach emphasizes social, economic, environmental, and political influences that affect the health of individuals in our society. In offering this model, Winett (1984) pointed out that the individual's behavior can be understood and analyzed within its interrelationship with broader environmental influence. The individual is not ignored but, rather, placed within a societal context (Sarason, 1981a, 1981b).

The ecobehavioral paradigm does not neglect or discard what is within the person. It is assumed that any environmental influence is mediated by a range of interactive, intraindividual, genetic, biological, cognitive, and behavioral-skill variables. However, the focus of concern for the ecobehavioral paradigm is the broader environmental influences and health behaviors of large population segments. (Winett, 1984, p. 148)

Investigators using this broader environmental approach observe that the health of an individual is influenced by the nature of the individual's interactions with family, relatives, friends, and co-workers (social networks) (Gottlieb, 1981). There is growing evidence that such factors as social connectedness (e.g., marriage, church membership) and the social support systems affect the amount of stress on the individual and consequent health problems (Felner et al., 1983). Although it might seem remote at first, public regulations as to the kind of information that is available to the public on foods, cigarettes, medicines, and medical services can assist the consumer in making more informed choices about health practices (Pertschuk, 1982).

There is another environmental source of stress leading to health problems with which most of us are involved, the *workplace*. Winett succinctly expressed this:

> . . . it is essential to understand how much work and its schedule determines the ebbs and flows of people's lives. . . . It is the schedule of work that dictates when people will arise, when they will eat, when they will socialize, and when they will sleep; it is the schedule of work that determines when and where there will be massive traffic jams and unacceptable air quality. It is the schedule of work and living and commuting patterns that determine the availability of time and constraints on engaging in some health-related behaviors. (1985, p. 152)

As an illustration of how the environment influences health, the issue of *safety* is certainly in the health psychology area and is also a major aspect of psychology in the community (see chapter 2). Psychological techniques have been increasingly applied to areas of safety to prevent injury and death in a variety of situations. The importance of safety-related behaviors is involved in many ways. As noted before, among adults, accidents are the fourth leading cause of death (after heart disease, cancer, and stroke). Accidents involving motor vehicles and work are the two categories with the highest death rates. For example, B. Sulzer-Azaroff and de Santamaria (1980) have developed a program in a small factory to reduce hazards leading to accidents such as obstructions of walkways or exits in the plant, exposed electrical circuits, and flammable materials.

In chapters 2 and 5 we further describe some of the applications of psychology, particularly behavioral, in the community and the workplace to influence techniques, procedures, and attitudes affecting the environmental impact on health behavior.

Epidemiological Approach

A useful approach to the relationship between behavior and disease is *epidemiology*, the study of the prevalence; etiology, or origin; and consequences of diseases (Brownell, 1982). Notice the new word (and concept) that enters our discussion as a consequence of this model, *disease*, in contrast with the notion of *health* basic to the ecobehavioral model just described. The focus is on large groups of subjects and the natural history of disease. Investigators Catalano and Dooley (1980) have used ecobehavioral research techniques to demonstrate a relationship between broad economic indexes of recession and recovery and indexes of health disorder. In effect, epidemiology asks What is the relationship between environmental events, such as changes in the number of individuals who smoke and the incidence of lung cancer in the population, over broad periods of time? Other epidemiological relationships would involve the relationship between consumption of certain dietary items such as salt or cholesterol-laden food and the incidence of heart disease. A further example would look at the relationship between the growth of the exercise industry (spas, swimming pools, media focus, health clubs, etc.) and the incidence of heart disease. The basic hypothesis for which there is growing evidence is that certain specific patterns of behavior, nutritional and physical, affect physiological factors, which in turn increase or decrease the likelihood of occurrence of physical diseases.

A major point in the health psychology field, frequently misunderstood by all of us, is that epidemiological data involve *probabilistic* relationships that might or might not hold for specific individuals, and, thus, change in the behavior of any specific individual will not necessarily prevent or cure his or her disease. Epidemiological researchers are interested in the long-range effects of behavior change on specific disorders in groups of persons. The epidemiological factors that then become the locus of study are the rates of *morbidity* (the presence of a specific disease) and *mortality* (the death rate) in the specific population being studied. The data derived from such studies then determine the impact and cost effectiveness of treatment programs.

Exercise and Health

A good example of the potentialities in and limitations of the epidemiological approach is in the area of exercise. The observation has been made, formally and informally, going back at least to the last century, that physically active individuals seem to live longer than those who are sedentary. There is a series of epidemiological studies, starting in the 1950s, that has compared mortality rates and coronary heart disease of individuals in various occupations involving differing amounts of physical activity (Brownell,

1982). These studies generally indicated that activity related to the work situation and leisure-time exercise reduced the risk of coronary heart disease. Further, the amount of activity and exercise can be minimal, such as walking at least five city blocks per day. However, as in almost every area of investigation, there are some studies that do *not* confirm this relationship between exercise and heart disease.

Even if the relationship between exercise and lowered risk for cardiovascular disorder were firmly established, it would not necessarily indicate cause and effect. It could be that susceptibility to heart disease influences the ability to exercise or to be active rather than vice versa, or both might be related to a third factor such as body constitution. Studies of the psychology of exercise are growing and are still equivocal. We are all willing to accept the idea that exercise makes us feel better, whether it is a question of providing us with extra energy or a psychological high via our improved self-concept. The studies relate physical activity to intellectual, psychological, social, and even work performance. The results and social implications of these studies have been cautiously summarized by Brownell (1982).

> To summarize the data on physiological and psychological changes with exercise: Definitive evidence is not yet in on whether exercise causes reduced risk for serious disease and improved psychological functioning. The weight of the imperfect evidence is impressive, but to place our faith in such evidence is to assume that weak data multiplied many times over constitutes strong evidence. At the risk of falling prey to this temptation, we must face the choice of encouraging exercise in sedentary persons or waiting for conclusive data which may be years in coming. We choose the liberal path and feel that exercise is probably beneficial. Therefore, studies on improving exercise patterns are important to the field of behavioral medicine. (p. 180)

The implications of Brownell's conclusion are that, even though the current "scientific" evidence is not conclusive, it never really is. Exercise and activity should be encouraged and even prescribed in various health-related situations. This brings us to one of the key issues in the health psychology field. When a series of behaviors is suggested to the individual to prevent or alleviate a physical disorder (e.g., nutrition, exercise, nonsmoking, medication), how is adherence to these behaviors established and maintained?

There are numerous studies indicating that drop-out rates in various cardiac rehabilitation programs are very high and similar to drop-out rates for patients in smoking, alcoholism, and heroin addiction programs. Thus, there is a field developing for applying psychological procedures to enhancing adherence to the doctor's orders. In effect, how do you get people to do what the experts think, and hope, is good for them?

One technique for enhancing adherence is that of *contracting*, a derivative of the token-economy programs described in chapter 3. In one such study of an aerobic exercise program, the subjects were required to deposit, in advance, some items of personal value that were returned when they earned points for complying with the requirements of the aerobic program (Wysocki, Hall, Iwata, & Riordan, 1979). In follow-up a year later, the subjects had continued to adhere to the exercise program. Variations of the contracting method, still clearly at an early stage, seem to offer some promise.

An interesting and important extension of the adherence studies is referred to as *life-style activity*. These are the daily activities involving ordinary routines such as walking, using stairs, and just plain moving about. In a series of studies (Brownell & Stunkard, 1980; Brownell Stunkard, & Albaum, 1980), investigators observed the usage of stairs or escalators in public places where these two modes of transportation were contiguous (in shopping malls, train stations, and bus terminals). Only 5% of the 45,000 individuals observed used the stairs. Further, among obese individuals, presumably those the most in need of such exercise, only 1% actually used the stairs. The investigators then put up an attractive poster ("Your heart needs exercise . . . here is your chance.") in front of the stairs and the escalator. The result was a tripling in the frequency of stair use. After removal of the sign, the effects lasted for 1 month and had completely disappeared after 3 months.

Thus, broad theoretical and investigatory approaches give us clues as to the complex relationship between human behavior and health and disease. We will illustrate psychological applications designed to affect this relationship in the areas of smoking, pain, cardiac functioning, and eating.

SMOKING BEHAVIOR

We are focusing on the applications of psychology designed to influence smoking behavior for a number of cogent reasons. Primarily, the issues involved are prototypical of all other areas of health psychology. The number of smokers in the United States is considerable including, probably, many of the readers of this chapter. The connection between smoking behavior and certain debilitating and often fatal health problems such as cardiovascular diseases, pulmonary diseases, and cancers *seems* to be clearly established. Smoking behavior can be understood, in part, in the context of the social, economic, and political systems of the country. Virtually every psychological technique extant has been applied to the attempt to stop smoking behavior. One comprehensive review in the early 1980s of current trends in the modification of cigarette dependence (Lichtenstein & Brown, 1982) cited over 250 studies, including 20 papers that were just *reviews*, on the control of smoking.

Social Context of Smoking Behavior

We feel that it is most appropriate to open a section on smoking behavior with the self-observation of a major author in American society. The appeal of smoking and the difficulty of permanently stopping are expressed by Norman Mailer (1984) in the context, of all things, of a mystery novel:

> For twelve years I had been trying to give up smoking. As Mark Twain said — and who does not know the remark? — "It's nothing to stop. I've quit a hundred times." I used to feel I had said it myself, for certainly I had tried on ten times ten occasions, once for a year, once for nine months, once for four months. Over and over again I gave them up, a hundred times over the years, but always I went back. For in my dreams, sooner or later I struck a match, brought flame to the lip, then took in all my hunger for existence with the first puff. I felt impaled on desire itself — those fiends trapped in my chest and screaming for one drag. Change the given!
>
> So I learned what addiction is. A beast had me by the throat and its vitals were in my lungs. I wrestled that devil for twelve years and sometimes I beat him back. (p. 4)

As a human behavior, tobacco smoking goes back to antiquity. The spirit of the enjoyment of smoking was further captured by Robert Burton in the classic text on human problem behavior *The Anatomy of Melancholy* (1621). "Tobacco, divine, rare, super excellent tobacco which gives far beyond all the panaceas, potable gold, and philosopher's stones, a sovirgn remedy to all diseases" (Raw, 1977). This nicely captures the attraction that smoking has had and continues to have. Virtually every study of smoking behavior emphasizes the tenacity and the difficulty of changing this "habit," "addiction," or "dependence." There is even controversy as to which of these labels is most appropriate.

In their introduction to a review of current developments "in the modification of cigarette dependence," Lichtenstein and Brown (1982) dramatically and succinctly presented the context for this major health-problem area.

> Cigarette smoking is the largest preventable cause of death in the U.S. Each year there are 80,000 deaths from lung cancer, 22,000 deaths from other cancers, up to 225,000 deaths from cardiovascular disease, and more than 19,000 deaths from pulmonary disease, all causally related to cigarette smoking. . . . the annual cost of health damage resulting from smoking is estimated to be $27 billion in medical care, absenteeism, decreased work productivity, and accidents. (p. 575)

The complexities involved in smoking behavior, of course, go well beyond simply labeling it an *addiction* or a *bad habit*. There are considerable social and economic influences affecting smoking behavior. For example, heavily involved in maintaining, and even in increasing, smoking behavior is a major American tobacco industry with strong economic incentives to reinforce and enhance smoking behavior (Kristein, 1984; Kristein, Arnold, & Wynder, 1977). Ironically, the U.S. government gives a very substantial yearly subsidy to tobacco growers. In that sense, we all bear some responsibility for the action of our government.

It should be noted that smoking by women has actually increased in the United States. Historically, smoking by women had a symbolic importance in the 1920s. It was considered immoral for women to smoke. The "originator" of behaviorism, John Watson (of our chapter 1), devised ads to attract women to smoking because he felt that women should not be castigated for smoking and had as much right as men to smoke. Later, in the 1960s, woman's smoking was symbolic of the sexual revolution, as manifested in the "You've come a long way baby" ad for Virginia Slims cigarettes (J. M. Matarazzo, 1982).

Smoking and Models of Human Behavior

Psychological interpretations and explanations are continually offered to explain the development and maintenance of smoking behavior (Tomkins, 1966). In their day of popularity, psychoanalysts were not loathe to interpret smoking as evidence of masochism (G. H. Green, 1923), as hostility toward parental figures, and even as symbolic masturbatory activity (Bergler, 1946). The standard intervention to cure such activity was, of course, long-term analytic psychotherapy, which would resolve relevant hidden conflicts.

The models of human behavior that have had most impact in stimulating attempts to affect smoking behavior are the behavioral, particularly the operant and the social-learning versions. For example, a social-learning model would emphasize imitation of parents, pressure of peers, pressure to conform to the group, and smoking as a symbol of independence from adult authority (Pomerleau, 1979).

Smoking as "Addiction"

It has recently been asserted by the Director of the National Institute on Drug Abuse, Dr. Richard Polin, that cigarette smoking is now the most serious and most widespread form of addiction *in the world*, even worse than heroin. The latest estimates of smoking habits in this country are that one third of American adults continue to puff away annually on 593 billion cigarettes. Four out of five of these smokers indicate that they really want to quit, but, even after many attempts, most are unable to do so.

Addiction is one explanation for this strange and disturbing phenomenon (Pomerleau & Pomerleau, 1984). Presumably, nicotine changes the availability of important brain chemicals involved in feelings of reward and well-being. Nicotine produces temporary improvements in task performance, improves memory, reduces anxiety, increases pain tolerance, and reduces hunger. The smoker learns to adjust nicotine intake to selectively enhance these effects by the type of puffing and the number of cigarettes smoked. Even though there is increasing evidence of physiological involvement in maintaining an addictive behavior such as smoking, it is increasingly clear that there is an interaction between smoking and environmental stimuli. For example, stressful situations, such as tasks requiring increased alertness, enhance the likelihood of smoking. Apparently, taking deep, full drags creates a more sedative, relaxing effect. It is even speculated that different personality types use smoking to reinforce preferred behavior patterns. Type A individuals, who are competitive and impatient, might take shorter and smaller puffs, to enhance arousal. On the other hand, Type B personalities, who are less concerned about achieving, might take larger puffs, to promote relaxation (Pomerleau & Pomerleau, 1984).

To develop reasonable intervention procedures, it is necessary to analyze smoking behavior first in terms of what is causing the harm in smoking. One such series of studies has involved analysis of just what elements are harmful in smoking. One model suggests that smokers physiologically regulate the amount of smoking to maintain a certain level of nicotine in the body (Schachter, 1977, 1979). This view implies the existence of a "nicostat" that regulates intake to keep nicotine at a constant level. A whole series of studies has been generated by such a pharmacological hypothesis, which would have implications for eventual control measures. Three other physiological measures that have been developed vary in intrusiveness, cost, and sensitivity — carbon monoxide, nicotine, and thiocyanate. The presence of such measures is useful in that they supplement and perhaps are even more sensitive than the usual measures of smoking behavior, which are self-report and reports of observers.

Prevention of Smoking

Perhaps the major development in the effort to decrease smoking has been the growth of programs aimed at preventing the onset of smoking in children and adolescents. We have certainly pointed out that smoking is a major health problem in adults. It comes as a shock and a disappointment that smoking is a major problem in children and adolescents. It has been estimated that 12% of all individuals between the ages of 12 and 18 smoke regularly and that about one fourth of females between 17 and 18 smoke regularly (Brownell, 1984). How does a society go about preventing the development of this very harmful behavior among its youth?

It is not simply a question of mere information, because surveys clearly indicate that the vast majority of teenagers are aware of the dangers of smoking and the relationship of smoking and eventual diseases. In fact, early-prevention studies with children focused on giving information on the dangers of smoking. These apparently were successful in conveying the information but *not* in preventing smoking. It soon became clear to psychologists that the initiation of smoking is related to social factors, particularly the influence of adult role models and peer pressure.

A somewhat more sophisticated approach has been developed by a group of investigators working out of universities at Stanford, Minnesota, and at Harvard (Hurd, Pattison, & Llamas, 1981; Telch, Killen, McAlister, Perry, & Maccoby, 1982). The program is called Counseling Leadership Against Smoking Pressure (CLASP) and differs from traditional health education approaches in that it does not emphasize the negative effects of smoking on health. It exposes students to the social pressures they will face and teaches them specific skills for dealing with these situations, and perhaps most importantly, it uses peers to teach the skills needed to resist pressure. It uses behavioral techniques of modeling, rehearsal, and role taking, rather than the lectures and movies so prevalent in other programs, and it attempts to develop a nonsmoking environment in an entire school rather than focusing on an individual classroom.

Brownell (1984) summarized the CLASP program as it has been applied to a variety of schools in Minnesota, California, and Massachusetts.

> These results are most promising. The programs can be done in an inexpensive fashion and the results are clinically meaningful as well as statistically significant. Large numbers of students can be reached. Most importantly, the long term results of these programs look very good . . . this is certainly an area worth pursuing. (p. 238)

Another example of a program oriented toward preventing smoking in children and adolescents is offered by the University of Houston (Evans et al., 1978). These investigators developed a series of videotapes portraying social pressures on youths to smoke and effective strategies for resisting these pressures and were evaluated in a seventh-grade classroom. The tapes also present information about the immediate physiological effects of smoking. The success of such programs in preventing smoking, however, appears to be minimal at best.

Intervention Procedures

One of the major controversies in the field of smoking prevention is the issue of the *goal* of the intervention procedure; total abstinence as against controlled smoking. This is also an issue in other areas of potentially harmful behaviors such as alcohol consumption. Based on the difficulty of achieving total cessation of smoking, some intervention procedures have emphasized the possibility of decreasing the rate and switching to cigarettes with less dangerous substances or a lower quantity of nicotine or tar.

A major intervention procedure is the development of broad community programs that include clinics offering encouragement and advice, both specific and nonspecific. The mass media technology permits the delivery of information and advice to entire communities.

There have been a variety of ways in which intervention procedures have been offered as solutions to the health hazards of smoking. One such categorization describes four different battlefronts (Lutzker & Martin, 1981). The first is an attempt to reduce the number of young smokers, the 12- to 18-year-olds. Major efforts have been through antismoking educational procedures in public schools. A second major area is to attempt to help people *stop* smoking, focusing on antismoking clinics in most major cities. These clinics apply the wide range of psychological principles and techniques described throughout the book. A third approach is to effect what might be called *controlled* smoking. For those individuals who cannot stop smoking, techniques are applied to control the number and type of cigarettes, the number of puffs, and other elements. Techniques applied include aversive procedures such as electric shock while smoking, pairing stale smoking air with smoking, satiation via rapid smoking, combining smoking with nausea pills, and more positive procedures such as training in self-control.

The fourth approach described by Lutzker and Martin for dealing with the health hazards of smoking is not at all psychological in nature. This is the continual attempt of the tobacco industry to develop a "safe cigarette" with lowered tar and nicotine content. Perhaps in this same category are the repeatedly published "denial" advertisements by the tobacco industry arguing that the scientific evidence for the linkage of smoking and diseases such as coronary heart disease is "inconclusive."

Most of the reviewers of the research on intervention procedures with smoking behavior note that the outcome data are permeated with methodological flaws. The major problem is that almost all research studies and clinical programs have had to rely upon self-report data, which are unverified, as their dependent measure. Even when physiological data are utilized, there literally is still great unreliability in correlating such measures with rate and number of cigarettes smoked.

Once you are dealing with self-reports, particularly of smoking cigarettes, you are forced to deal with such issues as underreporting due to implicit demand characteristics of the situation, emotional involvement resulting in bias of self-observations, and just plain unreliability of human observation, particularly when a specific number count is required.

Other methodological problems involve difficulty in attributing the cause of outcome results in large-scale smoking prevention studies. They are usually lacking the kinds of controls needed to answer the question of what really *caused* a decrement in smoking rates, when such indeed does occur.

We will describe in detail some of the efforts to decrease the incidence of smoking behavior in the community in a later section focusing on the *diffusion* of "good" health practices in a community. At this point we describe applications to other specific health problems.

CHRONIC PAIN

Most of us at one time or another have felt pain, a form of stress that involves interaction among physiological, psychological, and environmental components. A considerable range of psychological approaches has been utilized to alleviate this universal malady.

Pain that endures beyond the normal course of healing for a disease, or pain connected with a progressive disease is defined as *chronic pain*. It has been estimated that as many as 86 million Americans suffer from some type of chronic pain (Bonica, 1980). We are dealing with both individual and societal problems in terms of suffering, impact on families, time lost from employment, medical expenses, litigation costs, disability compensation, and utilization of health care resources.

> It has long been recognized that subjectively experienced pain is not solely dependent upon tissue damage or organic dysfunction. The intensity of pain reported and amount of pain behavior displayed seem to be influenced by a wide range of factors such as attention, anxiety, financial, cultural background, and environmental contingencies. Thus, the role of psychological processes, especially dysfunctional ones, in the etiology, exacerbation, and maintenance of chronic pain has received increasing attention. The advent of a multidimensional perspective on pain in contrast to a view that is based largely on sensory–physiological factors has resulted in a proliferation of mulitidisciplinary pain clinics (over 1,000 in the United States) that focus on all aspects of the pain experience both physical and psychological (Holzman & Turk, 1985, p. ix).

We will illustrate an application of a psychological approach to pain, derived from the behavioral model. Although certainly not the first, it has been the most comprehensive and derives from the broader psychological model.

The first systematic application of behavior techniques to treating chronic pain was developed by Fordyce (Fordyce, 1974; Fordyce & Steger, 1979). He distinguished between *respondent* pain caused by physiological distress and *operant* pain behaviors, which are learned and maintained by environmental reinforcements. These latter include behaviors such as moaning, taking medication, being physically inactive, and avoiding responsibilities such as work.

The approach of the operantly oriented psychologist is to rearrange environmental contingencies that influence pain behaviors. It has been observed that the report of pain elicits attention and sympathy from family, friends, and others. The individual reporting pain is able to avoid responsibility and possibly take medication that relieves unpleasant feelings such as anxiety and depression. From these obvious observations, an approach to alleviating pain developed. In the initial study of contingency management (Fordyce, 1974), the investigator trained nursing staff and patient spouses to use praise and attention to reinforce well behaviors and to avoid reinforcing patients' reports or exhibitions of pain. These environmental procedures were, of course, accompanied by medication, which was reduced over time. In these early studies, patients significantly improved physical activities, reports of pain, and usage of medication. More recently, such procedures in the "clinical management" of the pain patient have become components of a larger treatment package that includes feedback and relaxation.

Biofeedback is the generic term for a number of approaches using a variety of devices applied to different parts of the body. The basic element in biofeedback is the learning of self-control procedures. The individual learns to control specific bodily functions such as skin temperature, pulse, or alpha waves of the brain. It should be noted that biofeedback was initially considered the major approach to the treatment of pain, but more recently there is growing doubt as to its efficacy for controlling chronic pain (Turk, Meichenbaum, & Berman, 1979).

Relaxation procedures, a major component of the treatment approach to chronic pain, as well as to virtually every other health problem, continue to be useful and healthful. In effect, it is clear that relaxation represents a skill for coping with all stressful life situations, and there seems to be no evidence of any negative features to it.

Recent developments in pain management have involved the applications of a *cognitive* model that assumes the patient's attitudes, expectations, and beliefs influence how pain is experienced (Turk & Meichenbaum, 1984). The aim is to help the patient gain better control over the pain experience by changes in cognitions and thus to live more adaptively. As we indicated in chapter 1, this approach represents the latest wave of application of psychological theory to influence human behavior. One of the applications of the principles of the cognitive approach is the "stress inoculation" procedure of Meichenbaum and Turk (1976). A conceptual framework of pain, emphasizing the influence of thoughts and feelings on how pain is experienced, is presented to the patient. The individual is then taught coping skills for dealing with pain, which include way of diverting attention to the relabeling of sensations, the use of imagery, and, of course, the practice of relaxation. These skills are practiced in the laboratory, hospital, and home environments.

A note of caution must be added about these newer cognitive approaches to pain, as indeed, of all approaches, not only to pain but to almost all health problems.

> It is important not to lose sight of weaknesses in many of the studies on cognitive approaches. . . . Many have not used adequate controls, have not employed multiple measures of outcome, have not evaluated generalization, and have not followed patients beyond a brief treatment phase. However, the evidence that does exist appears positive. (Brownell, 1984, pp. 205–206)

The issues raised in the treatment of chronic pain are prototypical of all other human problems discussed throughout this book. It is clear now that chronic pain has multiple origins and is maintained by a complex series of factors. In order to substantially reduce this problem, a complex series of techniques and procedures must be used. In effect, a comprehensive program for managing pain has to be developed that includes many of the approaches described. For example, Follick, Zitter, and Ahern (1983) approached chronic pain with a comprehensive program combining behavior modification, physical therapy, co-joint marital therapy, and cognitive restructuring. Similar comprehensive programs have been developing in a large number of treatment settings.

CARDIAC DISORDERS

A major development in psychological theory has been the emergence of a concept of specific types of personalities, and Type A has become a particular favorite (Friedman, 1977; Friedman & Rosenman, 1974). In fact, the term Type A has become part of the popular American vocabulary. When we hear the term, it elicits an image of an individual with high drive and ambition, a strong sense of urgency, preoccupation with real or imagined deadlines, and an intense competitive drive. Of course, none of us are Type As, but the chap down the hall, "Watch out, he's a real Type A!"

The argument has developed, with some supporting data, that the Type A Behavior Pattern (TABP) is an independent risk factor for coronary heart disease (Rosenman, 1978). The origin of the TABP concept goes back to the psychosomatic hypotheses described earlier about the relationship between personality and physical disorders and the notion that there were coronary-prone individuals in terms of their unconscious conflicts (Alexander, 1950).

In the 1950s, two cardiologists, Meyer Friedman and Ray Rosenman, were so impressed with their observations of their postcoronary patients that they developed some hypotheses, behavioral rather than psychodynamic, about the personalities of their patients. Based on these observations, a number of studies developed of the relationship between the behavioral patterns of individuals and incidents of coronary disorders (Brand, Rosenman, Sholtz, & Friedman, 1976).

Once the broad parameters of Type A behavior were established, the next step, of course, was the development of intervention procedures designed to change characteristics of such behavior with a view to ascertaining the effects of such changes on the reoccurrence of coronary difficulties in these patients (Friedman et al., 1984; Glass, 1977; Roskies, Spevack, Surkis, Cohen, & Gilman, 1978; Suinn, 1975).

A major problem in the attempts to modify Type A behavior is that the change agents are dealing with a wide range of behavior, in effect, with a way of life. In contrast with modifying specific behaviors such as eating, drinking, or smoking, attempts to affect Type A behavior are dealing with a general life-style, hence the behavioral-change procedures require more complexity and subtlety, and even the methodology of evaluating the effects of treatment have to be reconsidered. Further, there are subtle ethical issues in even attempting treatment.

> Because the TABP is congruent with the values of our society, it may be impossible to permanently change the pattern in individuals unless we first change the environmental conditions that elicit and maintain this type of behavior. If this is so, classifying certain people as Type A and offering them treatment for the condition may simply create anxiety about this new health problem without providing the means of remedying it. (Roskies, 1980, pp. 300–301)

Further, to the extent that Type A behavior is an integral part of modern occupational careers, treatment programs could very well arouse realistic concern on the individual's part of diminished vocational achievement and its social and economic consequences. However, in one control study of U.S. Army officers, Type A behavior was drastically reduced with no evidence of diminished career effectiveness (Gill et al., 1985).

In a major study of modifying Type A behavior in coronary patients (Thoresen, Friedman, Gill, & Ulmer, 1982; Friedman et al., 1984) success has been reported in both changing Type A behavior and linking such changes with nonrecurrence of cardiac disorders. The techniques used in the alteration of Type A behavior were labled *cognitive social learning* and included self-control training, behavioral contracting, and cognitive and environmental restructuring. The more Type A behavior was reduced, the fewer cardiac recurrences, including death, took place.

EATING DISORDERS

It seems that in each of these sections we are emphasizing the ubiquitousness of the health area to which psychology is being applied. We all smoke or interact with people who do. We all feel pain at one time or another, and now we point out dramatically that we all eat. Included in the eating disorder category are all the problems associated with the eating process: eating too much, eating the "wrong" foods, not eating at all, eating and throwing up. These disorders have official labels such as *anorexia nervosa*, *bulimia*, and *obesity* (Agras, 1987).

Anorexia nervosa is a serious disorder, affecting primarily young women, in which the individual fears gaining weight, and there is a sharp weight loss to the point where it becomes life threatening. The first illustration of the application of the operant conditioning techniques to control the eating behavior of an anorexic was described by Bachrach, Erwin, and Mohr (1965). They were working with a 37-year-old woman whose weight had dropped from 120 lbs to 47 lbs at the time of her hospitalization. The following description of her appearance is dramatic and typical of severe cases of this eating disorder:

> The physical examination revealed a creature so cachetic and shrunken about her skeleton as to give the appearance of a poorly preserved mummy suddenly struck with the breath of life. Her pasty white skin was mottled a purple hue over her feet and stretched like so much heavy spider webbing about the bony prominences of her face. (p. 154)

To put it mildly, she was not in the best of shape. The problem for the investigators, very simply, was how to go about restoring eating behavior in this individual who was close to death.

Her treatment program exemplified the application of an operant conditioning/behavior modification approach. First, this involved an analysis of the individual's environment to determine what might be reinforcing contingencies. The patient was in an attractive hospital room with flowers, lovely view, radio, television, books, and access to visitors. To initiate the operant conditioning program, she was moved to a rather barren room in the psychiatric ward of the hospital. Each of the three investigators would take turns dining with her during daily mealtimes. They would then systematically reinforce all movements directed toward eating by doing such things as talking, smiling, and nodding. Over a period of time they would reinforce weight gain by introduction of desirable environmental stimuli such as a radio, a television set, and a phonograph. In effect, an informal reinforcement schedule was set up.

> When the patient lifted her fork to move toward spearing a piece of food, the experimenter would talk to her about something in which she might have some interest. The required response was then successively raised to lifting the food toward her mouth, chewing, and so forth" (Bachrach et al., 1965, p. 157).

As caloric intake increased, so did the nature of reinforcing events, such as family visits, walks on the grounds, and mail. After her discharge from the hospital, this same general approach was extended to her home environment with the cooperation and involvement of her family. At the time of the report, approximately 2 years after her hospitalization, her weight had increased to 85 lbs, and she was taking courses oriented toward a business career. This case became a classic in influencing future applications of behavioral procedures with anorexic individuals.

Bulimia is an eating disorder that has received the attention of professionals only in recent years (Pope & Hudson, 1984; Weiss, Katzman, & Wolchik, 1986). This disorder involves fear of obesity and episodic bouts of excessive intake of "fattening" foods followed by self-induced vomiting, and it occurs predominantly in females (primarily teenagers through the early 30s). It often occurs in conjunction with anorexia nervosa, complicating treatment.

As with any other problem behavior, the initial question is how did such a strange, self-defeating behavior develop? After a comprehensive review of the theories of the etiology of bulimia, Agras and Kirkley (1986) concluded that:

> There is evidence to support both a sociobehavioral and a biological explanation for the etiology of bulimia, and at present a biopsychosocial model which incorporates both perspectives seems most promising. It is possible that each theory explains the disorder in some subset of bulimic patients, or that the two forces interact together to produce bulimia.
>
> Certain biological conditions may prove to be risk factors for what is otherwise a learned behavior pattern. For example, within the current social context that encourages extreme thinness among young women, some may be prone to extreme dietary restraint and may be vulnerable to binge eating. (pp. 376–377)

It is clear that investigators are still at an early stage of theorizing. The first applications of psychological treatment were behavioral, conducted on an individual basis and aimed at control of eating habits (Logue, 1986). The goal was to normalize the patient's eating pattern and to incorporate eating of regularly scheduled meals with variety of foods. A group approach was described by Kirkley, Schneider, Agras, and Bachman (1985) in which a "cognitive–behavioral" group was instructed to make specific changes in their eating and vomiting behavior, while a "nondirective group" received no such instructions. The instructions were to increase eating regularly, to increase the variety of foods including previously avoided foods, to eat only when seated at the table and using utensils, and to use relaxation tapes.

Although the patients in the cognitive–behavioral treatment approach did have significantly greater decreases in binging and vomiting than the nondirected group, the differences did not continue to be significant. The authors pointed out that the results indicated that the behavioral techniques offered a "promising" approach. A major methodological concern, as in other disorders such as smoking, was that follow-up was based on self-reports, which may be dubious.

The third of these interrelated disorders is generally referred to as *obesity*, a far more professional-sounding term than just plain "fat." In an article in

Science titled "Obesity Declared a Disease," Kolata (1985) noted that: "A National Institute of Health consensus panel on the health implications of obesity has concluded that obesity is a potential killer" (p. 1019). A relationship between overweight and a variety of physical disorders has been tentatively established.

Approaches to affecting weight loss have emphasized *self-management*. For example, there are now a number of books, mostly behaviorally oriented, available in bookstores that deal with self-treating problems of obesity. Most of these have been written by researchers and clinicians who have much experience with overweight (e.g., *Permanent Weight Control*, Mahoney & Mahoney, 1976; *Take It Off and Keep It Off*, Jeffrey & Katz, 1977; *Act Thin, Stay Thin*, Stuart, 1978). There does not seem to be experimental evidence that one can follow the suggestions in these books and lose weight, and therefore the efficacy of such self-help books has been heatedly debated (Glasgow & Rosen, 1978).

In applying psychological approaches to any or all of the health problems discussed in this chapter, there is one predominant issue. The professional person knows what is *good* for your health and what is *bad*. But how does one persuade, influence, shape, modify the individual to *adhere*?

ADHERENCE

A major part of medical practice is devoted to encouraging and persuading patients to follow prescribed health-related activities. Some, in fact, argue that the most crucial issue facing modern medicine and practitioners of health psychology is adherence to or compliance with prescribed or suggested medical and behavioral regimens. Reviewers of the field have concluded that the research, thus far, has provided few guidelines for the practicing health care professional. Conflicting and negative results are quite usual. The few experiments devoted to applications of behavioral-change principles to compliance problems have been relatively successful. For example, Meyer and Henderson (1974) at the Stanford Heart Disease Institute reported on a project devoted to changing certain health-related behaviors of individuals with risk of heart disease.

A good example of the adherence problem can be found in the area of exercise. It seems to be quite clear at this point that a systematic exercise program increases the likelihood of good health. Yet survey data indicate that roughly two thirds of Americans do not exercise regularly (J. E. Martin & Dubbert, 1982). Reports of studies on cardiovascular risk modification, for those individuals in structured and prescribed exercise programs who certainly know that they should exercise, show adherence to be very low. Attrition in these types of programs ranges from 30 to 70% in the first 3 months, with further dropouts after 1 or 2 years. In view of the presumed benefits of a regular exercise program, it is remarkable that adherence to exercise is so poor, especially among those who presumably stand to benefit the most. There have been studies oriented to developing ways of improving short-term and long-term adherence to physical activity that used various behavioral techniques such as the buddy system, booster sessions, phone calls, modeling, contracting, goal setting, and coping self-statements. The results of these studies are still quite equivocal, primarily because of methodological difficulties.

DIFFUSION OF GOOD HEALTH PRACTICES

We have but to glance at our television sets or local newspapers to realize that we are living in an age in which we are constantly bombarded by news reports of the latest "scientific" findings about what is good or bad for our health and by promptings to eat properly and to exercise, all for our better health or to prevent this or that physical disease.

We have labeled this section *diffusion* to emphasize a major element in the health psychology field, the spreading of the influence process throughout the community to affect people's behavior in order to increase the prevention of major illnesses. The complexity of initiating and diffusing any health program is evidenced by Winett's (1984) analysis of organizations, which focuses on such aspects of the situation relevant to health behavior as (a) employee and management attitudes toward exercise and current practices (b) flexibility of work schedules, (c) places to change and dress, (d) potential and willingness to modify work settings for health and exercise programs, (e) potential costs and benefits to an organization of instituting exercise and well-being programs, given current performance, attendance, turnover, health, and disability figures. In effect, bringing health psychology to the community level involves, at the least, a complex aggregate of organizations, work settings, health care facilities, private providers, media, recreational settings, and facilities.

Bandura (1986) cited the Stanford Heart Disease Prevention Program as an illustration of the "social diffusion of innovations." In this program (Maccoby Farquhar, Wood, & Alexander, 1977; Farquhar, Magnus, & Maccoby, 1981), the mass media are used at a community level to convey information to the general public about how personal things such as nutrition, smoking, and exercise can effect the risk of premature heart disease. The focus is on teaching self-regulatory skills.

Major techniques in the diffusion and influence process require the use of self-help manuals and prime-time TV programs and the continuing use of telephone contacts with selected groups of individuals. The investigators focus on enhancing weight reduction, encouraging exercise, eliminating smoking, and changing eating and drinking habits to decrease consumptions of salt, saturated fat, cholesterol, and alcohol. One example of the influence process is a 30-second commercial aired on local TV stations that points out that fats in red meat can increase the risk of heart disease. The commercial presents a Japanese restaurant chef twirling his meat cleaver and removing the fat from a big juicy steak. The narrator then warns the viewer that at least half of the meat's fat is really hidden, so, if you must eat meat, eat smaller portions. A local supermarket cooperates in the program by putting flyers On How to Eat Less Salt and Making the Most of Snacks into grocery bags. In these studies, which are still underway, it has been clearly demonstrated that, in the communities receiving the media programs, there have been sharp reductions of heart disease problems, as compared with a control community that did not receive the information-diffusion program (Farquhar et al., 1977; Meyer et al., 1980).

In another example of the diffusion of good health procedures deriving from a psychological model, Elder, Abrams, and Carleton (1983) reported on their experiences with community-level applications in the Pawtucket Heart Health Program. They started with a theoretical base of social learning and self-control principles and applied them in the community. Based on these principles, the investigators developed a set of intervention procedures that guided their applications. They presented their procedures as a clear alternative to the traditional "medical model" that focuses on "curing" individuals who are "sick."

According to these principles, intervention procedures in a community should be behavioral-change oriented, community owned (input and control derived from members of the community in all phases of planning and implementation), easily adopted by all community members, flexible and adaptable, inexpensive, multilevel (consumers participating as individuals or as members of organizations), appropriate to interests and needs and acceptable to community members, focused on developing social support networks, evaluation oriented, and visible in the community. Such principles are, or course, applicable to any procedures utilized in any community for any purposes (see chapter 2).

One example of the program developed by the Pawtucket group involved training individuals who wanted to lead aerobic exercise programs at their own places of work, in churches, or in other social settings. In the first few months of the program, 20 leaders were trained from 11 different community organizations such as banks, factories, schools, and churches. A dozen exercise programs involving about 250 participants, run by these volunteers, were soon underway. This illustrates how community members can quickly become involved in doing the kinds of things that should decrease the likelihood of heart problems.

Other behavioral change group programs included working with problems of smoking, weight loss, nutrition, blood pressure, and stress and a general heart-health group covering all risk factors. The most popular groups were Up in Smoke, a mildly aversive program to stop smoking, and Learn to Be Lean, a weight-loss program.

The approach to smoking cessation of the Pawtucket group is of particular interest. Initial emphasis of the program was on developing task forces and risk-factor programs within specific churches, work sites, and other community organizations. However, at the end of 9 months, only one of these community organizations decided to begin a stop-smoking program. In view of the fact that over 45% of the community were smokers, the investigators decided that a community-wide intervention program was necessary. They tried to recruit as many participants as possible into the Up in Smoke program, which incorporated smoke holding and self-management techniques. The attraction (reinforcement) of joining such a program was a chance to participate in a lottery, which included as prizes trips to Atlantic City, membership at health spas, and free dinners at local restaurants. All of these efforts attracted 128 participants, and the program was underway.

Another example of community intervention by the Pawtucket group involved the broad goal of modifying the community's eating behaviors, specifically, the consumption of less sodium, fat, and cholesterol. The plan involved two broad strategies. The first was to increase the availability and marketing of *heart-healthy* food and to decrease the availability and marketing of unhealthy foods in the community. Second, the plan involved increasing consumer demand for heart-healthy foods. To accomplish the first, committees were set up to work with food vendors in the community to affect the availability and sales of specific food products. To affect consumer demands for the appropriate foods, group and individual self-help programs in nutrition and weight loss were set up. It is readily obvious that, with this approach, a considerable, and key, portion of the community became involved.

ETHICAL AND VALUE ISSUES

As in all fields of psychological application, major social, ethical, and value issues arise. In effect, whenever psychology is to be applied to influencing human behavior, the question arises For what? What is the goal of this behavior change, and what are the consequences for the individual and for the broader community and society in which the individual lives?

These issues in the health psychology field are dramatically and succinctly brought together in a paper by Joseph Matarazzo (1982), aptly titled "Behavioral Health's Challenge to Academic, Scientific, and Professional Psychology." Matarazzo noted that, following the first Surgeon General's Report in 1964 on the dangers to health of smoking, strong efforts were made to apply the principles and techniques of psychology and other disciplines to reduce smoking behavior. Because of the various educational and behavioral-change techniques applied, there was a sharp decrease of about 15% of *male* adult smokers of all ages. During the same period there was an increase in *female* adult smokers of approximately 5%. Matarazzo pointed out:

> Many experts agree with the American Cancer Society that this increase for females is eloquent testimony to the power of the advertisements that were carefully crafted with the help of psychologists who are specialists in the field of subliminal motivational psychology. Examples of these skillfully crafted slogans are, "You've come a long way, baby," with its strong but still subtle appeal to the women's liberation movement. The "Virginia Slims" brand name artfully takes advantage of the increasingly well-documented research finding that, for many female (and male) smokers, quitting the habit is associated with gaining weight. (Blitzer, Rimm, & Giefer, 1977, p. 6)

Matarazzo made an eloquent appeal to psychology, which admirably expresses both a value system and a challenge.

> Should not a greater portion of psychology's currently vast talents and resources be applied to stemming the health and financial costs associated with smoking by children and adults as just cited in the tables and figures? As the field which has the longest history in the study of human behavior, and especially individual behavior, psychology has the scientific knowledge base, the practical applied experience, and the institutional supports for individuals within it to begin to make important contributions immediately in preventing smoking among our country's youth and in helping adults who wish to quit to do so successfully. (p. 6)

It must be pointed out that a major ethical issue could be related to the possible side effects of large-scale implementation of social programs. Altering environmentally significant behavior on a large scale could have effects beyond those for which the program was designed. The larger the scale upon which social programs are implemented, the more serious the possible threat of unanticipated, undesirable side effects of the program. The eradication of a particular problem might introduce undesirable changes in other aspects of the system (e.g., Willems, 1974).

Another social and value issue involves questions of *rights* versus *duty and responsibility* in health care (Winett, 1984). An extreme rights position sees access to good health care as a basic entitlement of a citizen, regardless of cost, and a strong role for governmental agencies in enforcing the individual's "rights" to good health. An extreme duty-and-responsibility position sees health, in large measure, as a function of individual initiative and choice, and the government's role is therefore that of laissez faire.

The greatest causes of death today stem from such behaviors as smoking, drinking, overeating, and poor dietary practices. These result in diseases that are potentially preventable. An active government can emphasize these problems at the *legal level* with enforcement of laws, for example, concerning selling of cigarettes to minors.

THE FUTURE OF HEALTH PSYCHOLOGY

There are, of course, dangers in the rapid development of a new field (Brownell, 1984), among them, initial overoptimism and resultant disillusionment when initial expectancies are not fulfilled. There is a tendency to apply techniques to situations and individuals before reasonable evidence and data are in. There is the danger of overspecialization, which means too narrowly training in and focusing on detailed aspects of a situation, perhaps losing sight of the broad picture.

However, appropriate notes of caution are being expressed by leading investigators (Agras, 1982; Brownell, 1982, 1984; Hamburg, 1982; N. E. Miller, 1979; Schwartz, 1982). These show concern that techniques will be applied before data warrant, the focus of professionals will become too specialized, and subareas (e.g., behavioral cardiology) will develop with no theoretical rationale. In view of the importance of health psychology to all of us, as individuals and as a society, and the research skill and strong motivation of the investigators in this field, we are optimistic about its very positive future development.

5 Industrial Applications

In the 20th century, American business and industry has passed through four major stages, each one substantially changing many aspects of the workplace, basic employer–employee relationships, and the nature and meaning of work itself. In the *Scientific Management Era*, which began around 1900 and lasted until approximately 1910, emphasis in management was placed upon man–machine efficiency and fitting of the employee to the job via structured, authoritarian, supervisory leadership. The *Industrial Psychology Era*, which took place from about 1910 to 1925, also stressed efficiency of productivity but began more fully to discover the worker as a human being. If she or he didn't fit a given job, the characteristic firing and replacement of the Scientific Management Era was frequently replaced in this second stage by active efforts to train the worker to better fit the job at hand.

These orientations to the industrial worker and his or her productivity, however, eventually proved unsatisfactory in their results and combined with the rise of the labor union movement and the Great Depression to move American business and industry into its third major stage, the *Human Relations Era*. Lasting from approximately 1930 to the late 1950s, this era was marked by efforts to better understand and improve labor–management and worker–worker relationships. As the Western Electric Hawthorne studies (Mayo, 1933; Roethlisberger & Dickson, 1939), which helped shape this era, had suggested, employee satisfaction and social welfare appeared to be important influences upon productivity and hence became the major target of the Human Relations Era. The passage of three major laws in the 1960s and 1970s bearing upon the rights of employees—the Civil Rights Act of 1964, the Occupational Safety and Health Act of 1970, and the Employee Retirement Income Security Act of 1974—gave both structure and substance to a major new phase in American business and industry, the *Quality of Life Era*. Rowland and Ferris (1982) described this movement well:

> While the primary objective of the earlier eras was to maximize production by (1) restructuring the production process (i.e., division of labor and hierarchy of authority), (2) increasing technical or man-machine efficiency, (3) selecting

or modifying [training] the person to achieve a better job-person fit, and (4) improving human relationships at work, our society now began to witness a broader set of concerns . . . organizational efforts toward improving productivity continued, but these were supplemented with efforts toward providing equal employment opportunity; job enrichment; protection of privacy and freedom of speech; reduction of stress, drug abuse, alcoholism, and so forth; all of which demonstrated considerable interest in the employee as an individual. (p. 4)

Over the span of the almost 100 years collectively represented by these four periods in American business and industry, applied psychology has played first a small (e.g., time and motion studies in the Scientific Management Era), then a growing (e.g., aptitude and achievement testing in the Industrial Psychology Era) and quite substantial (e.g., testing, interviewing, and training programs in the Human Relations Era) role. At present, as the substance of this chapter will detail, psychology's effect upon the quality of life of the industrial worker or business employee is both broad and deep. We will consider, in turn, the efforts of the modern applied psychologist in the full span of relevant domains constituting entry into, performance in, and satisfaction at the American workplace. Our specific topics are human resources planning; job analysis; screening, selection, and placement techniques of biodata, testing, and interviewing; diverse training programs; organizational development; worker motivation and job satisfaction; performance appraisal; and modification of ineffective performance. It will become clear as we journey through these key areas of industrial function, that, along with clinical and educational applications of psychology (chapters 3 and 6, respectively), it is here, in the office, in the factory, in the executive suite, that applied psychologists have had their greatest impact.

PLANNING AND PREPARATION

Selection, training, performance appraisal, and the several other specific functions that applied psychologists affect in industrial settings are best carried out as a coordinated and integrated set of activities. For such coordination to occur, these several functions must optimally flow from carefully developed planning and preparation. The two major expressions of such prior, stage-setting activity common in many corporations are *human resource planning* and *job analysis*.

Human Resource Planning

Very much a characteristic of the Quality of Life Era in American industry, human resources planning is " . . . a process of analyzing an organization's human resource needs under changing conditions and developing the activities necessary to satisfy these needs" (Walker, 1980). As Cascio (1982) observed, human resources planning can also be viewed as an effort to antici-pate future demands on an organization and the personnel requirements associated with this demand. Drawing not only upon psychology, but also upon mathematics, economic theory, and other behavioral sciences, human resource planning concretely involves needs forecasting (planning and control of staffing), performance management (improvement of organizational and individual performance), and career management (development of individu-al careers). The actual planning efforts conducted within an organization to meet the needs, performance, and career-management goals specified can be long-term strategic planning, shorter-term tactical planning, or day-to-day operational planning. In all three instances, the psychologist's skills in as-sessment, training, prediction, and evaluation frequently play a significant role.

Job Analysis

Job analysis is an activity in which a given job is defined in terms of the behaviors necessary to perform it. A job analysis typically consists of two major elements: the job description, which lists the physical and environ-mental characteristics of the work to be done, and, especially relevant to the psychologist's expertise, the job specification, which is the personal employ-ee characteristics necessary to do the job. More specifically, the job descrip-tion component of a job analysis is likely to consist of a statement of procedures (tasks performed, machinery and materials used, nature and extent of supervision), working conditions (heat, noise, light, hazardous conditions), the job's social environment (nature of work group, amount of interpersonal interaction required), and the conditions of employment (hours, wages, pay schedule, fringe benefits, promotion opportunities). The job specification component of the job analysis (optimal employee charac-teristics), in turn, typically reports employee behaviors, skills, and interests necessary to perform the job well.

Not only does the applied psychologist often have a major role in plan-ning job analysis procedures, but he or she also frequently supervises or serves as the job analyst gathering the relevant information. Job analysis information is obtained from incumbents and supervisors or by the job analyst's actually performing the job. At times, recording devices, cameras, physiological measures, and similar mechanical means are also employed. The major methods of collecting job analysis information from these several sources, used at different times since job analyses were first performed in the early 1900s, are observation, individual or group interviews, question-naires, diaries, records of critical incidents, and other records of various types.

Job analysis information is especially central to the planning and preparation goals underlying so much of what occurs in industrial organizations. Table 5.1 summarizes the multipurpose value of such information. Note that almost all phases of production, personnel management, and employee satisfaction literally begin with and ideally follow from a satisfactory job analysis. One of its first uses in the employment process is employee selection.

> I hope this is the absolutely last midterm exam I ever take, thought Lenore, as she left the classroom after completing her Economics 412 examination. In less than 2 months, I'll be Lenore Corat, Bachelor of Business Administration, and then good-bye college and hello work. The 4 years at Capstone College had been real good ones, Lenore reflected, but, as she had gotten hooked into her business administration major, and especially her courses in personnel management and industrial psychology, she more and more itched to get out into the real world of work.
> Business administration majors were still in pretty decent demand, and Lenore's grades and recommendations were pretty good, so she hadn't had too much trouble so far arranging to see recruiters she wanted to see. That was good news. The bad news was that she really wasn't terribly excited about any of the four companies she'd interviewed with. Envirotech and Parks Unlimited stood for things she believed in, but had starting jobs and later job possibilities that didn't sound great. The Harris Corporation sounded much better from its literature, but their recruiter (she couldn't even remember his name) was so unpleasant and arrogant that it had really turned her off the company. The firm she interviewed with last Thursday, Universal Books, was still a possibility for her. She loved books and thought publishing might be a first-rate industry to work in, but Universal was huge. You could really get lost in a company that big. Tomorrow would be her fifth interview, with Artist's Press Publishers. They did great books, seemed to be just the right size—not too big, not too small—

Table **5.1.** Uses of Job Analysis Information

ORGANIZATION DESIGN	PERSONNEL ADMINISTRATION	WORK AND EQUIPMENT DESIGN	ADDITIONAL USES
Organizing Human-resource planning Role definition	Job evaluation Recruitment Selection Placement Orientation Training and personnel development Performance appraisal Promotions and transfers Career-path planning Labor relations	Engineering design Job design Methods improvement Safety	Vocational guidance Rehabilitation counseling Job classification systems Personnel research

Note. From *Applied Psychology in Personnel Management* (2nd ed., p. 49) by W. F. Cascio, 1982, Englewood Cliffs, NJ: Prentice-Hall. Copyright 1982 by Prentice-Hall, Inc. Reprinted by permission.

and the opening was in their personnel department. They could be the firm for me, Lenore thought, her enthusiasm growing at the prospect.

SELECTION

Background Information

It is a generally accepted principle in contemporary psychology that one of, if not the, best predictors of future behavior is the individual's past behavior, especially in similar settings. It is not surprising, therefore, that background data on prospective employees have in fact proven to be consistently superior to that obtained from the two other most widely used selection methods, interviewing and testing.

The usefulness of personal history data as a predictor of future behavior was underscored early in psychology, particularly by Allport's (1942) emphasis on the usefulness for such purposes of personal documents (letters, diaries, autobiographies) and Guthrie's (1944) stress on the predictive value of past affiliations. In American industry around the same period there began early efforts to objectively score employee application blanks. In a number of investigations, especially a long-term series of studies conducted at Standard Oil (Henry, 1966), such application-blank information as school achievement, leadership, early family relationships, personal goals, health, and leisure-time activities indeed proved predictively valuable in forecasting work performance. These several demonstrations led many companies to more fully objectify their application blanks, giving rise to the scored biodata form. Such forms, essentially standardized and objectively scorable, background information, application questionnaires, have found widespread acceptance in American industry. The Biographical Information Blank, the Biographical Data Form, and the Individual Background Survey are a few current examples. Cascio (1982) nicely summarized the important role of such information in the selection process.

> What is impressive is that indicators of past successes and accomplishments can be utilized in an objective way to identify persons with differing odds of being successful over the long term in their management career. People who have a prior record of achievement when they enter an organization are in excellent positions to profit from training opportunities and from challenging organizational environments. (p. 196)

The Interview

Although very serious questions have been raised about the validity of information gathered in the employment interview for predicting future on-the-job performance, this nevertheless continues to be the single most widely used selection technique. In fact, its use has even increased in recent years (in the face of an array of findings of bias, weakness, and poor validity about the interview), probably because of the difficult legal challenges raised in the last decade to a companion selection technique, psychological testing.

What are these weaknesses and sources of predictive invalidity? Several investigators (Carlson, 1970; Hakel, Ohnesorge, & Dunnette, 1970; Landy, 1973) have shown how powerful are the initial biases about the interviewee that the interviewer can bring to the interview, perhaps originating from an unfavorable letter of recommendation or an application-blank statement. Under such circumstances, the interviewee could be given less credit for past accomplishments, be held more personally responsible for past failures, and in the end be less likely to be offered the job for which she or he is applying.

A second preinterview source of interviewer bias is the other applicants interviewed immediately before the present one. Strong contrast effects often operate here. The "just average" job candidate interviewed immediately following two or three clearly below average ones tends to be evaluated very positively by the interviewer. Contrastingly, being interviewed following outstanding applicants often makes the applicant appear weaker than his or her own qualifications warrant. Once the interview actually begins, the first few minutes play a crucial role in influencing the interviewer's perceptions, observations, and later decisions about acceptance. Important here in determining the favorableness or unfavorableness of this *primacy effect* is the applicant's appearance and interpersonal skills when greeting the interviewer and in the opening discussion. The potential for interviewer bias continues throughout the interview. Hakel et al. (1970) noted that interviewers often devote considerable interview time to searching for negative information and give it disproportionate weight when they find it. Anderson (1960) found that interviewees were more likely to be hired after interviews in which the interviewer did a great deal of the talking. Though it is unclear whether this reflects interviewer bias, appropriate information exchange, or other factors, it is the case that the longer the interview, the more likely it is that the applicant will be hired. More generally, many preemployment interviews can be accurately described, as Cascio (1982) observed, as events in which interviewers develop a stereotype of a good applicant and then proceed to search for qualities that match or fail to match their stereotypes.

Given these several powerful effects of interviewer bias, as well as the fact that interviewers' behaviors and postinterview decisions can also be influenced by applicants' sex, educational level, age, physical attractiveness, and a host of nonverbal behaviors (Dipboye, Fromkin, & Wiback, 1975; Zikmund, Hitt, & Pickens, 1978), we must agree with Rowland and Ferris's (1982) depressing conclusion that:

> The research literature presents a veritable rogue's gallery of biases and other assorted effects through which interviewer decision-making can go wrong.

Individually, these studies lead to pessimism about the possibility of re-engineering the interview. Collectively, their impact is almost devastating. (p. 140)

Attempts to diminish these several sources of interview invalidity by means of interviewer training have generally been unsuccessful. Wexley, Sanders, and Yukl (1973), for example, showed that neither the use of warnings (lectures) nor anchoring (comparing applicants to a pre-set standard rather than to each other) reduced the frequency of the applicant-to-applicant contrast effects just described. A more hopeful direction has been to seek to add structure and standardization to the interview process and, thus, in a sense to diminish somewhat the opportunity for interviewers' biases and related effects to operate. Evidence in recent years, therefore, has shown improved predictive validity for the preemployment interview when " . . . the content is focused on job-related situational questions, job knowledge questions, work requirement questions . . . " (Perloff, Craft, & Perloff, 1984, p. 429).

Before concluding our discussion of the selection interview, we wish to note that, in addition to its information-gathering purpose (for the interviewer), it can also intentionally and unintentionally serve an information-providing function (for the interviewee). Just as interviewers can be appropriately and inappropriately responsive to applicant characteristics, applicants can form too hasty and erroneous impressions of both the recruiting interviewer and the company he or she represents, as a result of interviewer age, sex, race, style of delivery, and job title (Rynes, Heneman, & Schwab, 1980). Particularly helpful to an applicant's forming favorable impressions is a recruiting interviewer who is well-prepared in her or his knowledge of both the applicant and the job being applied for and who, in addition, is or has been an actual incumbent in that job.

In spite of very considerable reservations, we would not wish to recommend that preemployment interviews be eliminated from the employee selection process. When used in a structured format, perhaps somewhat analogous to a verbally administered questionnaire, they can make an important and relatively unbiased contribution to employee-selection decision making. Their proper role beyond this limited one must await further research and refinement.

Psychological Testing

Of the many varied functions performed by the applied psychologist in industrial settings, those associated with psychological testing are clearly most frequent. Test development, test administration, test interpretation, and research on test validation are the primary examples. Although the first psychological tests were not created by psychologists (Gideon and Plato advocated military aptitude testing centuries before psychology existed as a discipline), psychological testing has been with us for over 100 years.

In 1869, Galton began psychology's long interest in intelligence testing with his book *Hereditary Genius*, which presented a classification scheme based upon abilities. Shortly thereafter, Wundt began using reaction-time measures and tests of visual and auditory acuity as indexes of intelligence. This effort was greatly advanced by Binet in the same era, because he reconceptualized intelligence as consisting of more complex mental processes than had Wundt and, accordingly, developed tests of memory, attention, comprehension, imagination, and the like (see chapter 1). Munsterberg in 1913 brought this fledging movement into the industrial context in general, and employee selection in particular, by using a battery of tests available at the time to help select motormen for the Boston Railway Company. Psychological testing has blossomed fully since that early era, to gain a place of high prominence not only in industry, but also in school settings, clinical settings, and elsewhere. Its greatest boost for selection purposes came during World War I, at a time when the American Psychological Association (60,120 members in 1985) consisted of 336 people. Under the leadership of many of these early pioneers, 1,726,966 men were tested (for selection and classification purposes) as a part of the country's war effort.

In the period since these beginnings, the numbers and types of psychological tests employed in industry have expanded greatly. In a large, national survey done by the American Society for Personnel Administration in 1975, it was reported that approximately 60% of employers with over 25,000 employees and 40% of those with less than 100 employees used psychological tests. Current tests in major use follow.

Aptitude Tests
These tests measure the capacities of the individual for learning the skills and knowledge necessary to perform the job well.

Achievement Tests
Such tests measure proficiency or competencies already acquired in job skills and knowledge.

Interest Tests
Measured here are the activities of a vocational and avocational nature (e.g., mechanical, scientific, social welfare, clerical, business, esthetic) that an individual would prefer to engage in and enjoy engaging in.

Cognitive-Ability Tests
Descending from the early work on intelligence testing and the many efforts that followed to identify the factors or elements of which intelligence was

composed, these are measures of such abilities as word fluency, perceptual speed, memory, inductive reasoning, and comprehension.

Leadership Ability Tests

These tests have taken several forms, but most have sought to measure two central leadership dimensions: the task-oriented quality of initiating structure (defines and structures one's own and subordinates' roles) and the relationship-oriented quality of consideration (enhances mutual trust, shows respect for the ideas of others, considers others' feelings).

Personality Tests

These tests, as used in industry and elsewhere, have taken a particularly wide variety of forms. Designed to reflect enduring qualities, traits, or behavioral predispositions, their form has included questionnaires completed by others, self-report inventories, behavioral measures (described later), and projective techniques (i.e., ambiguous test stimuli onto which the person is held to cast or project individual qualities when responding).

Peer Assessment

These are test procedures by means of which selection and other information relevant to personnel decisions are obtained from other persons in, or applying to join, the work force. The three major forms of peer assessment are peer nomination (each person nominates one or more other persons as highest and lowest on a given dimension), peer rating (each member rates every other member on a given dimension or quality), and peer ranking (each member ranks every other member from best to worst).

Work-Sample Tests

Tests designed to obtain samples of the actual behaviors one is trying to predict have become quite widespread in contemporary psychology, and their major form in industrial settings has been work-sample tests, of which three in particular are especially popular. The *leaderless group discussion* is a procedure in which a group of candidates is asked to carry on a discussion for a period of time, no one is appointed leader, and raters observe and rate each person's performance. The *in-basket technique* is a procedure in which the testee is told about the organization involved, is asked to pretend he or she is now in a managerial position in that organization, and attempts to deal effectively with a variety of memos, letters, telephone calls, and other materials in an in-basket. *Business games* are a third prominent example of work-sample tests. These are primarily simulations in which the candidate is required to hire, fire, sell, deal with stress, or show other administrative skills in tasks consisting of human relations problems, running a warehouse, managing a stock market portfolio, and the like.

Assessment Centers

An especially prominent recent trend in industrial use of psychological testing has been the assessment center. Here, several of the techniques described thus far in this section, but especially varieties of behavioral or situational testing, are administered to small groups of candidates over a period of a few days, with their test behavior observed and rated by a panel of judges or assessors. Used first during World War II for the selection of secret agents and first utilized in American industry by AT&T in 1956, assessment centers are currently in widespread industrial use. A typical such center, as described by Cascio (1982), might aspire to measure:

1. Administrative skills, by the in-basket test
2. Interpersonal skills, by leaderless group discussion and manufacturing-problem business game
3. Intellectual ability, by paper-and-pencil ability tests
4. Stability of performance, by in-basket, leaderless group discussion, and manufacturing-problem business game
5. Work-oriented motivation, by projective tests, interviews, and simulations
6. Career orientation, by projective tests, interviews, and simulations

By means of the assessment center combined procedure, or via the individual psychological tests described earlier, we have painted a picture in this section of a large, energetic, and diverse activity engaged in by the applied psychologist in industry. This impression is generally correct, but there remains yet unmentioned one important facet to it, a facet quite necessary to a full understanding of the current status of psychological testing in American industry.

On August 25, 1978, a milestone in American industry's Quality of Life Era took place. The Equal Employment Opportunity Commission, the Department of Labor, and the Civil Service Commission jointly issued the *Uniform Guidelines on Employee Selection Procedures*, a watershed event in personnel practices and policy, with major implications for the psychologist in industry and especially his or her functions in connection with psychological testing. Among other stipulations, the guidelines required employers to validate a selection procedure (especially tests, but also recruiting procedures, background information forms, and interview procedures) when use of the procedure resulted in adverse impact upon any race, sex, or ethnic group.* The guidelines were originally designed to reduce discrimination in employment toward women and ethnic minority groups, but subsequent legislation

---

*Adverse impact is held to have occurred when the selection rate for one group for a given job is less than 80% of the selection rate for the group with the highest selection rate.

has explicitly extended them to the handicapped, Vietnam veterans, and persons between ages 40 and 70. What have been the effects of this important legislation? Some employers, rather than undertake the expensive and laborious task of test validation, have dropped or greatly reduced their use of psychological tests for employee selection. But many others have undertaken the test-validation effort, often leading to clearer understanding of job performance criteria of effectiveness, the creation of fairer psychological tests and test result usage, and, ultimately, substantially less discrimination in the American workplace.

The recruiting interview had gone really well with Artist's Press, Lenore thought. In fact, when it was over, she almost felt that she and Mary Jane Thomas, the interviewer, were old friends. Lenore's interests and the firm's came together particularly well. It sounded very much like Lenore could learn most major aspects of what Artist's Press did, but especially develop expertise in personnel work, her main interest. Mary Jane, the recruiter, was in the personnel department there herself and seemed pretty frank and honest about the people, the company, the work itself, and the chances to advance and grow. The more Lenore thought about it, the more interested in Artist's Press she became.

One month before graduation, the letter came. Artist's Press was "very pleased" with her credentials and interview, and "very much" wanted to proceed at her "earliest convenience" to the next steps in their "possible hiring" procedure—completion of their detailed background information data form, an interview at the company's main office with the personnel manager ("My boss-to-be?" wondered Lenore), and some psychological tests they wanted her to take ("Would they be the very same tests I learned about in my second industrial psychology course?"). Lenore was getting a little apprehensive and very excited. Artist's Press could be it!

TRAINING

Changing the Individual

Once an organization has determined its personnel needs via human resources planning, defined the jobs to be filled via job analysis, and selected and hired persons to fill the jobs thus defined, it can turn to the next opportunity to maximize employee–job fit, or congruence, namely employee training. Training has been defined as a planned activity designed to bring about a relatively permanent change in employee knowledge, skills, attitudes, or social behavior. An organization's training needs can be determined through a variety of avenues: advisory committees, attitude surveys, employee interviews, exit interviews, management requests, observation of on-the-job behaviors, performance appraisals, skill tests, grievances, customer complaints, accidents, downtime, and product quality.

Each of these sources could signal arenas of employee deficiency or organizational weakness. Yet to go from awareness that training is needed to the actual selection and implementation of a training program is not a simple matter. Not only, as we shall see, are there many alternative training methods from which to choose—each perhaps best for different kinds of training goals, and each differing from the others in the type of employee for whom it is the most effective training approach—but also there exists a fundamental problem that goes to the heart of training in industrial settings. The problem is the difficulty experienced if one seeks to select a training approach based on sound, demonstrated *evidence* of its effectiveness. Although some training program evaluation research does exist and is useful in this all-important regard, most decisions about industrial training are based on anecdotal impressions, hearsay, word of mouth, or faddishness. As Campbell (1971) expressed it:

> . . . it is faddish to an extreme. The fads center around the introduction of new techniques and follow a characteristic pattern. A new technique appears on the horizon and develops a large stable of advocates who first describe its "successful" use in a number of situations. A second wave of advocates busy themselves trying out numerous modifications of the basic technique. A few empirical studies may be carried out to demonstrate that the method "works." Then the inevitable backlash sets in and a few vocal opponents begin to criticize the usefulness of the technique, most often in the absence of data. Such criticism typically has little effect. What does have an effect is the appearance of another new technique and a repetition of the same cycle. (pp. 565–566)

Faddish popularity and actual effectiveness frequently do not correspond. It is crucial, therefore, that the applied psychologist in industry devote considerably more effort and energy to careful and systematic evaluation of employee training methods.

With this serious problem of faddishness a reality that must be taken into account, and with the need for rigorous evaluation research thus proclaimed, the training effort must go forward nevertheless. How shall the selection of a particular method occur? Moses (1980) suggested that a given technique is adequate to the extent that it provides the basic conditions for effective learning to take place. To accomplish this, he proposed that the technique should:

1. Motivate the trainee to improve his or her performance
2. Clearly illustrate the desired skills
3. Provide for the learner's active participation
4. Provide an opportunity to practice
5. Provide feedback on performance
6. Provide means for the trainee to be reinforced while learning
7. Be structured from simple to complex tasks
8. Enable the trainee to transfer what is learned in training to the actual work situation

These are excellent technique-selection criteria, well worth aiming for as the goals of an employee training program. All of the specific techniques indicated later meet several of these objectives; very few meet all of them.

Industrial training techniques can be organized into categories of approaches in a number of ways. Dunnette's (1976) presentation arranges approaches into content techniques designed to impart knowledge on a cognitive level (lectures, audiovisual, auto-instructional), process techniques intended to change attitudes and develop self-awareness (role playing, sensitivity training), and mixed techniques, which seek both information acquisition and attitude change (case studies, simulations). Cascio's (1982) training-approach schema is particularly comprehensive. He described on-the-job, information presentation, and simulation methods.

On-the-Job Training Methods
These are perhaps the most commonly used methods of employee training, apparently of value at both basic skills and management-development levels. These methods include:

1. Orientation training, which is on-the-job training during the initial weeks of employment
2. Apprenticeships, which are more extended initial training experiences, often involving the active tutoring and coaching by an experienced employee
3. Vestibule training, which duplicates exactly the materials and equipment used on the job, but which takes place away from the actual job setting
4. Job rotation, in which the employee serves as incumbent in a sequence of jobs within the organization, often graded in difficulty or complexity
5. Committee assignments, in which the employee is exposed to several positions within the company, without actually being rotated through those positions

Information Presentation Methods
1. Lectures
2. Conferences
3. Correspondence courses
4. Reading lists
5. Audiovisual methods (movie, video)
6. Systematic observation
7. Programmed instruction
8. Computer assisted instruction

Simulation Methods
1. Case methods
2. Critical incidents methods
3. Role playing

4. Programmed group exercises
5. Situational tasks

Although it is beyond our purpose here to describe in depth these several approaches to industrial training, there are two we wish to single out for further examination. Although each clearly reflects our own biases, highlighting their potential value here grows primarily from the fact that these are two approaches to training that, unlike most, do rest on a reasonably firm basis of experimental support for their effectiveness.

Behavior Modification

Behavior modification is the application of the techniques and findings of experimental psychology to applied problems. As almost all other chapters of this book make clear, this application has been extensive and very often successful. In the early 1970s, behavior modification entered the industrial training arena. At the heart of this approach lies the belief that most complex human behaviors are learned, and, by altering either the conditions preceding the behavior or, especially, the consequences following it, that behavior can be altered and a new behavior or behavior pattern can be learned. Much of the applied science of behavior modification, therefore, is devoted to examining the most effective ways of altering consequences, for example, by providing new, better, more immediate, more frequent, or better-scheduled rewards or reinforcements or by withholding such rewards in order to diminish other behaviors. By means of systematically rewarding appropriate or desirable behaviors, withholding reward or extinguishing inappropriate or undesirable behaviors, or altering antecedent conditions, a wide variety of industry-relevant behaviors have been successfully altered. As Tosti noted, in the book *Industrial Behavior Modification* (O'Brien, Dickinson, & Rosow, 1982):

> Among the factors that make industrial behavior modification especially relevant to today's environment are. . . . Behavior technology is a measurement-based approach to behavior change. . . . The focus on objective measurement of change allows a realistic assessment of the success of an intervention. It can be used at any level in an organization. . . . It can be incorporated into the organization's operating system. . . . Perhaps one of the most valuable features of industrial behavior modification is its broad applicability. (p. IX)

Behavior Modeling

From the work of Bandura (1969) and his research group it became clear that the success of efforts to alter individual behavior of diverse types could be increased considerably if, in addition to altering antecedent conditions and modifying consequences, the trainer also concretely illustrated the desired skills, provided ample opportunity for active participation and practice by the trainee, and supplied both systematic feedback and specific procedures to enhance the likelihood of transfer of skills learned to the workplace. In 1974, we brought this combined training approach to industry, then labeled *Applied Learning*, now typically termed *behavior modeling* (A. P. Goldstein & Sorcher, 1974). At General Electric, Agway, AT&T, and other locations, we implemented and evaluated a four-phase training program designed, in this case with management trainees, to teach such skills as:

1. Orienting a new employee
2. Teaching the job
3. Motivating the poor performer
4. Correcting inadequate work quantity
5. Correcting inadequate work quality
5. Reducing absenteeism among disadvantaged workers
7. Reducing turnover among disadvantaged workers
8. Handling a racial discrimination complaint
9. Handling a reverse discrimination complaint
10. Reducing resentment toward the female supervisor
11. Discussing personal work habits with an employee
12. Discussing formal corrective action with an employee
13. Giving recognition to the average employee
14. Overcoming resistance to change
15. Reducing evaluation resistance
16. Delegating responsibility
17. Conducting a performance review

In the Applied Learning (behavior modeling) training program, trainees are (a) shown several examples of expert use of the behaviors constituting the skills in which they are weak or lacking (*modeling*); (b) given several guided opportunities to practice and rehearse these competent skill behaviors (*role playing*); (c) provided with praise, reinstruction, and related feedback on how well their role playing of the skill matched the expert model's portrayal of it (*performance feedback*); and (d) encouraged to engage in a series of activities designed to increase the chances that skills learned in the training setting will endure and be available for use when needed at the work site (*transfer training*).

It is our prediction that these two soundly grounded training approaches, behavior modification and behavior modeling, will increasingly be utilized as the training approaches of choice in more and more segments of American industry.

Changing the Organization

Training in industrial organizations could be directed not only toward change in individual employees, but also toward the organization, or large subdivisions of it, as a whole. This orientation to change, known as *organi-*

zational development, grew originally from a research program (The Hawthorne studies) conducted in the 1930s at the Western Electric Company, from which it was concluded that interpersonal relationships at the workplace often influence satisfaction and productivity considerably more than hours of work, rest breaks, noise, ventilation, music, or other physical job factors. The blossoming of the Human Relations Era in American industry from the 1930s to the 1950s and the popularity in the 1950s of certain job satisfaction–oriented theories of worker motivation helped the organizational development movement grow further.

The organizational development strategy was given tactical substance by the appearance in 1947 of the technique for effecting change that became its major approach, the interpersonal sensitivity laboratory training group. This approach, popularly known as the T-group, was originated by Bradford, Benne, and Lippitt at the National Training Laboratories in Bethel, Maine. Beer (1976) described the T-group as:

> . . . a small, unstructured, face-to-face group ranging in size from approximately ten to fifteen individuals. . . . No activities or agenda are planned. A trainer is present as a resource, guide and model, but not as a formal leader or chairman. With no structure planned and with no prior common experiences to discuss, group members' own behavior exhibited in their struggle to deal with the lack of structure becomes the agenda. "Here and now" behavior, in the language of T-group, is the subject matter for learning. The main mechanism for learning is nonevaluative feedback received by each individual from the group members. This feedback creates a certain amount of anxiety and tension which causes the individual to unfreeze and begin to consider alternative values, attitudes, and behaviors. (p. 940)

As a result of T-group participation, individuals are held to become more aware of the interpersonal impact of their own behavior and more sensitive to the behavior of others and to change aspects of their own behavior and attitudes. Of direct relevance to organizational development, individuals might more fully understand group process, participate more, be more willing to take creative risks, and more effectively engage in conflict management. Although evaluation research has indeed demonstrated the occurrence of these several beneficial outcomes of T-group participation (Buchanan, 1969; Campbell & Dunnett, 1968), as with all other training interventions, transfer of newly learned skills and attitudes from the training setting to the work environment is a much less reliable finding (Argyris, 1971; Beer & Kleisath, 1967).*

---

*In recent years, a highly promising technology of transfer-enhancing techniques has begun to be developed. These are procedures originated in the experimental psychology laboratory that have subsequently been adapted and evaluated for their effectiveness in enhancing the transfer of skills learned in training settings to such applied settings as industry, schools, clinics, and elsewhere. A detailed description of these procedures is provided in A. P. Goldstein and Kanfer (1979) and Karoly and Steffan (1980).

In addition to its main expression, the T-group, a number of additional techniques have emerged as part of the organizational development movement. Some are *diagnostic* interventions, designed to discern organizational strengths and problems; others, like the T-group itself, are process interventions, designed to alter important aspects of the organizational system and its functioning. Diagnostic interventions include:

1. *Survey feedback.* By means of questionnaire, interview, or both, information about relevant organizational issues is gathered by the psychologist or other organizational consultant and analyzed, interpreted, and fed back to the appropriate organizational figures.
2. *The confrontation meeting.* These are organizational problem-solving sessions, usually called in response to particular crisis situations.
3. *Sensing.* This is an unstructured group interview designed to enable the organizational development consultant to learn about the feelings and attitudes of on-line (or other) employees.
4. *The manager's diagnostic meeting.* Like the confrontation meeting, but staffed by supervisory personnel and their assistants.
5. *The family group diagnostic meeting.* This is the meeting of a work group to gather information about its own functioning, critique its performance, and plan appropriate changes.
6. *The organizational mirror.* This is a procedure whereby the consultant gathers and presents to the organization or organizational subsection information gathered from important sources the organization affects such as customers or suppliers.

Process interventions, in addition to the T-group, include:

1. *Team building.* Growing out of the confrontational and diagnostic meetings described above, team building stresses self-examination, problem confrontation, and goal-setting activities. Their usual target is changes in interpersonal process, trust, communication, and decision making and the reduction of barriers to effective organizational functioning.

2. *Interpersonal interventions.* Designed to deal with interdepartmental and interindividual conflict, process interventions aim at altering poor communication, jurisdictional ambiguities, task-interdependence problems, and the like. Included here are the T-group itself and such variations on the T-group as the Intergroup Laboratory (Blake & Mouton, 1964), the 3D procedure (Golembiewski & Blumberg, 1967), and the Merger Laboratory (Blansfield, Blake, & Mouton, 1964).

In addition to those several diagnostic and process interventions designed to enhance organizational development by optimizing the quality of interpersonal process within the organization, it should be noted that the character of an organization has also been shown to change substantially as a result of two other types of interventions, usually called *environmental interventions*. One is *job enrichment*, in which, contrary to the Scientific Management Era strategy of dividing jobs into simple, specialized, repetitive tasks, the organization follows the Quality of Life strategy of adding job responsibility, in which the worker performs a longer and more varied sequence of tasks; schedules, inspects, and tests her or his own work; sets up and maintains her or his own equipment; and could be part of an autonomous work group responsible for completion of the total work task. The second environmental intervention shown to substantially affect organizational character is the company's *pay system*. Beer (1976) remarked that an especially good example of a pay system that has significantly influenced organizational behavior in many settings is the Scanlon Plan (Lesieur 1958). This most widely used payment incentive plan involves joint participation by workers and management in cost saving and profit sharing. Both organizational climate and organizational productivity have been shown to be substantially influenced by this shared approach to worker payment.

Lenore had worked at several part-time jobs during her college years: cashier at a department store, sales clerk at a bookstore, counselor in a day camp. But now that she had finished her first day on the job at Artist's Press, work seemed like a brand new experience she had never had before. They had really seemed interested in her doing well, and, even during this very first day, her opinions seemed to interest the people she was working with. In the middle of all her excitement, though, Lenore realized she'd be having to handle some regular responsibilities at Artist's, and that some of the work might get kind of boring and routine, and that not everyone in the personnel department was a terrific person, and that she'd better get her alarm clock fixed if she wanted to get to work on time every day.

Three months passed, and passed rather quickly for Lenore at Artist's Press. She'd begun to feel a bit at home there. Maybe a little less excited but also a little more optimistic about a possible long-term future for herself there. A good bit of the work asked of her was routine—record keeping, report checking, looking stuff up—but much of it was new to her. Even the material she'd learned in school was somehow different, kind of transformed, when it was used here in a real business.

It took Lenore by surprise, a very pleasant surprise, when Mary Jane (who turned out to be her immediate supervisor) told her that at Artist's Press an employee's first 6 months are considered an informal probationary period and that, for new employees who look especially promising, there is the opportunity to apply for Artist's junior management training program. Mary Jane said that Lenore looked well on her way to qualifying and, if her work performance stayed this good for the next 3 months, Lenore would very probably be invited to join the next training sequence when it began in March. The program, Mary Jane added, was a combination of three rounds of behavior-modeling management-skills training and an 18-month sequence of job rotation through several departments within the company. The more Lenore thought about it, the more she hoped she'd be invited.

EMPLOYEE MOTIVATION AND JOB SATISFACTION

Clark Hull, one of America's most influential psychologists, demonstrated in detail in his 1943 book *Principles of Behavior* that an individual's behavior was an end product of several factors, chief among them being skill level, or ability (Hull's Habit Strength), and motivation (Hull's Drive). There have been many similar such assertions and findings since Hull. With proper selection and adequate individual and organizational training, the employee is likely to possess adequate skill levels for effective organizational performance. But what of his or her motivation? A number of work-related factors have typically been identified as major employee-motivation incentives and employee job satisfaction sources:

1. Work attributes, including intrinsic interest, variety, opportunity to use one's skills, opportunity for new learning, difficulty, amount of work, responsibility, control over work methods and pace, complexity, and opportunity for job enrichment
2. Pay, including its absolute amount and perceived fairness, method of payment, and comparative amount in relation to one's age, seniority, education, experience, effort expenditure, output quantity and quality, job challenge, and job responsibility
3. Promotion opportunities, their basis, fairness, and frequency
4. Recognition, including credit for work done and praise for accomplishment
5. Working conditions, including hours, rest breaks, temperature, noise, ventilation, light, humidity, location vis-à-vis home, cleanliness, physical layout, tools, and equipment
6. Supervision, its considerateness, fairness, style, and technical and administrative skill
7. Coworkers, their friendliness, helpfulness, and competence

To summarize, in the words of Locke (1976):

> Job satisfaction [and motivation] results from the attainment of values which are compatible with one's needs. Among the most important values or conditions conducive to job satisfaction are: (1) mentally challenging work with which the individual can cope successfully; (2) personal interest in the work itself; (3) work which is not too physically tiring; (4) rewards for performance which are just, informative, and in line with the individual's personal aspirations; (5) working conditions which are compatible with that individual's physical needs and which facilitate the accomplishment of his work goals. (6) high self-esteem on the part of the employee; (7) agents in the work place who help the employee to attain job values such as interesting work, pay, and promotions whose basic values are similar to his own and who minimize role conflict and ambiguity. (p. 1319)

Employee motivation and job satisfaction have been measured in a number of ways, including observation of overt behavior, rating scales, projective techniques, and, as illustrated in Table 5.2, action-tendency structured interviews.

Although efforts to more fully understand worker motivation and job satisfaction have relied on a variety of perspectives such as reinforcement theories, need theories, expectancy theories, two of the more influential approaches have been those put forth, respectively, by Maslow and Herzberg. Maslow's (1970) Need Hierarchy Theory proposes five basic levels of human needs: *physiological* needs, including air, food, water; *safety* needs, which include freedom from physical threats, economic security, and so on; *love and belongingness* needs; *esteem* needs, such as the needs for recognition, approval, mastery, and achievement; and the need for *self-actualization*, which involves fulfilling one's capabilities and aspirations. Maslow posited that these needs are ordered or hierarchically arranged in potency (as just listed), such that the less prepotent needs are neither desired nor sought until the more prepotent needs are satisfied or fulfilled. Although subsequent

TABLE 5.2. Sample Items for an Action-Tendency Interview Schedule for Job Satisfaction

1. When you wake up in the morning, do you feel reluctant to go to work?
2. Do you ever feel reluctant to go home from work at night because of the enjoyment you are getting from your job?
3. Do you often feel like going to lunch at work sooner than you do?
4. Do you feel like taking a coffee or rest break more often than you should?
5. Do you ever wish you could work at your job on evenings or weekends?
6. Are you sometimes reluctant to leave your job to go on a vacation?
7. When you are on vacation, do you ever look forward to getting back to work?
8. Do you ever wake up at night with the urge to go to work right then and there?
9. Do you ever wish holidays or weekends would get over with so that you could go back to work?
10. If you were starting over in your working career, would you lean toward taking the same type of job you have now?
11. Would you be tempted to recommend your present job to a friend with the same interests and education as yours?
12. Do you ever feel like just walking out on this job for good?
13. When you are at work, do you ever wish you could be somewhere else?
14. Do you think you will be reluctant to retire when the time comes, if you still have this same job?
15. Do you ever feel like working right through lunch break?
16. Do you ever feel like going home early from this job?
17. When you are on your way to work, do you ever feel like going somewhere else instead?
18. How would you feel about working overtime at this job without extra pay?
19. If you inherited a million dollars tomorrow, how would you feel about keeping this job?
20. Would you like to find a better job than this one as soon as possible?

Note. From "Nature and Causes of Job Satisfaction" by E. A. Locke in *Handbook of Industrial and Organizational Psychology* (p. 1336) edited by M. D. Dunnette, 1976, New York: Wiley Interscience. Copyright 1976 by Wiley Interscience. Reprinted by permission.

research has demonstrated only mixed support in industrial contexts for Maslow's perspective (Alderfer, 1972; Wahba & Birdwell, 1976), it has nevertheless continued to have a substantial impact on thinking and planning about worker motivation and job satisfaction in American industry.

In 1959, Herzberg, Mausner, and Snyderman, conducted a study of 200 engineers and accountants, who were asked to describe a time when they felt especially satisfied with their jobs and a time when they felt especially dissatisfied. Incidents involving factors intrinsic to the work itself — responsibility, recognition, advancement, a sense of achievement, and growth — were frequently mentioned as sources of job satisfaction. Herzberg et al. termed these *motivators*. Incidents classified as involving supervision received, interpersonal relations on the job, working conditions, company policies and salary, that is, the context in which the work is performed or factors extrinsic to the job itself, were frequently mentioned as sources of job dissatisfaction. These were labeled *hygiene* factors. As Locke (1976) noted,

> Thus, the theory argues that job satisfaction and dissatisfaction result from different causes; satisfaction depends on Motivators while dissatisfaction is the result of Hygiene factors. . . . The Hygiene factors operate only to frustrate or fulfill man's physical needs, while the Motivators serve to fulfill or frustrate man's growth needs. (p. 1310)

Human relations training, improved compensation arrangements, and better working conditions have (since the onset of the Human Relations Era) long been recognized as reducing job dissatisfaction. The motivation-hygiene theory of Herzberg et al. (1959), in contrast, enhanced the concern with motivation factors, especially in the form of job redesign, as the chief means of enhancing job satisfaction. Job redesign has found several concrete expressions, most of which are one form or another of job enrichment such as enhanced responsibility, recognition, autonomy, and sense of achievement.

The industrial employee, appropriately selected, adequately trained, and sufficiently motivated will ideally function on the job in a manner leading to high levels of productivity and job satisfaction. In this chapter's final two sections, we will consider how employee performance can be competently and fairly evaluated and, if found wanting, how ineffective performance can be improved.

PERFORMANCE APPRAISAL

Performance appraisal is a systematic description of an individual's job-relevant strengths and weaknesses. The individual conducting the appraisal could be a peer of the employee, an immediate supervisor, a subordinate, a client served by the employee, a panel of raters, or the employee himself or herself. Several performance-appraisal methods have been used:

1. *Ranking.* The rater orders all ratees from highest to lowest or best to worst on an array of job-performance characteristics.
2. *Paired comparisons.* All ratees are paired with all other ratees, the rater chooses the best of each pair, and the ratee's ranking becomes the number of times she or he is chosen the superior of the pair.
3. *Forced distribution.* The rater distributes all ratees into a normal distribution on the particular job-performance characteristics.
4. *Narrative essay.* This is a highly subjective but often richly detailed description of employee performance.
5. *Behavior checklist.* The rater is provided with a list of descriptive statements of job-relevant behaviors, on each of which she or he rates the employee.
6. *Critical incidents.* These are observer reports of especially positive or especially negative work-related employee behaviors.
7. *Graphic rating scales.* These are quantified and standardized measures on which scale points are unambiguously defined or anchored for the rater.

In addition to these several types of subjective performance-appraisal information, a number of objective performance-appraisal measures have been employed, for instance, from sales income, units produced, number of errors, amount of scrap, tardiness, absenteeism, turnovers, and accidents. Much of the research conducted by the applied psychologist in the area has focused not only upon the central question of how adequately the various subjective and objective measures of performance appraisal reflect actual on-the-job competence, but also upon how best to reduce the several types of biases and distortions typically associated with many of these measures. These include raters who are characteristically too lenient in their ratings, too severe, too oriented toward a central tendency (i.e., little spread in ratings), too subject to a halo effect (i.e., too influenced by global impressions when rating), and too subject to proximity or logical errors when rating (i.e., adjacent traits or logically related traits on a rating scale erroneously assigned similar ratings). When measurement errors such as these are minimized, a competent performance appraisal can result. Such appraisals have found a valuable place in American industry. As Cascio (1982) and Rowland and Ferris (1982) noted, performance appraisals may be used for both evaluation purposes and coaching or development purposes. When they are used as an evaluation tool, results can provide feedback to employees about their work performance, provide feedback to the organization regarding hiring and training needs, be useful in developing compensation criteria (pay bonuses, raises), and help contribute to discharge, retention, and promotion decisions. When used as a coaching and development tool, performance appraisals can help motivate employees, improve their performance, provide a basis for examining career plans and opportunities, and strengthen employer–employee relations. Performance appraisals, when well planned, conducted, and utilized, can indeed serve as an especially valuable and multipurpose tool.

IMPROVING INEFFECTIVE PERFORMANCE

The factors contributing to less than optimal levels of employee performance are many and varied. Some are characteristics of the worker; other factors concern the family, work group, company, or larger societal context in which the employee works. Miner (1975) comprehensively listed these several sources of ineffective employee performance (Table 5.3).

The consequences of these many sources of ineffective employee performance take many forms, for example, absenteeism, turnover, repetitive accidents, alcoholism, drug addiction, and a variety of stress disorders. Each of these several manifestations of poor quality work and low levels of worker job-related motivation and job satisfaction presents major personnel and personnel management problems. Absenteeism, for example, results in approximately 400 million lost workdays each year in American industry, or approximately 5 days per employee. There is more absenteeism in urban than in rural settings, more among smokers than nonsmokers, more in larger than smaller companies. It increases around holidays, and absenteeism rates tend to drop for female employees over the course of their careers but increase for males over theirs. Perhaps a series of clues about how to reduce absenteeism is found in the knowledge that, although absenteeism level does not appear to correlate with employee's level of compensation, growth potential of the job, work load, or amount of required overtime, it is associated with the quality of physical working conditions and employee attitudes toward both immediate supervisor and immediate group of co-workers. Absenteeism is also clearly associated with alcoholism, drug addiction, and an array of personal problems.

Employee turnover might be a second major outcome of the many factors that cause ineffective employee performance. As with absenteeism, possible means for its reduction are suggested by the factors with which it is associated. Turnover rate correlates with wages, age of employee, time on the job, quality of working conditions, attitudes toward management, amount of required overtime, job content, working hours, and satisfaction with immediate supervision.

Alcoholism, drug addiction, various stress disorders, repetitive accidents, and other personal and interpersonal problems are all serious and major sources or correlates of ineffective employee performance. Their cost in personal unhappiness, physical pain, lost wages, and company profits is immense. American industry has employed a wide variety of approaches to reduce such personal and financial costs. Locke (1976) commented:

A great variety of corrective procedures may be used in an attempt to move

TABLE 5.3. Sources of Ineffective Employee Performance

1. Intelligence and job knowledge
   a. Insufficient verbal ability
   b. Insufficient special ability other than verbal
   c. Insufficient job knowledge
   d. Defect of judgment or memory
2. Emotions and emotional illness
   a. Continuing disruptive emotion (anxiety, depression, anger, excitement, shame, guilt, jealousy)
   b. Psychosis (with anxiety, depression, anger, etc., predominating)
   c. Neurosis (with anxiety, depression, anger, etc., predominating)
   d. Alcoholism and drug problems
3. Individual motivation to work
   a. Strong motives frustrated at work
   b. Unintegrated means to satisfy motives
   c. Excessively low personal work standards
4. Physical characteristics and disorders
   a. Physical illness or handicap, including brain damage
   b. Physical disorders of emotional origin
   c. Inappropriate physical characteristics
   d. Insufficient muscular or sensory ability
5. Family ties
   a. Family crises
   b. Separation from an emotionally significant family
   c. Social isolation
   d. Predominance of family consideration over work demands
6. The groups at work
   a. Negative consequences associated with group cohesion
   b. Ineffective management
   c. Inappropriate managerial standards or criteria
7. The company
   a. Insufficient organizational action
   b. Placement error
   c. Organizational overpermissiveness
   d. Excessive span of control
   e. Inappropriate organizational standards or criteria
8. Society and its values
   a. Application of legal sanctions
   b. Enforcement of cultural values by means not connected with administration of the law
   c. Conflict between job demands and cultural values as individually held (equity, freedom, morality, etc.)
9. Situational forces
   a. Negative consequences of economic forces
   b. Negative consequences of geographic location
   c. Detrimental conditions of work
   d. Excessive danger
   e. Problems in the work itself

Note. From "Management of Ineffective Performance" by J. B. Miner and J. F. Brewer in *Handbook of Industrial and Organizational Psychology* (p. 998) edited by M. D. Dunnette, 1976, New York: Wiley Interscience. Copyright 1976 by Wiley Interscience. Reprinted by permission.

performance to an effective level. Among these are job redesign, promotion, transfer, demotion, management development, training, changes in supervision, changes in compensation, personnel policy modification, threats, disciplinary actions, counseling, medical treatment, and psychotherapy. The nature of the corrective procedure that will prove effective depends on the strategic factors causing performance failure. (p. 1013)

In chapter 3 of this book, dealing with interventions targeted to improving psychological health and in chapter 4, dealing with applied psychological intervention to improve physical health, we elaborate considerably on the important role of the applied psychologist in developing, implementing, and evaluating not just means to enhance an individual's efficiency as an employee, but also a wide array of other avenues for personal growth, effectiveness, and satisfaction.

As Lenore looked back on her 3 years at Artist's Press, she thought with satisfaction of mostly happy and growthful times. The junior management training had been especially interesting and valuable. It was almost as if all the courses of her undergraduate major, one by one, had come alive and been made real by her 3-months-at-a-time job rotation through Artist's accounting, production, editorial, warehouse, sales, and senior management departments. Mary Jane had just moved on to another company, and Lenore thought she had a good chance of landing her Assistant to the Manager's position.

Not everything was ideal. Her salary hadn't grown as fast as she had hoped, because it was Artist's policy to pretty much freeze salaries when the person was on management rotation. And her office was more of a cubicle than a real office, though that would change if she got Mary Jane's old job. And she wasn't thrilled with the amount of drinking that almost seemed to go hand in hand with the job. She'd bet that at least two or three of her colleagues were firm alcoholics. But mostly it was fine. She basically liked the company, and the company basically liked her. Though she'd gotten a job feeler from Universal Books, it seemed all the more certain that Artist's Press was where her future rested.

---

6 Educational Applications

INTRODUCTION

Although we have been discussing the application of psychology in a wide range of areas, it could well be that it is the education process that has the most impact on all of our lives. We use the phrase *education process* because of the broad and complex issues involved and the continuing nature of our interaction with this process as students, teachers, parents, and community members. The very nature of what constitutes the classroom is changing as the role of textbooks and traditional teaching is sharply evolving and changing.

The influence of psychology in and on the classroom and on the process of education has had a long and honorable history. We will describe the development of the major fields involved in the application of psychology, *educational psychology* and *school psychology*. This is followed by a description of the applications of psychological theory and research in the classroom. We then focus on one theoretical formulation, a very basic one, that of learning. After all, it does make sense that a theory of learning should be involved with classrooms, because presumably learning is the basic purpose of the classroom.

We illustrate the linking of several streams of psychological theory in an approach to the classroom we label *environmental design*, because we are biased toward and familiar with this psychological application (M. Krasner, 1980). We emphasize theoretical formulations and historical context because these are basic elements in understanding and applying psychology in current and future classrooms, and we illustrate them with specific techniques applied directly in the classroom such as token economy and personalized systems of instruction (PSI), which anticipated the later emergence of the computer in the classroom. As with each area of application, we discuss the value implications of psychological applications to the educational system. Throughout we intersperse reminiscences of Alice Smith, a woman who just retired after 40 years of teaching. Of course, Alice and her experiences symbolize many of the educational issues covered in the chapter.

Alice Retires

Some might say it was the highlight of her life. Alice Smith was seated on the platform of the auditorium at the local community center. Singing her praises were a whole group of community big shots; the superintendent of schools, the president of the school board, even a member of the State Assembly, a principal or two, and lots of teachers and friends. She was actually retiring after 40 years as an elementary school teacher in the middle grades. During the soaring psalms, mostly to the school system by the administrators, Alice found her thoughts wandering to a long life as a student, as a teacher, and as a parent. She would look at her husband, the psychologist in the family, and think of their hectic and exciting life built around the classroom.

It seems to us most appropriate to share the reminiscences of Alice Smith after her 40 years of teaching. She has come into personal contact with the impact of psychology on education as a student, a teacher, a parent, a community member, and a taxpayer (as most of us have) and also as the wife of a psychologist. For many aspects of her rich life we will cite examples of psychology's contributions.

PSYCHOLOGISTS IN EDUCATION

In discussing the application of psychology to education we start with descriptions of the labels utilized by psychologists involved in the schooling process such as school psychologists and educational psychologists. There are many psychologists whose research and applications articulate with the educational scene, including clinical psychologists, experimental psychologists, social psychologists, counseling psychologists, community psychologists, and developmental psychologists. It is clear, of course, that the educational process is influenced by applications from virtually every area of psychology.

The school psychologists and the educational psychologists have much in common in terms of training and functioning. However, they are clearly differentiated in terms of the focus of their application, as evidenced by the fact that school psychology and educational psychology are two separate divisions in the structure of the American Psychological Association.

The *school psychologist* works in the school itself, serving as a consultant to other educational personnel, working directly with students by administering various psychological tests, and conducting assessment-oriented interviews with students, teachers, parents, and others significantly involved with specific students. The kinds of situations school psychologists deal with vary considerably but tend to focus on behavioral problems that are disruptive to classroom activities. The school psychologist also works with students who have problems involving emotional adjustment and specific learning difficulties (e.g., in reading or arithmetic) and students who have unique handicaps or special abilities (e.g., those who are "gifted") that affect their placement in and adjustment to the school setting.

The *educational psychologist* is more likely to be located on the faculty of a school of education or on the staff of an educational research organization. Generally, this person concentrates on teacher training or research in such areas as the psychology of learning and motivation and measurement and test development. Current textbooks on the subject of educational psychology are oriented toward offering the prospective teacher a comprehensive introduction to those areas of psychology that are most relevant for the teacher to understand and to apply (e.g., Baldwin, 1982; Cronbach, 1977; Hudgins et al., 1983; Jackson, 1968; Lindgren, 1980; Reilly, Lewis, & Tanner 1983).

It has been in the area of test construction and in the development of statistical methods to analyze test results that educational psychologists have greatly influenced the direction and impact of the educational process. Once into the issues of testing, psychologists often become involved with the influence of coaching and practice on test results and issues of test anxiety.

Psychologists of all types and fields are prone to build and join professional organizations representing their viewpoints. For example, Takanishi, De-Leon, and Pallak (1983) reviewed the contributions of psychology to education in the context of the relationship between professional organizations (such as the American Psychological Association or the American Education Research Association) and federal agencies (such as the National Institute of Education) that disperse funds for research. Takanishi et al. made their case for psychology thus:

> Psychology as a science and a profession has most likely had its most important impact on schools through the accumulation and application of research knowledge. As with any area of scientific endeavor, there have been continuing debates about the validity of research, and the past two decades have seen controversies as to whether the application of knowledge has actually led to individual and social benefits (Cronbach, 1975). Furthermore, our understanding of the processes by which research knowledge enters educational practice remains rudimentary. (p. 996)

In this context they described examples of systematic examinations of the use of psychological knowledge in education. They cited the report of Suppes (1978) to the National Academy of Education that offered case examples of psychological applications that have influenced educational procedures: development of psychological tests, Thorndike's vocabulary research, Skinner's programmed instruction and behavior modification research, impact of psychoanalytic theories on elementary education, contribution of psycholinguistics to second-language education, research on gifted and talented children, use of human relations research in the professional preparation of teachers and administrators, architectural design of educational environments. This list serves as a broad framework for psychological contributions and influences on education. But to more clearly understand these developments, we must put them in a historical context.

HISTORICAL CONTEXT

As we have previously pointed out, the generally acknowledged father of applied psychology was Hugh Munsterberg. The following passage from Moskowitz (1977) illustrates the moderate priority Munsterberg gave to education as the locus of applying psychology:

> In the introduction to *On the Witness Stand*, Munsterberg (1908) outlined the major fields of applied psychology: "The time for . . . Applied Psychology is surely near, and work has been started from most various sides. Those fields of practical life which come first in question may be said to be education, medicine, art, economics, and law" (p. 9). Having tackled medicine and the law, he next turned back to education. Of the five "fields of practical life" that were to make up his applied psychology, educational psychology received the weakest treatment. In a period when Thorndike and Dewey were reshaping education, Munsterberg remained the stalwart defender of 19th century tradition. His enthusiasm for the German educational system never wavered, and he was almost blind to new principles and techniques. (p. 833)

The application of psychology to the educational process clearly goes back a long way, even earlier than the Munsterbergian era. Perhaps the first text to combine the terms *psychology* and *education* was an 1885 book by an Englishman, James Sully, called *Outlines of Psychology With Special Reference to the Theory of Education*. Initially, during the 1890s that part of teacher training that emphasized psychological content was labeled *genetic psychology* or *child study*. In 1903, Edward R. Thorndike published the first edition of his *Educational Psychology*, providing a term that became the label for this field and for the concept linking the emerging field of psychology with the process of education, which, in the United States at least, goes back to the one-room schoolhouses existing at the time of the American Revolution.

The actual practice of school psychology started in 1896, with the establishment of the first psychological clinic (see chapter 3) at the University of Pennsylvania by Lightner Witmer (J. L. French, 1984). This clinic was founded to study and treat mentally or morally retarded children and those with physical defects. Witmer's clinic became a model for others around the country in the early 1900s and was the major source of influence on those working with children with learning problems. The first psychological clinic in a public school system, called the Bureau of Child Study and Pedagogic Investigation, was established in 1899 in Chicago. Thus, the early clinics set the model for the application of psychology to work with children who had a wide range of problems in the educational system. Psychological clinics in university settings grew quite rapidly, whereas clinics physically located in public schools grew very slowly. The focus in both settings was on problem behaviors.

Just what was the school psychology of that era? Actually, a number of then current streams of research in psychology were merging in this new field. One of these developments was that of *testing*, or, more generally, assessment. This stream is usually traced back to Sir Francis Galton, considered by some the father of testing, who was particularly noted for his introduction of the statistical concepts of correlation and regression to the mean. The first individual to be labeled *school psychologist* was probably Arnold Gesell, around 1915. Early practitioners, even trained psychologists, had titles such as Binet testers, examiners, or child study specialists. The initial "mental tests" were attempts to differentiate bright, normal, and dull children. Besides mental ability, there were tests developed of sensory motor performance, memory, attention, perception, motor functioning, and computational and verbal skills. The first Binet–Simon scale of intelligence was published in 1905 and was unique for its time in its concern for normative data.

Another link between psychology and education was the field generally called *developmental psychology*. It was the psychologist G. Stanley Hall who was most instrumental in initiating this field of study of the individual child. Children were studied through questionnaires and observation. Child welfare research stations developed in the 1920s, systematic research on children was undertaken, and even a publication outlet, *The Journal of Educational Research*, appeared in 1920.

Still another link between education and psychology is that of counseling and vocational guidance. Actually these two have evolved into two separate paths, both involving systematic application of and training in psychological principles. Thus, one way of approaching the applications of psychology to the education field is via the development of the professional fields described in the previous section.

Finally, and most important, there is the stream of application that can best be labeled *Thorndikian*. Thorndike's writing in the early 1900s argued that psychology could and would contribute to every aspect of education. He especially emphasized the idea that studies in human learning would contribute to the enhancement of methods of teaching. He also emphasized the use of assessment procedures to test out the efficacy of various teaching methods. A series of standardized tests (arithmetic, reading, composition, spelling) quickly became available after 1905. Thorndike's doctoral dissertation established the *law of effect*, which was to become one of the basic elements in learning theory applications in the classroom. His studies on learning produced considerable material useful for the theories of instruction in his *Principles of Teaching* (1906). He offered illustrations on the topics of attention, reasoning, feeling, and moral training. He also dealt with the design and choice of teaching materials, the organization of instruction, the ways of adjusting to individual differences in the classroom, and the methodology of judging student progress. It was through his efforts that research in psychology became the basis of classroom application.

Cremin (1961), in his classic history of the development of the American school systems (aptly entitled *The Transformation of the School*), summarized Thorndike's influence and, in effect, presented it as a prototype of psychological applications in the classroom by indicating that

> . . . no aspect of public-school teaching during the first quarter of the twentieth century remained unaffected by his influence . . . Ultimately, Thorndike's goal was a comprehensive science of pedagogy in which all education could be based. His faith in quantified methods was unbounded, and he was quoted ad nauseam to the effect that everything that exists exists in quantity and can be measured. Beginning with the notion that the methods of education could be vastly improved by science, he came slowly to the conviction that the aims, too, might well be scientifically determined. (p. 114)

Thus, Thorndike set in motion the systematic utilization of psychology, viewed as a "scientific" discipline, in education. This is not to imply that after Thorndike all was well and that psychology would save the day for education. Throughout its history, psychology has been a fractionated discipline with many diverse theories of human behavior competing for ascendancy. This has been increasingly so as psychology has grown through the years in the number of professionals identified with the discipline.

In many ways the issues arising from the application of psychology to education are prototypical of the application of psychology to any of the areas described in this book. However, the problems are more intense, because the process of education involves all of us, as individuals and as a society, and there is no way of avoiding it.

Two of the major divisive issues that go back to Thorndike, and even earlier, are the relationship between a so-called *scientific* discipline and a clearly *applied* field and the theoretical view of the *nature* of human nature. Thorndike, and many other psychologists, viewed psychology as a scientific discipline whose major function was to gather data for and develop general principles of human behavior, particularly laws of *learning*. Then such laws of behavior could be applied in any situation involving human beings, including the classroom. The opposing view is that general laws of behavior, developed in the laboratory, are not independent of the environment in which the individual is functioning. Thus, general principles involving behavior in the classroom must include specific classroom variables. This issue goes to the heart of what is applied psychology.

The second divisive issue, involving the basic theoretical formulations of human nature, can in effect, be conceptualized in terms of the perennial nature-versus-nurture controversy. Thorndike believed in the existence of a certain number of "original" tendencies or instincts. Opposing theorists, some of whom were labeled *behaviorists*, hypothesized virtually no innate tendencies. The nature–nurture controversy manifests itself most dramatically in the area and consequences of intelligence testing.

ON VIEWS AND IMPACTS

We will be describing the impact on education of various theoretical psychological approaches, with the emphasis on behaviorism and at least a passing reference to humanism and psychoanalysis. But as we have stressed throughout this book, *psychology* primarily refers to the behavior of individuals whose training and identification is in the field of psychology. Thus, in this section we will briefly examine the views and impacts on the classroom of such key psychologists as Jean Piaget, Erik Erikson, Carl Rogers, and Abraham Maslow.

Piaget (1926, 1981) observed four stages of cognitive development in children. Cognitive stages are a characteristic pattern of mental operation (thinking) of a child that is qualitatively different from that of children in other age groups. The four stages, which are in a continuous process of unfolding, are:

1. *Sensory motor stage*. The first 2 years of life, in which the infant discovers basic facts about the world
2. *Preoperational period*. From 2 to 7 years of age, in which the child begins to utilize symbols to represent objects and events
3. *Concrete operations*. From 7 to 11 or 12 years of age, in which logical thought processes develop
4. *Formal operations*. From about 12 to 16 years of age, in which the ability to do abstract thinking occurs.

A Piagetian view of the child would thus tend to emphasize the fact that inner biological events and their interaction with the environment determine the development of thought processes (Modgil & Modgil, 1982; Rosen, 1985). The child is seen as an active agent constructing the various mental schemes that will enable an understanding of, and a way of dealing with, the environment. A more behavioral-oriented psychologist would argue that the child is learning sets of rules that are progressively more complex, rather than being the site of the unfolding of an inborn timetable. One can readily envision very real differences in teaching techniques as a result of these two broad models of behavior.

Erik Erikson (1963) postulated the existence of eight stages of emotional development and characterized them by the kinds of psychosocial crises likely to occur in those stages. If each crisis is handled successfully by teacher, parent, or both, the child is able to move on to the next stage. For example, the psychosocial crisis in adolescence would involve issues of identity. Teachers must be aware of the crisis the student is then undergoing and handle it appropriately. Such an approach places the teacher in the position of therapist, in effect, placing greater pressure on the teacher.

The title of Carl Rogers' 1969 book on education, *Freedom to Learn*, succinctly expresses his views. He argued that the classroom climate must be such that students are free to learn. In effect, the teacher's role is not to "teach" but rather to provide a minimal structure in the classroom and to encourage individual responsibility. The classroom should, of course, reflect the warmth and empathy Rogers considered basic to providing the atmosphere of "unconditional positive regard," in which the child was completely free to learn.

Abraham Maslow (1954) also postulated a "needs hierarchy" of physiological, safety, love, and belongingness and esteem "needs." The ultimate for the individual was to become fulfilled, or "self-actualized." The teacher must then be aware of what is basically motivating the student and must help satisfy the child's needs. For example, the teacher must recognize a child's need for feeling safe and secure. Again, the pressure is on the teacher to be a therapist.

INTELLIGENCE IN THE CLASSROOM

The area of psychological application to education that has created the most controversy is that of intelligence testing. The very concept of an intelligence quotient (IQ) and its measurement by tests was first initiated by the French psychologist, Alfred Binet. He was involved with the problem of identifying children in the Paris elementary schools who were unable to benefit from school instruction because of low intellectual capacity, in order to place them in appropriate classes. He developed a concept of *mental age*, which meant the age level at which a child actually performed. A ratio was developed between the child's level of performance (MA) and the child's chronological age (CA). A 7-year-old child performing at the 7-year level would have a mental age of seven. The child's IQ would then be the mental age divided by the chronological age (7), multiplied by 100 (to avoid decimals), to give an IQ of 100. Thus was developed the formula:

$$\frac{100 \text{ MA}}{\text{CA}} = \text{IQ}$$

The "average" child would then have an IQ of 100. Scores beyond 100 would indicate a higher degree of intelligence, and those below 100 would indicate a below-normal intelligence. Binet devised a series of tests to measure the child's performance. There have been a series of revisions of this original scale, especially the 1916 Stanford–Binet scale by Lewis Terman, who adopted Binet's work for usage with American children. Actually, it was Terman's 1916 Stanford–Binet scale that was the first test to utilize the IQ ratio, because Binet's early test had only used mental age as a basic yardstick.

The Stanford–Binet test is an *individual* intelligence test, meaning that it can be administered to only one child at a time. It has to be administered by a professional psychologist (usually a school psychologist) well trained in individual testing, and it is used to make a clinical evaluation of a particular child's problem behaviors. Clearly, time and expense are involved. The group intelligence test, which can be administered to a large group of students, evolved from an instrument (The Army Alpha) devised to test individuals for leadership in the Armed Forces during World War I. Group intelligence testing was introduced into the educational systems on a large scale during the 1920s. Educators use them as the basis of ability grouping and as a way of evaluating the learning process. The concept of homogeneous grouping, placing pupils in classes of approximately the same level of intelligence, became popular in the belief that it was in the best interest of the child to learn at the same rate as her or his peers.

To put it mildly, the use of intelligence testing and the concept of an IQ have been very controversial in the education scene and more broadly, in American society (Eysenck & Kamin, 1981; Getsels & Jackson, 1962). Among the basic issues are: What is intelligence and how much of "it" is measured by a test and how much is created by a test? Does the teacher's knowledge of an IQ score influence expectations for performance in the classroom (the Pygmalion Effect of Rosenthal & Jacobson, 1968)? What is the relationship, if any, between IQ and personality? Do IQ scores correlate with real-world behavior? Can a single score such as an IQ really be considered a definitive index to the competence and performance of an individual student?

The broader issues involved in the application of intelligence testing in the school situation, of course, bring us back again to the nature–nurture controversy that has affected and afflicted our society (Gould, 1977; Jensen, 1972, 1980). At this point we will only allude to this controversy and again point out the link between psychological applications in almost any context and the society at large. The very fact of conceiving of and measuring a concept called intelligence, however, has had perhaps the greatest of social impacts.

APPLICATIONS OF THEORY AND RESEARCH

The major link of psychology and education is the application in the classroom of theory and research derived from psychological laboratories. Virtually every development in psychology has had some impact in the classroom, mediated through a whole host of formal and informal procedures such as college courses, in-service training, internships, workshops, conferences, preparations for competency-based tests, licensing, and supervisory observations.

A problem arises at this point. It would indeed be ideal if psychology were a unified discipline producing a continually growing output of knowledge that could be applied to the classroom. However, as we (and many others) have pointed out, in reality, psychology, on a theoretical level, is a discipline badly split as to the nature of human nature. "Basic" research (laboratory or field) and subsequent application derive from the theoretical orientation (and value system) of the investigator.

A book aptly entitled *Four Psychologies Applied to Education: Freudian, Behavioral, Humanistic, Transpersonal* (Roberts, 1975) nicely illustrates this point. Specific material covered in each section differs sharply from that of the others, especially in terms of language, concepts, and ideas. Freudians speak of the "latency period" (in a chapter by Anna Freud, no less), behaviorists talk of "behavioral self control," humanists discuss "personal growth," and transpersonal advocates discuss "fantasy and imagination." Nor is there much likelihood of terminology overlapping. Certainly these four do not exhaust the theoretical frameworks of psychology that have been applied to education, such as Gestalt, Piagetian, and others. Further, each of these general orientations has spawned splinter groups.

One of the major problems in psychology is definitional. No matter what the approach—behaviorist, humanist, psychoanalytic—there are continual differences among practitioners of any particular model as to how to define it. As an illustration of the relationship between theory and application, we will briefly describe the humanistic approach. The humanist, as the name implies, emphasizes human welfare and "good" values. The emphasis in the classroom is on the development of human relations skills, education of the "whole" individual, and the importance of emotions (the affective domain) in education (Maslow, 1954).

Roberts (1975) captured the spirit of humanistic applications and some differences among models by noting that:

> Besides stressing human relations, or group dynamics, humanistic educators see other human abilities that we under-teach in schools. In addition to the cognitive skills and social relations, humanistic educators try to plan classes that help us improve our abilities to perceive, feel, move, wonder, intuit, sense, create, fantasize, imagine, and experience. . . . one of the humanistic roles of the teacher is to assist students to learn what they want to when they want to. This is the *teacher* as *humanistic facilitator* to help people meet their higher, human needs, rather than the teacher as a Freudian counselor or behavioral engineer. (p. 291)

In addition to these theoretical differences, psychology is divided into a series of specific fields such as experimental, clinical, social, developmental, personality, physiological, child, forensic, counseling and, of course, educational. Each of these fields produces a vast array of theory, research, and applications with implications for, and direct applications in, the classroom. To convey the scope of this material, we list just a few of the topics that appear in various texts on educational psychology (e.g., Amabile & Stubbs, 1982; Farley & Gordon, 1981): applications of psychological tests; the testing movement in America; the concept and testing of intelligence; the IQ controversy; assessment (of individuals and of programs); programed instruction; The computer; accountability; token economy; open education; teacher expectation, symbolized by the classic *Pygmalion in the Classroom* (R. Rosenthal & Jacobson, 1968); atypical children; school violence (Goldstein, Apter, & Harootunian, 1983); motivation; perception; thinking; concept formation; conditioning; learning theory; verbal learning; self-management; discipline; teacher characteristics; teacher training; merit pay; community involvement; teacher unions. Psychology has been applied to every variation of behavior in the classroom, school, community, and society.

Alice as a Student

Alice could not help thinking of when she had been in elementary school. It was in a small, rural school in the Midwest. Her parents were immigrants who had gone into farming, knew nothing about education, and were not in a position to advise her. There was much talk of how bad economic conditions were. She later learned that she had grown up in the Depression. Her most vivid recollections were of two teachers, women of course. One she remembered warmly; the other with bitterness and constant warnings of "no talking, sit still, get rid of that gum." Yet she remembered there was a sense of excitement as a student in what she later learned was a one-room schoolhouse. So much was happening in this large room.

Alice could still remember her education courses as an undergraduate in a small Kansas college. Almost from the beginning, as far back as she could remember, she had wanted to be a teacher. In fact, what other profession could a woman go into? The courses made it perfectly clear that the training really involved the application of the psychology of the day. She could still remember the big names they threw out such as Thorndike, Hall, James, and, of course, John Dewey. It was Dewey's ideas that excited her the most.

After graduating from college, Alice had been determined to become a real teacher. Think of it, to be able to teach young children and help develop a human mind. What else could an ambitious woman do? So off she went to the big city, New York, and enrolled at the teachers college that was most renowned for having the two major proponents of psychology applications to education, Dewey and Thorndike. She learned a lot and thoroughly enjoyed her 2 years there, particularly meeting Ted, a graduate student in psychology, of all things. The merging of psychology and education occurred at both a theoretical and a practical level.

Learning Theory

No term is simpler or more complex or more basic to psychology and education than the concept of *learning*. Thus we should start with a clear-cut definition of learning. As with most other aspects of psychology and education, this is easier said than done, because there is a tendency for investigators to be idiosyncratic in their definitions and conceptualizations of what material is to be included in their fields. The field of learning is a classic example of this, because the term itself is frequently used to encompass almost every kind of activity in which there could be some change in individual performance. It might even be argued that *application* is synonymous with learning.

Hilgard and Bower's (1966) review of theories of learning is the classic text influencing the training of most current investigators. They defined learning as "the process by which an activity originates or is changed through reacting to an encountered situation, provided that the characteristics of the change in activity cannot be explained on the basis of native response tendencies, maturation, or temporary states of the organism (e.g., fatigue, drugs, etc.)" (p. 2). The authors themselves pointed out that this definition is "not formally satisfactory because of the many undefined terms in it" (p. 2). In fact, this is a definition by exclusion. If a change in behavior cannot be accounted for by a species-specific reflex, by maturation, by fatigue, or by drugs, then we can call it *learning*.

A more useful approach is to deal with the "conditions of learning" (Gagné, 1970). Gagné used this term as the title of a book that discussed what was known about the process of learning that could be put to use in designing better education. He defined learning as "a change in human disposition or capability which can be retained, and which is not simply ascribable to the process of growth" (p. 3). With such a definition, he focused on dealing with *sets of circumstances* that exist when learning occurs. From Gagné's point of view, learning must be linked to a design of instruction through consideration of the different kinds of capabilities being learned. This is a broader and more meaningful way to look upon the learning situation, in contrast with more formal learning theories, because it views the classroom situation in terms of *interaction* between various sets of stimuli.

The vast majority of learning research in the laboratory and in the classroom is usually intended to test specific hypotheses derived from a particular theory. This is an important point to note when evaluating the implications of learning studies for the education field, because the studies were usually designed for one purpose, theory testing, but they are frequently misapplied to another purpose, namely, processes in the classroom.

Theories of learning are usually labeled in terms of the individual most prominent in their formulation or by a key concept in the theory. There are the learning theories of Thorndike, Pavlov, Guthrie, Skinner, Hull, Tolman, and even Freud. There are learning theories labeled connectionism, classical conditioning, contiguous conditioning, trial-and-error learning, operant conditioning, reinforcement theory, verbal-association learning, sign learning, gestalt learning, insight learning, discovery learning, functionalism, mathematical learning theory, and information processing. We will briefly review several of these concepts because all have had impact on the classroom, and it should be clear that none of these theories is mutually exclusive. It is usually their proponents who have strong vested interests in maintaining their individuality.

Perhaps the earliest theory was that of the associationists, who argue that learning takes place by the *contiguity of events* and then is enhanced by repetition of these contiguous events. Some of the historical names associated with this theory, and later variations, are John Stuart Mill, William James, and John Dewey.

The concept of *trial-and-error* learning developed from the early experimental work of Thorndike (1931) and his law of effect (correct responses are strengthened by being followed immediately by an event that results in a "satisfied state of affairs").

Theories based on *conditioned response*, which involve the establishment of new signal–response connections, are based on Pavlov's (1928) classical laboratory work with dogs. They were popularized by Watson's (1919) view of learning as involving the establishment of conditioned responses in the nervous system and by his attempt to apply them to human problem behaviors.

Finally, there is *reinforcement theory*, a view of learning that cuts across, and could be related to, each of the previously described approaches, although it is most compatible with the law of effect. To add to the confusion, there are several definitions of reinforcement and several reinforcement theories with sharp differences among them. One branch of this theory developed through Hull, Spence, and Miller, and it links reinforcement with motivation. It views human beings as being motivated by fundamental drives such as hunger, which, when reduced by some satisfaction or reward, result in learning. Skinner's view (1953) of reinforcement is different from these in that a response that one might want the individual to learn must be made *contingent* on certain subsequent stimulus conditions. Skinnerian *operant conditioning* is based upon the observation that a behavior followed by a reinforcing stimulus is more likely to recur in the future. The concept of *social learning* via modeling of behavior has had considerable impact on the educational field (Bandura, 1977a, 1977b, 1982, 1984).

An intermediate concept of learning, which at least warrants mention because it is also influencing current research, is that of *learning by discovery*. Forerunners of learning by discovery include Rousseau, Montessori, and Dewey. A clear-cut definition is virtually impossible. The term *discovery* is often used to denote a hypothetical intervening cognitive event.

Alice in the Classroom

Alice vividly remembered her first years in front of the class. Actually there was a note of bitterness in these thoughts. She had so much to teach and give, but it was not to be. It was clear that schooling did not rank high in the children's lives. Throughout the day they would leave their seats, wander about the room, talk across the room, and generally be disruptive. Alice felt so frustrated because she had so much to teach, if only they would let her. In discussing the situation with her fellow teachers, who were not sympathetic, the answer was clear: "restore" discipline. Ted was also very "helpful" in psychologizing and explaining the behavior of the children in the classroom as "acting out their problems at home."

Throughout her graduate years, Alice was taught that education was really applied psychology and that she would be using psychological principles in her own classroom. She was always inclined to think that she was dealing with common sense. But she was to learn the truth from the gentleman she married after a brief courtship during graduate school. He was a clinical psychologist and a true believer in psychology. Through the early years, while she was struggling to maintain "discipline" in her classroom, each evening he would carefully explain to her how she could apply learning-theory principles in her class to maintain order.

Somehow it eventually all came together: the early Dewey influence, her visits to British primary schools, Ted's constant urging to apply learning principles, some exciting new books on education, years of her own experiences and development, continued discussions with several like-minded teachers, encouragement from administrators, and cooperation from and with parents. Alice and several colleagues initiated a program called *Open Wing* which involved applying the "best" of psychological theories in a carefully designed group of classrooms. Then there followed years of the greatest satisfaction to Alice, her fellow teachers, the many children who participated, the parents, the administrators, and even Ted.

Classroom Applications

We will describe classroom applications of psychological principles by focusing on an approach, *environmental design*, which integrates the theory and research of a number of the investigators already mentioned such as Dewey, Skinner, and Piaget. This approach is very compatible with the experiences and practices of Alice, particularly in her later years. In presenting her description of the applications of psychology in her classroom, M. Krasner (1980) placed her approach in the context of "the mutual interaction of an open education teacher and a purveyor of applied psychology whose professional roots are in clinical/behavioral psychology" (p. 303). Alice and Ted, of course, would resonate to such a combination.

The application of techniques derived from behavioral and learning models of behavior in the classroom is not idiosyncratic to Krasner but reflects a major aspect of the current educational scene in the United States. For example, Ruggles and LeBlanc (1982), in a chapter on "Behavior Analysis

Procedures in Classroom Teaching," cited approximately 300 references, and the number of publications on behavioral applications in the classroom is growing ever more rapidly.

Krasner placed her environmental-design approach in the context of three streams of psychological influence in the classroom: behavioral, progressive, and environmental. The theoretical formulation of the behavioral stream revolves about that popular psychological term, *learning*. Although most of Thorndike's linkage of learning and instructional theory to the classroom environment, described previously, would apply today, the current "behavioral influences" can be traced to Skinner (1938; 1983) and to other operant investigators (K. D. O'Leary & O'Leary, 1977).

Many of the developments in education involving the classroom from the mid-1970s to the mid-1980s have been influenced by this behavioral stream, such as the teaching machine, programmed learning, computer-assisted instruction, behavioral objectives, behavior modification, token economy, competency-based teacher education, accountability, contracting, peer teaching, and microteaching. We will discuss some of these in a later section.

Progressive Education

A second major stream of influence derived from psychology with applications in the classroom is that of *progressive education*, which has had considerable impact on environmentally designed classroom programs. Perhaps the major difference in the progressive stream, as against the behavioral, is the clear avowal of the linkage of value and social belief systems in classroom applications. Once again we turn to Cremin (1961), who noted the following four elements in progressive education that express the basic principles of the application of psychology in the context of a social value system:

> First, it meant broadening the program and function of the school to include direct concern for health, vocation, and the quality of family and community life.
> Second, it meant applying in the classroom the pedagogical principles derived from new scientific research in psychology and the social sciences.
> Third, it meant tailoring instruction more and more to the different kinds and classes of children who were being brought within the purview of the school.
> Finally, Progressivism implied the radical faith that culture could be democratized without being vulgarized, the faith that everyone could share not only in the benefits of the new sciences but in the pursuit of the arts as well. (pp. vii, ix)

The most influential psychologist in the progressive stream was John Dewey (1859–1954). There might be some surprise that Dewey was a psychologist, because he is most noted for being a philosopher. Yet his training in graduate school and his early professional role in academia labeled him a psychologist. Further, in his early days, psychology and philosophy were considered to be one field. It was only late in the last decade of the 19th century that psychology established itself as a separate discipline, an event that should never have happened, because the two fields are still integral to each other.

In 1894 Dewey was appointed Head of Psychology at the University of Chicago. He had been attracted to this university because education, philosophy, and psychology were all in one department, and he clearly envisioned an integration of these three fields. In 1896 he wrote a paper that became a classic influence on the direction of American psychology, "The Reflex Arc Concept in Psychology." Dewey's concept of the reflex arc was of a coordinated unit that had to be viewed as a whole rather than as dichotomous concepts, such as stimulus–response, then becoming popular. In his approach, behavior cannot be isolated from the environmental context in which it occurs.

Dewey was determined to apply his version of psychological theory to the educational process in a real classroom, and so he established a laboratory school at the university (which lasted from 1896 to 1904) (Mayhew & Edwards, 1936). He viewed this as a site for the application of psychology analogous to the laboratory used in science courses. The effort to merge theory and practice was the major characteristic of Dewey's entire professional career. His view of the application of psychology in the classroom was strongly influenced by his philosophical beliefs and his sensitivity to social concerns.

The aim of Dewey's work was to encourage the application of scientific method and critical thinking to social and moral beliefs and practices. It seemed to him that the primary obstacle to this was the view that theories and ideas are positive entities, logically derived and not subject to empirical testing. Therefore, he concentrated on the development of a logical system that would tie theory and practice (like mind and body) into a unified whole. For Dewey, the modern science of his day was a perfect example of the interplay and unity of theory and practice. Ideas are the "mind's" response to problematic situations and guide further observations to be made of the situation. Observations (direct experience with the situation) in turn shape new ideas concerning the problem. Thus, Dewey stressed the idea that the goal of education was to teach students the skills and attitudes needed to develop their ability to solve problems. Consequently, he felt that school curricula should not, as they traditionally had done, emphasize the learning of facts and fixed ideas, but rather should stress the learning of a *method* for obtaining facts for oneself and reasoning out one's own ideas about the world.

Progressive education, as influenced by Dewey, attempted to reform traditional education, in which the teacher lectured and the students copied, learned by heart, and recited. Students sat at desks that were fastened to the floor and needed permission to speak or even move. Dewey stressed the importance of the individual child progressing at his or her own pace, the importance of the child developing interest in the subject matter, and, most important of all, the child *learn by doing* and by direct contact with people, places, and things. Dewey's strong belief in the desirability of a liberal democratic social order influenced the broad nature of classroom structure, emphasizing greater freedom, informality, and activity on the part of the child, who would be able to gather materials from many sources and who would work in small groups with other children. This was training the student to live in and contribute to a democratic society.

It seems quite clear that Alice was very much influenced by Dewey's ideas, particularly because Alice received her graduate training at the university (Columbia) where Dewey spent a large portion of his academic life. The open-education approach that Alice espoused in her classroom was certainly influenced by the concepts of Dewey. On the theoretical level, other psychologists, particularly Piaget (1926), were foremost shapers of what has become *open education*. This approach to the classroom as a process closely links the notion of desirability of achieving valued social behavior, competency, and skill with the notion of designing the learning environment to achieve these valued objectives. More and more, the teacher realizes that she or he must talk in terms of goals and purpose for every design or feature that is put into the environment. In effect, the teacher carries out a *functional analysis of behavior*, to use a favorite behavioral term, in planning a classroom environment.

Open Education

Open education, as it developed in the United States in the 1960s and 1970s, was a creation of both the progressive movement and the enthusiastic reports on British primary schools by educators and journalists (Featherstone, 1971; Giaconia & Hedges, 1982; Horwitz, 1979; Plowden, 1967; Rogers, 1970; Silberman, 1970).

The psychological principles that were the bases of applications in the open-education classroom derived in large part from environmental, Gestalt, developmental, and behavioral psychology. The major elements of open education were the integrated day, the individualized instruction, and the systematic design of the usage of people and space. The integrated day encompassed a *total environment* in which there was a blurring of distinctions among subject matters and between the inside and outside environments of the classroom. In effect, the integrated day involved having available in the classroom environment a wide variety of stimuli and learning conditions to make the learning situation interesting, exciting, meaningful, and reinforcing to the child, and thus to integrate elements of the principles of all of the psychological theories involved.

Open education was clearly designed to maximize the likelihood of each individual child's learning at his or her own pace, using the individual's own base rate as a yardstick to measure learning. In effect, the teacher designed the individual learning environment for each of the children in the class. Thus, by carefully structuring the open classroom, the teacher also was applying the basic principles of behavior modification (Drucker, 1972). The individual child learned to program himself or herself according to a behaviorist scheme in which reinforcements were built into every aspect of the environment (i.e., the tools, playthings, human participants, materials, and experiences) with which the teacher had carefully planned the classroom.

Illustrative of the teacher using her or his behavior in a deliberate attempt to modify children's behavior so as to maximize the learning experience of the individual child is the description of an open classroom in action by Nyquist and Hawes (1972). The children are at work in a variety of activity areas under their own initiative, talk freely, and move about in classroom and corridors, and " . . . as they work, their teacher moves among them helping, suggesting, questioning, observing, commenting, evaluating, encouraging, comforting, and when needed, ordering. The teacher plays a key role by knowing each child thoroughly and guiding his development as a unique and complex individual" (p. 1).

Environmental Psychology

The third context of psychological research applied to the classroom in Krasner's environmental design approach is *environmental*, or *ecological* (Ittelson et al., 1984; Moos & Insel, 1974; Sarason, 1982, 1983; Sommer, 1969). The research concentrates on the impact on behavior of environmental settings and events. Barker (1968) expressed it well:

> We found, in short, that we could predict some aspects of children's behavior more adequately from knowledge of the behavior characteristics of the drugstores, arithmetic classes, and basketball games they inhabited than from knowledge of the behavior tendencies of particular children. (p. 4)

The Teacher as Applied Psychologist

In effect, the classroom teacher is the exemplar of the applied psychologist. From the three streams of interaction between psychology and education—behavioral, progressive, and environmental—comes a set of principles that places the teacher in the difficult role of integrator of theory, research, and practice.

1. *The teacher as planner of the environment.* The teacher states her or his objectives in behavioral terms, to achieve specific behavioral objectives with *each* student. This is an operational way of defining and evaluating *individualized instruction*, a key concept. The teacher thus systematically utilizes behavior, her or his own and that of other adults and children, in and out of the classroom and the physical environment to affect the learning in each child.

2. *The teacher as source of value and model of a socially responsible individual.* The teacher is sufficiently aware of her or his own values (personal preferences) so that the students can be helped to recognize that values enter into virtually every situation involving human behavior.

3. *The teacher as continual self-trainer.* The teacher keeps a journal as a useful source of self-observation and utilizes reactions from peers, principal, and students as a source of feedback to change her or his own behavior. Community resources such as teacher centers, college courses, and workshops are used to improve classroom teaching skills.

4. *The teacher as participant-observer.* The teacher observes and records, as a continuous, ongoing process, the relationship between her or his own behavior and that of the pupils.

5. *The training of students in techniques of observation and self-observation.* In effect, the student is trained to be a psychologcial investigator applying psychological research in the classroom.

6. *The application of specific behavior-modification techniques in the classroom to achieve behavioral objectives in children.* The teacher becomes skilled in the multitude of techniques derived from psychology to affect what takes place in the classroom.

7. *The design of physical environments as learning environments.* The teacher utilizes spatial arrangement of furniture and materials to achieve individual behavioral objectives. A multitude of media, including films, tape recorders, cameras, and phonographs, are used in creating specific learning-environment areas in science, social science, math, language arts, art, and music.

8. *The teacher as resource administrator.* The environmental-design teacher utilizes appropriate classroom, school, and community resources as necessary to achieve her or his objectives and as a backup to enhance the effectiveness of her or his procedures. These include peers, administrators, guidance people, school psychologists, consultants, university resources, teacher centers, and books.

BEHAVIOR MODIFICATION IN THE CLASSROOM

At this point we are going into detail for a number of reasons about an approach to applying psychology in the classroom, behavior modification. The specific applications derive from a broader psychological theory, and, in that sense, this approach is analogous to other approaches in that the specifics of what takes place in the classroom derive from a broader psychological theory, and many of the issues are prototypical of all classroom applications. However, the behavioral approach has been more detailed and systematically researched and is more controversial than other approaches.

The literature on the applications of psychology, particularly studies with the straightforward *behavior modification* label, to the classroom are voluminous. Ruggles and LeBlanc (1982) have classified these studies into those involving ways of maintaining order in the classroom, those analyzing the effects of contingent relationships on the amount and correctness of work produced by the children in the classroom, and those investigating the effects of influencing teachers' instructions and discriminative stimulus materials on children's learning of academic skills.

It is of interest to note that Ruggles and LeBlanc, in reviewing the considerable research on "maintenance of classroom order" also, in effect, defended the goals of such research, which is to enhance order in the classroom. The basic philosophy is that there must be order in the classroom for children to "learn." "Teachers should be encouraged to use reinforcement and even mild forms of punishment for response-decrement procedures to control the social climate of the classroom so that learning can occur and creativity can be enhanced" (p. 988). The major critique of this philosophy of the goals of the classroom was expressed in the title of a Winett and Winkler (1972) paper "Current Behavior Modification in the Classroom: Be Still, Be Quiet, Be Docile." We have earlier described, in Krasner's environmental-design approach, a very different conceptualization of the learning process in which the student learns by being an active participant in the total environment rather than a passive recipient of knowledge in a well-ordered environment.

There is now a considerable amount of research, labeled *behavior modification*, that focuses on techniques the teacher can use in fostering the goal of maintaining order, including paying attention to desired behavior, offering access to preferred activities, and using token reinforcement systems.

We will describe in detail the development of token-economy programs in the classroom because they are representative of the gradual extension of theory and research in behavioral psychology into the classroom. Further, token economy illustrates ways in which a carefully planned environment can be developed to achieve the goals of the teacher, whatever these might be.

In presenting token economy as a planned environment in social institutions, especially in the classroom, the notion we must dispel is that we are reviewing a brand *new* procedure, radically departing from the past, implicitly promising salvation for the many problems of education and of society. Token economy developed in mental hospitals and spread to other social institutions including the classroom. But the general notion of *planning the environment* so as to shape and maintain "desirable" behavior was an integral part of the scheme of the planners of the first mental hospitals (and other "correctional" institutions) in this country in the early 19th century (Rothman, 1971).

Nor can the use of positive reinforcement (the major element in token economy) in the classroom be considered new, because the use of rewards for academic performance has a long educational history. Further, the principles of token economy are the same as those of the money economy within which we all function. Yet a token-economy program as a *systematic* and *planned* approach should help clarify and influence the educational and social issues that are implicitly and explicitly part of the classroom scene.

We must emphasize that, in most instances, a teacher does not explicitly verbalize "I am now going to apply a token economy (or behavior modification) in my classroom." Rather, more often than not, the teacher is not aware of the label *token economy* or that he or she is applying "psychological principles" to the classroom. Rather, what is being done is common sense, based on living and learning in our society. One "rewards" the behavior of the student that is considered desirable, correct, and beneficial. In effect, the teacher is doing what comes naturally and assumes that the student will respond appropriately.

Token economy, as eventually applied in the classroom, derived from the behavior modification streams of operant conditioning and utopian planning (L. Krasner, 1971). The landmarks of this stream were early laboratory studies by Skinner (1938); application to the simple behaviors of psychotic patients in a state hospital (Lindsley, Skinner, & Solomon, 1953); applications to preschool and mentally retarded children by Bijou and his co-workers (Bijou, Peterson, Harris, Allen, & Johnston, 1969); token-economy classrooms with the mentally retarded (Birnbrauer, Bijou, Wolf, & Kidder, 1965; Birnbrauer & Lawler, 1964) and with delinquents (H. L. Cohen, 1968); application of operant conditioning to autistic children by Ferster (Ferster & DeMyer, 1965) and by Lovaas (1968); and use of tokens as reinforcers in a reading program with children, by Staats, Minke, Finley, Wolf, and Brooks (1964).

Token Economy in the Classroom—Theory

The previous section offered illustrations of token economy in the classroom. At this point we examine the general principles involved, to help us understand and develop useful classroom procedures. In applying the principles of behavior change in the classroom, one begins with systematic *observation* of the behavior of the people for whom the program is intended and the *consequences* of their behavior in the specific situation in which it is occurring. This could be in the classroom, on a hospital ward, in the home, or in the community. The unit of observation goes beyond the specific act of an individual to include the response elicited from the environment by the behavior. Thus it is insufficient to observe that a child "left his seat." The full observational unit is that the child left his seat, the teacher said, "Go back to your seat," three children laughed, and another child started to leave her seat.

Second, there is the *designation* of certain specific behaviors as *desirable*, hence reinforceable. This includes behaviors such as those on a hospital ward of dressing oneself or making a bed and those in a classroom of staying in one's seat or raising one's hand. These behaviors are usually those someone (teacher, ward nurse, or individual) determines to be socially useful and of initial low frequency. We stress the value decisions implicit in deciding that a certain behavior (e.g., staying in a seat) is desirable.

In their classic critique of the application of psychology via behavior modification in the classroom, as previously mentioned, Winett and Winkler (1972) reviewed publications in the *Journal of Applied Behavior Analysis* from 1968 to 1970 in which behavior modification was applied to relatively normal classrooms. "Our purpose was not to evaluate specific techniques that were either reinforced or in various ways prescribed" (p. 500). They cited, as illustrative, a study by Thomas, Becker, and Armstrong (1968) that sought to rigorously classify "appropriate" and "inappropriate" behavior and that was a prototype for future studies. Labeled *inappropriate* were such behaviors as getting out of the seat, standing up, walking around, running, hopping, skipping, jumping, moving chairs, racking chairs, tapping feet, rattling papers, carrying on a conversation with other children, crying, singing, whistling, laughing, turning head or body toward another person, showing objects to another child, and looking at another child. *Appropriate* behavior included attending to the teacher, raising a hand and waiting for the teacher to respond, working in the seat on a workbook, and following along in a reading text.

It is quite clear that the desirable behaviors tend in the direction of quietness and nonmovement, whereas the undesirable behaviors tend in the direction of movement and interactive stimulation. It would appear that the behavior modification approach in the classroom as typified by token economy has been used to support the implicit behaviors held desirable as part of the traditional school approach. Winett and Winkler drew this bleak picture of current goals:

> Just what do those present goals seem to be? Taken as a fairly accurate indication of what public schools deemed the "model" child, these studies described this pupil as one who stays glued to his seat and desk all day, continually looks at his teacher, or his text/workbook, does not talk to, or in fact look at, other

children, does not talk unless asked to by the teacher, hopefully does not laugh or sing (or at the wrong time), and assuredly passes silently in halls. (1972, p. 501)

The issue of target behavior is not peripheral, but central, to the application of token economy in the classroom, as it is to every application of psychological procedures. Many of the early applications of behavior modification in the classroom, particularly in the mid-1960s, were attempts to demonstrate that, indeed, the application of learning principles could change behavior. The particular behavior was selected on the basis of its being readily observable, countable, and of importance to the teacher. Little regard was given to evaluating the desirability of the behaviors themselves. Eventually social and ethical implications of target behavior became inreasingly more focal.

A third element is the determination of what environmental events serve as *reinforcers* for the individual. What are the good things in life for these individuals? What are they willing to work for? For the hospitalized adult, it might include a bed, a pass, or a chance to sit in a favorite chair. For the child in the classroom, it might include candy, toys, or a chance to go on an interesting trip.

In discussing the use of reinforcers in token economy and other planned environments, there are two aspects that must be considered. The tokens per se only serve as discriminative stimuli, which stand for, or are symbolic of, some other object or event. Theoretically, the tokens take on reinforcing properties because of the desirability of the backup reinforcers for which they stand. Yet, it is clear from observation that tokens do take on reinforcing properties of their own. The clearest analog of this is the individual who works for money far beyond his or her needs. The token money becomes highly desirable for itself.

Among the variety of actual tokens used are check marks, stars, rings, chips, and tags. K. D. O'Leary and Drabman (1971, p. 389) listed the desirable properties of the tokens themselves: Their value should be readily understood; they should be easy to dispense; they should be easily transportable from the place of dispensing to the area of exchange; they should be identifiable as the property of a particular child; they should require minimal bookkeeping duties for the teacher; they should be dispensable in a manner that diverts as little attention as possible from academic matters; they should have some relevance to real currency if one's desire is to teach mathematical or economic skills that will be functional outside the classroom; and, they should be dispensable frequently enough to insure proper shaping of desired behavior.

As for the backup reinforcers themselves, every conceivable object or event that can be considered desirable can and has been used. These include such diverse objects as candy, food, clothing, watches, and access to such events as movies, sports contests, and circuses. Once it becomes clear that reinforcers do not necessarily mean material objects, but can include opportunities to do certain things, go places (e.g. movies, dances), and do many different kinds of things, then it is clear that reinforcers are stimuli (used in the sense of stimulation). Stimulation is basic to living. We could even argue that stimulation, unless it is aversive, is rewarding per se.

The planned, or open-classroom, environmental design approach is a way of organizing the natural reinforcers in the environment so as to maximize the likelihood of learning taking place. The introduction of tokens per se might speed up the process or make it more explicit for those who have not yet learned or have mislearned the relationship between their behavior and its environmental consequences.

The fourth element in a token economy is the *medium of exchange*, the token that connects elements two and three. The token stands for the back-up reinforcer. It can act as a discriminative or reinforcing stimulus, or both. The token can be a real, tangible object such as a plastic card or a green stamp that one can handle (e.g., money is a medium of exchange in our larger society), or it can be a mark on a piece of paper, a grade, or a point scored that the individual knows is there but to which he or she has no direct access. Despite the label of token economy, the tokens themselves are merely a gimmick, a training device to help teachers and others in the classroom learn how to observe behavior and its consequences, how to use their own behavior in a reinforcing manner, how to respond contingently, and how to arrange the environment so as to maximize the possibility of the individual child's receiving reinforcing stimuli at the appropriate time.

The fifth element is the *exchange rules*. The planning of a token economy must specify the economic relationship between the amount of tokens an individual earns and the cost of the good things in life. If a person can earn only 10 tokens a day (at most), and the cheapest item that can be purchased costs 100 tokens, the system will not work. Conversely, if the student can earn 100 tokens and can take care of all her or his desires for only 10 tokens, the system will not work either. We must take into consideration the economic constraints that determine the value and effects of specific reinforcers. At this point, we begin to develop a very complex relationship, which is analogous to what occurs to all of us in our everyday life as we try to figure out various ways of budgeting money in our real-life economic system.

The use of reward itself in the classroom is, of course, not new, but the *systematic* use of contingent reinforcement by a teacher trained in the procedure does represent a basic change. The principle behind the use of tokens in the classroom, contingency reinforcement of desirable alternative behaviors, is the same as in mental hospitals, but, of course, there are issues unique to the nature of the classroom, which we have been describing.

Token Economy in the Classroom—Illustration

Ayllon and Azrin (1965, 1968) reported the results of the first use of a token-economy program in a psychiatric hospital ward. Based on the principles of this mental hospital program, K. D. O'Leary and Becker (1968) introduced the use of a token-reinforcement program in a class ($N = 17$) of children with behavior problems in a public school. Thus, as is often the case, the initial application of a psychological procedure was with children with some kind of problem. Observations were focused on the eight most disruptive children. Two observers recorded behaviors labeled *deviant* (for example pushing, talking, making a noise, and chewing gum) every 30 seconds for $1^1/2$ hours on 3 days a week. Behaviors manifested during the observation periods were classified either *disruptive* or *nondisruptive*.

On the first day of training, the experimenter put the following words on the blackboard: "In Seat, Face Front, Raise Hand, Working, Pay Attention, Desk Clear." The experimenter then explained that tokens would be given for these behaviors and that the tokens could be exchanged for backup reinforcers of candy, comics, perfume, and so on. The teacher, during several brief class interludes, rated the extent to which each child had met the criteria.

For the first 3 days, tokens were exchanged at the end of each period. Tokens were then accumulated before being cashed in, first for 2 days, then for 3 days, finally for 4 days. The process was designed to gradually fade out the backup reinforcer, so that the more desirable reinforcement of teacher's praise would take over. In addition, group points, exchangeable for ice cream, were awarded for quietness of the group during the rating period. Further techniques of verbal praise, ignoring (extinction), and time out from reinforcement were used when appropriate. During the baseline observation period, the disruptive-deviant behavior ranged from 66 to 91% of the observations. This disruptive behavior dropped to a range of from 4 to 32% during the period of token training. The authors concluded that "with the introduction of the token reinforcement system, a dramatic, abrupt reduction in deviant behavior occurred. . . . The program was equally successful for all children observed, and repeated anecdotal evidence suggested that the children's appropriate behavior generalized to other situations" (K. D. O'Leary & Becker, 1968, p. 637).

This program contained most of the elements that were to characterize future token programs in the "normal" classroom and that had appeared in the earlier mental hospital and mental retardation applications, namely, systematic observation; explicit selection of desired behaviors, with the assistance of the teacher, as alternatives to undesirable behavior; the exchange system; training of the teacher in his or her new role; use of additional behavior-influencing techniques such as social reinforcement; and careful charting of behavior by trained observers.

The questions asked in more recent token-economy programs in the class-room have become more subtle and complex. Kistner et al. (1982) did a systematic study of the "contrast effects" of the token economy. Such a study investigates the effects on classrooms in the same school in which a special program, such as a token-economy program, is *not* introduced. It is clear that children's behavior and attitudes toward themselves and toward the teacher are affected by *not* having the special, applied psychology program. What are the contrast effects when an incentive program, a token-economy program, or a gifted and talented program is introduced elsewhere in the school? The Kistner et al. study, one of the first to look at this effect, found that there were indeed consequences in other classrooms. Clearly, we are dealing with school *systems* and are moving beyond the by-now ancient focus on the one-to-one relationship in the classroom.

In an interesting variation of the, by-now, traditional behavioral applica-tion was a study in which children were taught to modify teacher behavior (Graubard & Rosenberg, 1974). Their take-off point was previously report-ed studies of teacher behavior in the classroom that had observed that natural rates of teacher disapproval exceeded rates of approval (White, 1975). Graubard and Rosenberg (1974) reported several studies in which children were taught to modify the teacher's behavior. In one study, students in special education classes (12 to 15 years of age) were taught to make eye contact with the teacher while asking for help and to make comments such as, "It makes me feel good when you praise me." The results indicated a large increase in positive teacher behavior and a sharp decrease in negative behav-ior.

These types of studies clearly demonstrate that the interaction in the classroom between teacher and student is a two-way process. The teacher might be attempting to influence the student's behavior, but the student is also influencing the teacher, as in any interpersonal situation.

GENERALIZATION

Behavior changes only in a social context. The question then is, Does behav-ior generalize from one social situation to another? Although both laborato-ry and individual case studies with operant procedures have attempted to approach problems of generalization across time (Do changes in the morn-ing carry over to the afternoon?) and across situations (Does change in the classroom extend to the home?), most of the token-economy programs have not attempted such measures.

The key observation on the problem of generalization is that of D. M. Baer, Wolf, and Risley (1968) that " . . . generalization should be pro-grammed rather than expected or lamented" (p. 97). It seems clear that the token programs, with a few exceptions, do not result in generalized behavioral change in other situations. But most of the studies were not intended or designed to bring about change in other situations.

K. D. O'Leary and Drabman (1971) offered a list of 10 procedures useful in enhancing generalization, which were utilized in many subsequent studies (e.g. Kazdin, 1977):

> Provide a good academic program, since in many cases you may be dealing with deficient academic repertoires, not behavior disorders. . . . Give the child the expectation that he is capable of doing well by exaggerating excitement when the child succeeds and pointing out that if he works hard he can succeed. . . . Have the children aid in the selection of the behaviors to be reinforced and as the program progresses, have the children involved in the specification of contingencies. . . . Teach the children that academic achievement will "pay off . . . ." Involve the parents. . . . Withdraw the token and backup reinforcers gradually and utilize other "natural" reinforcers existing within the classroom setting, such as privileges. . . . Reinforce the children in a variety of situations and reduce the discrimination between reinforced and non-reinforced situations. . . . Prepare teachers in the regular class to praise and shape the children's behavior as they are phased back into the regular classes. . . . Look at the school system as a large-scale token system with the distribution of token and backup reinforcers and extending from the school board to the superintendent, to the principle, to the teacher, and finally to the children. (K. D. O'Leary & Drabman, 1971, p. 395)

VALUE SYSTEMS

We have used the token-economy program as a major example of the application in the classroom of psychological (in this case, behavioral) principles based in large part on laboratory studies, mainly with animals. To the extent that a teacher must be creative in planning a total classroom environment, these applications are analogous to and consistent with the environmental-design approach.

In any case, the philosophical and theoretical base of application in the classroom of token economy and other behavioral procedures is the use of positive reinforcement. At this point, we reluctantly describe the use of aversive procedures in the classroom. We say *reluctantly* to emphasize the relationship between the value systems of the investigators and the procedures used in research and application. Although there is now general agreement that punitive procedures are undesirable in the classroom, within the behavioral stream such procedures subtly enter the classroom under different terms such as response decrement, reprimands, response cost, and time-out. Aversive procedures involve the use of penalties, fines, negative reinforcements (e.g., staying after school until assignment is completed), and time-out from positive reinforcement. There has not been a large amount of behavioral research in this general area. However, there is almost a reluctance in avoiding such research, as expressed by Gardner (1969), who laments that punishment procedures are often avoided "not on the basis of an objective evaluation of scientific data but on the basis of ethical, philosophical, and sociopolitical considerations" (p. 88).

This view was more specifically spelled out by Ruggles and LeBlanc in their summary of their comprehensive review of behavioral techniques applied in the classroom. They pointed out that the current behavioral technology that can be used to maintain order in the classroom is vast. However, sometimes a "resistance" occurs to the use of such procedures, on the basis that the children's "creativity and openness" would be stifled. They agreed that creativity should be fostered. However, in their view, "bedlam" in the class prevents the teacher from fostering creativity. Thus:

> . . . teachers should be encouraged to use reinforcement and even mild forms of punishment or response-decrement procedures to control the social climate of the classroom so that learning can occur and creativity can be enhanced. Research outcomes that indicate optimal procedures for controlling classroom behavior are currently sufficient for prescriptions to be developed for teachers to use when problems develop. It needs only to be done. (1982, p. 988)

This view neatly illustrates the belief that the "social climate" of the classroom and the learning process can be differentiated, as against the view, which we share, that they are integral and cannot be separated.

Alice Sums It Up

So now it was all over. Alice had enjoyed it, at least most of it. Certainly the sense of self-satisfaction was linked with the feeling that she had been a vital figure in the lives of many children. Despite the *Zeitgeist* of pessimism about education, and the future in general, that pervaded society, she felt optimistic about the future. She felt that this optimism was beautifully captured in the title of a book written by Gilbert Highet in 1976, *The Immortal Profession: The Joys of Teaching and Learning.* Indeed, she had known both!

THE FUTURE OF PSYCHOLOGY IN EDUCATION

As the fields of application of psychology to education continue to grow extensively, we are impressed by the process of change in theoretical orientations and consequent applications of techniques. In the behavioral field, a most recent development, with major implications for the future, is the growth of a systems approach.

In his annual review of the previous year's developments, Franks (1984b) headed a chapter section "Behavior Modification and the School System." He made the very cogent observation that this particular section heading deliberately included the word *system.* "Ten years ago, most school behavior modification consisted either of traditional one-to-one procedures carried out in the classroom or psychologist's office or some form of straightforward classroom or school-wide token economy" (p. 277). Franks noted that, as behavioral strategies become increasingly sophisticated, "it becomes virtually impossible to think in terms of one-to-one direct S-R relationships" (p. 277). In education, as in other areas and fields of application, psychologists are increasingly focusing on approaches to systems (Hannafin & Witt, 1983; Piersel & Gutkin, 1983). However, Franks observed that there has not yet emerged a behaviorally compatible, clearly articulated theory of systems.

Earlier, Franks (1984a) had noted, perhaps overoptimistically, that the mechanistic application of behavioral principles in the classroom "would seem to be at an end." He contended that "thoughtful" behaviorists are asking broad questions as to the social implications of the educational process and the role of behavioral principles in the broader social context (Kazdin, 1982; Lahey & Rubinoff, 1981). In effect, as we have been emphasizing throughout this chapter, the goals of the application of psychology in the classroom cannot be separated from the broader social aims of the educational process. Franks cited examples of the more recent explorations of societal influences affecting psychological procedures in the classroom. Rose (1981) analyzed the "societal pressures" that continue to maintain aversive procedures, such as corporal punishment in the classroom, despite the lack of evidence that it is effective.

In presenting our illustrations of psychology applied to education, we merely skimmed the surface. For example, we have alluded to, but not delved into details of, the continuing controversy about the application of psychological tests (IQ tests, achievement tests, and aptitude tests) in the educational system and the societal ramifications of such applications. There is a considerable amount of psychological research on human behavior (e.g., motivation, sensation, perception, creativity, personality, concept formation, memory, child development) that is certainly pertinent to the classroom. Other relevant research areas would provide studies of characteristics of the teachers, effective teaching methods, technology hardware (computers) and assessment of educational achievement. There is the whole important area of the atypical child (special education) including learning-disabled, developmentally disabled, physically disabled, and the socially and emotionally disabled. There are even some arguments for the special field of study of the "gifted and talented."

We can only hope that the future of psychology applied to education will lie in directions called for in the past, specifically by John Dewey in his 1899 Presidential Address to the American Psychological Association (cited by Seymour Sarason in his incisive 1983 critique *Schooling in America*): "Theory and application are inseparable from each other and from the social and value context in which they develop and are applied" (p. 49).

7 Legal Applications

At approximately 8:20 p.m. on the evening of October 27, the Tempo Service Station at the corner of 12th Street and East Main was held up. Ted Aronso, the attendant on duty, was severely pistol whipped and is currently in Center City Hospital in guarded condition, with head injuries, a broken nose, and possible internal bleeding. According to Jack Elmo, the station owner, $1,260 is reported to be missing, and two vending machines were damaged. Officers Carl Bemstrom and Samuel Brown, responding to the reported robbery and assault, picked up George Harris, described as a 19-year-old white male, a few blocks from the Tempo Station shortly before 9:00 p.m. The officers said that they arrested Mr. Harris, now being held at the 44th precinct lockup, because of information about the alleged perpetrator obtained from a customer who was at the station at the time of the reported robbery.

This chapter is about psychology and the law. Our goal is to describe how psychological theory and research have been applied, and might be applied, to the concerns of the police, the courts, the prison, and several other aspects of the legal process. Most applications of psychology to the law have been in connection with criminal justice, and that will be our emphasis in this chapter. We will follow George Harris, alleged to have committed armed robbery and assault and battery, through the several stages of legal processing that constitute America's criminal justice system. At each stage we will present and examine psychology's actual and possible contribution to the better understanding and more effective functioning of that part of the system. We will consider the police who arrested George Harris, their selection, training, and management of stress. Psychological studies of police techniques for identifying perpetrators, such as the lineup or mug books, will be examined. The psychological assessment of alleged criminals such as Mr. Harris will also be covered. We will include evaluations used to determine the individual's competence to stand trial, his or her degree of responsibility for the criminal act, and predictions of future dangerousness.

We will examine psychology's contribution to the trial, as it helps us better understand the judge, the lawyers, and especially the jury and how they decide the fate of the accused. What influences them, and how do they, in turn, influence each other? What are the effects of the size of the jury, how they are seated, and the judge's instructions to them? Do various characteristics of the defendant and the witnesses influence jurors' decisions, such as race, sex, and attractiveness? Can eyewitness testimony always be trusted, or never, or only sometimes? If sometimes, when? How can lying by the defendant or witnesses best be detected, by polygraph, voice characteristics, nonverbal behavior, or hypnosis? If the defendant is convicted, what does psychology tell us about his or her alternative futures such as probation, imprisonment, parole? Psychologists engaged in prison work conduct classification, treatment, and research. What is the nature of this work, and how well or poorly does it fit the broader context of contemporary corrections? These are the kinds of questions this chapter will address, as we look over George Harris' shoulder as he enters and passes through the American criminal justice system.

HISTORY

Experimental psychology was still a relatively young science when the first call came to try to apply its theories and results to legal procedure and concerns. Hugo Munsterberg wrote in his 1908 book *On the Witness Stand* about the likely value of psychological research on perception and memory for evaluating the accuracy of eyewitness testimony. Although, as we shall see, this is a suggestion that blossomed into very considerable applied research approximately 60 years later, most experimental psychologists in the early part of the century did not share Munsterberg's enthusiasm for seeking real-world applications of laboratory findings, to the law or elsewhere.

Although a serious marriage between psychology and the law did begin in the 1960s, the 50 years between this point and Munsterberg's book were largely a nonproductive period for those seeking to relate the two fields. Some sporadic efforts did take place, however. In 1909, Healy established the first psychological clinic associated with a juvenile court, the Juvenile Psychopathic Institute in Chicago. In 1918, the State of New Jersey originated the first prison classification system in the United States. Hutchins (a lawyer) and Slesinger (a psychologist) collaborated in 1929 to write about the psychology of evidence. A few others also wrote important books during this period, mostly concerned with one or another aspect of the criminal justice system. Burt's (1925) book *The Young Delinquent* was an effort to use psychodynamic ideas to explain juvenile delinquency. A similar viewpoint on crime in general appeared in *The Criminal, The Judge, and The Public* a few years later (Alexander & Staub, 1931). Glueck and Glueck's (1930) longitudinal study of the development of juvenile delinquency, Karpman's (1933) intensive case study of different types of criminals, Burt's (1931) *Legal Psychology*, and Lindner and Selinger's (1947) *Handbook of Correctional Psychology* are the main examples of this sporadic effort.

Matters took a very different, and much, much more active, turn in the 1960s. The climate for a substantial viewing of the law through psychological glasses became much more supportive. Federal-level concern, and funding, for criminal justice research increased greatly, as did a general trend in the social sciences toward greater respectability for applied research. Not very much had happened before this period, not only because psychology was looking elsewhere, but also because the legal profession had not been especially receptive to the perspectives and findings of psychology. This reluctance also began to change considerably in this period. Thus, both psychology and the law came, in the 1960s, to more fully believe that many of the fundamental assumptions and procedures at the heart of the legal process were psychological in nature, such as perception, memory, decision making, group dynamics, and behavior under stress. This chapter will examine this more recent beginning union of psychology and the law in considerable detail.

Officer Carl Bemstrom, 9 years on the force, and Officer Samuel Brown, a rookie of 3 months, came upon George Harris the night they arrested him by a combination of good police work and sheer luck. Carl knew how to secure and examine a crime scene; question witnesses, even those under great stress, to get usable information quickly; and systematically scour an area seeking an alleged perpetrator. And Samuel was learning quickly.

How do people like Carl and Sam come to be police officers? How are they trained? Is the daily work of the officer as stressful as the popular press suggests? These are among the several questions about the police segment of the criminal justice system that applied psychologists have sought to answer.

POLICE SELECTION

A brief glance at the origins of police selection will help us view more clearly current efforts of psychology in this arena. Chenoweth (1961), looking back 150 years, described these origins.

On September 29, 1829, the Metropolitan Police of London, England, entered upon their first day of duty. Of the first 2,800 men recruited into that organization, at least 2,238 (or approximately 80%) had to be dismissed from the force. All 2,800 officers had been hand-picked by a very careful system of selection. Each candidate had to submit three written testimonials of character, one of them being from his last employer; the writers of these testimonials were personally interviewed. If a candidate passed through this stage, he reported for a medical examination, which in practice meant an inquiry into both his physical qualifications and his general intelligence. Less than one in three of the applicants was successful in passing through this stage. Those who did were then interviewed by an experienced personnel officer who eliminated the candidates obviously not suited to police work and passed the survivors on to the first two Commissioners of the Metropolitan Police, who again interviewed the remaining candidates. The disapproval of either Commissioner was sufficient to reject the candidate.

The above technique for the evaluation of police applicants was originated over 130 years ago; it is still the basic examining procedure used by many police agencies today. In it we may glimpse the seeds which were subsequently transformed into our present methodology of assessment; the personal references, the background investigations, the physical and mental tests, the oral interview. (p. 232)

Procedures for selecting police were, if anything, *less* adequate when police departments were first established in the United States. Toch (1979) noted that friends and relatives of political figures were very often "selected"; given a badge, a gun, and a book of regulations; and sent off to work. Over the years, as the police selection process has become less political and, in aspiration if not too often in reality, more scientific, the selection procedures hinted at in London of 1829 have become considerably more refined.

In most American cities, the process now begins with public announcements (newspapers, television) by the civil service examiner of expected openings, along with age, health, and citizenship requirements. Applicants then take the appropriate civil service examination and, if they achieve more than a specified cutting score, undergo some or all of the steps involved in a background investigation, psychological and physical testing, and face-to-face interviews. It is quite common that the testing and interview components of this selection sequence are conducted by a psychologist. The psychological testing could seek to evaluate intelligence, aptitude, interests, and personality. The tests themselves could be inventories, questionnaires, performance tasks, projective tests (in which the applicant responds to ambiguous test materials by supposedly "projecting" her or his personality into the perception and interpretation of them), and, in recent years, situational tests (in which the applicant is actually put in challenging re-creations of situations very similar to those she or he will face on the job and then observed for responses). Psychological tests, of whatever type, are essentially devices used to measure current behavior in order to predict future behavior.

What are the police behaviors the psychologist should seek to predict with his or her tests and interviews? Stotland and Berberich (1979) suggested decision making, human relations skills, emotional maturity, communication skills, and resistance to stress. Although this list certainly sounds reasonable, it, unfortunately, is as much speculation as fact. Psychologists and others have strong *beliefs* about the psychological qualities that make a good police officer, but they have rather little hard evidence. Furthermore, some of the qualities of successful police officers might in fact be considerably more subtle than one would estimate at first glance. Levy (1973), for example commented,

> Unless and until we know which emotional components militate against satisfactory police work, it is a waste of time, energy, and money to seek the candidates with the greatest amount of "emotional stability." It is emotional *suitability*, not emotional stability we should be seeking. (p. 27)

Thus, the use of psychological procedures for police selection has come a long way from its inadequate beginnings, but much remains to be done. Job analysis and critical-incidents studies that identify the key qualities of successful police officers are the first major step. Rather little of such research has already been conducted. Then, what psychologists call *predictive validity research* must follow. These are studies in which specific test results and interview information are examined to determine how well their presence or absence predicts the qualities of good police officers identified in the job analysis and critical incidents research. According to Lefkowitz (1977), only a few such predictive validity studies of police selection, a very small beginning, had been conducted by the late 1970s. We have come a long way from the London of 1829, but we still have a good distance to go.

POLICE TRAINING

Most police training occurs either in a police academy, when the officer-to-be is still a recruit, or on the job, after academy training. One comprehensive example of a police academy curriculum, revealing the scope and depth of topics that could ideally constitute a training program, was provided by Bristow (1971) (Table 7.1). Note that there are several topics whose teaching would benefit from the involvement of the applied psychologist.

On-the-job police training occurs in a variety of ways and in a variety of settings. It can be as simple as a two-page training bulletin or training key or a 5-minute minilecture during roll call, to informal observation and coaching by a more senior officer while on road patrol, to formal week-long (or more) seminars and workshops devoted to special topics. In recent years many of these special workshops, conducted by psychologists, have dealt with such topics as terrorism and hostage negotiation procedures, community relations, handling of group conflict, dealing with emotionally disturbed or intoxicated citizens, strategies and techniques for effectively resolving the most dangerous type of police call (A. P. Goldstein, Monti, Sardino, & Green, 1979), the domestic dispute, and means of controlling and reducing police stress.

TABLE **7.1.** Basic Curriculum of the Police

	TIME	
TITLE	*HOURS*	*MINUTES*
Organization and Functions of Law Enforcement Agencies	7	30
Ethics and Conduct	2	0
Constitutional Law and Civil Liberties	5	0
Court Systems and Procedures	12	30
Law of Search and Seizure	21	15
Testifying in Court	21	30
Detention and Arrest	29	30
Recognize Criminal Violations	46	30
Illegal Firearms	5	0
Principles of Evidence	30	15
Recognition of Evidence	8	0
Collection and Preservation of Evidence	17	30
Housebreaking and Burglary Investigation	3	30
Searches and Raids	15	0
Search Vehicles	4	30
News Media	1	30
Sources of Information	3	0
Interviewing	22	0
Note Taking	4	0
Report Writing	10	30
Recognize and Dispose of Bombs and Explosives	5	0
Photography	7	30
Radio Communications	8	0
Fingerprinting	5	0
Missing or Wanted Persons	4	0
Description and Identification	6	0
Human Relations	25	0
Appraising Crowds and Mobs	16	45
Control Crowds and Mobs	39	0
Surveillance	13	0
Standard and Advanced First Aid	30	0
Recognize and Handle Ill, Injured, and Dead	25	0
Operation of Police Vehicle	32	0
Roadblocks	10	0
Physical Defense Tactics	65	0
Defense Equipment	18	30
Firearms	42	0
Total Training Time	622′	15″

Note. From *Police Supervision Readings* (p. 287) by A. P. Bristow, 1971, Springfield, IL: Charles C Thomas. Copyright 1971 by Charles C Thomas. Reprinted by permission.

POLICE STRESS

It had been a tough week for Officers Bemstrom and Brown, though not very different from most weeks. They spent most of Monday in court, waiting to testify about an arrest they had made a few weeks earlier, but they were never called to the stand. Tuesday morning they found out that another officer in the department, a friend of Carl's, had put his revolver in his mouth over the weekend and blown his brains out. That was the third suicide of a fellow officer in Carl's precinct since he had gotten there. Nothing happened Wednesday—just a boring, empty, routine day. Carl's stomach bothered him a lot that day, and he made a mental note to see the department's physician.

All hell broke loose on Thursday. There had been a big fire in a downtown lumberyard when they came on duty at 4:00 p.m. and Carl and Samuel had helped redirect traffic. Then a really tricky domestic dispute call came around 6:00 p.m. Samuel was a bit surprised over this one, because most of the family fights in this neighborhood came on the weekend. Samuel came within 2 in. of getting hit in the head by a flying ashtray. No counseling or arbitration on this call. They arrested the husband. The officers were wolfing down a quick, late supper when the Tempo station robbery call came in to them around 8:35. They knew that the perpetrator was armed and dangerous, so the 20 minutes between the call and their arrest of George Harris seemed like 2 days long all by itself. When they signed in on Friday, it wasn't congratulations for the Harris arrest that were waiting for them, but Supplementary Regulations Bulletin 714A, spelling out in no uncertain terms that officers of the 44th precinct had recently been too casual in the care and wearing of their uniforms and that such sloppiness was to cease immediately. The worst part of the day, the worst part of *any* day for the police officer, came on Friday afternoon. Two bodies were discovered in a shed in the lumberyard that had burned the day before, and Carl and Samuel were assigned the death notification responsibility for one of them. As they drove to the address, Samuel kept imagining what the victim's wife might say when he told her . . .

Police work is indeed stressful work, and psychology has made a substantial contribution to both understanding the nature and sources of stress, and developing ways of alleviating its intensity and negative consequences. Bartol (1983) listed the following common types of stress on police: lack of supervisory support, complexity and unpredictability of police work, diversity of role demands constituting the job of police officer (e.g., on-the-spot judge, counselor, peacemaker, service-provider, physical protector), shift work, social isolation, physical danger, negative public image, family and marital conflict, and departmental overregulation and restrictions on behavior. Kroes, Margolis, and Hurrell (1974) added to this list inactivity and boredom, punctuated with hyperactivity and job overload, red tape, pay inequities, court rulings and scheduling and perceived court leniency for perpetrators, and more. It would be difficult to identify other occupations so broadly, diversely, and continuously stressful.

Of course, it has long been established (Selye, 1956) that stress can help a person become alert and mobilized and thus deal more effectively with his or her environment. Although this beneficial effect of stress can in fact occur *in the short run*, continued stress has clearly negative effects: " . . . no organism can exist in a prolonged state of alarm. Under such conditions, resistance is undercut and disease states, including emotional and physical symptoms, occur" (Stotland & Berberich, 1979, p. 58). This is precisely the negative outcome for many American police officers. Compared with the general population, as well as with almost any other profession, police rates are higher for alcoholism, divorce, suicide, depression, and a wide variety of stress-related physical problems such as headaches, ulcers, and hypertension. Psychologists have helped develop and evaluate several apparently effective treatment methods for this broad variety of stress reactions, including cognitive stress inoculation, biofeedback, progressive relaxation, systematic desensitization, autogenics, and visualization. These stress-remediation techniques are described and evaluated in more detail in the chapters on "Clinical Applications" (chapter 3) and "Health Applications" (chapter 4).

THE LINEUP

After his arrest on October 27, George Harris was booked at the 44th precinct and held for his preliminary hearing. The booking process included fingerprinting, taking front-view and profile photographs of his face (mug shots), and interviewing him for identifying and background information. The county prosecutor, judging that enough evidence appeared to exist to proceed further, issued a formal complaint (warrant) against George Harris and scheduled his preliminary hearing for the October 30.

At the hearing, formal charges were read to Harris by the judge, who, in spite of a claim to the contrary by Cindy Gayle, Harris' court-appointed attorney, ruled that enough evidence existed for Harris to be officially charged with armed robbery and assault and battery and held over for formal trial. Because part of the charge against Harris included the alleged assault and battery against the station attendant, the judge also ruled that bail be set quite high, at $50,000. After the hearing, Ms. Gayle urged Harris to plea-bargain, expecting that the prosecutor would be willing to accept a guilty plea to a lesser charge. But Harris refused, loudly protested his innocence, and insisted he be allowed to have his day in court. In the weeks that followed, Ms. Gayle and the prosecutor assigned to the trial, Assistant District Attorney Allen Hanson, prepared their cases. As part of his efforts, DA Hanson arranged for Harris to appear for a lineup on December 3 at the second-floor observation room of the city jail in which he was being held.

Having witnesses to a crime view possible perpetrators in a lineup (or in mug shots) is but one of several examples of the use of eyewitness testimony in the trial process. Such testimony has been the target of considerable psychological research. Penrod, Loftus, and Winkler (1982) described the ideal eyewitness as an individual who "(a) perceived all that transpired during the [target] event, (b) accurately encoded these perceptions, (c) exhaustively stored the encoded perceptions in memory, and (d) fully and accurately retrieved the encodings from memory in the form of later reports" (p. 121). Unfortunately, this ideal is rarely even approximated, because substantial inaccuracies can occur at each stage of the memory process: encoding, storage, and retrieval.

Encoding

When witnessing a crime or other event, a person's ability to encode (move from perception to storage) what he or she sees, hears, or perceives is influenced by several factors: the frequency of the event, his or her exposure time to it, its complexity and organization, and event stressfulness and seriousness. Research on eyewitness testimony has shown that greater frequency of exposure (Sanders & Warnick, 1979), greater time of exposure (Read, 1979), the more organized or meaningful the event (Mandler, 1980), and the more serious the apparent crime being perpetrated (Leippe, Wells, & Ostrom, 1978) result in greater accuracy of eyewitness identification. What is encoded? In a study of 100 street crimes, eyewitnesses reported, in order of frequency, the perpetrator's sex, age, height, build, race, weight, complexion, hair color, and eye color.

It is certainly not just qualities of the event that determine what is encoded and how accurately, but also qualities of the witness. Witness expectations, stereotypes, cultural biases, and prior information about the event influence what is perceived and encoded. In a complex manner, accuracy of encoding is also influenced by the stressfulness of the event for the witness. Events of low and high stressfulness are encoded less well than moderately stressful events. As can be seen from these several results, a great many factors associated with either the event or the witness can adversely affect the accuracy of information encoding. A parallel conclusion may be drawn for the next stage of the memory process, storage.

Storage

Some of psychology's oldest research findings are directly relevant to the storage component of memory and to accuracy of identification in the police lineup in particular. One hundred years ago, Ebbinghaus (1885) demonstrated the existence of a forgetting curve, in which considerable information is forgotten shortly after an event, followed by the more gradual loss of additional information as further time passes. Thus, the longer the storage period, the more forgetting occurs. New information learned after the event, during the storage period, also actively and negatively influences the storage process. With regard to the police lineup, for example, innocent persons (those not at the crime) whose pictures happen to be included in the mug-shot books looked over by the witness after the crime but before the lineup are more likely to be incorrectly identified as perpetrators of the crime (Brown, Deffenbacher, & Sturgill, 1977).

Retrieval

As was true for encoding and storage, there exist several sources of possible inaccuracy when the witness seeks to retrieve and report his or her recollection of an event. The specific retrieval questions asked, for example, can cause distortion. Unbiased instructions to the witness at a police lineup ("The perpetrator might be in this lineup"), as compared with biased instructions, ("The perpetrator is in this lineup"), led to a greater number of both accurate identifications when the perpetrator was in fact present (unbiased, 83%; biased, 75%) and accurate rejections when the perpetrator was not present (unbiased, 67%; biased, 22%). Those persons besides the possible perpetrator who appear in the lineup also influence retrieval accuracy. Researchers (e.g., Wells, Leippe, & Ostrom, 1979) have distinguished between the nominal and functional size of lineups. Nominal size denotes simply how many people are in a given lineup. Functional size pertains to how many people who are similar to the perpetrator in at least some important, observable way appear in the lineup. The greater the functional size, that is, the more other persons appear who are not immediately and consistently ruled out by the viewers, the lower the retrieval accuracy. Multiple retrievals are a further source of retrieval inaccuracy. Retelling an event or reidentifying an alleged perpetrator leads to systematically clearer and clearer statements and more and more certainty and confidence in one's (perhaps incorrect) identification with each repetition. The nature of the crime itself also affects the retrieval process. It has been shown that the more serious the crime, the greater the likelihood of a false lineup identification (Malpass, Devine, & Bergen, 1980).

We see, therefore, that at each stage of the memory process—encoding, storage, and retrieval—there exist sources of inaccuracy associated with the event itself, the passage of time, competing information, and the witness herself or himself. It should not surprise us, therefore, to learn that, in the several studies examining eyewitness accuracy, the amount of correct identifications in lineups was always less than 50% and frequently less than 20% (Buckhout, 1974, 1975; Buckhout, Alper, Chern, Silverberg, & Slomovitz, 1974). We concur with Bartol's (1983) observation:

> Eyewitness research has continually found that memory is highly malleable and easily subject to change and distortion. Apparently, humans continually alter and reconstruct their memory of past experiences in light of present experiences, rather than store past events permanently and unchangingly in memory. (p. 171)

PRETRIAL PREPARATION: JUDGES AND JURIES

Paul Hisarta was feeling really nervous as he approached the city jail. He had never been there, or to any jail, before and certainly had never been a viewer of a police lineup before. Paul had simply been unlucky enough to be buying gasoline at the Tempo station when all hell broke loose that day. There was also something else that bothered Paul. Ted Aronso, the station attendant, had not responded well to treatment and was still in the hospital, in and out of a sort of coma. He not only couldn't come to the lineup, but he was in no condition to even look at mug books in the hospital. DA Hanson had let Paul know in no uncertain terms that "the whole ball game" was riding on his identification.

One hour later it was all over. It happened so fast, Paul thought. Paraded them in. "Is he there?" "Yes, it's number three." "Are you sure?" "Yes, I am. " Fill out one more form. Then, "thank you, we'll be in touch."

Ms. Gayle, Harris' attorney, wasted no time. She was at the lineup, saw its outcome, understood its consequences for her client, and proceeded to seek expert support for what would be her main defense strategy: the claim that George Harris, because of his mental condition at the time of the crime, was not guilty by reason of insanity.

Judges

There are approximately 17,000 full-time judges in the United States presiding over trials at the federal, state, and county levels. States vary in the procedures used for establishing new judgeships, some relying on election, others on merit selection or political appointment. Winick's (1979) description of judicial functioning gives a clear sense of the judge's overriding role in the trial process:

> The judge is the umpire in the courtroom. . . . By his rulings on specific applications of law, the judge contributes toward the record of the trial. . . . The subpoena powers of the judge enable him to compel the production of records and the appearance and testimony of witnesses. It is the duty of the judge to maintain order and discipline, and to control the conduct of attorneys and other participants in a trial. The judge's power to set aside verdicts, to direct verdicts, and to rule on the various motions of counsel, enables him to dominate the course of litigation. (p. 77)

In spite of the judge's singular importance, he or she has only rarely been the target of psychological study, apparently in large measure due to inaccessability. Only a few relevant psychological findings have been reported concerning judicial decision making and judicial influence upon jury decision making. Later in this chapter, we will learn the several ways in which jurors' deliberations and decisions are importantly influenced by defendant characteristics. Judges, in contrast, appear to be more singularly responsive to evidence and considerably less influenced in their sentencing decisions by defendants' sex, age, social class, and (with some regional exceptions) race

(Hagan, 1974). Juries, on the average, are more willing to acquit defendants than are judges (Kalven & Zeisel, 1966), but some jury verdicts are influenced by subtle (and perhaps not so subtle) "leanings" of the judge that become evident during the trial. Kerr and Bray (1982) showed that jurors were more likely to acquit, the more respectful the judge was to the defense attorney. The more the judge favored the prosecution, the more likely a jury decision to convict. Beyond these few findings, the psychology of the judge is little known and, thus, is a valuable target of future research.

Jury Selection

A central component of the American legal system is the representative jury. In theory, and partly in fact, the typical American jury reflects the nature and diversity of the community in which the trial occurs. The usual first step in selecting a jury (called the *venire* or "to come when called") is to constitute a pool of potential jurors from voter registration lists. Because citizens who are young, poor, or minority members are underrepresented on such lists, the degree to which the juror pool selected actually represents the community is thus reduced. Once selected from the voter registration list, potential jurors are sent a jury questionnaire by the jury commission. The pool is further reduced at this point by questionnaire responses, through the disqualification of those who cannot read, cannot speak the language, are employed in criminal justice occupations, or have criminal records. Those for whom jury duty might be an undue hardship on themselves or their clients may be exempted from the pool, such as physicians and nurses. Once the juror pool is constituted in this manner, the next stage in juror selection is the *voir dire*, or, the choosing of the actual jury from the panel or pool.

The voir dire, in operation, is a questioning of potential jurors by the prosecution and the defense. Either attorney may excuse any given panel member up to a set number, on a peremptory basis (no explanation needed) or for cause (because of clear juror bias, for example). As this last sentence suggests, the purported goal of the voir dire is to select a fair and unbiased jury. In reality, it has been shown that, in the typical voir dire, only 20% of the usual half-hour devoted to each panelist is spent on questions designed to identify trial-relevant biases. Eighty percent of the voir dire looks as if the trial has already begun! The attorneys conducting the voir dire spend most of their time seeking to indoctrinate the panelist, commenting on points of law, ingratiating themselves, forewarning jurors about given items of evidence, and engaging in similar behaviors. For these reasons, as well as because of its considerable cost in time and money, in some jurisdictions the amount of attorney questioning is limited by the court or, more drastically, the voir dire is conducted by himself or herself. How well does the voir dire system work, whether conducted by attorneys or judges? Prevailing opinion (there is little evidence) concludes that it probably eliminates the openly prejudiced and sensitizes those selected to trying to set aside their prejudices when deliberating (Blunk & Sales, 1977; Suggs & Sales, 1978).

The American legal system, in all its particulars, proceeds on an adversarial basis, in which two opposing sides, refereed and directed by a judge, actively seek to convince a jury that their versions of the truth are more accurate. The adversarial approach differs markedly, for example, from the much less competitive orientation of the inquisitorial judicial format popular in several European countries. Lind (1982), for example, observed,

> In a French trial, the questioning of witnesses is conducted almost exclusively by the presiding judge. The judge interrogates the disputing parties and witnesses, referring frequently to a dossier that has been prepared by a court official who investigated the case. Although the parties probably have partisan attorneys present at the trial, it is evident that control over the presentation of evidence and arguments is firmly in the hands of the judge. (p. 14)

We have briefly pointed to these two contrasting legal orientations and procedural formats in order to underscore the crucial assumption underlying American adversarial legal orientation. It is the belief that skilled and energetic partisan advocacy on the part of both sides to a trial, more fully than other approaches, yields the fullest hearing of the facts, the fairest bases for deliberation, and the most just verdict. It is in this adversarial context that there began in 1968 one of psychology's most controversial contributions to legal process, systematic, or scientific, jury selection. Systematic jury selection is the use of psychological techniques to obtain a final jury likely to be most favorable to one's own side and least favorable to the opposition. This is the identical goal already sought by attorneys preparing for trial, but the means utilized are rather different. Instead of the attorney's usual unsystematic interview of voir dire panelists, the psychologist conducting a systematic jury selection might use

1. Surveys of the community in which the trial is to take place, in order to identify characteristics of persons who favor one's own side as well as the opposition, so that voir dire panelists with the same or similar qualities favoring one's own side can be accepted
2. Information networks, that is, sources in the community who know and are willing to describe the actual jury panel members (attorneys or their representatives may not contact panel members directly, as this would constitute jury tampering)
3. Juror ratings, in which the psychologist observes the voir dire, draws "clinical impressionlike" conclusions, based upon panelist answers and nonverbal behavior, and advises the attorney for whom he or she is consulting accordingly
4. Small-group research findings, to draw conclusions about how a given

panelist might behave and vote in the context of the particular jury being selected, for example, how responsive the potential juror might be to the status of others and his or her likely alliances, resistance to conformity pressure, and so forth.

Adequate research examining the effectiveness of systematic jury selection has yet to be conducted. The anecdotal and experiential evidence examining its effectiveness appears to be largely positive, beginning with its first uses in the 1968 trial of Black Panther Huey Newton and the 1972 trial of the Berrigan brothers. In reality, it has been used very infrequently, probably in part because of expense. Given its infrequent use, and given its apparent success when it has been used, the high degree of impassioned objection to it is rather remarkable. Some appear to hold, and hold strongly, that American jurisprudence works best when aspects of its process are left ambiguous. Were we somehow to be more scientifically certain in our voir dire selections, these opponents of systematic selection hold, either the voir dire system would collapse from failure to select or juries would be selected that were singularly biased as a function of whose psychological consultants were more competent.

Although this particular instance of the use of reasonably scientific bases for shaping courtroom procedure has yet to be resolved, it is not the only illustration of controversy over science in the legal process that might be cited. As we saw earlier in this chapter, there exists a very considerable amount of psychological research evidence pointing to the frequent inaccuracy of eyewitness testimony, yet it remains almost sacred as a basis for decision making in the American courtroom. Yet the polygraph, whose accuracy for deception detection when used by a skilled operator has been demonstrated in at least a moderate number of studies, is inadmissible in most judicial jurisdictions. We can see, therefore, that although the marriage of psychology and the law is in part far from complete because psychology has often had little to offer, it is also true that at least in some of the instances when it did, the courtroom door has been locked.

THE TRIAL: THE PROSECUTION

The voir dire was now over, and, as DA Hanson faced the assembled jury for the first time and looked them over as a group, he felt he had used his challenges reasonably well. This was a jury, he believed, he could convince. As he rose to address the jury with his opening statement, and glanced at defense attorney Gayle as he strode past her, he had a passing thought of pleasure that in the American court the prosecution speaks first on opening and second on closing. A "prosecution sandwich" he mused.

His statement to the jury was strong. Hanson skillfully yet simply promised them an impressive parade of evidence against George Harris. He said there was motivation he would prove, because Harris had lost his job 8 months earlier and was up against it financially. There was an eyewitness, he promised, who had unequivocally identified Harris as the perpetrator at a police lineup. And there was, according to a report filed by the arresting officers, $1,300 in Harris' pocket at the time of arrest. "How would someone out of work almost a year explain that?" Hanson asked the jury. Yes, there was motivation, a witness, and what certainly was the stolen money, Hanson held. What there most definitely was not, he concluded passionately, was a reasonable doubt that George Harris was guilty of the crimes of armed robbery and assault and battery.

Defense Attorney Gayle then had her turn, devoted largely to preparing the jury for her later presentation of evidence in support of the insanity defense. Her skill in doing so clearly matched Hanson's, thus promising quite a court-room battle ahead.

Hanson then called his first witness.

Testimony

Applied psychologists have studied witness testimony in considerable detail, finding much to offer both the student of courtroom behavior and the practicing attorney. A crucial aspect of witness behavior is the witness' credibility. It has been demonstrated (Mehrabian & Williams, 1969) that higher degrees of communicator credibility are associated with a conversational delivery, a minimum of nonfluencies, a moderate to slightly rapid speaking rate, a lower pitch, a variety of intonation, eye contact, moderate use of gestures, and a somewhat extroverted style. Witnesses not only influence others (e.g., the jury) as a function of such qualities as their credibility, but they also are open to influence.

In our earlier discussion of the police lineup, we noted the several ways in which the encoding, storage, and retrieval phases of the memory process might be influenced or distorted by both new information received by the person and his or her internal processing of information. At the trial stage, the examining (or cross-examining) attorney's questions could cause similar memory distortions. Loftus (1975) showed that incidental mention in the attorney's question of such, in fact, absent details about an event as a "stop sign" or "passing the barn" increased the degree to which witnesses mentioned a stop sign or a barn in later testimony. In a related demonstration of question-induced bias, Loftus and Palmer (1974) demonstrated that the intensity of the descriptive term used by the questioner when inquiring about a speeding accident directly influenced the witnesses' average estimates of the vehicle's speed, namely "smashed" (40.8 mph), "collided" (39.3 mph), "bumped" (38.1 mph), "hit" (34 mph) and "contacted" (31.8 mph).

What about the witness whose testimony is in error not because of faulty memory or examiner questioning bias but, instead, because of deliberate deception? Four major areas of deception detection have been explored, the polygraph or lie detector, hypnosis, voice indicators, and nonverbal cues.

The Polygraph

The polygraph is a device composed of three (or more) instruments designed to record on a moving paper chart any changes in skin conductance of electrical currents (the galvanometer), in respiration (the pneumograph), and in blood volume and pulse rate (the cardiophysmograph). Two forms of examiner questioning are most common in current use of the polygraph. With the *control question technique*, the examiner asks not only questions about the alleged crime or event, but also other questions (control questions) designed to elicit guilt or anxiety in the subject. If the subject is telling the truth, users of this approach claim, then polygraph response to control questions should be greater than response to event questions. If the subject is lying, then the opposite should be the result. In the *guilty knowledge technique*, an approach being employed with increasing frequency in recent years, the subject is asked questions about the event whose answers could be known only to the perpetrator. The subject's responses to such questions are then compared with responses to diverse control questions.

Across several investigations (Barland & Raskin, 1973; Horvath, 1977; Raskin & Hare, 1978) polygraph accuracy, especially its skin-conductance component, has been shown to be between 70 and 90% correct. Although there is no evidence that certain types of persons, described in terms of age, sex, previous arrests, polygraph experience, or Minnesota Multiphasic Personality Inventories (MMPI) profile, can beat the polygraph, there is a series of countermeasures that some subjects have successfully used to deceive the polygraph and its operator. These include such techniques as mental distraction; dissociation from the questioning by doing a repetitive, monotonous task; posing and answering one's own questions during the exam; thinking erotic, embarrassing, or painful thoughts; flexing various muscles; and taking depressant drugs. Critics of polygraph use point out that the high levels of accuracy reported in polygraph evaluation research reflect its use at its best, not its typical employment with often less experienced examiners. False alarm rates under these latter circumstances, it is suggested, are considerably higher than the reported 10 to 20%. Nevertheless, on balance it appears that the polygraph, when used by a skilled operator and considered in combination with other evidence, can make a substantial contribution to discerning the truthfulness of courtroom testimony. It is, therefore, unfortunate that most courts in the United States rarely allow polygraph evidence, an especially puzzling stance given their willingness to accept information based on such often less valid sources of evidence as psychological tests, interviews, and eyewitness testimony. Perhaps, as Bartol (1983) noted, we see here a philosophical problem, in that the polygraph brings to the court-room an aura of absolutes that runs counter to " . . . the traditional judicial process, its adversarial nature, and the fact that the system thrives on debate and uncertainty" (p. 208).

Hypnosis

Hypnosis has been employed in legal contexts in a number of different ways. One is *hypnotic screening* during the voir dire, used to detect panelists' prejudice or bias. A second is to help determine the *mental state* of an accused individual at the time of an alleged crime. Hypnosis has also been used to help prepare the *anxious witness* with posthypnotic relaxation sug-gestions. Finally, in its most common legal usage, hypnosis has been em-ployed to *improve the process of remembering*. Much like polygraph use, this procedure has engendered considerable controversy. But, unlike investi-gations examining polygraph use, research evaluating the success of hypnosis-aided remembering has not been supportive (Barber & Calverley, 1966; Cooper & London, 1973; Dhanens & Lundy, 1975).

As M. C. Smith (1983) reported, what has been shown is that, under hypnosis, witnesses are more suggestible and show a greater tendency to agree with the interrogator. Because of these findings, and the growing trend for courts to reject hypnosis-aided testimony, psychology has recently sought nonhypnotic means of enhancing memory. Two such procedures that appear quite promising are reinstatement of context and experimental hypermnesia. Studies of reinstatement of context (Bower, 1981; Malpass et al., 1980; S. M. Smith, 1979) show that providing the individual with information about the context in which an event originally occurred serves to improve his or her recollection of that event. Such memory-enhancing cues have included physi-cal location, room size, objects and persons present, odors, sounds, temper-ature, lighting, and other contextual dimensions. Experimental hypermne-sia is the second promising means of improving recollection (Erdelyi & Kleinbard, 1978). When a person who has tried to recall all he or she can about an event is asked, after the passage of a period of time, to attempt yet one more recall, it often happens that additional information is indeed retrieved. Interestingly, this improved recall with repeated attempts might be what occurs when someone is hypnotized and asked to recall events. When he or she succeeds in doing so, hypnosis gets the credit, but hypermnesia could be responsible.

Voice Characteristics

As a rough guide to deception detection via vocal cues, it has been shown that many individuals, when lying, show (a) reticence, reflected in fewer total words and shorter statements than when they are telling the truth; (b) vagueness, as shown by a restricted verbal code, that is, fewer *different* words, fewer facts, broader generalities; and (c) negative emotion, or, more disparaging remarks and fewer group references (Knapp, Hart, & Dennis, 1974; Mehrabian, 1971). An attempt to make much more specific and exact use of voice qualities in detecting lying has emerged in recent years in the form of voiceprints (Bartol, 1983; Schwitzgebel & Schwitzgebel, 1980). These are oscillographic representations of spoken sounds that supposedly identify unique elements of an individual's vocalizations. Neither the legal profession nor the psychological research community has accepted the validity of this approach. Research shows voice detection by this means to be no better than chance in identifying deception (Hollien, 1980; Kubis, 1973; Yarmey, 1979).

Nonverbal Characteristics
The individual's nonverbal behavior has also been the target of research on deception. Although hands and feet appear to be special sources of information about deception, mostly because individuals who are simulating seem to concentrate their nonverbal deception efforts on their facial expressions, it is nevertheless true that the face has been the main focus of psychological research to date on nonverbal detection of deception. We refer in particular to Ekman and Friesen's (1974) studies of the leakage of facial cues of deception. They proposed four types of facial leakage cues:

Morphological. These are changes in the configuration, shape, or dimensions of facial features accomplished by the deceiver's using such techniques as modulation (making the expression more or less intense) and falsification, in which, in the viewer's perspective, the features constituting the configuration "don't fit." With regard, for example, to efforts to simulate sadness, Ekman and Friesen (1974) commented:

> When sadness is simulated, it will probably be shown in the lower face and a downward cast of the eyes. The absence of the sad brow/forehead and upper eyelid would be a good clue that the sadness was simulated. . . . the sad brow/forehead is a particularly reliable indicator that sadness is genuinely felt, because this expression is hard to make voluntarily . . . (p. 149)

Temporal. In a manner parallel to the morphological discordance of facial features, temporal discordances may also provide important leakage cues. How long a given facial expression takes to appear in a particular context, how long it remains on the face, and how long it takes to disappear are each matters of facial expression timing that may serve as leakage cues to deception.

Location. The occurrence and spacing of a facial expression in relation to ongoing conversation, body movement, and related unfolding events may provide further leakage information. As with morphological and temporal cues, the interpersonal context in which the facial expression is displayed will influence in important ways the interpretation of location cues to deception.

Micro-expressions. A final type of cue, especially to those efforts to deceive that involve falsifying the emotion one is experiencing, are very brief expressive interruptions. The micro-expression (accurately expressing what one is actually feeling) may occur just before, during, or just after the appearance of the deceptive (i.e., deintensified, neutralized, intensified, or masked) emotion.

What can be said in conclusion about this diverse information on witness testimony? We have seen that eyewitness recollection can be faulty and is open to biasing influence by the substance and form of questions asked by the attorneys. And, aside from the (inadmissable in most courts) polygraph, its truthfulness or falsity is difficult to detect when the witness is seeking to deceive. Perhaps our most appropriate conclusion is to concur with A. G. Goldstein (1977), who suggested "eyewitness personal identification testimony should be inadmissable unless corroborated by facts associated with another class of evidence. . . . multiple eyewitnesses may be as unreliable as single eyewitnesses" (p. 237).

THE TRIAL: THE DEFENSE

Ms. Gayle did her best, if not to fully discredit the witnesses for the prosecution, at least to begin raising reasonable doubts about certain aspects of their testimony. Her effort to make eyewitness Hisarta sound confused or contradictory in his recounting of what he had seen had gone well, she felt. And she had even been able to get from both arresting officers a smattering of testimony about how George had behaved in peculiar ways at the time of his arrest.

When her turn came to begin calling witnesses, she lost no time starting to make concrete her "not guilty by reason of insanity" defense. First, two neighborhood witnesses testified about George sitting out all night on his front steps, not answering at times when they'd say hello, or breaking off conversations in mid-sentence, and a string of other mild oddities in his behavior. Then two more witnesses were heard, one who claimed to have bought George's television set from him the day before the alleged robbery, a second making similar claims about what he described as "George's fine watch." The second witness also added that George had tried hard to sell him the shoes George was wearing at the time. These were double-barreled witnesses for Ms. Gayle. The selling of personal possessions was at least a little odd, and, along with other such sales she purported that George had made on the street in the days immediately before the robbery, they helped explain the $1,300 found in his pocket at the time of arrest.

George's wife testified about their family troubles, his moodiness, his bursts of anger, and the times he'd just sit in the living room, sometimes for hours, not talking to others or doing anything, but just sitting.

Ms. Gayle was ready to call her main witness, psychologist Susan Peth, long a recognized expert in examining for the insanity defense.

In the relatively few years since it has become fairly common for psychologists to serve as expert witness in the American courtroom, they have testified in relation to an impressively broad array of concerns: competence to stand trial, criminal responsibility (insanity), opinion sampling, drug addiction, sex offenses, child custody, adoption, jury selection, capacity to testify, brain injury, memory and perception (as they bear upon accuracy of eyewitness testimony), impact of media programming, employment selection practices, and more. Most frequently, however, the psychologist as expert witness has meant psychological testing at one of three possible points in the trial process. Is the defendant, the psychologist might be asked to help determine, competent to stand trial? That is, prior to the decision that a trial will in fact occur, the court may request that the defendant's psychological and intellectual capacity be examined, to ascertain whether she or he understands the charges, comprehends the legal proceedings, and is able to communicate with her or his attorney. During the trial, the second possible occasion for psychological evaluation, the psychologist could be called upon to help determine criminal responsibility. The insanity defense, or, more exactly, the plea of not guilty by reason of insanity, is in essence a plea claiming that the defendant was "insane" (a legal, not a psychological term) at the time of the crime and hence not responsible for her or his behavior. As Bartol (1983) clarified, according to law:

> . . . if a person chooses to do evil through the exercise of his or her free will, that person is exercising criminal responsibility. Insanity is the legal term which refers to an "excusing condition" from criminal responsibility. Thus, if a person is "insane" at the time of an illegal action, in most states he or she would not be guilty of the crime. (p. 115)

Criminal responsibility, and the psychologist's role in its determination, will be the primary focus of the present section. Further into this chapter, we will detail later (in the criminal justice process) utilizations of such expertise. These will include psychological testing employed to aid the court in making optimal sentencing decisions, that is, providing psychological information as part of a presentence evaluation to assist the judge in selecting among a suspended sentence, probation, incarceration, and hospitalization, and the use of test-derived information in prison settings for prisoner classification, treatment, or parole decision-making purposes.

The judgment of not guilty by reason of insanity is a difficult and, as we will see, controversial determination to make. Various standards, or rules, have been utilized as the criteria against which to make this judgment: the M'Naughton Rule (Leifer, 1964; Marshall, 1968), the Durham Rule (Bartol, 1983; Brooks, 1974), and the Model Penal Code Rule (American Law Institute, 1962). Though the M'Naughton Rule came first, and the other two were intended as improved revisions, they have not for the most part fulfilled this aspiration. In most states, the M'Naughton Rule is still in effect. Simply put, it holds that a defendant will be held not criminally responsible if he or she committed an illegal act (a) without knowing what he or she was doing at the time, and (b) without knowing right from wrong in the moral sense. These two features are sometimes described as the cognitive element of the rule, that is, that to be found guilty (held responsible) the person must understand the nature of the act and the fact that it was wrong. Several states have added a second element, a volitional one known as the *irresistible impulse test*. In this added condition for excusing responsibility "a defendant will be classed as insane if the governing power of his mind has been otherwise than voluntarily so completely destroyed that his actions are not subject to it, but are beyond his control" (Saks, 1977, p. 47).

The insanity plea is not raised often. It is used in only about 1% of criminal cases brought to trial in the United States. In California, for example, there were over a quarter of a million felony arrests and 39,000 felony convictions in 1980, but only 259 defendants were found not guilty by reason of insanity. Those defendants who raise the insanity plea tend to be predominantly white, have less than a high school education, and are often unemployed, semiskilled, and unmarried. Not only is it a plea that is not raised very often, but also, when it is, more often than not it is unsuccessful. Interestingly, those categories of defendants who tend to make successful use of the insanity plea are mothers who have committed infanticide and police officers involved in off-duty killings. Though relatively few in number, those acquitted on this basis, that is, excused or exculpated on the basis of absence of responsibility, are viewed by some as justifying in a sense the use of imprisonment for the other 99% — those who are held to know what they did, to know right from wrong, and to not be responding to an irresistible impulse.

How do psychologists typically utilize their evaluation expertise to help support or refute a plea of not guilty by reason of insanity? Since the first use of expert testimony on insanity by a psychologist in 1940 (*People v. Hawthorne*, see Comment, 1979), the acceptability of the psychologist as expert witness for this purpose has been a stormy affair. The American Psychiatric Association, in particular, has raised a steady series of objections to the admissibility of such testimony. Psychologists, however, do appear to have their unique contribution to offer such deliberations, and approximately half of the states in the United States now have statutory provisions admitting psychological evidence on insanity.

As suggested earlier, the retrospective determination of a defendant's mental state at the time a crime was committed, such determination being made at the later time of trial with the fallible interviewing and testing tools of psychiatry and psychology, is a difficult determination to make. For the psychologist, such an evaluation for criminal responsibility has typically involved the use of objective (e.g., MMPI, intelligence test) and projective (e.g., Rorschach, Sentence Completion Test) testing, supplemented by interviews with the defendant and perhaps other significant persons in his or her life, and with attention also to aspects of the defendant's history. The psychological testing component of the psychologist's contribution to determining criminal responsibility has generally been of mixed value. Test results indeed provide a measure of relevant information, but many psychological tests are of modest validity, and psychological reports based upon such tests have often contained too much inference, overgeneralization, and reliance on the implicit belief that behavior results exclusively from the person's personality, rather than taking the more accurate view that what one does (of a criminal or noncriminal nature) is a result of *both* characteristics of the person and the situational and environmental influences acting upon him or her.

As with much of its applied work, however, this application of psychology to the legal process benefits from continuing research activity. As a result of such research, not only have the quality of psychological testing and its relevance to criminal responsibility determinations gradually improved, but also two more sophisticated and highly promising psychological approaches to the evaluation of insanity have recently emerged. One relates to the more accurate use of life history information in criminal responsibility determinations; the second substantially improves the adequacy of both interview content and format used for this same purpose.

The first innovation is the "discriminant function" work of Jaffee (1981). In this highly comprehensive approach, personal history, interview, and psychological test results on two groups of defendants (one group found not guilty by reason of insanity (NGRI), the other group held criminally responsible for their crimes) were examined to determine which specific information reliably differentiated between, or discriminated, the two groups. The NGRI group proved to be significantly older, better educated, and the recipients of significantly more psychiatric hospitalizations in the past than the criminally responsible group. The latter, as compared with the NGRI group, had higher resources (e.g., married, employed) scores, more serious criminal histories, more criminal charges associated with the crime that was the focus of the evaluation and, in the past, they had committed less impulsive crimes. The Jaffe (1981) study did not find psychological test (MMPI) discriminators of the two groups.

As noted, because more or less standard psychological testing has in actual practice and research (as in the Jaffe study) often proved too fallible and nondiscriminating, some psychologists have turned instead to efforts to rigorously improve the interview format typically employed in NGRI determinations. As Rogers, Seman, and Wasyliw (1983) observed,

Traditional methods for completing insanity evaluations have involved individualistic and unvalidated approaches. As a result, there has been increased criticism of the scientific basis of such evaluations, and an argument to disinvolve psychologists and psychiatrists from criminal court proceedings. In response to a dearth of scientific research in this area, Rogers and his associates developed the RCRAS (Rogers Criminal Responsibility Assessment Scales) as one systematic and empirical approach to insanity evaluations. (p. 554)

The RCRAS was constructed in response to the American Law Institute (1962) standard for insanity, which implies that an insane defendant would show one or more of the following characteristics: (a) reliability, in the sense of relative absence of malingering; (b) evidence of severe organic disorder, (c) evidence of severe mental disorder, or psychopathology; (d) diminished cognitive control, that is, diminished awareness that she or he had committed a crime; and (e) diminished behavioral control, that is, diminished self-control over his or her crime-related behavior. The RCRAS is a structured interview sequence in which these five insanity-related domains are systematically examined and combined to arrive at a judgment with regard to criminal responsibility. To be sure, psychologists and, especially, psychiatrists have interviewed defendants for the past several decades, asking questions in all of the RCRAS areas and more. What is new and different and encouraging here is the effort by Rogers and his group to carefully develop and standardize the interview content and format, tie it closely to the components of one of the most widely accepted legal definitions of insanity, and then to rigorously and quite extensively test the discriminant validity of RCRAS-determined insanity decisions against other, independent, criteria of insanity. It is quite encouraging, in this chapter largely devoted to the relevance of the science of psychology to the practice of law, to note that these tests of RCRAS in fact turned out quite satisfactorily (Rogers & Cavanaugh, 1980, 1981; Rogers, Dolmetsch, & Cavanaugh, 1981; Rogers, Wasyliw, & Cavanaugh, 1984), and in fact have served to stimulate similar efforts by others (Slobogin, Melton, & Showalter, 1984).

As noted, the insanity defense is controversial. Some believe it to be a ruse or an unjustified means of escaping justified punishment. Such feelings seem to run particularly strong when the insanity plea is utilized, especially utilized successfully, by persons seeking to harm major public figures. In the aftermath of John Hinckley's exculpation from responsibility by reason of insanity for his shooting of President Reagan, nine states abolished the insanity defense, added the perhaps politically satisfying but philosophically contradictory possible verdict "guilty but insane," or did both. Psychology and psychiatry have attacked the insanity defense on at least a few grounds. One is that it is an often unmeetable challenge to ask the tools of these professions (tests, interviews, etc.) to establish at the time of trial the state of a defendant's psychological intellectual capacity at a considerably earlier date, when the crime occurred. A second grows from the manner in which the adversarial system leads to opposing experts, for prosecution and defense, battling in court over the alleged psychological state of the defendant at the time of the crime. These often-embarrassing encounters have led some to suggest that, if expert testimony is used, it should be used optimally in an inquisitorial and not adversarial manner (that is, experts consult with the judge). A third objection, bearing upon the irresistible-impulse addition to the M'Naughton Rule, is that no research evidence exists to suggest that any behavior is "irresistible" or totally out of the individual's control. Even more widely, many segments of the mental health professions have challenged the major philosophical and legal assumption underlying the concept of insanity (as well as most of criminal law), namely the notion of free will. Because of these beliefs, many now support the view that the insanity plea should be severely modified or even abolished. Bartol (1983) noted:

> In most cases, law adheres to the common sense view that behavior is a matter of free choice; it is the actor's act. However, when there is a suspicion of mental defect, law provides special consideration for acts which may have been the product of the defect and hence out of the actor's control and choice; the mental disease is responsible and the actor is its victim. Is this special consideration valid? There is little empirical evidence to support the assumption that mental illness robs an individual of control and free will (Morse, 1978). In terms of our present knowledge, there is little reason to believe that any behavior, non-crazy or crazy, is ever irresistible. Crazy people behave normally most of the time and in many ways. In addition, between crazy periods crazy people are not reliably distinguishable from normal people. (p. 124)

JURY DELIBERATION

Allie Rosen was tired. The trial had lasted only 3 1/2 weeks, but somehow it seemed longer. Most of it was interesting, but he didn't like being away from his job for so long. At the end, he thought he had pretty much made up his mind. Paul Hisarta's testimony, actually saying he saw Harris do it, was pretty convincing. And the two cops wouldn't have arrested him if he didn't at least act suspicious. Besides, when Harris himself testified, he seemed kind of sleazy. Just the kind of guy who might hold up a gas station. All that stuff about insanity didn't carry too much weight with Allie. He knew what crazy was; he'd visited his uncle at the state hospital four or five times. *That* was crazy. Harris was crazy like a fox!

Allie was kind of thrown, though, by the instructions the judge gave them just before sending them all off to the jury room. He didn't understand some of the words the judge used, especially the instructions about burden of proof being on the DA. Harris sure seemed guilty, and his lawyer had to prove otherwise. And how in hell could he ignore things that a witness had said right out loud. How could he make believe that something that had happened had never happened? Allie wished the judge had explained some of all this more clearly, and at the beginning of the trial, not now. As the jury walked to the jury room to begin their deliberations, Allie wondered why they hadn't been allowed to chat with each other about the evidence during the trial, and why *they* couldn't ask the witnesses questions, or even be allowed to take notes (like he used to do in school) during the trial so that he wouldn't forget

things. Strange rules they've got here, he thought, as he sat down at a big
rectangular table.

Jury Size and Decision Rules

Although only about 8% of all criminal cases are decided by a jury, in the
United States about 3,000 different courts (criminal and civil) use approximately 20 million juror days each year. Six percent of the general population
will be called for jury duty at some time in their lives. Although 12 jurors
has been the size of the American jury, the only size, since the use of juries
began in the 19th century (Winick, 1979), in recent years some jurisdictions
have been experimenting with the use of alternative sizes, particularly with
juries of six. Bartol (1983) pointed out that, in experimental studies of the
effects of jury size, small juries (6 people), as compared with large ones (12
people), allowed more participation for each individual, had fewer women
or minorities, and, in general, examined the evidence presented less carefully. The large juries provide more skills and knowledge, are potentially a
more representative cross section of the community, and provide more opportunity for a viable minority opinion (but also a powerful majority opinion) to emerge. It has been estimated that small and large juries would
disagree in their verdicts about 14% of the time (Lempert, 1975).

It is not only the size of the jury that has recently become the focus of
experimentation, but also their decision rule (Kalven & Zeisel, 1966; Saks,
1977). In the traditional decision format, the unanimous jury, all must agree
for a decision to be reached. In quorum-decision formats, some proportion
of the members of the jury is necessary for a verdict.

Research has shown that quorum juries, as compared with juries needing
unanimity for a verdict, show better recall of arguments and higher levels of
communication among its members, but they often stop deliberating when
they reach the required majority. Thus, the quorum jury provides less opportunity than those requiring unanimity for dissenters to have their say. Although unanimous juries are more likely to become hung, they do, therefore, allow for greater presentation and examination of minority viewpoints.

Communication Patterns

Davis, Keer, Atkin, Holt, and Meek (1975), and Gordon (1968) have
shown that the individual selected by the jury at the outset of its deliberations to serve as foreperson is likely to be male rather than female, to have
prior experience as a juror, to be of higher occupational status, and to be
seated at one of the end positions at the jury's rectangular table. In his
behavior, the typical foreman assumes a moderator's role, concerned with
maintaining rules of procedure and facilitating the jury's deliberation, rather

than advocating a particular point of view. Seating position is associated not only with foreman selection, but also apparently with the behavior of the other jurors as well (Hawkins, 1962). Those in the end positions participate most actively in the jury's discussion, those seated at the table's corners tend to be least active. Higher juror levels of occupational status and education are also associated with higher rates of participation. There is no apparent relationship between level of participation and juror age, although, anticipating our later discussion of jury decision making, jurors under 30 years of age tend to be more lenient in the verdicts they support than those over 30 years of age.

During the jury's deliberations, the communication flow is such that, early in the process, most comments are directed toward the jury as a whole or to those in apparent agreement with oneself (Chester, 1970). As the deliberations progress and opposing factions become clearer, statements are increasingly directed toward members who disagree with one's own viewpoint. The actual content of what is discussed is diverse. According to James (1959), the breakdown in the typical jury is juror opinions on facts of the case (29%), comments on the process of deliberation (26%), personal experiences (22%), references to testimony (15%), and references to the judge's instructions (8%). Content of statements, of course, varies from juror to juror. Less well-educated jurors appear to devote more of their comments to testimony, personal experiences, and their opinions; better-educated jurors focus relatively more on jury procedures and the judge's instructions. Juries also often discuss testimony or other matters that have been explicitly prohibited by the judge's charge to them. They have also often been shown to discuss, although it is not a part of their responsibility, the consequences for the defendant of a guilty verdict, that is, the verdict is a jury matter and sentencing, in most jurisdictions, is a prerogative of the court.

Defendant Characteristics

Though it is clearly *evidence* that looms largest in the typical juror's decision making (Dane & Wrightsman, 1982), jurors also tend to be responsive to a variety of defendant characteristics. Defendant *gender* (E. Green, 1961; Kalven & Zeisel, 1966) is one such influential quality relevant to the verdict reached. Men are five times more likely than women, for example, to be convicted of spouse murder. In laboratory research on juror behavior, conviction for grand larceny results in shorter sentences for women offenders than for men. The defendant's *physical attractiveness* is a second outcome-relevant characteristic (Mitchell & Byrne, 1972; Reynolds & Sanders, 1973). Less attractive defendants tend to receive longer sentences, at least in experimental studies of courtroom decision making. Physically attractive defendants are more likely to be acquitted, unless their attractiveness was used as a part of the crime, as in a swindle. Highly authoritarian jurors tend to be most influenced in their decision making by defendant attractiveness. Defendants whose victims were attractive receive harsher sentences, again in laboratory and not actual courtroom settings, than do those whose victims are unattractive. On both counts, defendant attractiveness and victim attractiveness, jurors are more influenced than are judges.

Defendant *race* is a third characteristic associated with juror decision making (Bell, 1973). In all too many American jurisdictions, blacks are more likely to be convicted than whites, and they are more likely to receive longer sentences. In addition, black defendants whose victims were white are treated more harshly by many jurors than are blacks whose victims were black. *Aspects of the crime* itself also influence the juror (Dane & Wrightsman, 1982; Savitsky & Sim, 1974). Was it committed alone? Presence of an accomplice leads to a more lenient juror response. Who did the planning? Defendants who play a central role in planning a crime receive longer sentences than do those who serve as accomplices. Is there more than one charge against the defendant? If the evidence is strong on one charge, jurors are less likely to convict on the second charge. Was there much suffering by the victim? The more the victim suffered, the longer the suggested sentence by the juror.

An especially important influence upon juror thinking and decision making is the defendant's *behavior during the trial* (Monahan & Loftus, 1982; Rumsey, 1976). The defendant is more likely to be found guilty if he or she appears in court in custody (e.g., in jail clothing and handcuffs) rather than on bail (e.g., in civilian clothes, without handcuffs); if extenuating circumstances relevant to the crime are presented by the defendant rather than by an impartial other person; if the defendant protests his or her innocence too extensively; or if the defendant fails to appear remorseful about the criminal behavior.

Decision Making

We have seen thus far that, in addition to the (highly influential) trial evidence, there are several factors that help shape the jury's verdict. These include the size of the jury, its decision rule (unanimous or quorum), its communication pattern, and such defendant characteristics as gender, attractiveness, race, and behavior at the time of both the crime and the trial. There are still further influences on juror decisons. One is juror bias. Toch (1979) reported that, on the average, 25% of all jurors believe an accused person is guilty; otherwise the accused wouldn't be charged. Thirty-six percent, he added, believe the defendant is responsible for proving his or her innocence, rather than that the state has to prove the defendant guilty. Juror decisions are also influenced by knowledge of a prior record on the part of the defendant. Awareness of a prior record increases juror belief that the evidence against the defendant is strong, decreases juror willingness to dismiss damaging evidence, and increases the likelihood of a guilty verdict.

Seventy-four percent of all juries deliberate for less than 2 hours. Thirty percent reach a unanimous decision on their first vote. In 90% of the instances, the final verdict favors the view held by the majority on the jury's first vote. Seldom, therefore, does a position held initially by a minority of the jury prevail. Ninety-five percent of all juries do reach a verdict. When it is reached, the judge agrees with the jury's decision about 75% of the time, with most disagreements occurring when the defendant is acquitted (Kalven & Zeisel, 1966).

The Verdict

The jury filed back in and moved quickly into the jury box. Ms. Gayle noticed that not one of them made eye contact with her or with George Harris. A bad, bad sign, she thought. The silence in the courtroom was the loudest she had ever heard. DA Hanson sat silent and still, learning forward with the trace of a confident smile on his face. When all were seated, Judge Bruce asked Harris to stand. He and Ms. Gayle slowly rose to their feet. Harris swayed perceptibly, and Ms. Gayle quickly wondered if he was about to faint.

Judge Bruce: "Has the jury reached a verdict?"
Foreman Rosen: "We have, your honor."
Judge Bruce: "How do you find?"
Foreman Rosen: "On the charge of armed robbery, guilty, your honor. On the charge of assault and battery, guilty, your honor."

On the 27th of May, 7 months to the day after the crime for which he was convicted, George Harris was sentenced to serve 9 to 15 years in Stanton State Penitentiary.

PRISON AND PAROLE

There are several actual and possible roles for the applied psychologist in, and with reference to, the contemporary prison. For custodial placement, vocational, treatment, or other purposes, classification based upon psychological testing is often employed. Although the shining goal of rehabilitation is more than slightly tarnished in many American prisons, psychological treatment in one or more of its diverse forms remains a service frequently provided by the staff or consulting psychologist. Finally, psychology plays a substantial role in contemporary corrections by applying its research expertise to the myriad of often controversial issues and innovations that characterize prison life. In this section we wish to examine these several classification, treatment, and research examples of modern applied psychology.

Classification

The effort to classify offenders in meaningful and utilitarian ways has a long and full history in the criminal justice literature. Megargee and Bohn (1979) noted that:

> For over a hundred years, behavioral scientists from several disciplines have been formulating typologies to categorize juvenile delinquents and adult offenders. Anthropologists, sociologists, criminologists, psychoanalysts, and psychologists—some using deductive heuristic methods, others inductive quantitative procedures—have divided the heterogeneous array of offenders up, down, sideways, and across on the basis of their body builds, offense history, social class, language patterns, psychodynamics, and virtually any other aspect of human beings that can be measured or observed, as well as many that cannot. (p. 25)

A classification system of value for a correctional setting is essentially a procedure for grouping or categorizing offenders (or probationers or parolees) that has direct implications for how the offenders are dealt with; which prison they are sent to, which type of custody in the prison they are placed in, which type of treatment they are offered or assigned to, and so on. Ideally, the classification system would be:

1. Objective and standardized
2. Unambiguous in its category definitions
3. Comprehensive, so that all or most offenders fit into one category or another
4. Simple, rapid, and economical, so that assignment to category can be done readily by nontechnical staff
5. Reliable, so that different raters are likely to arrive at the same classification for any given offender
6. Valid, in that it can be shown that offenders placed in each category actually possess the attributes the assignment purports they do
7. Mutually exclusive, so that any given offender fits in one, and only one, of the classification system's categories
8. Dynamic, so that significant changes in an individual can be reflected in parallel changes in classification category
9. Relevant to treatment assignment and outcome, so that there is a high likelihood of a "good prescriptive fit" between the offender and his or her treatment regime

Although a few come close, none of the diverse offender classification systems developed during the past century meets all of these criteria. Table 7.2 lists the several approaches that have been taken to offender classification.

Megargee and Bohn (1979) have carefully reviewed and evaluated these and other approaches to offender classification and, correctly we feel, concluded that

TABLE 7.2. Approaches to Offender Classification

TYPE OF CLASSIFICATION	*MAJOR EXAMPLES*
Constitutional/Physiological	Lombroso (Lindesmith & Dunham, 1941)
	Kretschmer (1925)
	Sheldon, Hartle, & McDermott (1949)
Type of offense	National Advisory Committee on
	Criminal Justice Standards and Goals
	(1973)
	Guttmacher (1960)
Type of repetitive crime pattern	Roebuck (1967)
Degree of deviance	A. Morris (1965)
	Cavan (1955)
Criminal career patterns	Glaser (1972)
	Clinard & Quinney (1973)
	Gibbons (1975)
Subculture and reference group	Sutherland (1939)
	Cloward & Ohlin (1960)
	Sykes (1958)
Social class	Ferdinand (1966)
	Rubenfeld (1965)
Psychoanalytic	Friedlander (1947)
	Sanford (1947)
	S. K. Weinberg (1952)
Development level	Hunt et al. (1972)
	Warren (1976)
Empirical/Statistical	Jenkins (1943)
	Quay (1964)
	Megargee & Bohn (1979)

Despite the proliferation of typologies, using a variety of approaches and data bases, there is no system currently available that meets the need for a broadly applicable, economical, reliable, and valid classification system for adult offenders in the variety of settings. . . . The vast majority of the typologies surveyed are far removed from application, designed more for textbooks and theoretical discussions of crime and criminals than in aiding differential decision making for correctional management and treatment. (p. 71)

Megargee and Bohn's (1979) response to this state of affairs was to seek to create a new classification system to meet and correct most of these criticisms. Their effort, still in progress, has been a largely successful one. Their approach rests primarily upon offender responses to the psychological test mentioned earlier, the MMPI, a standardized personality inventory consisting of 566 true–false items. It is a self-administered test whose results typically yield 14 scored scales, 10 of which are clinical scales measuring different dimensions of the testee's personality, and 4 of which are validity scales measuring test-taking attitudes (see Table 7.3).

The 14 MMPI scales are usually not evaluated singly, but together, for their overall patterns and configurations. Megargee and Bohn (1979) have

TABLE 7.3. Minnesota Multiphasic Personality Inventory Scale Descriptions

SCALE	NAME	NO. OF ITEMS	DESCRIPTION
		Validity Scales	
Abbreviation			
Qu	Cannot say	—	Total number of items the test taker marks "true," "false," or omits.
L	Lie	15	Measures deliberate attempts by the subject to present himself or herself in a good light.
F	Frequency or infrequency	64	Represents items rarely answered in the scored directions by normals. Indicates random responding or deliberate attempts by subject to present himself or herself in a bad light.
K	Correction	30	Indicates a general test-taking attitude of defensiveness about psychological weaknesses. The K-score is used as a correction to certain clinical scales (1, 4, 7, 8, 9) to improve their ability to discriminate normal from abnormal profiles.
		Clinical Scales	
Number and Abbreviation			
1 (Hs)	Hypochondriasis	33	Reflects abnormal concern over bodily functions and preoccupation with physical complaints.
2 (D)	Depression	60	Reflects a pessimistic world view, feelings of hopelessness and self-depreciation, possible considerations of suicide.
3 (Hy)	Hysteria	60	Measures tendency to use physical or mental symptoms to avoid stressful conflicts, often accompanied by unwillingness to accept adult responsibilities.
4 (Pd)	Psychopathic deviate	50	Measures tendency toward conflicts with authority figures, disregard of social conventions and laws, inability to learn from experience, and shallowness in personal attachments; the most frequently elevated scale among juvenile delinquent and criminal populations.
5 (Mf)	Masculinity-femininity	60	Differentiates tendency toward traditional masculine or feminine interests, attitudes, and forms of self-expression.
6 (Pa)	Paranoia	40	Reflects abnormal suspiciousness and sensitivity, possible delusions of persecution or grandeur.
7 (Pt)	Psychasthenia	48	Measures tendency toward obsessive ruminations, guilty feelings, anxiety, indecision and worrying, and compulsive ritualistic behavior.
8 (Sc)	Schizophrenia	78	Reflects bizarre or unusual thinking and behavior, interpersonal withdrawal and alienation, inappropriate affect, possible hallucinations or delusions.
9 (Ma)	Hypomania	46	Reflects high activity level, often without productivity; emotional agitation; possible euphoria and flight of ideas.
0 (Si)	Social introversion	70	Reflects shyness, social withdrawal and insecurity, and disinterest in others.

Note. From *Classifying Criminal Offenders: A New System Based on the MMPI* (pp. 77–78) by E. I. Megargee and M. J. Bohn, Jr., 1979, Beverly Hills, CA: Sage Publications. Copyright 1979 by Sage. Reprinted by permission.

administered the MMPI to several thousand offenders in diverse correctional settings, in an ongoing research effort to answer the following questions, questions that follow the sequence of hurdles one may profitably tackle when developing a new classification system:

(1) Do the MMPI profiles of youthful offenders in a federal correctional institution fall into distinct groups or clusters?

(2) Are such groups reliable? That is, does one obtain the same basic groupings in different samples?

(3) Is it possible for a clinician to sort individual MMPI profiles into such groups reliably?

(4) Is it possible to define such groups operationally so that other clinicians, or even a computer, can sort individual MMPI profiles validly?

(5) Assuming that an MMPI-based system can be derived and reliable classification is possible, do such groups differ significantly on non-MMPI variables, for example, in their life styles, social history, behavior, and dynamics?

(6) If the groups do differ in their behavior, are there clear implications for treatment?

(7) Is such treatment effective? Does each group respond better to the prescribed treatment than to other treatment modes?

(8) Can a system derived on data collected on incarcerated youthful offenders in a federal institution be generalized to offenders in other settings who differ in age, sex, and offense patterns?

(Megargee & Bohn, 1979, pp. 82–83)

The experimental results of this research program reveal very considerable progress toward the valid, reliable, economical, and prescriptively useful classification system that was its goal. Megargee and Bohn noted that:

The results indicated that the MMPI profiles of youthful offenders did appear to fall into [ten] reliable, natural groupings, and that the investigators could formulate guidelines or rules that would permit them to classify individual MMPI profiles into these types reliably. (p. 91)

In addition to differentiating the 10 types on the basis of their history and past behavior, the typology was shown to have considerable pragmatic value, as the types were found to differ significantly in their subsequent adjustment to and achievement in the institution, and even in their rates of recidivism following release. (p. 174)

This important, and in some ways exemplary, applied psychology research program continues today in its developmental efforts.

Treatment

Though its roots in prison history are long and deep, treatment, as a guiding philosophy and functional goal in prisoner management, began to flower most fully in the 1950s, as the medical-model belief grew that those committing crimes against society were "sick" and, therefore, in need of appropriate, rehabilitative care. Prior to this era, in what Irwin (1980) described as the "Big House" phase of American penology, a much more singularly custody-oriented philosophy dominated prison administration. One did one's time; "treatment" in most of its later forms essentially did not exist. In the 1950s penal philosophy changed, and with it the Big House changed also and became America's "correctional institutions." Central to this change was the heavily increased use of the indeterminate sentence, a term of imprisonment with either no minimum or maximum (e.g., from one day to life) or a fixed minimum and maximum (e.g., from 5 to 20 years).

At the heart of this new sentencing philosophy was the belief and aspiration, unfortunately far from realized in subsequent years, that such sentencing, when accompanied by appropriate classification and treatment, enabled the prisoner to be rehabilitated or cured, and when, and only when, this state was achieved, he would be paroled or released. In fact, classification has been used more for custodial placement than for determining optimal treatments, treatments have been used more for aiding prisoner management within the institution than for hastening the appropriate time of release or assisting in community adjustment. The indeterminate sentence itself, a fine idea in the abstract, has resulted in great prisoner bitterness about perceived arbitrariness and inconsistency in its use; great difficulty for parole boards in judging when a prisoner is no longer dangerous to society or is otherwise "rehabilitated"; great unfairness, in that length of sentence became based on expectations of future behavior rather than on the crime committed; and longer sentences, on the average, than when determinate sentencing, (e.g., flat or fixed times) was used.

But these failures and misuses of classification, treatment, and the indeterminate sentence itself were still in the future. In the 1950s and 1960s treatment still seemed to be *the* answer. The forms prison rehabilitation treatment took were quite diverse. At the broadest level, treatment was vocational, academic, or therapeutic, the last being the primary concern of the psychologist. *Milieu therapy*, or the therapeutic community, was among the first approaches used. *Group counseling* has been the most common; *behavior modification* the most controversial. For different reasons, worth illustrating here, none of these three approaches "worked" in the sense that it did not yield substantial numbers of rehabilitated prisoners or low rates of recidivism. An understanding of why these approaches failed will help explain the near-demise of the rehabilitation approach more generally.

The therapeutic community was, at its heart, an effort to reorganize and reorient at least certain major aspects of prison life to give prisoners more of a sense of responsibility for themselves, ideally beginning to prepare them for later independent community functioning. But added responsibility or power for the prisoner had to come from someone else's supply, and custodially oriented, conservative prison officials and employees overtly and covertly sabotaged the effort. As Irwin (1980) explained, "policy makers, administrators and staff continued to demand that the main purpose of prison, taking precedence over such rehabilitation, was punishment, control and restraint of prisoners" (p. 46).

Group counseling fared no better. Though the most frequently used rehabilitation approach, its leaders were quite typically poorly trained, and, as with all treatments provided to help one change enough to secure one's parole from prison, prisoner participation all too often became impression-management. As Bartol (1983) comments, "institutional treatment suffers from the faulty logic that psychological change can be coerced. Traditional forms of psychological treatment have been successful only when subjects were willing and motivated to participate" (p. 295).

Behavior modification, in our view potentially the most effective rehabilitative approach, has paradoxically fared the worst in prison settings. In addition to a small but highly publicized number of instances of its misuse, behavior modification early on acquired a particularly bad reputation, because it was confused with such totally unrelated procedures as psychosurgery and chemical or electrical aversion techniques (behavior modification is the application of laboratory-derived procedures for enhancing human learning). And, as with the methods just described, it also failed because all too many prison staff essentially did not want rehabilitation to succeed.

Many other forms of psychological treatment have been employed in prison settings. These include individual psychotherapy of diverse types (Adams, 1961; Lipton, Martinson, & Wilks, 1975), reality therapy (Glasser, 1965), guided group interaction (McCorkle, Elias, & Bixby, 1958), positive peer culture (Vorrath & Brendtro, 1974), and several types of group psychotherapy (Lipton et al., 1975). These and related approaches have suffered in their outcomes from the political and philosophical difficulties we have noted.

It is our firm belief that the death of rehabilitation in most segments of the American penal system was far too premature. We believe rehabilitation can work with many prisoners, but that, as both an operating philosophy and a treatment reality, it never received fair, extended, and appropriate trials. Psychological treatments of diverse types do change offender behavior in ways that increase functioning effectiveness and personal satisfaction, *if* the treatments are used prescriptively. As T. Palmer (1978) and A. P. Goldstein and Stein (1976) have put forth elsewhere, there is evidence to believe that, although no treatments work with all offenders, almost all treatments work with some. It is our task as applied psychologists, therefore, to conduct the kinds of research that enable us to classify prisoners in ways relevant to assigning them to optimal treatments—prisoner A to group therapy, prisoner B to behavior modification, and so forth.

Such differential treatment work has barely begun, but what has been conducted appears especially promising (T. Palmer, 1978; Warren, 1974). Optimally, treatment would be offered voluntarily, and prisoners could seek it or not noncoercively, in a manner not relevant to parole decisions. The possibility of such voluntarism and avoidance of the use of treatment for institutional management purposes would obviously be enhanced to the degree that American society made greater use of alternatives to incarceration, by diverting certain types of offenders (again, a classification problem) from prison altogether. Nonviolent criminals and offenders in victimless crimes certainly ought to be considered for such a possibility. There are many other sentencing alternatives available that similarly could provide new and unexplored opportunities for noncoercive, voluntary, noninstitutional uses of psychological treatments: graduated release, work furlough, home release, halfway house, reentry centers, transitional centers, and so forth. Crucial to the success of the treatment process, as demonstrated all too well by its failure, is the role of the prison staff and other criminal justice agents in the offender's life. It must be made not only possible and desirable, but also regularly rewarding, for staff to accept, encourage, and aid prisoners' psychological change, not so much in ways that enhance institutional management, but much more clearly related to effective, competent, and satisfying functioning in nonprison, community settings. Such staff reorientation is indeed a major research, administrative, and psychological challenge.

Research

Along with the purported failure of rehabilitation, or, as we prefer, the failure to use and evaluate rehabilitation approaches fully and fairly, several other forces of the late 1960s and 1970s combined to change the typical American prison system once again, this time from the correctional institution to the volatile and violent contemporary prison. Increased use of diversion and other alternatives to incarceration meant that an ever greater percentage of those sent to prison had engaged in violent crimes. Violent gangs organized along ethnic lines, first on the outside and then in prison, came to exist in and then dominate the prison population. Prisoner strikes, the prisoner rights movement, the black power movement, the fading of the older prisoner power structure, increased recidivism, longer sentences, crowded conditions, and the more explicit reemergence of the custody orientation to penology all directly or indirectly came together to change the American prison in new and often frightening ways. Gang fighting, attacks on guards, indiscriminate attacks on fellow prisoners, and full-scale prison rioting increased. As Irwin (1980) comments:

Today the respected public prison figure . . . stands ready to kill to protect himself, maintains strong loyalties to some small group of other convicts (invariably of his own race), and will rob and attack or at least tolerate his friends' robbing and attacking other weak independents or their foes. He openly and stubbornly opposes the administration, even if this results in harsh punishment. Finally, he is extremely assertive of his masculine sexuality. . . . Today prisoners who embrace versions of this ideal and live according to it . . . dominate the indigenous life of the large violent prisons. They control the contraband distribution systems, prison politics, the public areas of the prison, and any pan-prison activities, such as demonstrations and prisoner representative organizations. (p. 195)

This depiction of the modern American prison substantially helps set the priority research agenda for the applied psychologist concerned with prison functioning. Violence must be the number-one topic. Its causes, its control, and the creation of alternatives to it are research avenues well worth pursuing. One of the more enduring theories about the causes of human aggression points to frustration in its various forms as the responsible agent. In a penal context, the sources of frustration are both diverse and plentiful: loss of freedom, separation from loved ones, moral rejection by the free community, crowding, lack of privacy, excessive noise, idleness, physical and homosexual threat, many and often arbitrary rules and regulations, enforced deference, helplessness and dependency, and more. For too long researchers have looked mostly *in the person* — his or her personality, character, history — to understand why violence occurs. Future research on prison violence would ideally examine carefully the several sources of *environmental* frustration we have just listed. Regarding the control of aggression, and creating alternative behaviors to it, there now exists a series of highly promising new treatment directions that appear to be well worth pursuing. These include anger-control training (Novaco, 1975), cognitive-stress inoculation (Meichenbaum & Jaremko, 1983), and psychological skills training (A. P. Goldstein, 1981). Each is clearly worthy of considerable research effort.

In addition to the study of classification, treatment, prison living conditions, and prison violence, there remains a wide host of other aspects of contemporary corrections deserving the research scrutiny of the applied psychologist. Perhaps most important among these priorities, in terms of their potential consequences for positive impact upon the correctional process, are research on the selection and training of prison personnel, the consequences of different approaches to sentencing, alternatives to incarceration and, of special relevance to parole decisions, the prediction of dangerousness.

> Ten and a half years had passed. George Harris was now almost 30 years old, although on most days he felt much older. It had been a terrible 10½ years. Stanton might not have been the worst prison in the state, but it had been

plenty bad for George. For most of his sentence so far, he'd shared a two-man cell with two other men. He'd been raped twice, had his nose and jaw broken once, and voluntarily spent almost a year out of the general population and in protective custody after getting on the wrong side of the most powerful gang in his cell block. Three years ago he made a sort of knife from a piece of metal he stole from the license plate shop, and he'd carried it with him ever since whenever he could.

Visitors never came to see George, except, once in a while, his uncle. Time passed very, very slowly. There wasn't much to do at Stanton. He lifted weights some, got his arms tattooed, watched a lot of television, tried reading law books once or twice, but he mostly hung out, spaced out, and passively watched the days, months, and years drift by. Ten and a half years had passed.

Early in the ninth year of his sentence, George came up for parole consideration. It went badly. Although Mr. Aronso, the victim of George's assault, had long since fully recovered, the violence of his crime still weighed heavily with the parole board. Their decision was not to parole. Now, a year and a half later, George was about to come before them again.

Parole is the conditional release of inmates from prison back to the community after a portion of their sentence has been served. As of 1984, there were approximately 300,000 juveniles and adults on parole in the United States, under the supervision of over 2,000 separate parole agencies. Most such agencies function under the jurisdiction of state departments of corrections. Parole boards usually start to review inmates after one third of their sentences are served. If parole is granted, it is almost always under certain conditions and stipulations, mostly concerned with a stable home environment, potential employment, and likely risk to the community. The number and reasonableness of such parole conditions vary greatly from one jurisdiction to another. The conditions might specifically include obtaining and keeping a job, attending academic or vocational schools, participating in drug or alcoholism counseling, attending church, reporting in daily, and not drinking, signing contracts, associating with former prisoners, moving one's residence, voting, or traveling out of state. The typical parolee in recent years has received an average of 13 such conditions.

The use of parole began in 16th-century England, with the granting of reprieves and stays of execution to criminals who were physically fit for employment overseas, to work in the American colonies. A more graduated, transitional system of parole emerged in certain other European countries. Ireland (Smykla, 1984), for example, moved prisoners stepwise from strict imprisonment to government labor (chain gangs) to individual labor to "tickets of leave" involving first a conditional, and then a full, pardon. The first parole ("good time") law in the United States appeared in New York in 1817, with its major implementation being at the Elmira (New York) Reformatory in 1876. Sentences there were indeterminate, their length a function of good behavior, and postrelease parole supervision heavily emphasized gainful employment. The use of parole spread across the United States, and, by 1929, all states utilized it. Smykla (1984) asserted that parole became widespread not because its use facilitated rehabilitation or reduced recidivism, but because it helped prison administrators (via good-behavior-enhancing chances of parole) maintain a more peaceful and orderly prison environment, helped district attorneys plea-bargain (longer sentences were more attractive to defendants if the possibility of earlier parole existed), and helped the community, in that it extended supervision and surveillance of ex-inmates into their community's functioning.

There are two major problems with the parole process, however. It often doesn't work fairly and effectively before the inmate's release, and it often doesn't work fairly and effectively after the inmate's release. The parole decision-making process prior to an inmate's release suffers, first of all, from all the difficulties associated with its companion procedure, the indeterminate sentence. The parole decision can be highly arbitrary, capricious, and the result of a changing and prejudicial decision-making process. As we saw earlier, this process helps distort the meaning of treatment and rehabilitation in a prison context, and, to a substantial degree, denies or diminishes the legal due process to which the inmate is entitled because the parole board, not a trial judge, actually determines the length of sentence.

An especially strong objection to the parole process has been raised regarding the degree to which it reflects not only the inmate's past behavior, crime, and in-prison behavior, but also, many believe quite unfairly, what he is or is not likely to do in the future. This latter basis for reaching a parole decision is held to be unjust not only because it is an example of preventive detention (holding someone in prison longer because of something he or she might do, rather than for a crime actually committed), but also because psychological research consistently demonstrates great difficulty in predicting dangerousness. Essentially without exception, studies have failed in their diverse efforts to predict future dangerousness. In fact, as Bartol (1983) explained, even " . . . the most sophisticated methods yield 60 to 70% false positives, i.e., people said to be dangerous who are not" (p. 104).

Dangerousness is so difficult to predict for several reasons. First, violent behavior on the part of even the more chronically aggressive person is still an infrequent and perhaps rare event, and rare events of any type are difficult to predict. Second, there has only been modest progress in identifying those factors in the person's history and personality that are causatively related to violence. Third, although we do not yet know enough about qualities of a person that predict future violence, we know even less about environmental qualities conducive to such behavior. In fact, psychological research has looked at environments for such purposes far too little in the past, a perspective that is changing in recent years. We now know that *while in prison*, a person's likelihood of engaging in violent behavior is a function not only of qualities of that person, but also of such environmental attributes as the prison's noise level, crowdedness, opportunity for privacy, turnover of inmates, internal traffic (cell-changing frequency), and overall size. To the extent that future psychological research yields analogous information about aggression-encouraging qualities of nonprison environments might our predictions of dangerousness improve.

As matters stand at the present, psychological research has identified some variables of *groups* of individuals more likely to behave violently (age, sex, race, socioeconomic status, drug and alcohol abuse), but this information has not yet proven useful in predicting the future dangerousness of any given *individual* (Monahan, 1981). The same is true for childhood characteristics of individuals who later, as adults, behave violently. On the average, but again of little value in predicting individual violence, adults who behave violently are more likely to have been children who received little mothering, were enuretic, set fires, were cruel to animals, and were abused by one or both parents (R. Goldstein, 1974; Hellman & Blackman, 1966). History of mental illness or current mental illness are *not* predictive of violence, as such persons have been shown to commit acts of violence no more frequently than do persons not so labeled. As is true for all behaviors, perhaps the best single predictor of future violence, weak as it might be, is past violent behaviors. Interestingly, and appropriately, we feel, given the inadequate state of knowledge in this area, the State of Alabama has adopted an approach to prison classification we feel could have much to teach those concerned with parole decisions.

> The Alabama model demanded that compelling behavioral evidence of violent action be documented before an inmate could be categorized as dangerous. . . . In essence, this model attended only to the severity, frequency and recency of overt acts of violence against others. Classifications were made on those "more visible" criteria, and not on what experts thought about the clinical dynamics of an inmate's mind or emotions. (Smykla, 1984, pp. 190–191)

We noted earlier that there were serious problems associated with the parole process both at the decision-making stage, which we have examined, and after an inmate's release to community supervision. There are several problems associated with this latter phase. Parole officers are poorly trained, poorly paid, and usually burdened with caseloads so large that only cursory supervision is possible. When rendering supervision, they are typically caught in the conflicting roles of cop and counselor, mandated to carry out both supervision helpful to the ex-inmate and surveillance helpful to the community. Perhaps most consequential about the postrelease phase of the parole process is the absence of evidence that the sequence of indeterminate sentencing–rehabilitative treatment has had any beneficial effect on recidivism rates. Clearly, there is a strong movement in the United States to abolish this process and, instead of indeterminate sentencing, treatment, and parole, use determinate sentencing in which both a fixed length of sentence and a fixed reduction in sentence for good behavior are stipulated at the posttrial sentencing.

As we sought to make clear in our discussion of the ways in which rehabilitative treatments have yet to receive full and fair trials, we also feel parole to be a valuable legal process whose perhaps imminent demise is due more to its misuse or inadequate implementation than its inherent weaknesses. We agree with Smykla (1984), who urged that new and different life be breathed into the parole process. In such new and probably more adequate form, parole would be more decentralized, parole officers would do less one-on-one casework and invest more time and energy in identifying and mobilizing community resources of value to the parolee, and greater emphasis would be placed upon finding or developing jobs for ex-inmates. Just as we held earlier that inmates in prison needed a diverse array of prescriptively assigned rehabilitative treatment, we now assert that parole will work best when it is viewed and prescriptively utilized as but one of many alternative means for dealing with offenders. Other alternatives proposed by Smykla (1984) in this regard included community service orders, day fines, monetary restitution, neighborhood justice arbitration, nonresidential and residential care centers, work release, graduated release and such split sentences (a combination of incarceration and community supervision) as shock probation (90 days of incarceration followed by parole eligibility), and weekend jail. The alternatives are many. To nonprescriptively move in any single direction, be it determinate sentencing or any other, will inevitably lead to yet more injustice in America's criminal justice system.

> The sunlight temporarily blinded George Harris, as he stepped through Stanton prison's main door into the world of free men. Almost 11 years of his life gone. His uncle leaned against his car, waiting for George. George walked over, silently hugged the old man, and then quickly got in the car. As they drove away down Riverton Street toward the city, George never looked back.

THE FUTURE OF PSYCHOLOGY AND THE LAW

As we noted at the beginning of this chapter, psychology and law largely went their separate ways until recent decades. Their interaction began in earnest in the 1960s, and, since that time, a growing number of applied psychologists have by their research and direct services made important, if beginning, contributions to both our understanding of the legal process and its effective functioning. Their concerns have been varied: selection and training of police; reduction of police officer stress; jury selection; accuracy of eyewitness testimony; detection of deception; effects of defendant and witness characteristics; jury deliberation and decision-making processes; jury size, decision, decision rules, and communication patterns; use of psychological evaluations to help establish competence to stand trial and criminal responsibility; offender sentencing alternatives; classification and treatment in prison settings; prison conditions and prison violence; prediction of dangerousness; parole and other forms of community supervision, and still other related topics. All of these domains of psychological–legal interest are clearly worthy of continued public and professional concern and debate, as well as rigorous study and experimentation.

There are yet additional concerns of a psychological and legal nature that might profitably occupy the future attention of the applied psychologist. A small sampling of these topics includes research on

1. The development of legal and moral thinking in children (Tapp & Levine, 1977)
2. The law-breaking process (Farrington, Hawkins, & Lloyd-Bostock, 1979)
3. Witness and bystander behavior (Latane & Darley, 1970)
4. Qualities of perpetrators of crime who do and do not get apprehended (Farrington, Hawkins, & Lloyd-Bostock, 1979)
5. Qualities of resilient youth, such as those growing up in high delinquency areas who do not become juvenile delinquents themselves (Gable, 1985)
6. The (usually well-hidden) plea-bargaining process (Lind, 1982)
7. Legal language and means of enhancing its understandability (Danet, 1980)
8. Such alternatives to trial as mediation, arbitration, and negotiation (Lind, 1982)
9. Parents' and children's legal rights (Tapp, 1977)
10. The use of alternative jury formats such as twin juries and science juries. (Saks, 1982)
11. Domains of law other than criminal justice, such as labor law, tax law, contract law, and torts (Monahan & Loftus, 1982).

In realms such as these, as well as in most of its other particulars, the law is at root a human endeavor. Psychology is the science of human behavior. There remains much for the applied psychologist to contribute.

8 Sports Applications

1992 FINAL LEAGUE STANDINGS NORTHEASTERN LEAGUE				
Team	Wins	Losses	Percent	Games Behind
Manhattan Maulers	57	27	.679	—
Port Jefferson Jesters	50	34	.595	7
Newark Eagles	46	39	.541	11 1/2
Coney Island Cyclones	41	43	.488	16
Norristown Rockets	39	47	.453	19
Harrisburg Blues	36	46	.439	20
Camden Sluggers	33	49	.402	23

The serious and sustained interest of applied psychologists in sports and athletic performance is, compared with other fields of applied psychology, largely a recent development. To be sure, a few early examples of such interest exist, but only a very few. The earliest seems to be the work of Tripplett in 1897, occurring at a time when psychology was especially concerned with motor learning and performance. Tripplett's research was among the first to examine the effects of an audience on motor behavior (a topic we return to later in this chapter), in this case, competitive bicycling. In the 1920s, Coleman Griffith at the University of Illinois conducted the first sustained sports psychology research program. Using the research methods of that era, among other topics he studied the "automatic triggering of responses" with Harold "Red" Grange as his research subject; through correspondence with Knute Rockne he gathered subjective information regarding athlete motivation. He established the Athletic Research Laboratory at the University of Illinois in 1925 and published the books *Psychology of Coaching* (1926) and *Psychology and Athletics* (1928), based largely on the studies conducted there and on his own creative speculations. Coleman Griffith, for these several reasons, is usually thought of as the father of sports psychology.

In the years between the 1920s and the 1970s, very little research or writing in sports psychology took place in the United States, and what did occur was of relatively modest theoretical or applied value (e.g., on self-administered personality inventories). Most of the relevant research during this period was conducted in the Soviet Union and Eastern Europe on such topics as motor learning, cardiorespiratory fitness, strength development, muscular endurance, and related topics. Even including these exceptions, the degree to which psychological findings and methods of research had been applied to athletic activities by the early 1970s was meager indeed. As Straub (1980) observed,

> The mind is sport science's last frontier. All other systems have been extensively used to improve athletes' performance . . . the physiology of muscle contraction . . . nutrition . . . kinesiology, the science of human movement . . . the design of equipment, human engineering . . . even the athlete's blood has been sampled and his/her biorhythms charted. Only the mind seems to have been neglected. (p. 13)

In the early 1970s, this pattern of relative neglect began to change. With the encouragement and collaboration of both physical educators working in academic settings and the management and players on professional athletic teams in several sports, a broad spectrum of concerns relevant to athletic behavior became the target of applied psychological research and theory. It is these several topics that will be the focus of this chapter; research on team leadership, player personality and motivation, determinants of athletic performance and psychological interventions for improving such performance, aggression in sports, team cohesiveness, and a host of related concerns. A great deal of interesting research of considerable applied value has gone on in a relatively short period of time, research we now wish to present and examine.

Arthur Larsen, owner of the Coney Island Cyclones, was unhappy with their fourth-place finish last year and was determined to do something about it. On December 1, after a long search and much consideration, he took the first step. Larsen called a press conference and announced that the team's manager, Oscar Barnes, was fired. Effective immediately, the Cyclones' manager for the 1993 season would be Tony Scarpo, the just-retired center fielder from their parent major-league team.

LEADERSHIP

The topic of leadership has long been an active concern of the applied psychologist, especially in industrial and business contexts. Only recently has such concern been directed toward the manager, the coach, the team captain, or the emergent leader in athletics. Historically, leadership, in athletics or elsewhere, has largely been viewed as a quality of the leader, either something the leader inherited or was born with or was trained for. The "Great Man" theory of leadership, popular until the 1940s, is a prominent example of such a viewpoint. This view gave rise to a widespread, energetic, and largely unsuccessful hunt for reliable "leadership personality traits." As with the general failure of extensive psychological research to discover reliable personality correlates of superior athletic performance, so too with leadership, whether in athletics or elsewhere. To be sure, beliefs about leader personality traits abound. As Straub (1980) notes, for example:

> The traditional view of successful coaches is that they are dominant, authoritarian, hardworking, artless, tough minded and manipulative. They are also thought to be task-oriented rather than player-centered . . . as leaders, most coaches believe in strong discipline, rigid rules, extrinsic motivation, and impersonal approaches toward their players. (p. 385)

In contrast with this view of effective leadership as due to internal qualities of the leader, modern psychological thinking takes a predominantly *situational* view of leadership. Carron (1980) succinctly presented this viewpoint in his observation:

> . . . it is [now] generally accepted that there are no inherent traits or dispositions within an individual which contribute to ascendancy and maintenance of leadership. Instead, it is believed that the specific requirements of different situations dictate the particular leadership qualities which will be most effective. (pp. 126–127)

Such situational thinking about leadership leads to two research tasks. The first is identification of the specific *behaviors*, not traits, characteristic of acts of leadership, and then the prescriptive determination of which leader behaviors are optimal for which players and which athletic situations. Successful leadership, in this effort, then, becomes a matter of matching leader behaviors with appropriate situations (players, events) in which the behaviors would ideally be used.

The Ohio State Leadership Studies (Hemphill & Coons, 1957) identified the following behaviors as constituting what leaders actually do: initiation, membership, representation, integration, organization, domination, communication, recognition, and production. Consistent with a view that holds effective leadership to vary with the situation, Chelladurai and Saleh (1978) reexamined the Ohio State results in an athletic context. Leadership in the sport of amateur hockey appeared to be reflected in five types of behavior, as Table 8.1 elaborates. Though their language is somewhat different, the Ohio State and Chelladurai and Saleh studies both yielded similar dimensions of leadership behavior, some largely task-oriented in focus, others more concerned with interpersonal relationship aspects of the team or other group being led.

Just as progress has been made in identifying leader behaviors to be optimally matched to situations, so too has at least beginning progress been

TABLE 8.1. Leader Behavior Dimensions in Sport

DIMENSION	DESCRIPTION
Training behavior	Behavior aimed at improving the performance level of the athletes by emphasizing and facilitating hard and strenuous training, clarifying the relationships among the members
Autocratic behavior	Tendency of the coach to set himself (herself), apart from the athletes, and to make all decisions by himself (herself)
Democratic behavior	Behavior of the coach that allows greater participation by the athletes in deciding on group goals, practice methods, and game tactics and strategies
Social support behavior	Behavior of the coach indicating his (her) concern for individual athletes and their welfare and for positive group atmosphere
Rewarding behavior	Behavior of the coach that provides reinforcement for an athlete by recognizing and rewarding good performance

Note. Adapted from "Preferred Leadership in Sport" by P. Chelladurai and S. D. Saleh, 1978, *Canadian Journal of Applied Sport Sciences*, 3, 85–97.

made in our ability to describe and categorize aspects of the athletic situation to which such matches could ideally be made. Straub (1980) suggested that effective matching of leader behaviors with situations would incorporate not only the major situational feature to which effective leaders should respond differentially, the player himself or herself, but also the sport, the team, team standing, time of season, time of game, and whether the athletes are on an interacting team (e.g., basketball, football) or a coaching team (e.g., track, tennis). In more direct emphasis on player characteristics that optimally require different coaching leadership behaviors, Carron (1980) stressed the player's centrality in the team's decision-making process (e.g., quarterbacks, catchers, and playmaking guards often require similar coaching) and the degree of stress a player is undergoing at the moment (e.g., the greater the stress, the more acceptable and appropriate might be authoritarian leadership behaviors). In a nonathletic leadership research context, Schutz (1958) has shown leadership effectiveness to be maximized when leader and led are compatible to the degree that each wishes to express to others and receive from others three basic types of interpersonal behavior: inclusion, affection, and control. Carron and Bennett (1977) and Cratty (1981) have creatively illustrated the manner in which this general finding might also apply in a sports context.

To be sure, the prescriptive, situation-specific view of optimal leadership behavior as applied to athletics is in its infancy. It is important to note, however, that this approach to maximizing the effectiveness of leadership has been shown to be highly successful in other applied psychological arenas including industry (Hersey & Blanchard, 1969, 1977; G. G. Stern, 1970), education (Cronbach & Snow, 1977; D. E. Hunt, 1971), and psychotherapy (A. P. Goldstein, 1978; Goldstein & Stein, 1976; Magaro, 1969). We strongly suspect that further research will yield similar positive support for this view of leadership, whether the leader is a baseball team manager, a football team coach, a hockey team player-captain, or a similar sports figure.

Tomorrow was the first game of the exhibition season. Tony Scarpo was enjoying a quiet moment, thinking how hectic the last 3 months had been. No sooner had he signed the contract to manage the Cyclones last December, than Art Larsen let him know in no uncertain terms that he wanted a winner in 1993. Not 5 years from now, or even 2, but this very next year. Larsen promised he'd put his checkbook to work, to help Scarpo build a winning team—trades, hirings, firings, up from the farm system, whatever it took. Scarpo had taken him at his word. Hank Watkins, the hotshot young left fielder had been bought from Roanoke. Red Wingo, a kid with a golden glove if there ever was one, was brought up from Syracuse. Some sending down had to go on also, but Scarpo bit the bullet, told himself it went with the territory, and let several players go. In all, there were 11 new faces on the 25-man team he had built when Scarpo got them all together for the first day of spring training. He wondered who would be good, who would be great, and who would he be letting go next year at this time?

PERSONALITY AND ATHLETIC PERFORMANCE

Dozens, perhaps hundreds, of investigations have been conducted in the search for personality characteristics of successful athletes. Such research has ventured into baseball, football, cross-country skiing, golf, karate, marathon running, swimming, scuba diving, tennis, track, wrestling, and parachuting. These studies have compared athletes versus nonathletes, athletes differing in ability level, athletes from different sports, team versus individual sport athletes, combative versus noncombative sport athletes, and athletes from different institutions. This search for personality differences, examined across many, many, different personality traits would, if successful, provide exceedingly valuable information for the screening, recruitment, selection, and training of athletes. If successful players in a given sport were shown to usually possess personality characteristics A, B, C, and D, such persons might, with great potential benefit to a team, be actively sought, bought, and taught, and a pennant might result! Or, at least, that was the applied researcher's dream. For the most part, however, reality proved to be quite different. To be sure, some personality qualities of successful athletes were identified. Suinn (1980b) and others pointed to high extroversion and low neuroticism as two such frequently found traits. Ogilvie (1976) singled out self-discipline, dominance, stability, venturesomeness, and capacity for emotional control. Browne and Mahoney (1984) commented,

> . . . in general, the successful athlete will score higher than the less successful one on personality attributes of assertion, dominance, aggression, reservation,

self-sufficiency, and need for achievement, and he/she will score lower on
. . . emotionality, anxiety, depression, schizoid features, fatigue and confusion. (p. 610)

Many more such findings could be cited, but almost all proved to be
single-study, test-specific, nonreplicable results. Two reasons clearly exist for
this disappointing research outcome. First, most such research was weak in
both conception and design. Conceptually, the research strategy governing
much of the personality and performance research effort was, as Ryan
(1968) noted:

> . . . of the shotgun variety. By that I mean the investigator grabbed the nearest
> and most convenient personality test, and the closest sports group, and with
> little or no theoretical basis for their selection, fired into the air to see what
> they could bring down. It isn't surprising that firing into the air at different
> times and at different places, and using different ammunition, should result in
> different findings. In fact, it would be surprising if the results weren't contra-
> dictory and confusing. (p. 17)

And so they are largely just that, contradictory and confusing. Experimental design weaknesses in this body of research appear to be unusually
plentiful, including, according to Carron (1980); Horsfall, Fisher, and
Morris, (1980); Martens (1976); and Suinn (1980a):

1. Inadequately defined and operationalized variables, for example, focus
   on abnormality and deficiency rather than personality strengths
2. Poor sampling procedures, for example, what defines "an athlete"
3. Inappropriate selection of measures, for example, "choice by scale title,"
   poor validity and reliability, response sets
4. Investigator expectancy effects, for example, investigator expectancies
   influencing subject responses
5. Inappropriate statistical analyses, for example, use of multiple *t* tests
6. Interpretive errors in explaining results, for example, leveling, ignoring
   nondifferences, noncriticalness, implying causation from correlation, inadequate social validity

Beyond such weaknesses of design and execution, it seems to us that the
major failure of personality-performance research is its basic, underlying
assumption that enduring personality traits of the athlete are so substantially associated with athletic ability and performance that such a predictive
relationship is reliably obtainable. As we saw was the case with efforts
aimed at identifying leaders in athletic contexts and elsewhere, one cannot
do so simply on the basis of personality-trait predictors. Athletic performance certainly derives in part from such qualities of the athlete, but apparently only in small part. Results indicate that level of athletic performance
also grows from other characteristics of the person (e.g., motivation, anxi-

ety, competitiveness, a variety of physical attributes) and his or her situation, or, the total athletic context in which the performance is inacted (e.g., home or away; size of audience; audience communications; score of game; standing in league; communications from manager, coach, teammates, opposition players). The interaction of these variables with one another and with such person variables as those just noted is also an important influence. The interactionist view of personality, in which overt behavior is a joint result of enduring personality characteristics and a wide host of situational or contextual influences, appears very much to apply also to athletic performance.

Finally, were these several reservations and salient criticisms not enough, the search for personality correlates of athletic performance may be faulted on yet one additional basis. Kroll (1976) has cogently pointed out that, even were such relationships to be reliably found, one still cannot conclude that the *meaning* of the correlations involved is that persons with certain personality traits select and excel in particular sports. High positive correlations between one or more traits and outstanding performance might, alternatively, reflect situations in which (a) players in a sport share no common personality characteristics at first, but through personality modification of those remaining in the sport and attrition of those who don't, those who remain are homogeneously high on the trait(s), or (b) there are common personality characteristics among rookies, but through personality modification and attrition, veterans possess very different personality traits. In either instance, a strong, positive correlation of personality trait and performance would be of no value for the recruitment, selection, assignment, and training purposes noted earlier as lying at the heart of the applied interest in this subarea of sports psychology. Thus, we can broadly conclude that personality-performance research, its extensiveness notwithstanding, has thus far yielded exceedingly little payoff for either the applied researcher or the athletic practitioner. It is hoped that its recent move toward an interactionist, person-times-situation perspective will enhance its future applied value for both.

Sixteen wins, seven losses, Tony bragged to no one in particular. He sat in the locker-room, the last exhibition game now over. The new kids had done fine, at least most of them. Starting the preseason with five straight wins seemed to pump everyone up at first. Next Tuesday it would start for real, and Tony wondered how he'd keep them giving that little extra that seemed to make a big difference. "Hell," he thought, "what am I worried about? Most of these guys can hardly wait for the season to begin."

MOTIVATION

Motivation is defined in psychology as that state that gives both direction and intensity to behavior. For the applied psychologist concerned with athletic motivation, direction and intensity translate into the directionality question, Why does someone choose to become an athlete and engage in athletics in the first place? and the intensity question, Why, after having chosen to do so, does one persist energetically in athletic behaviors?

Direction

Alderman (1980) proposed a comprehensive listing of needs, or incentives, that might motivate young athletes to choose to engage in sports activities:

1. *Affiliation.* Making or maintaining friendships, social intercourse
2. *Power.* The opportunity to influence or control others
3. *Independence.* The chance to do things on one's own
4. *Stress.* Activities characterized by excitement, tension, action, or pressure
5. *Excellence.* The opportunity to do something well
6. *Success.* The chance to receive extrinsic reward, for example, approval, status, trophies
7. *Aggression.* The opportunity to dominate, subdue, or intimidate

Across large samples of youngsters differing in age, culture, and the major sport in which they were participating, Alderman (1980) found affiliation and excellence to be the strongest and most consistent motivators, stress incentives to be a consistent third, and aggression and independence to be relatively unimportant. The investigators proposed that the applied motivational significance of this research, for coaches of young athletes in particular, is the desirability of keeping the sports context both social and interpersonally pleasant and a setting that provides opportunities for the expression of individual excellence.

Youngblood and Suinn (1980) addressed a similar question in their research, namely, What needs are involved in becoming and remaining an athlete? Their Motivational Assessment Scale, as Table 8.2 details, presents 19 possible categories of athletic motivation. Such a measurement approach offers not only a potential means of measuring the motivational bases for an individual's sports participation, but also an *individualizing* device by means of which the coach can understand how best to increase the motivation of a given athlete by means of his or her individual channels of motivational accessability. As Youngblood and Suinn (1980) explained,

> Using the [individual motivational] profile approach, the coach might instead [of a pep talk for everybody] elect to offer personal support for the athlete characterized by high Social Approval scores, discuss the rival competition with the athlete high on Competition, inquire about the personal or career development of the athlete with high emphasis on Family, set and plot training goals for the competitor who emphasizes Success Achievement. . . . (p. 77)

The Motivational Assessment Scale, although relatively new and still in need of empirical scrutiny to establish its validity and reliability, clearly points us

TABLE **8.2.** Motivational Categories

Category 1: Social Approval
a. Parental approval
b. Peer approval
c. Opposite sex approval
d. Coach approval
e. Same sex approval

Category 2: Competition
a. Against time
b. Against fellow team members
c. Competing rather than practicing
d. Against rival teams
e. Defeating specific competitors

Category 3: Self-mastery
a. Mentally push yourself farther
b. Achieve control of mind over body
c. Feeling more in control of body movements
d. More control of personal emotions
e. Learn new skills

Category 4: Life-Style
a. Family participation
b. Habit
c. Lack of something better to do
d. Introduced to activity at early age
e. Parents decided for you

Category 5: Fear of Failure
a. Critical comments from others
b. What others might say
c. Self-criticism
d. Finish in last place
e. How others view your performances

Category 6: Physical Fitness and Health
a. Feel healthier
b. Increased muscle tone
c. Keep in good shape
d. Greater physical strength
e. Sense of physical well-being

Category 7. Friendship and Personal Associations
a. Fellow team members
b. Meeting other competitors at contests
c. Meeting other teams' coaches
d. Meeting athletes of other sports
e. Meeting famous athletes

Category 8: Success and Achievement
a. Achieve more in practice
b. Being a participant in an important contest
c. Achieve in training periods

d. Achieve personal goals
e. Setting higher levels of achievement

Category 9: Tangible Payoffs
a. Athletic scholarship
b. Travel
c. Extra awards (extra coaching, equipment, etc.)
d. Athletic awards
e. Chance for better life (job, money, etc.)

Category 10: Recognition
a. By peers
b. By the public
c. By younger persons
d. By older persons
e. By special people

Category 11: Intimidation/Control
a. By the coach giving instructions
b. By the coach being angry
c. By the coach directing your training
d. By the coach criticizing severely
e. By the coach telling you exactly what to do

Category 12: Heterosexuality
a. Being more attractive to the opposite sex
b. Dating because of athletics
c. Athletics having positive effect on social life
d. Getting more dates
e. Being dated because you are an athlete

Category 13: Competing Conditions/ Crowds
a. Competing before a large enthusiastic audience
b. The crowd focusing on your event
c. Being viewed as the "favorite"
d. Crowd watching you only
e. Competing with lots of noise and fanfare

Category 14: Independence/Individuality
a. Deciding your own training schedule
b. Practice alone
c. Few rules/requirements about training
d. Help coach decide training schedule
e. Viewed as an individual or team member

Category 15: "Family"
a. "Family" belonging in team situations
b. Being able to talk to athletic personnel
c. Athletic personnel being a substitute family
d. Confide in athletic personnel

(*continued*)

TABLE **8.2.** (*Continued*)

e. Close relationship with coaches, teammates, etc.	**Category 18: Self Direction / Awareness** a. Getting a focus in life b. Greater sense of confidence
Category 16: Emotional Release a. Competing bringing sense of calmness b. Letting your feelings take action c. Feeling exhilarated d. Being in athletic situation being pleasing e. "Let it all hang out" in athletic competition	c. Knowing better what direction to follow d. Feeling better about yourself as a person e. Feeling you are "special" **Category 19: Understanding Reasons** a. Coach explains purpose of your training b. Coach explains reasons for changing your techniques
Category 17: Status a. Others view you as more important b. Others put you on a higher level c. Others look up to you d. Others treat you with more respect e. You feeling more important	c. Coach explains reasons for training regulations d. Coach explains his directives e. Coach explains his actions regarding your competing

Note. From "A Behavioral Assessment of Motivation" by D. Youngblood and R. M. Suinn in *Psychology in Sports* (pp. 74–75) edited by R. M. Suinn, 1980, Minneapolis, MN: Burgess Publishing Co. Copyright 1980 by Burgess. Reprinted by permission.

in the valuable direction of both individualized sources of motivation and correspondingly individualized channels for its enhancement.

Intensity

Are higher levels of motivation, in terms of intensity and arousal, always better? Does energizing or "pumping up" the athlete inevitably mean better sports performance? According to coaching folklore, the answer is usually yes, and the pervasive use of the psyching-up pep talk is the result. According to psychological research, however, the answer, instead, is "it depends."

There have been two alternative views in psychology regarding the relationship of motivation to performance (Figure 8.1.). The first, the *drive theory* position, straightforwardly predicts a linear relationship between the two. In other words, as motivation, drive, or arousal increases, performance increases correspondingly. The alternative position, known as the *Inverted U* or *Yerkes–Dodson Law*, predicts a curvilinear relationship between motivation and performance. That is, both low and high levels of arousal are associated with low levels of performance; moderate arousal correlates with high performance levels. Interestingly, research examining which of the two views is more factually accurate has convincingly demonstrated *both* to be correct, depending upon the type of behavior being performed. For athletic performance requiring extreme effort, speed, strength, or persistence for success, such as running, shot put, and blocking, the drive theory prediction is correct. Here, wise strategy for the athlete is "the more the better," and psyching-up is the appropriate tactic for the coach. The picture is quite different, however, for athletic responses characterized by complexity, control, flexibility, or coordinated movements. Here the Inverted-U prediction is quite accurate, and the quarterback, wide receiver, baseball pitcher, or basketball player, all of whose tasks require such coordinated and complex performance for success, might, as often as not, need psyching down, rather than psyching up, at the hands of the coach or manager. Table 8.3. elaborates this prescriptive motivational viewpoint further, indicating a full array of athletic behaviors and the optimum arousal level associated with each.

Such an individualized view of motivation, as a function of the demands of the particular sport (Table 8.3.), can be extended further to include the proficiency level of the athlete (Suinn, 1980b). The optimal level of arousal for any given athlete varies with her or his level of skill. High levels of arousal should generally be avoided when a skill is new and many errors are still being made. High levels of arousal should generally be sought when a

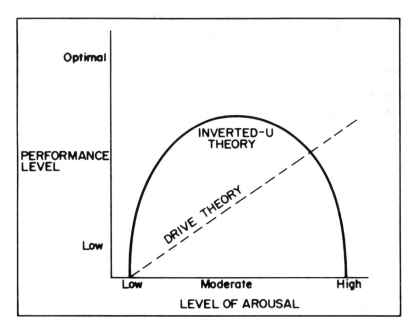

FIGURE 8.1. A comparison of the Drive Theory and the Inverted-U Theory. (From *Sports Psychology: An Analysis of Athlete Behavior* (p. 107) by W. F. Straub, 1980, Ithaca, NY: Mouvement Publications. Copyright 1980 by Mouvement. Reprinted by permission.)

TABLE **8.3.** Optimum Arousal Level for Some Typical Sports Skills

LEVEL OF AROUSAL	SPORTS SKILLS
#5 (Extremely excited)	Football blocking and tackling Performance on the Rogers' PFI test Running (220 yards to 440 yards) Sit up, push up, or bent arm hang test Weight lifting
# 4	Running long jump Running very short and long races Shot put Swimming races Wrestling and judo
# 3	Basketball skills Boxing High jumping Most gymnastic skills Soccer skills
# 2	Baseball pitchers and batters Fancy dives Fencing Football quarterback Tennis
#1 (Slight arousal)	Archery and bowling Basketball free throw Field goal kicking Golf putting and short irons Skating figure 8s
0(Normal state)	

Note. From "Emotional Arousal and Motor Performance" by J. B. Oxendine in *Psychology in Sports* (p. 109) edited by R. M. Suinn, 1980, Minneapolis, MN: Burgess Publishing Co. Copyright 1980 by Burgess. Reprinted by permission.

skill is well developed and few errors are being made. These prescriptive recommendations follow directly from Drive Theory research, which shows that drive or arousal potentiates dominant responses, that is, those behaviors most probable in the athlete's behavioral repertoire. Errors are frequent during the early stages of learning, hence high drive results in still more of them. In the later stages of learning, error-free performance dominates; thus high drive will result in even more skilled performance.

We have proposed that the level of an athlete's arousal be optimally matched to both the task demands of his or her sport and the level of proficiency at the sport that the athlete displays. It is interesting to note that reaching such an optimal motivational level (by moving up or down) might most desirably be something the athlete can accomplish on his or her own, rather than through the efforts of a coach or a manager. Bunker (1978) reported separate studies of olympic gymnastic qualifiers, springboard divers, and parachutists, each of which found that

> . . . the more successful athletes were able to reduce their arousal levels in the crucial moments just prior to competition, while the less successful failed to do so. . . . These results suggest that it may not be the absolute level of arousal, but the ability of athletes to control that level, which governs actual sports performance. (p. 111)

Although we would not wish to go as far as Bunker's conclusion, it seems quite appropriate to conclude that the effect of athlete motivation on performance is far more complicated than the simple notion of more is better that we noted earlier. The nature of the concrete tasks required of the athlete for successful performance, his or her level of proficiency, and the degree to which his or her arousal level is self-managed influence (a) what motivational level is optimal; (b) how, and if, a coach or manager ought to seek to alter motivational level; and (c) the success of the sports performance itself.

Optimal Coaching Strategies

We have already suggested that the effective coach approaches his or her players, and any motivational goals he or she sets regarding them, in an individualized, prescriptive manner. The simple notion that each player is an individual, requiring differential, or tailored, motivational coaching is a truism requiring a creative and discerning coaching response. Others have provided additional guidelines, reasonably well-based in psychological theory or research, of substantial potential value for optimizing athlete motivation. R. N. Singer (1972) and Duquin (1980) each took a broad, multisource view of the development of athletic motivation and, correspondingly, offered a spectrum of coaching recommendations. R. N. Singer (1972) suggested that an athlete's motivation stems from (a) qualities of the person such as need for achievement, approval, and failure avoidance; (b) societal sources such as cultural influences and social expectancies; (c) the activity itself and its complexity, demands, appeal, and meaningfulness; and (d) the specific athletic situation, that is, its location, audience, score, standings. Based upon this multisource perspective, Singer recommended the following as optimal coaching strategies:

1. Help the athlete set personally high but attainable, specific goals.
2. Supply appropriate reinforcement and feedback.
3. Enhance training perseverance by means of varied drills, individualized training, and encouragement of self-regulation.
4. Develop practice situations that simulate as much as possible the actual sports situation.
5. Seek to enhance athlete self-confidence not only by generous use of social

approval, but also by avoidance of berating or other self-concept diminishment.

6. Seek to help the athlete view the training program as meaningful and relevant to his or her goals.

7. Encourage the development of intrinsic motivation.

Picking up from Singer's last suggestion, Duquin's (1980) recommendations add further to a sound panel of strategies for optimal motivational coaching. Athletic persistence is more likely, he proposed, if:

1. The athlete is process oriented, that is, intrinsically motivated and concerned with the sports process and its opportunity for competition, skill development, tension release and health maintenance, and not unduly extrinsically motivated, that is, dependent on objective indices of success such as the actual victory, helmet decals, trophies, medals.

2. The group or team atmosphere is supportive, cohesive, enhancing of personal development, clear in its expectations, and responsive to change.

3. The activity is successful in the majority of cases, and the success is attributable to *internal* sources, for example, effort and ability, not luck, the coach, the opponent's weaknesses.

4. Unsuccessful instances are seen as subjectively profitable, for the information they provide about one's own and one's opponent's strengths and weaknesses.

5. Failure is attributed to unstable factors, for example, luck, the coach, the opponent's strength, lack of effort and not lack of ability or task difficulty. Perseverance here may be aided because unstable factors often change or can be changed.

The literature on coaching is quite substantial. Most of it is anecdote, experience, and folklore. As with all other forms of leadership behavior, we believe its effectiveness can be placed upon a sound, scientific foundation. The several suggestions for optimal coaching in this section on athlete motivation are a mere beginning in this desired direction, and more such work will surely be forthcoming as its value finds concrete expression on contemporary sports' playing fields and stadiums.

NORTHEASTERN LEAGUE STANDINGS April 27, 1993				
Team	Wins	Losses	Percentage	Games Behind
Newark Eagles	14	7	.700	—
Manhattan Maulers	13	8	.650	1
Norristown Rockets	10	10	.500	3 1/2
Coney Island Cyclones	8	12	.400	5 1/2
Harrisburg Blues	8	13	.380	6
Port Jefferson Jesters	7	14	.333	7
Camden Sluggers	5	16	.238	9

They'd been so good in exhibition games, but there they sat, in fourth place, right where they had ended up last year. The season was only 3 1/2 weeks old, but Tony felt more and more like the Cyclones might be heading into trouble. It was no solace that their arch-rivals, the Jesters, were in even worse trouble. Two of the rookies Tony was counting on most didn't seem able to hit a decent curveball, and his "golden glove" second baseman had already made four errors. Jeff Petrie, his 8-year veteran first baseman, a class act if there ever was one, was going to be out for 2 weeks with a broken toe.

Scarpo's mind drifted briefly into pleasant thoughts of strangling Willie Harris from Camden, who had stepped on Petrie's foot and done the damage. But with all this, and even with the team acting sort of edgy and kind of uncertain in spots, Tony was planning no changes . . . for now. The raw material is here, he thought, reflecting on spring training and their exhibition record. We're having a bit of a rocky start, but the best thing to do now seemed to be to just sit still and ride it out.

OTHER DETERMINANTS OF ATHLETIC PERFORMANCE

In addition to coaching or managerial leadership and athlete personality and motivation, there remain several additional influences upon athletic performance that have been the focus of psychological inquiry. It is to these further sources of athletic success and failure that we now turn.

Components of Athletic Performance

It will aid considerably our understanding of further determinants of athletic performance, the focus of this section, and means for remediating inadequate performance, the topic of a later section, if, following Suinn's (1980b) example, we seek to identify and examine the separate processes or components that collectively constitute athletic performance. We will elaborate in a later section upon the remediation techniques mentioned in the following list. We wish to list such intervention here, however, to once again highlight the *prescriptive* theme presented earlier. Here we stress the fact that whatever intervention is appropriate is very much determined by that component of the athletic performance process with which the athlete is having difficulty. Suinn's (1980) component analysis proposes five sequential responses as constituting correct athletic performance.

1. *Isolated motor responses.* These are the physical actions learned and shaped through observation, coaching, and practice such as the swimmer's turn at the end of the pool, the basketball player's feint left and cut right, the football tackle's body block. Suinn suggests that flaws in technique, that is, incorrect isolated motor responses, can be remediated by intensified technique coaching, use of videotape feedback, and body awareness training.

2. *Preparatory or arousal responses.* These are the psyching-up or psyching-down preparations mentioned in our earlier discussion of athlete motivation. Psyching-up, when arousal level is too low and performance too

flat, might be aided, according to Suinn (1980), by taking trial runs, talking to or about a competitor, talking to oneself about bettering last times or accomplishments, setting personal goals, and a variety of coach-offered energizing talks and activities. Psyching-down, when arousal is too high and performance thus disrupted and poorly coordinated, might be accomplished by relaxation training, autogenic training, meditation, or the use of biofeedback techniques.

3. *Adapting motor responses to other events.* In almost all sports, the athlete's performance is influenced by, and must adjust to, the athletic performance of unfolding events. Sometimes this is the behavior of opponents or teammates, other times it is physical stimuli such as slalom courses in skiing, other autos in racing. Particularly helpful in remediating difficulties in this sphere might be techniques that assist the athlete in refocusing attention, from broad to narrow or narrow to broad and from internal to external or external to internal.

4. *Linking responses.* Isolated motor responses, in the context of athlete arousal and adaptation to others' behavior, must be joined together into a chain of smoothly coordinated and sequenced behaviors to form the complete athletic performance. A tailback's 20-yard run, a play-making guard's setting up and executing a successful pick and roll, a second baseman's enacting a successful double play are examples of linking responses. Visual–motor behavioral rehearsal (Suinn, 1976), to be discussed along with other interventions later in this chapter, is of apparent value in efforts to correct performance deficiencies involving inadequate linking responses.

5. *Cognitive responses.* The cognitive-response component of athletic performance might include (a) cue-instructional thoughts such as telling oneself "calm," "steady," "go," (b) strategy such as planning to execute a daring rather than a conservative gymnastic routine or deciding how best to "psych-out" or compete against a given opponent, and (c) focused attentional responses involving narrowing of one's attention to the athletic task at hand. Suinn (1980b) suggested that the negative thinking that impedes success-related cognitive responses could be dealt with by training athletes to think thoughts incompatible with negativism (e.g., "I am able to relax"), by techniques of positive self-instruction (e.g., "I will hit the ball solidly"), and by reframing (e.g., "pain means I'm giving it maximum effort").

> The main point . . . is that it is possible to conceptualize sports performance into various component parts and that such an analysis gives direction for the application of a variety of psychological methods. Training programs then become tailor-made to the particular component that needs attention. Further, the conceptualization points out that different athletes have different needs, some being more influenced by cognitive factors, others more by arousal level, others more by emotional factors. Psychological methods, to be useful, must be appropriate for the person and for the situation. (p. 36)

Suinn's components conceptualization of athletic performance appears to be very useful for prescriptive coaching purposes, and it is, more generally, a view of performance of considerable operational value for the study of such behavior. Most of its focus, however, is upon events internal to the athlete himself or herself—what he or she does, thinks, feels. In our earlier discussion of athlete personality and athletic leadership, we stressed the view that athletic (or any) performance is a joint function of qualities of the performer and qualities of the situation in which he or she performs. We would like now to reemphasize the important contribution of athletic performance of situational events by discussing two final determinants of such performance, both external to the athlete, namely, attentional demands inherent in the task or sport itself and the influence on performance of the audience.

Attentional Demands

Nideffer (1980) has proposed that different sports, and different positions within the same sport, vary in the attentional focus they require for successful athletic performance. He suggested that the attentional focus necessary for optimal responding varies along two dimensions, broad versus narrow and internal versus external. Nideffer (1980) defined these continua.

> A broad external focus is useful when the individual needs to be aware of and able to respond to a complex, rapidly changing environment. In addition to the quarterback example, a three on two fast break in basketball, a double play in baseball, or playing linebacker in football would all demand the ability to have a broad external focus. Situations where a narrow external focus would be useful would include hitting and pitching in baseball, golf, bowling, etc. In almost any situation where only one stimulus (e.g., ball or pins) is relevant, an internal focus can be important for rehearsal of tasks, reflection, and preparation for a game, as well as for endurance. For example, distance runners can use the ability to narrow their attention and focus internally as a means of directing thought to the mechanics of running (to a rhythm), thus increasing pain tolerance by not attending to the painful cues. (p. 232)

To satisfactorily measure these qualities of attentional focus, Nideffer (1980) developed the Test of Attentional and Interpersonal Style (Nideffer, 1976). This measure yields a pattern of subscales directly relevant to athletic performance, as Table 8.4 indicates.

As an example of the significant deterministic effect of attentional focus on athletic performance, Nideffer (1980) provided a hypothetical profile of a baseball player with high scores on OET and OIT and a low NAR score.

> . . . let's look at some of the difficulties a hitter with this profile has. First, he has great difficulty narrowing attention and focusing on the ball. Instead, when focused externally, he is aware of everything from the crowd noises to the movement of players on the field. Such a broad focus makes it difficult to concentrate on hitting the ball. Another problem occurs because he doesn't

Table 8.4. Attentional Subscale Definitions

BET (Broad-External)
The higher the score, the more the individual's answers indicate that he deals effectively with a large number of external stimuli. He has a broad external focus that is effective.

OET (External Overload)
The higher the score, the more the individual's answers indicate that he makes mistakes because he is overloaded and distracted by external stimuli. He has difficulty narrowing attention when he needs to.

BIT (Broad-Internal)
The higher the score, the more the individual indicates that he is able to think about several things at once when it is appropriate to do so. He has a broad-internal focus.

OIT (Internal Overload)
The higher the score, the more the individual indicates that he makes mistakes because he thinks about too many things at once. He is interfered with by his own thoughts and feelings.

NAR (Narrow Effective Focus)
High scorers indicate that they are able to narrow attention effectively when the situation calls for it

RED (Errors of Underinclusion)
High scorers have chronically narrowed attention. They make mistakes because they cannot broaden attention when they need to.

Note. From "The Relationship of Attention and Anxiety to Performance" by R. M. Nideffer in *Sports psychology* (p. 283) edited by R. M. Suinn, Minneapolis, MN: Burgess Publishing Co. Copyright 1980 by Burgess. Reprinted by permission.

balance his internal and external attention. Instead, he becomes trapped in his thoughts and responds to what is going on around him without thinking. In this case he may be so busy trying to analyze the situation, in an attempt to predict the next pitch, that he doesn't realize that the pitcher is already in his windup. The result is that he isn't ready when the ball arrives. He fails to shift to an external focus when he needs that kind of focus. (p. 285)

A final word regarding athlete attentional focus and task demands is appropriate before we move on to other situational determinants of athletic performance. Much has been made in recent years of *inner* athletics (inner tennis, inner golf, etc.). The view has been promoted, based exclusively on anecdote and experience and not on empirical evidence, that athletic performance is maximized if the athlete allows "Self 2" to take command of his or her game, Self 2 being the "unconscious automatic doer," in contrast with Self 1, the "conscious, analytic teller." Gallway (1974), the chief promoter of this perspective, urged upon athletes an attentional stance characterized by nonjudgmental awareness. As Browne and Mahoney (1984) put it,

Performance is at its best during these flow episodes in which athletes often report feeling as if they were in a trance. They report experiencing (a) dissociation and intense concentration, often being unaware of their surroundings at these times, (b) feeling neither fatigue nor pain, (c) perceptual changes which include time-slowing and object enlargement, and (d) feeling unusual power and control. (p. 612)

Clearly, research is warranted to ascertain whether such an attentional set in fact enhances athletic performance and, if so, prescriptively for which athletes, in which sports, and under which game circumstances.

Audience Effects

We opened this chapter with reference to what apparently is historically the first sports psychology research project, Tripplett's (1897) investigation of the influence of an audience on competitive bicycling. He indeed found such "social facilitation" to be operating, i.e., the presence of an audience enhanced cycling speed. In the several subsequent studies on this topic that have followed, results have been mixed. Sometimes the presence of an audience has been shown to facilitate athletic performance, sometimes it apparently detracts from performance, and sometimes an audience appears to be irrelevant to the success or failure of the athlete. Zajonc (1976) has sought to resolve this discrepancy in findings by reference to a fact we described earlier in this chapter; an audience raises performer arousal, and arousal increases the frequency of whatever responses are dominant. For the more error-prone, still-learning rookie, audience-caused heightened arousal can thus result in deterioration of athletic performance. For the less error-prone, experienced veteran, audience-caused, heightened arousal potentiates the response of successful athletic performance. The general finding here, as A. C. Fisher (1976) wrote, is simply that " . . . performance is facilitated but learning is impaired by the presence of spectators" (p. 6).

But are the effects of an audience in fact due to "the mere presence of spectators?" Cottrell, Sekerak, Wack, and Rittle (1968) suggested, and Klinger (1969) confirmed, that, in fact, it was not "mere presence" of others that seemed to influence performer drive or arousal, but instead the performers' perception that the audience was a potential source of positive or negative evaluation of his or her performance. When others were present, in Klinger's study, but could not evaluate the performer's responses, no effects on quality of performance were found. Yet, as so often happens in psychological research, simple truths and uncomplicated generalizations are hard to come by. Burwitz and Newell (1976), in contrast with Klinger (1969), in fact, later found that, at least for the performers in their study, mere presence with no opportunity for evaluation *was* a significant influence upon performer behavior. Audience effects have been an active target of psychological research. The contrast between the Burwitz and Klinger results is matched by other contrasting outcomes, all of which point to the broad conclusion that, although the presence of an audience might indeed effect performer behavior, whether it does so, and the nature and direction of the influence, depend upon several characteristics of the audience, the performer, and the athletic task. Concretely, specific parameters shown to influence audience effects include

1. Audience parameters
   (a) Size
   (b) Messages to performer, e.g., noise, facial expressions
   (c) Psychological distance, e.g., familiar versus strangers
   (d) Physical proximity, e.g., close versus distant
   (e) Sex of audience
2. Performer parameters
   (a) Perception that audience is/isn't evaluating him or her
   (b) Degree of stressful anticipation
   (c) Skill level
   (d) Personality characteristics
3. Task parameters
   (a) Position played
   (b) Task complexity

The full nature of the influence of these several parameters on performer behavior, and the identification of further such parameters, is a challenging task for future research. The research already conducted, however, not only has begun to reveal when an audience will and will not affect athletic performance, but once again clearly illustrates the requirement that we consider both the performer and his or her situation (in this case, the audience) in seeking to predict or enhance athletic behavior.

NORTHEASTERN LEAGUE STANDINGS May 24, 1993				
Team	Wins	Losses	Percentage	Games Behind
Manhattan Maulers	23	13	.638	—
Newark Eagles	22	13	.628	$^{1}/_{2}$
Norristown Rockets	19	17	.527	4
Harrisburg Blues	17	20	.459	$6^{1}/_{2}$
Coney Island Cyclones	16	21	.432	$7^{1}/_{2}$
Port Jefferson Jesters	14	23	.377	$9^{1}/_{2}$
Camden Sluggers	10	26	.279	13

Fifth place and going nowhere. The season was a third over now, and Tony knew he had trouble. And, in case he forgot, owner Larsen called him twice a day now with reminders. He let Larsen know as clearly as he could that *he* was managing the team, not Larsen. But the team was doing lousy, and they had all better produce soon, or Larsen would be finding a replacement. The Cyclones had played everyone in the league now, so Tony had seen all the opposition firsthand. Tony was a fine judge of talent and still felt the Cyclones could be contenders, but they just couldn't seem to put it all together. When they got decent hitting, the pitching was lousy. When the pitching was good, there seemed to be no hitting. Tony had begun shuffling the lineup, but he had to be careful not to do too much of it. "I've got to build confidence and hang in with these guys a little longer," he thought. So far, the fans had mostly stuck with the club, but he was beginning to hear things on and off from the crowd that he didn't like and that he knew sure wouldn't help his team. Tomorrow was the first of three road games against the Maulers. "Some days it doesn't rain but it pours."

AGGRESSION

History

Sports violence by both participants and spectators is most certainly as old as sports itself. Guttman (1983) traced the growth of gladiatorial violence, starting with one-on-one contests, usually to the death, in 246 B.C., to events over the ensuing decades involving literally thousands of gladiators at a time and often as many of the audience. Chariot races, also a regular sporting event of this era, were also usually blood-letting occasions. Atyeo (1981), in a comprehensive but dismaying litany on the marriage of athletics and aggression down through the ages, mustered such historical examples of the tenacity of this marriage as cockfighting, baiting (e.g., dogs against other species, lions against bulls), ratting, jousting, sword-and-buckler (a small shield), quarterstaffing (a 6- to 8-ft pole used for head bashing), backswording, cudgeling, foil play, bare knuckle toe-to-toe boxing, and such more modern expressions of sports violence as football, soccer, lacrosse, boxing, and ice hockey.

Lest one think of sports violence as an uncivilized quality of past eras, a few statistics will very much show it to be a phenomenon of today. Atyeo (1981) reported that "Each year American sportsmen and sportswomen sustain a staggering total of 20 million injuries serious enough to be treated by a doctor. Of these 20 million, 6 million leave lasting and permanent reminders ranging from scars to paraplegia to death" (p. 11). From 1931 to 1965, there were 642 football fatalities in the United States. In 1977, according to M. C. Smith (1983), there were 318,000 football injuries requiring emergency room treatment. Boxing and hockey yield similar "body counts." M. C. Smith (1983), tracing the centrality of violence in organized hockey, commented that, as players get older, fewer team openings are available to them. "One of the most important [skills] . . . is the willingness and ability to employ and withstand illegal physical coercion . . . It's an extra skill almost" (p. 188).

MAP—H

Types of Sports Violence

A few applied psychologists have attempted to describe and categorize different sports in terms of their characteristic degrees of violence. Atyeo (1981) suggested (a) combat sports (e.g., boxing, wrestling), (b) killing sports (e.g., hunting, bullfighting), (c) heavy contact sports (e.g., football, hockey), and (d) risk sports (e.g., motor racing). M. C. Smith (1983) offered the sports violence continuum:

1. *Brutal body contact.* The aggression displayed falls within the formal rules of the given sport and is more or less accepted as a literal "part of the game."
2. *Borderline violence.* As above, this is athlete aggression generally accepted as customary, but in this instance is, nevertheless, a violation of the particular sport's regulations (e.g., the fistfight in hockey or the late hit in football).
3. *Quasicriminal violence.* These are acts of aggression that violate both the sport's rules and the sport's customs, and that are generally not acceptable to its participants (e.g., a devastating punch, an attack severe enough to be termed as assault).
4. *Criminal violence.* Aggressive acts in this category violate not only the sport's regulations and traditions of acceptable behavior, but also the law. Rather than being handled internally by team or league officials, these are acts appropriately responded to by law enforcement agencies.

Sports violence most certainly is not limited to its participants. Perhaps almost as often, spectators are involved. Vamplew (1983) proposed five sources of athletic event spectator aggression:

1. Frustration disorders, that is, when physical or visual access to the game or its playing, refereeing, or outcome thwart fan expectations.
2. Outlawry, that is, use of the opportunity presented by a sports event by chronically aggressive persons (e.g., youth gangs) to engage in antisocial acting-out.
3. Remonstrance, that is, use of a sporting event to express a political grievance.
4. Confrontation, that is, aggressive interactions between rival religious, ethnic, geographic or national subgroups of spectators.
5. Expressive, that is, as a result of the intense emotional arousal that may accompany or result from a team victory or defeat, a very close game, or unexpected turns of events.

Causes of Sports Violence

Freischlag and Schmidke (1980) suggested that useful predictors of fan violence include strong attachment to the performer(s), unrealistically high expectations of team performance, seemingly biased or incompetent officiating, early fouling, and a low-scoring game. An especially cogent perspective on the causes of sports violence, both player and spectator, was provided by Mark, Bryant, and Lehman (1983). For players, they placed causative emphasis upon being aggressed against by another participant and what they termed "perceived injustice," defined as "a discrepancy between one's outcome and what one believes one is entitled to, between what happened and 'what should have happened' according to fair rules" (p. 83). In support of this conclusion, they cited M. D. Smith's (1980) study of 68 accounts of player violence reported in a large city newspaper over a 10-year span. Prior assaultive behavior by another athlete was the most common immediate precipitant of participant violence; an unpopular decision by an official, or perceived injustice, ranked second. Mark et al.'s (1983) fuller view of the antecedants of sports aggression is particularly valuable:

> A review of social psychological research on aggression reveals many other characteristics of sports events [in addition to perceived injustice] which may serve to increase the likelihood of aggression in both fans and participants. Indeed, in some sports, the athletic arena and grandstands seem almost as though they were designed to maximize most of these conditions: participants and spectators alike experience [high levels of] physiological arousal . . . generally sports fans are crowded together . . . are relatively anonymous and deindividuated . . . many of them have consumed more than a small dose of alcohol . . . the very act of viewing an aggressive athletic event may promote hostility . . . sports participants typically compete before an audience, maximizing their ego defensiveness regarding performance . . . crowds often taunt or verbally abuse players for perceived errors . . . large amounts of money are usually at stake. (p. 89)

Thus, as we saw with athletic performance itself and athletic motivation, with aggression in the context of athletics the sources are multifaceted and complex. Any efforts to seek to alter such behavior, as we shall see later in this section, must similarly be multifaceted and complex. However, before turning to the section's final topic, the reduction of sports violence, one additional matter must be addressed, namely, the tenacious and very widely held but scientifically unsupported belief in sports violence as catharsis.

Catharsis

Catharsis is the draining off, venting, or purging of an emotion, an experience that purportedly occurs vicariously, by observing and empathically identifying with another person, or directly via one's own behavior. The concept of catharsis first appeared in the vicarious sense, in connection with the reported emotion-purging experience of the audience at early Greek drama. The Freudian (1950) view and that of Lorenz (1966), reflecting the ethologist's perspective, were more direct with regard to aggression. Freud wrote that "there is a continuous welling up of destructive impulses within the individual representing an outgrowth of the death instinct" (p. 160).

Lorenz held that in both animals and humans "aggressive energy is continuously being generated within the species member and seeks periodic release" (p. 161). In these views, therefore, aggression is inevitable, and the best one can accomplish is to direct, channel, or regulate its periodic release or discharge via a socially acceptable, minimally injurious, "aggressive" act such as debates, the space race, and, of direct relevance to this chapter, competitive sports. Proctor and Eckerd (1976) presented this viewpoint clearly.

> People's emotions are similar to steam locomotives. If you build a fire in the boiler of a locomotive, keep raising the steam pressure and let it sit on the tracks, sooner or later something will blow. However, if you take it and spin the wheels and toot the whistle, the steam pressure can be kept at a safe level. Spectator sports give John Q. Citizen a socially acceptable way to lower his steam pressure by allowing him to spin his wheels and toot his whistle. (p. 83)

The view of aggression as stored, constantly growing energy that, if directly or vicariously vented, leaves less of it in the person's reservoir is a very widely held belief in contemporary thinking. Is it correct? Let us see what applied psychological research has shown. Such research has been both abundant and of several types.

Static Comparisons

One research approach is to simply compare the aggressiveness levels of persons who do or do not regularly engage in aggressive activities. If the catharsis notion is correct, those who do, having vented, should show less aggression. Zillmann, Bryant, and Sopolsky (1979) compared contact-sport athletes (in football and wrestling) with noncontact-sport athletes (in swimming and tennis) with nonathletes, and they found no between-group differences on behavioral measures of aggression. Le Unes and Nation (1981) compared football players and nonathletes in the same way, and Ostrow (1974) did so with tennis players and nonathletes. Their results matched Zillmann et al.'s in that there were no between-group differences on aggression, or, to say it another way, there was no evidence that the expression of aggression reduces its occurrence.

Before–After Comparisons

These are applied psychological studies in which two groups are identified or randomly constituted, and one is given the opportunity to aggress. If the catharsis concept is correct, the after comparisons should reveal that the group permitted to express aggression is less aggressive than the comparison group. Ostrow (1974) and Ryan (1970) each conducted this type of study and found no support for such an effect. More surprisingly, three other before–after comparison studies of catharsis found an opposite effect! Persons permitted to behave aggressively afterward become more aggressive, not less so, as the catharsis concept would predict. This result emerged in

Hornberger's (1959) study in which some research subjects were required to hammer nails, in Loew's (1967) requiring some subjects to say a series of aggressive words, and in Patterson's (1974) comparison of football players and physical education students before and after the football season. Compared with their respective nonaggressive comparison groups, the nail hammerers, the aggression verbalizers, and the football players all became more aggressive—the direct opposite of a catharsis effect. J. H. Goldstein and Arms (1971) measured aggression level in randomly selected fans just before and after an Army–Navy football game. Contrary to experiencing catharsis, fans of both winners and losers increased their level of aggression after the game to more than before the game. The investigators' comment: "Exposure to the aggression of others seemingly acts to weaken one's internal mechanisms controlling the expression of similar behavior" (p. 165). Arms, Russell, and Sandilands (1979) replicated this result and showed, furthermore, that fan aggression increased after football and hockey matches (aggressive sports) but not after a swim meet (a nonaggressive sport).

Archival Studies
These are examinations of short-term or long-term records of aggression-expressing sports and other events that, if catharsis is a real phenomenon, should reveal its decrease over the course of the event. In five separate archival studies, Russell (1981) showed the opposite of a cathartic effect. Because catharsis by definition predicts that aggression should decrease as it is expressed, progressively less should occur as an athletic event progresses. In fact, aggression *increased* as the games progressed. A similar anticathartic result emerged in Russell's (1983) tracking of aggression between two teams the more times they met over a season: more, and not less, aggression took place. The early proponents of competitive sports as an ideal venting ground for human aggression saw sports in their grand vision as a substitute for war. Unfortunately, this cathartic vision, too, fails to find research support in archival studies of this phenomenon. Sipes (1973) showed a positive relationship, not the negative one the catharsis concept would predict, between the degree to which combatant sports existed in a society and its degree of involvement in wars, conflicts, revolutions, and similar events. Similarly, Keefer, Goldstein, and Kasiary (1983) found a positive correlation between whether a country participated in the Olympics and the number of athletes it sent, on the one hand, and the number of wars in which it participated and its number of months at war.

Laboratory Studies
Fully consistent with the research outcomes reported previously, Berkowitz (1964) conducted a series of investigations in which research subjects were or were not shown either brutal but staged sports violence (e.g., the fight

scene from the movie *The Champion*) or equally brutal actual fights from hockey, football, and basketball. In all instances, those viewing the aggressive scenes, compared with nonviewing control group subjects, significantly increased their own levels of aggression.

The conclusion is clear: catharsis is a myth. Sports violence increases participant and spectator violence, not decreases it. As Goranson (1970) aptly suggested:

> I think that this is one of those rare occasions in behavioral research where an unqualified conclusion is warranted. The observation of violence does not reduce aggressiveness. . . . Observed violence serves to facilitate the expression of aggression, rather than reduce aggression by "draining off aggressive energy!" (p. 12)

Reduction of Sports Violence

We have observed throughout this chapter that sports violence arises from many sources: the participants, the fans, the coaches and managers, the officiating, the mass media, the community traditions, and so forth. Any serious effort to reduce such excessive violence must simultaneously operate on several of these sources. Suggestions for doing so have been many and varied and ranged from the concrete and practical to the abstract and unrealistic. Presented next is a compilation of suggestions for reducing sports violence, some already in place, others proposed, from the writings of Carron (1980), Freischlag and Schmidke (1980), J. H. Goldstein (1983), and Mark et al. (1983).

Participants
1. Foster positive interaction with opposing players such as the end-of-game handshake.
2. Increase sanctions (fines, suspension) for violent behavior.
3. Reduce financial incentives and other rewards for violent performance.
4. Make equipment changes to increase physical protection of athletes.
5. Use positive reinforcement for nonaggressive, skilled performance.

Spectators
1. Lower unrealistically high expectations of team performance.
2. Sell tickets more cheaply, on a family plan.
3. Increase restrictions on the sale and use of alcoholic beverages and on gambling.
4. Play the national anthem after the game.
5. Arrange that not all spectators leave at the same time, for instance, have postgame concerts or several games in succession.

6. Increase police presence and other control agents, such as gatemen and stewards.

Coaches
1. Make coaches aware of evidence that players perform more poorly when aggressive.
2. Have coaches model positive interactions with opposition players and coaches.
3. Avoid negative or inflammatory comments.
4. Help players perceive opposition positively, for their fair play, respect for rules, effort.
5. Provide positive reinforcement for nonaggressive, skilled performance.

Officials
1. Make officiating fairer by better selection, training, and monitoring of officials.
2. Make officiating seem fairer by publicizing official selection, training, and monitoring procedures.
3. Improve official–fan communication, to explain rulings.
4. Increase use of technological aids such as instant TV replay and ground sensors in tennis.
5. Strictly enforce current rules.

Mass Media
1. Show professional sports on TV only, without live audiences.
2. Temper sports announcers' commentaries.
3. Increase programming of noncompetitive sports.
4. Diminish camera coverage of participant altercations.
5. Reduce media exploitation of existing or potential antagonisms such as regional, class, or ethnic rivalries.

Architectural/Technological
1. Use steel fencing to separate fans from players or rival groups of fans.
2. Use dry moats between fans and playing field and between rival groups of fans.
3. Use dogs to contain and restrain boisterous groups of fans.
4. Unobtrusively monitor fans by TV.

These suggestions are both creative and nonexhaustive. Violence need not be a central ingredient of enjoyable athletic performance. Clearly, significant contributions of applied psychology to sports are its continuing concern with identifying the sources of high levels of aggression in athletics and the hunt for effective means of reducing it.

NORTHEASTERN LEAGUE STANDINGS
June 16, 1993

Team	Wins	Losses	Percentage	Games Behind
Manhattan Maulers	33	19	.634	—
Newark Eagles	33	19	.634	—
Harrisburg Blues	29	23	.557	4
Norristown Rockets	26	26	.500	7
Coney Island Cyclones	26	27	.490	7½
Port Jefferson Jesters	20	33	.377	13½
Camden Sluggers	16	37	.301	17½

Tony sat sullenly in his motel room, watching the Cyclones on the local TV station. It was the last day of his 5-day suspension, and he'd be glad to get back in uniform and get down to the ballpark. He could sure use more spirited playing from some of the guys on the team, but the awful brawl with the Jesters Friday night was spirit of the wrong kind. Beanballs, a thrown bat, a third baseman with a broken nose, two fans arrested, and himself tossed out and suspended for 5 days! Tony had never meant to throw his cap in Umpire Bartnel's face, it just sort of happened. The whole team had been on a short fuse for at least 2 weeks, ever since the Eagles swept them in a four-game series. The beanball from the Jesters just sort of lit the fuse.

"We're pretty much at rock bottom now," Tony thought, "maybe there really is no place to go but up." Petrie's slump just might be ending, at least he was 2 for 5 today. And Kryzwiki's sore arm might be history too. He'd nursed it for over 2 weeks but really let loose in yesterday's game. Tony seemed to be having a little wave of optimism, even though they were still in fifth place, a feeling he hadn't had in a good long while. The phone rang, and it was Art Larsen calling to suggest that the team hire Kay Gunther, a psychologist Larsen had heard had really helped the Denver Stars in the Rocky Mountain League. Tony had mixed feelings about this one. Anything or anyone that could help would be welcomed, but how would the guys feel about a "shrink" in the locker room?

BEHAVIOR MODIFICATION

Psychologists are relatively recent visitors to the sports locker room. An occasional team has hired a hypnotist, a meditator, an EST consultant, or a devotee of one or another difficult-to-validate phenomenological approach to improving sports performance and motivation. In recent years, however, the primary sports psychological consultant has been the behavior modification specialist. G. L. Martin and Hrycaiko (1983) noted in this connection:

> The psychology of sport traditionally has been presented and studied within the framework of a phenomenological perspective. . . . As a result, studies of sports and athletics have dealt primarily with such variables as drive, determination, guts, winning attitude, desire, and self-concept—all hypothetical con-

structs which do not lend themselves to experimental analysis. Coaches do not have a scientifically derived data base to guide them in decision making. Pep talks, lectures, yelling at players for mistakes, and assigning extra laps, push ups, or other aversive conditioning activities for poor performance are all employed by most coaches despite the fact none of these basic coaching techniques has been validated experimentally. In a landmark book, Rushall and Siedentop (1972) described and called for an applied behavior analysis of sports and physical education. (p. 226)

Their call has been answered. Since the publication of *The Development and Control of Behavior in Sport and Physical Education* (Rushall & Siedentop, 1972), a great deal of behavioral research and several books describing diverse behavior modification techniques for improving sports performance and motivation have appeared. These include *Behavior Modification and Coaching* (G. L. Martin & Hrycaiko, 1983), *Sport Psychology: An Analysis of Athlete Behavior* (Straub, 1980), *Cognitive Sport Psychology* (Straub & Williams, 1984), and *Psychology in Sports* (Suinn, 1980a). Clearly, a technology for the modification of sports-participant behavior has rapidly begun to emerge. The specific procedures constituting this technology, to be implemented by the psychologist consultant, the manager, or coach are as follows:

1. *Positive reinforcement.* Any event or object that, when presented after the occurrence of a given behavior, increases the likelihood of that behavior's occurring again. Positive reinforcement can be tangible (points, helmet decals, money), social (praise, approval), or self-generated.
2. *Shaping.* Positive reinforcement of a presently emitted behavior in such a way as to cause it to change by successive approximation to a final, desired behavior not originally in the person's repertoire.
3. *Chaining.* Similar to shaping in that both aim at conditioning a complex behavioral act not yet emitted by the athlete. In shaping, some component(s) of the behavior is gradually changed over trials. In chaining, a number of component behaviors are linked together.
4. *Extinction.* The removal of any event or object that when presented after the occurrence of a given behavior, increases the likelihood of that behavior's occurring again. Extinction is typically implemented by simply ignoring the undesired behavior.
5. *Time-out.* The removal of the individual from sources of reinforcement, usually to a neutral, quiet location for a brief period of time.
6. *Response cost.* The removal from the individual of tangible reinforcers already in their possession (points, tokens, or other negotiable reinforcers) or of privileges they have earned or expect to earn.
7. *Fading.* Gradual change of cues or stimuli controlling a response so that the response eventually occurs to a completely or partially new set of cues.

8. *Prompting*. Similar to instructing (which usually occurs *before* the action takes place) and feedback (which usually occurs *after* the action), prompting typically provides the athlete with how-to performance information *during* the athletic activity.

9. *Performance feedback*. Providing information of a constructively critical, corrective, or approving manner to the performer regarding the nature and satisfactoriness of his or her just-completed athletic performance.

10. *Self-monitoring*. Systematic tracking and recording by the individual of his or her own discrete behaviors, usually with special attention to their rate or intensity.

11. *Self-instructions*. Statements the individual is taught to say to himself or herself to provide direction, enhance motivation, reduce anxiety, dispute negative thoughts, or otherwise influence the causes of good and poor athletic performance.

12. *Deep-muscle relaxation*. A systematic procedure involving the progressive tensing and relaxing of all major muscle groups as a means of heightening kinesthetic awareness and tension–relaxation self-control, thus providing the individual with the ability to readily become relaxed as he or she wishes.

13. *Modeling*. Asking the athlete to closely observe the live, audiovisual, or pictoral presentation, typically in vivid, concrete, stepwise form, of the correct manner of enacting a given athletic act.

14. *Imaginal rehearsal*. Covert practice of the specific component behaviors constituting a given athletic performance, seeking to reflect correct enactment of the behaviors in the correct sequence.

15. *Behavioral rehearsal*. Overt practice of the specific component behaviors constituting a given athletic performance, seeking to reflect correct enactment of the behaviors in the correct sequence.

16. *Thought stopping*. A type of self-instruction directively targeted to counter fearful, anxious, self-esteem diminishing, or other negative thoughts likely to lessen the probability of successful sports performance.

17. *Response-induction aids*. Special equipment that could reduce the perceived discrepancy between the athlete's current and desired performance.

In a real sense, these several behavior modification procedures should be viewed as ingredients in the sports psychologist's pharmacy. As with a competent pharmacist, which procedures or combinations of procedures the sports psychologist "prescribes" for any given player or team varies accordingly to what the apparent difficulty is. The hyper-anxious player, the inadequately motivated player, the player in a slump or with an overly broad attentional focus, the player constantly imagining errors she or he will commit, the team with low morale or high dissension or poor cohesiveness each requires a different selection of behavior modification ingredients. Since the Rushall and Siedentop (1972) book appeared, a substantial number of such behavior modification applications by sports psychologists have in fact been conducted and evaluated. The combined outcome of such evaluation research, as we will see, is highly encouraging of the continued application and evaluation of this full array of behavior modification techniques in the context of organized sports.

As noted previously a number of the evaluation studies in this context have focused upon single-behavior modification interventions; others have examined the potency of intervention combinations. In an example of the former, Komaki and Barnett (1983) investigated the effects of positive reinforcement on competence of football-play execution. The players were children, 9-year old members of a Pop Warner football team's offensive backfield. Three frequently run plays—an option, a power sweep, an offtackle counterplay—were each broken into five behavioral steps. Positive reinforcement for one play after another was provided after steps reflecting desired play execution. Youngsters gained in performance by an average of 20% after the staggered introduction of this behavior modification intervention. At an adult level, McKenzie and Rushall (1983) demonstrated similar effectiveness for positive reinforcement, in the form of coach attention and praise, for increasing attendance at practice and number of laps (voluntarily) swum by college swim team members. Jones (1977) developed an approach to the use of positive reinforcement in basketball in which an off-court observer, using a bullhorn, awarded points to individual players for such desired behaviors as rebounding; moving to good position without the ball; and executing a good pass, screen, or pick. The team was given a token that was exchangeable for cokes, T-shirts, and the like for every 20 points earned. Jones reported a sharp increase, as a result of this intervention, in the occurrence of desired game behaviors.

Intervention "packages," or combinations, vary from simple sets (usually positive reinforcement plus one other intervention) to considerably more complex four- or five-procedure sequences. Positive reinforcement plus response cost was the set employed by A. C. Fisher (1976) in a study taking Jones's (1977) effort one procedure further. Fisher developed a basketball-effectiveness scoring sheet for each player, giving or taking away points for forcing a jump ball (+), causing a jump ball (−), stealing the ball (+), giving the ball up by interception (−), and so on. This intervention also appeared to improve subsequent game performance. Most coaches, quite like most parents, employers, and classroom teachers, reward with attention when the target individual shows undesirable behavior. These and related investigations of the use of positive reinforcement to enhance sports performance clearly underscore the value of an opposite coaching strategy, namely, "catch them being good."

An intervention combination study reported by G. L. Martin, LePage, and Koop (1983) illustrates another important aspect of the use of positive reinforcement. In his successful use, based upon anecdotal evidence, of prompting, positive reinforcement, performance feedback, and self-monitoring, reinforcements were dispensed on a group basis, an option of considerable relevance for team sports. If all or most members of the swim team showed "good news behaviors" (e.g., being on time for practice, pushing hard even when the coach wasn't looking, practicing correct form on strokes and turns, encouraging teamates), reinforcers were provided as the team decided.

Allison and Ayllon (1983) tested the effectiveness of prompting, positive reinforcement, and time-out on (a) blocking in football; (b) backward walking, front handsprings, and reverse kips in gymnastics; and (c) forehand, backhand, and serve in tennis. In all three sports, significant performance gains up to 10 times baseline were obtained. In general, the growth in sports contexts of use of behavior modification intervention packages, such as the sampling of combinations just presented, paralleled their growing use in other contexts. In sports, their use usually was a *training* effort to improve athletic competence; outside of sports the effort was often more one of *therapy* to resolve disordered behavior problems. Though the goals were rather different in sports and nonsports contexts, advances in the technology and effectiveness of behavior modification outside of sports were rapidly and often creatively incorporated into the sports setting and used quite effectively there also.

Perhaps the prime example of this influence upon the growth of sports behavior modification began to occur in the mid-1970s as behavior modification in general became increasingly cognitive. In addition to being pushed and pulled by reinforcements provided or removed, people's behavior and its modification was increasingly seen as also resulting from their cognitive processing of events, such as through use of imagery, self-instructions, observation of others, mental rehearsal, attentional focus, elaborated thoughts, and stopped thoughts. A number of new behavior modification intervention combinations appeared, reflecting this new perspective, and became important additions to the sports psychologist's pharmacy. Suinn (1976) reported both case studies and empirical research on a sequence he labeled *visuo-motor behavioral rehearsal*. In this approach to improving sports performance, the athlete is first taught how to engage in deep muscle relaxation and then provided with training in imaginal rehearsal. This imagery component requires the person to visualize the complete athletic event as he or she would actually perform it. Visual-motor behavioral rehearsal has been shown to benefit positively the downhill performance of Olympic skiers (Suinn,

1976), foul shooting (+ 10% in home games; + 15% in away games) bas-ketball performance (Lane, 1980), football kicking distance (Titley, 1980), and karate performance (R. S. Weinberg, Seabourne, & Jackson, 1983).

Other promising behavior modification intervention combinations that include one or more cognitive components are Kirschenbaum and Bale's (1980) "brain power golf" (deep-muscle relaxation, imaginal rehearsal, self-monitoring, and self-instructions), Wenz and Strong's (1980) self-regulation approach (deep-muscle relaxation, imaginal rehearsal, autogenic phrases, and biofeedback training), E. Hall and Purvis's (1980) anxiety management combination (deep-muscle relaxation, imaginal rehearsal, thought stopping, biofeedback training), and Mahoney's (1984) recommended intervention for enhancing the athlete's sense of self-efficacy (response induction aids, imagi-nal rehearsal, direct reassurance, modeling, self-statement modification) and for psyching up (focused concentration, adrenalyzing imagery, and self-statements) and lowering arousal (deep-muscle relaxation, calming self-statements, deep-breathing exercises).

The positive initial evaluative evidence reported for these several behavior modification sequences is, in our view, strongly encouraging of the contin-ued use and study of behavior modification in athletic settings. Ideally, such work will aim at ever more effective and prescriptive combinations of proce-dures, combinations tailored to particular difficulties, people, teams, or sports. The future of this effort seems particularly bright.

NORTHEASTERN LEAGUE STANDINGS
July 10, 1993

Team	Wins	Losses	Percentage	Games Behind
Newark Eagles	42	26	.617	—
Manhattan Maulers	41	27	.602	1
Coney Island Cyclones	39	30	.565	3½
Harrisburg Blues	37	32	.536	5½
Norristown Rockets	33	35	.455	9
Port Jefferson Jesters	26	43	.376	16½
Camden Sluggers	20	49	.289	22½

It was like exhibition season all over again. The Cyclones had won 13 of the last 16 games, and it looked like there might be no stopping them. The team had caught fire and hit .303 since mid-June. The pitching was in a terrific groove. Five of the last six games had been finished by the starting pitcher. Tony wasn't sure exactly what had turned the team around. He'd take some of the credit for sure, especially because he got most of the blame when they were playing badly. "Fair is fair" he thought. The shrink didn't hurt any either. That relaxation stuff really got the guys loose. And imagining doing it all just right really seemed to make it happen, at least for some of his players. Tony wasn't sure just how far this team could go. They had shot up to third in just a

> few weeks, and they were as hot as he'd seen a team. But the Eagles and the Maulers sure weren't patsies. Well, smiled Tony, we're sure going to make a hell of a run for it now!

FUTURE DIRECTIONS

The concerns of the sports psychologist are many and varied. In this chapter we have examined psychological research on and application to several of their chief targets of interest, including sports leadership, components of athletic performance, athlete personality and motivation, sources and control of sports violence, and the application of behavior modification procedures to enhance sports performance. In addition to these major areas of applied psychological interest, additional facets of the athletic enterprise have begun to come under the scrutiny of psychological research. Some, as above, also relate to the enhancement of sports performance. Others relate to broader issues in American society. This final section of this chapter is devoted to these additional facets. They represent many of the important future directions for the applied psychological field of sports psychology.

Team Cohesiveness

Does team cohesiveness, usually defined as the degree to which players like each other, like the team as a whole, and want to remain a member of it, influence sports performance? Do more cohesive teams win more often? Or is it the case, instead, that teams that win more often are more cohesive? Several investigators working at different times and in different sports have fairly consistently found a cohesiveness–performance correlation. Although this relationship seems well established, its direction of causality is less clear. In some instances, it seems, cohesiveness enhances outcome; in others, outcome enhances cohesiveness. D. Gill and Martens (1977) suggested that cohesiveness influences performance more in sports involving interaction teams (e.g., baseball, basketball, football) than in sports with coacting teams (e.g., tennis, bowling, track). Martens and Peterson (1976) have appropriately reminded us that, even when team cohesiveness does influence sports performance, it is but one of several outcome-determining variables:

> . . . it is not contended that cohesiveness is the primary factor in successful basketball performance. The ability of the players and their opponents, the quality of coaching, the officials, and many other factors contribute to the effectiveness of a team. Our finding, however, does suggest that higher levels of cohesiveness are associated with greater success and satisfaction. (p. 53)

To the extent that team cohesiveness can heighten the quality of performance, there are several routes by which it can be maximized. Browne and Mahoney (1984) suggested open communication between players and coach and among players; coach fairness; shared goal setting; relative homogeneity among players in skill level, aspiration level, and value systems; external threat or pressure from other teams; continuity and stability of team membership; and, as noted, successful game outcomes. Tutko and Richards (1971) add, as still further means of enhancing team cohesiveness, having players become familiar with each other's responsibilities, having players observe and even try out each other's positions, developing pride in team subunits, and scheduling regular player–coach meetings to develop a spirit of participation.

Martens, Landers, and Loy (1980) aid us further in this cohesiveness-enhancement direction by proposing that cohesiveness, as usually defined in terms of liking or attraction, is an oversimplification. Instead, they suggest, cohesiveness reflects several dimensions of the player's perception of his or her team: interpersonal attraction, personal power or influence, value of membership, sense of belonging, enjoyment, teamwork, and closeness. Martens et al. (1980) captured this more expansive and, we believe, more accurate, multidimensional definition of cohesiveness in their Sports Cohesiveness Questionnare (Table 8.5.). Inherent in their definitional and measurement perspective is, we believe, some especially valuable leads for the future study of team cohesiveness in athletic contexts, including the more fine-grained, prescriptive question of whether different dimensions of cohe-

TABLE 8.5. Cohesion Items for the Martens, Landers, and Loy Sports Cohesiveness Questionnaire

ITEM	QUESTION
Interpersonal Attraction	On what type of friendship basis are you with each member of your team
Personal Power or Influence	For many reasons some of the members of a team are more influential than others. How much influence do you believe each of the other members of your team have with the coach and other teammates?
Value of Membership	Compared to other groups that you belong to, how much do you value your membership on this team?
Sense of Belonging	How strong a sense of belonging do you believe you have to this team?
Enjoyment	How much do you like competing with this particular team?
Teamwork	How good do you think the teamwork is on your team?
Closeness	How closely knit do you think your team is?

Note. "Sports Cohesiveness Questionnaire" by R. Martens, D. M. Landers, and J. Loy in *Social Psychology of Sport* (p. 238) edited by A. V. Carron, 1980, Ithaca, NY: Mouvement Publications. Copyright 1980 by Mouvement. Reprinted by permission.

siveness influence outcome differentially in different sports and with different players.

Transfer and Maintenance

Throughout this chapter we have examined a number of established and potential influences upon sports performance. If we assume that a combination of good coaching, high-level skills, optimal motivational level, maximal team cohesiveness, minimal interference from negative thoughts or events, and other forces combine to yield in any given player or team an outstanding quality of athletic performance, our applied task is still not complete. If outstanding performance is shown at practice, we must meet the challenge of *transferring* its occurrence to the actual game. If outstanding performance is shown during actual athletic contests, we still face the need to have it continue, or *maintain*, over time and future games. Changing sports performance for the better is clearly a difficult challenge. Causing it to transfer and maintain is even more difficult to accomplish. Attention can flag, motivation can diminish, the opposition can "get the player's number," physical energy level can decrease over a long season, personality concerns can prove distracting, or other antitransfer, antimaintenance causes can arise. Coaching lore is not very sophisticated for these purposes, and applied psychology is only slightly better. Together, a few valuable suggestions have emerged for purposes of transfer enhancement and maintenance enhancement, but clearly this is a primary domain in great need of additional applied psychological research. For now, one can only recount that transfer and maintenance of athletic skills can be promoted by:

1. Spaced, rather than massed, practice sessions
2. Overlearning, or, the continued practice of successful skills to the point at which they are experienced under game conditions as automatic
3. Replicated game conditions during practice, such as provision of game noises and even verbal harassment via broadcasting or a live audience, practice under diverse weather conditions, and shooting of fouls after a tiring scrimage
4. Provision of as much actual game time as possible to each player
5. Training routines designed to replicate the tension and arousal levels of actual game performance
6. Continued coaching attention to positive reinforcement, performance feedback, team cohesiveness, and related performance enhancers.

Beyond these few examples, not much of the beginning technology for enhancing transfer and maintenance that has emerged in other fields of applied psychology (A. P. Goldstein & Kanfer, 1979; Karoly & Steffan, 1980) has yet filtered into sports psychology. It is a need whose time has clearly come.

Special Populations

Organized sports serve several purposes: as entertainment, a business, and as an event that affects its participants in ways both known and unknown. In almost all sections of this chapter we have taken a prescriptive viewpoint. Different athletes and different sports require different styles of leadership, have different personalities, develop different sources of team cohesiveness, and so forth. In a similar fashion, different segments of society vary in what sports means to them and can do for them. Reis and Jelsma (1980) have written at length about the woman athlete and her special needs, problems, and opportunities. They highlighted the different meaning sports hold for men and women, the fear of athletic success that can occur in a sex-typing society, the role of self-fulfilling prophecies, and the views of sportswomen on the place of competition versus cooperation in both sports and American society. Brown (1980) wrote feelingly about the black athlete and his or her special needs, problems, and opportunities. In his provocative section "The Jock Trap: How the Black Athlete Gets Caught" he highlighted the seductive appeal of organized sports for many young black athletes and the personal and educational price many youngsters eventually pay for their sports participation.

Browne and Mahoney (1984), in contrast, highlighted with another population a series of potential benefits from sports participation. Given that many individuals report enjoying such benefits in their own sports participation as enhanced body awareness and image, time out from daily routines, a sense of belonging to a group with shared values and interests, and a rise in self-esteem from setting and reaching personal goals, Browne and Mahoney suggested that, for these several reasons, such participation might be especially beneficial for that large number of citizens suffering from depression, obesity, alcoholism, headache, and asthma or those who are undergoing cardiac rehabilitation. Browne and Mahoney, it is clear, feel sports participation can have a broad range of positive effects on the individual's mood, health, personality, and development.

Orlick, concerned with the effects of sports participation on children, has feared that quite the opposite happens far too often. As is clear in his books *Winning Through Cooperation* (Orlick, 1978) and *Every Kid Can Win* (Orlick & Botterill, 1975), Orlick felt that organized sports as typically carried out are basically organized to fit the needs of adults, not children, and thus have a serious negative effect on the social and psychological development of young children. In particular, he pointed to:

1. A competitive reward system (based on game score) that yields a winner and a loser, thus guaranteeing for those who are frequent losers an experience of negative appraisal by others and perhaps both rejection and withdrawal from participation.

2. Elitism, for instance, a system in which 100 children are urged to try

out, and 85 are cut to form a team of 15. Orlick and Botterill (1975) wrote:

> Elimination is . . . the most critical problem which exists in children's sports. It is absurd that on the one hand we feel that sports are good for kids, and on the other hand we set up a system which eliminates poorer performers, girls, late-maturing boys, kids who are not aggressive, and so on. (pp. 15–16)
> We should field as many teams as there are interested kids to fill them. . . . It is comparable to a doctor refusing to treat his sickest patients to insure that his win–loss record is good. Those people seeking athletic participation who are cut off may be the ones who could benefit most from this experience. (p. 17)

3. A negative effect on character development. Contrary to the popular belief that "sports builds character," the little existing research evidence shows just the opposite. Sports participation very often leads to a *decrease* in such prosocial behaviors as sharing (Barnett & Bryan, 1974), helping (McGuire & Thomas, 1975), and fairness (Webb, 1969), and, reciprocally, competitive sports participation might increase an array of antisocial or egocentric behaviors in children (Berkowitz, 1973; Gelfand & Hartman, 1978).

If, as Orlick and his collaborators proposed, excessive organization along the lines of adult athletics, competition, elitism, and character maldevelopment are what's wrong with children's sports participation, what are his recommended solutions? Orlick and his colleagues, with the aid of children's advice, have been exceedingly creative in this regard, developing for themselves and others to evaluate a long series of suggested novel modifications for children's sports:

1. Emphasis is on the means for "winning," not only in terms of game score, but also in gaining friends, respect, trust, confidence, satisfaction, knowledge, skills, and health.
2. The establishment of realistic and attainable goals is encouraged, such as by having the child compete against his own earlier performance.
3. Every one who wishes to play can.
4. Games are played cross-court, cross-ice, etc. (three games simultaneously), so that all can get sufficient playing time.
5. Everyone gets to play an equal amount of time.
6. Everyone gets a turn at being team captain.
7. Each child is given the opportunity to play each position.
8. Skill emphasis is on self-improvement.
9. No goals are counted, no points awarded, no records kept of leading scorers, no official score is kept.
10. Children are involved in the planning, leadership, and evaluation of the activity.
11. Extrinsic rewards (trophies, awards) are de-emphasized; intrinsic rewards are highlighted.

12. There is active encouragement of cooperative skills.
13. More co-educational games are used.
14. There is more use of games in which every child must touch the ball/ puck at least once before a teammate can take a shot.
15. Use of multiball, multigoal games.
16. Use of penalty shots rather than penalties.
17. Emotional or physical outbursts, especially toward officials, are not tolerated.
18. Expulsion from the game results for any deliberate attempt to injure another player.
19. Individual penalties are not announced, to minimize the reinforcement of attention.
20. All players shake hands with all opposing players after the game.
21. Coaches should be selected based upon their teaching ability, values and attitudes, rather than their personal athletic accomplishments.

Orlick and his collaborators have provided us with a very attractive yet very challenging agenda for future action. It is hoped that applied psychologists interested in obtaining maximum benefit for society from their efforts will respond energetically.

NORTHEASTERN LEAGUE STANDINGS August 18, 1993				
Team	Wins	Losses	Percentage	Games Behind
Newark Eagles	63	37	.630	—
Coney Island Cyclones	63	37	.630	—
Manhattan Maulers	59	41	.590	4
Norristown Rockets	52	48	.520	11
Harrisburg Blues	50	50	.500	13
Port Jefferson Jesters	38	62	.380	25
Camden Sluggers	31	69	.310	27

"No matter what happens now," Tony said so that everyone in the dugout could hear, "this is a championship team." It just had to be one of baseball's greatest stretch drives—fifth place at midseason, tied for first at the end. And now it all came down to this one playoff game.

Becker was pitching for the Eagles and had again retired the Cyclones in order. He seemed almost as strong in the eighth inning as when the game started. Watkins had doubled-in a run for the Cyclones in the second, but they had only two scattered singles since. Les Kryzwicki, a damned fine pitcher himself (and being born and raised in Coney Island, easily the most popular Cyclone) had given up an unearned run in the fourth, and now Wallace's home run in the top of the ninth. Eagles 2, Cyclones 1, and only three outs left for the Cyclones. Talk about going down to the wire!

Coach Ben Anderson reminded Tony of the 1951 New York Giants and how they had won it all in the last inning of their play-off game. "It *can* be done, it *will* be done!" Anderson shouted. Red Wingo was up first for the Cyclones. The count went to 2 and 1. On the next pitch, Wingo hit a sharp line drive right at the mound. Becker managed to get his glove down, but the ball deflected toward third, and Wingo was safe at first well before the third baseman's off-balance throw. Kryzwicki was due up next, but Tony sent up Harris Brown to hit for him instead. Brown was probably the slowest runner on the Cyclones, but a real bull who could hit the ball a mile. He went for Becker's first pitch and did hit it a mile . . . straight up. Tony's stomach sank, as the ball came down just in front of home plate, an easy out for the Eagle's catcher. Nate Krause, the Cyclone's left fielder, was the next batter. Nate hadn't been hitting well lately, and Tony thought about pinch hitting for him also. But Nate had so much talent and so much smarts about the game, that Tony decided to gamble and leave him in.

Becker's first pitch was high and inside, *very* inside, almost knocking Nate down. He came back with a fastball, low and outside, just over the plate. One ball, one strike. Nate quickly thought, "An off-speed pitch or a curve ball would usually come next. Bet he crosses me with another low, outside fastball." And so it was. Nate was ready for it. Nate was looking for it. Nate hit it with a solid crack of the bat that he felt throughout his body.

The ball left Nate's bat like a shot, heading to right field, and Nate left home plate toward first in pretty much the same way. The adrenalin had kicked into high gear, and Nate felt himself flying as he rounded first and tore toward second. He stole a quick glance toward right field and saw the ball bounce off the wall and *past* Fletcher, the Eagle's right fielder. Lord, he thought, I'm going to make it all the way to third! He rounded second and flew toward third. When he was half-way there, Wingo crossed home plate with the tying run. Nate looked at Coach Anderson in the box behind third. His face was as red as a beet. He was bent over, arms spread, hands down, yelling "slide, slide, slide!" Nate knew it would be close; Fletcher had a pretty decent arm. Nate strained every muscle in his body. About 10 ft from the bag he took off, launching himself like some sort of human rocket, aimed straight at third base. The ball arrived only a split second after Nate, and, when the dust settled, it was Eagles 2, Cyclones 2, with a bruised, dirty, and deliriously happy Nate on third.

Tony had to think fast. Jeff Petrie was the next batter, and that was just fine. Jeff was solid, batting .302 for the season, and a pretty versatile guy. The percentage call here was simple. Let Jeff hit away. All we need is a long fly ball. Nate will tag up, and it's all ours. The Eagles weren't going to make it that easy though, and Becker threw the first pitch to Jeff intentionally 4 ft wide of the plate. They were walking Jeff, hoping to set up a doubleplay and go into extra innings.

Nate was on third, Jeff Petrie on first, and the Cyclone's batter was the third man in their lineup, Juan Torres, their third baseman. A long fly ball will still sew it up, thought Tony. Then something caught his eye, and it made Tony catch his breath! Len Brakus, the Eagles' third baseman, was playing too deep. He should be in, way in for a play at the plate, and he wasn't. A bunt, a bunt, a suicide squeeze bunt thought Tony. If Torres can lay it down, the pennant is ours. It would have to be on the first pitch, before Brakus or someone else on the Eagles realized the mistake. Tony wiped his right arm across his chest three times, and Coach Anderson caught the signal and passed it on to both Nate at third and Torres at the plate. Becker stretched, pumped, and threw. Nate began his one-way charge toward home, no turning back possible. Torres's hand slid down the bat, and he turned to bunt the ball. Tony felt frozen in time and space, as if he were an actor in some old, slow-motion movie. He hardly heard the 15,000 screaming fans. Brakus realized his mistake and headed toward the plate, but it was too late. Torres met the ball perfectly, softly, and it dribbled off his bat toward third.

Nate was smoke flying toward home. The Eagles' catcher Sal Tinto stepped in front of the plate, blocking it from invaders. Brakus grabbed the ball with his bare hand and, off-balance, on the fly, threw it as hard as he could toward home. Tinto had 30 lb on Nate and was built like a battleship, but Nate had 90 running feet of momentum on this side. Nate, the ball, and Tinto all seemed to arrive at the same moment, in one grand explosion at home plate. The $1/4$ second it took for Jeff Riley, the home-plate umpire, to signal safe seemed like an eternity to Tony. But the arms were outstretched; safe it was.

Now Tony heard the crowd. He hugged a dazed Nate Krause, as Torres jumped on his back screaming. It was over. They had done it. The Cyclones had won the pennant.

Epilogue

This book has been a journey through human behavior. Wherever people live, work, play, learn, relate to one another, or seek to improve their physical or mental health, the applied psychologist has been there. His or her purpose has been to seek deeper understanding of cause and effect, greater effectiveness in reaching important human goals, and higher levels of human satisfaction. By means of creative speculation, systematic research, and skilled intervention, the applied psychologist has for nearly 100 years made significant contributions to the human condition.

As our text demonstrates, a number of these applied contributions have been in traditional, long-standing arenas of psychological interest: the clinic, the school, the world of business and industry. In these settings, as well as in the newer domains of application, the applied psychologist has sought to both better understand the interacting human forces and enhance human satisfaction and efficiency. In recent years, as we have shown, these efforts have extended into the courts and criminal justice settings, the sports arena, the general hospital, and the community. The impact of this body of psychological experimentation and application on the daily lives of all of us is very substantial. As J. D. Matarazzo (1984), for example, pointed out with regard to our health:

> The recent focus on enhancing health and wellness has helped spawn a major white-collar industry, which has attracted tens of thousands of new workers during the past 25 years and has helped give birth to hundreds of new companies and enterprises offering ways for healthy individuals to lose weight, stop smoking, tone flabby muscles, and improve their cardiovascular systems, as well as ways to inoculate them against stress at work and at home. This development in the direction of health enhancement represents a major break with the whole of the past history of humankind, in which survival and recovery from illness were paramount goals. (p. 3)

This same dramatic observation, with slight changes in the numbers involved, could be made about the growth, development, and social and economic impact of the application of psychology in many of the other areas of our lives discussed in this volume.

Psychology has entered into every phase of the educational scene. The teacher has been exposed to psychological theories throughout formal and informal training situations. Psychological theories, particularly involving the learning process, have affected every aspect of the school curriculum. The individual child in the classroom has been the target of conceptual and experimental research to explain and promote his or her development and behavior. Most recently, psychologists are conceptualizing students, teachers, parents, administration, and commmunity as a total system. This new approach will have considerable impact in the future on specific classroom applications and their community implications. An especially important future goal of the application of psychology to education should be to help attract to the role of teacher individuals who view teaching as an exciting and prestigeful endeavor, commensurate with functioning in that most important role in society, that of training the citizens of the future.

In the community and environmental areas extension of the scope of what the psychologist seeks to understand and improve is ever expanding and offers the most exciting of possibilities for change and betterment in our world. For example, a fairly recent edition of a text on environmental psychology (J. D. Fisher, Bell, & Baum, 1984) includes applications to stress in catastrophes and disasters, housing for the aged, work environments, hospitals, museums, prisons, public transportation, recreational settings, and virtually every environmental setting in which human beings participate. The focus of community applications has increasingly shifted from the treatment of pathological dysfunction to improvement of living and working conditions, as well as to helping the individual feel in control of her or his environment, and thus to prevention of the ills (physical, mental, and environmental) that plague us all.

This new emphasis on prevention and growth has also been clearly evidenced in the areas of health, mental health, education, industry, sports, and forensic psychology. It would seem clear that prevention (of illness, insanity, crime, inefficiency, social deterioration, pollution, etc.) is far more desirable than the treatment of already existing personal and social disorders. But once applied psychologists become involved in "prevention," they perforce are involved in influencing public policy and the legal system, and thus their situation and aspiration become far more complex. Ah, for the good old days of treating "sick" people; life was so much simpler.

We have been emphasizing throughout this volume that we are dealing with the behavior of applied psychologists as individuals. A major influence on such behavior, in fact on the behavior of all of us, is the expectancy (faith, belief, hope) that the procedures being applied can actually change (help, prevent, alleviate) human problems. The applied psychologist must have the theoretical training and technical competence that would lead to such effective application.

Thus, a major element in the future of applied psychology is the professional training of the appliers. There is currently considerable ferment about the process of training and accreditation of applied psychologists (Boll, 1985). The relevant issues go deep into the nature of the field of psychology itself. How should an applied psychologist be trained? What should be the relationship between basic and applied psychology? What is the best way to develop and enhance socially desirable ethical and value systems? Should the formal accreditation of training programs, by the American Psychological Association, be extended beyond the current clinical and counseling psychology areas to such fields as health psychology, industrial psychology, and forensic psychology? The implications of these issues go beyond the mere training of psychologists into the fabric of American society, because the values, goals, and procedures that go into the training of applied psychologists will have repercussions for the current and next generation of inhabitants of this society.

At this point we must offer at least a small note of caution in this highly optimistic view of the growth of applied psychology. The scientific influence in our training pushes us to note that, in the multitude of studies in the applied fields of psychology, there are frequent failures to replicate findings, poor experimental designs, low reliability, and even negative results. In effect, many applications simply are not effective or are questionable in their effects. There is the danger of giving the impression that effective ways to change human behavior are now completely developed, leaving only the task of extending them to newer and newer settings.

This is clearly not the case. Although the scientific basis of applied psychology and the resultant efforts of its many practitioners have grown greatly in rigor, competence, and effectiveness as its history has unfolded since the era of Munsterberg, there remains much to be done. Important items for a future agenda are better and more inclusive psychological theories, more adequately chosen and utilized experimental designs, greater openness to the use of a range of experimental designs (quantitative, qualitative, quasi-experimental) in examining the effectiveness of psychological applications, more sophisticated and more reliable measurement of application success and failure, and greater concern with the social validity of applications carried out.

THE FUTURE

There is no area of human behavior not affected by applied psychology, from art to zoology, including even such diverse fields as humor (Chapman & Foot, 1977), the mystery novel (L. Krasner, 1983), lie detection (Ekman & Friesen, 1974), and science (Mahoney, 1976). For example, to add to such already established fields as the history, philosophy, and sociology of science, there is now emerging a psychology of science (L. Krasner & Houts, 1984) that is, in effect, the psychology of the scientist (Roe, 1961). The impression that applied psychology is everywhere is certainly true.

Are we willing to make predictions? The obvious one is that the field of applied psychology will continue to grow in terms of publications, organizations, aspects of human life affected, and consequent influence on society. The positive possibilities and possible dangers of the growth and development of applied psychology were tersely captured in a 1972 article in *Psychology Today* by Kenneth Goodall, commenting on the then rapidly developing growth of applications of the Skinnerian operant conditioning version of behaviorism that have epitomized all other applications of psychology. In describing the "shapers at work," Goodall noted that

> They take Skinnerian principles out of the pigeon cage and put them into practice out where people live and work and play and suffer and learn, . . . in classrooms, kitchens, mental hospitals, rehabilitation wards, prisons, churches, reform schools, nursing homes, day-care centers, factories, movie theaters, national parks, community mental health centers, recreation centers and in the house next door. (p. 53)

Goodall described the growth of behavioral applications in the decades of the 1930s to the 1970s as they moved from experimentation through treatment to prevention. For example, target subjects in the 1930s were individuals, target subjects in the 1970s were "whole schools, neighborhoods, whole countries, the general public." Of special interest to us from our current time perspective is Goodall's projection for the year 2001. In that not-so-distant year the target subjects of these energetic appliers would be "everyone," the behavior shapers would be "everyone," the target behaviors would be "all kinds," the environments involved would be "everywhere," and the behavioral products would be a "happy productive culture without war, poverty, or pollution" (pp. 62–63).

On that upbeat note, and in the hope that we are at least substantially moving in that direction, we end this journey through modern applied psychology.

References

Acker, L. E. (1980). On the training of mediators in behavior modification. In G. L. Martin & J. G. Osborne (Eds.), *Helping in the community: Behavioral applications*. New York: Plenum.

Adams, S. (1961). *Assessment of the psychiatric treatment program, phase 1* (Research Report No. 21). Sacramento, CA: California Youth Authority.

Adkins, W. R. (1974). Life coping skills: A fifth curriculum. *Teachers College Record, 75*, 507–526.

Agras, W. S. (1967). Behavior therapy in the management of chronic schizophrenia. *American Journal of Psychiatry, 124*, 240–243.

Agras, W. S. (1982). Behavioral medicine in the 1980s: Nonrandom connections. *Journal of Consulting and Clinical Psychology, 50*, 797–803.

Agras, W. S. (in press). *Eating disorders: Management of obesity, bulimia, and anorexia nervosa*. Elmsford, NY: Pergamon.

Agras, W. S., & Kirkley, B. G. (1986). Bulimia: Theories of etiology. In K. D. Brownell & J. P. Foreyt (Eds.), *Handbook of eating disorders: Physiology, psychology, and treatment of obesity, anorexia, and bulimia*. New York: Basic Books.

Alderfer, C. P. (1972). *Existence, relatedness, and growth: Human needs in organizational settings*. New York: Free Press.

Alderman, R. B. (1980). Strategies for motivating young athletes. In W. F. Straub (Ed.), *Sports psychology: An analysis of athlete behavior*. Ithaca, NY: Mouvement.

Alexander, F. (1939). Psychoanalytic study of a case of essential hypertension. *Psychosomatic Medicine, 1*, 139–152.

Alexander, F. (1950). *Psychosomatic medicine: Its principles and applications*. New York: Norton.

Alexander, F., & Staub, H. (1931). *The criminal, the judge, and the public*. New York: Macmillan.

Allison, M. G., & Ayllon, T. (1983). Behavioral coaching in the development of skills in football, gymnastics and tennis. In G. L. Martin & D. Hyrcaiko (Eds.), *Behavioral modification and coaching*. Springfield, IL: Charles C Thomas.

Allport, G. W. (1942). The use of personal documents in psychological science. *Social Science Research Council Bulletin, 49*.

Altman, I. (1975). *The environment and social behavior: Privacy, space, territory, crowding*. San Francisco: Brooks/Cole.

Amabile, L., & Stubbs, B. (1982). *Psychological research in the classroom: Issues for educators and researchers*. Elmsford, NY: Pergamon.

American Heritage Dictionary of the English Language. (1976). Boston: Houghton Mifflin.

American Law Institute. (1962). *Model penal code, proposed official draft*. Philadelphia, PA: Author.

Anastasi, A. (1979). *Fields of applied psychology* (2nd ed.). New York: McGraw-Hill.

Anderson, C. W. (1960). The relation between speaking times and decision in the employment interview. *Journal of Applied Psychology, 44*, 267–268.

Apfelbaum, D. (1958). *Dimensions of transference in psychotherapy*. Berkeley, CA: University of California Press.

Appel, V. H. (1960). Client expectancies about counseling in a university counseling center. Paper presented at the meeting of the Western Psychological Association, San Jose, CA.

Argyris, C. (1971). *Management and organizational development: The path from Xa to Xb*. New York: McGraw-Hill.

Arms, R. L., Russell, G. W., & Sandilands, M. L. (1979). Effects of viewing aggressive sports on the hostility of spectators. *Social Psychology Quarterly, 42*, 275–279.

Arnkoff, D. B. (1982). Common and specific factors in cognitive therapy. In M. Lambert (Ed.), *A guide to psychotherapy and patient relationship*. Homewood, IL: Dow Jones-Irwin.

Atthowe, J. M., & Krasner, L. (1968). A preliminary report on the application of contingent reinforcement procedures (token economy on a "chronic" psychiatric ward). *Journal of Abnormal Psychology, 73*, 37–43.

Atyeo, D. (1981). *Violence in sports*. New York: Van Nostrand.

Ayllon, T., & Azrin, N. H. (1965). The measurement and reinforcement of behavior of psychotics. *Journal of the Experimental Analysis of Behavior, 8*, 357–387.

Ayllon, T., & Azrin, N. H. (1968).*The token economy: A motivational system for therapy and rehabilitation*. New York: Appleton-Century-Crofts.

Ayllon, T., & Michael, J. (1959). The psychiatric nurse as a behavioral engineer. *Journal of the Experimental Analysis of Behavior, 2*, 323–326.

Azrin, N. H. (1977). A strategy for applied research: Learning based but outcome oriented. *American Psychologist, 32*, 140–149.

Bachrach, A. J., Erwin, W. J., & Mohr, J. P. (1965). The control of eating behavior in an anorexic by operant conditioning techniques. In L. P. Ullmann & L. Krasner (Eds.), *Case studies in behavior modification*. New York: Holt, Rinehart & Winston.

Baer, D. E. (1979). On the relation between basic and applied research. In A. C. Catania & T. A. Brigham (Eds.), *Handbook of applied behavior analysis*. New York: Irvington.

Baer, D. M. (1984). *Modern behavior analysis*. Paper presented at the Fourth Annual Kansas Students' Conference, Pittsburgh State University.

Baer, D. M., Wolf, M. M., & Risley, T. R. (1968). Some current dimensions of applied behavior analyses. *Journal of Applied Behavior Analyses, 1*, 91–97.

Baldwin, J. (1982). *Psychology applied to the art of teaching*. Norwalk, CT: Appleton-Century-Crofts.

Bandura, A. (1969). *Principles of behavior modification*. New York: Holt, Rinehart & Winston.

Bandura, A. (1977a). Self-efficacy: Toward a unifying theory of behavioral change. *Psychological Review, 84*, 191–215.

Bandura, A. (1977b). *Social learning theory.* Englewood Cliffs, NJ: Prentice-Hall.

Bandura, A. (1982). Self-efficacy mechanism in human agency. *American Psychologist, 37,* 122–147.

Bandura, A. (1984). Model of causality in social learning theory. In S. Sukemune (Ed.), *Advances in social learning theory.* Tokyo: Kanekoshoho.

Bandura, A. (1985). *Social foundations of thought and action: A social cognitive theory.* Englewood Cliffs, NJ: Prentice-Hall.

Bandura, A. (1986). *Social foundations of thought and action: A social cognitive theory.* Englewood Cliffs, NJ: Prentice-Hall.

Bandura, A., Jeffery, R. W., & Wright, C. L. (1974). Efficacy of participant modeling as a function of response induction aids. *Journal of Abnormal Psychology, 83,* 56–64.

Barber, T. X., & Calverly, D. S. (1966). Effects on recall of hypnotic induction, motivational suggestions and suggested regression: A methodological and experimental analysis. *Journal of Abnormal Psychology, 71,* 169–180.

Barker, R. G. (1968). *Ecological psychology: Concepts and methods for studying the environment of human behavior.* Stanford, CA: Stanford University Press.

Barker, R. G., & Wright, H. F. (1955). *Midwest and its children: The psychological ecology of an American town.* New York: Harper & Row. (Reprinted 1971 by Archon Books, Handen, CT.)

Barland, G. H., & Raskin, D. C. (1973). Detection of deception. In W. F. Prokasy & D. C. Raskin (Eds.), *Electrodermal activity in psychological research.* New York: Academic.

Barnett, M., & Bryan, J. (1974). Effects of competition with outcome feedback on children's helping behavior. *Developmental Psychology, 10,* 838–842.

Barrett-Lennard, G. T. (1962). Dimensions of therapist response as causal factors in therapeutic change. *Psychological Monographs, 75,* 1–36.

Bartol, C. R. (1983). *Psychology and American law.* Belmont, CA: Wadsworth.

Beck, A. (1976). *Cognitive therapy and the emotional disorders.* New York: International Universities Press.

Beer, M. (1976). The technology of organizational development. In M. D. Dunnettee (Ed.), *Handbook of industrial and organizational psychology.* Chicago: Rand McNally.

Beer, M., & Kleisath, S. (1967). *The effects of the managerial grid lab on organizational and leadership dimensions.* Paper presented at the meeting of the American Psychological Association, Washington, DC.

Beier, E. G. (1966). *The silent language of psychotherapy.* Chicago: Aldine.

Belar, C. D., Deardorff, W. W., & Kelly, K. E. (in press). *The practice of clinical health psychology.* Elmsford, NY: Pergamon.

Bell, D. A., Jr. (1973). Racism in American courts: Causes for black disruption or despair? *California Law Review, 61,* 165–203.

Bergler, E. (1946). Psychopathology of compulsive smoking. *Psychiatric Quarterly, 20,* 297–321.

Berkowitz, L. (1964). The effects of observing violence. *Scientific American, 210,* 35–41.

Berkowitz, L. (1973). Sports, competition, and aggression. In I. William & L. Wankel (Eds.), *Fourth Canadian symposium on psychology of motor learning and sport.* Ottawa: University of Ottawa.

Berrien, F. K. (1948). *Practical psychology.* New York: Macmillan.

Bijou, S. W., Peterson, R. F., Harris, F. R., Allen, K. E., & Johnston, M. (1969). Methodology for experimental studies of young children in natural settings. *Psychological Record, 19,* 177–210.

Birnbrauer, J. S., Bijou, S. W., Wolf, M. M., & Kidder, J. D. (1965). Programmed instruction in the classroom. In L. P. Ullmann & L. Krasner (Eds.), *Case studies in behavior modification*. New York: Holt, Rinehart & Winston.

Birnbrauer, J. S., & Lawler, J. (1964). Token reinforcement for learning. *Mental Retardation, 2*, 275–279.

Blake, R. R., & Mouton, J. S. (1964). *The managerial grid*. Houston, TX: Gulf Publishing.

Blanchard, E. G. (1982). Behavioral medicine: Past, present and future. *Journal of Consulting and Clinical Psychology, 50*, 795-796.

Blansfield, M. G., Blake, R. R., & Mouton, J. S. (1964). The merger laboratory. *Training Directors Journal, 18*, 2–10.

Blitzer, P. H., Rimm, A. A., & Giefer, E. E. (1977). The effect of cessation of smoking on body weight in 57,032 women: Cross-sectional and longitudinal analyses. *Journal of Chronic Diseases, 30*, 415–429.

Blunk, R., & Sales, B. (1977). Persuasion during the voir dire. In B. Sales (Ed.), *Psychology in the legal process*. Englewood Cliffs, NJ: Prentice-Hall.

Boll, T. J. (1985). Graduate education in psychology: Time for a change? *American Psychologist, 40*, 1029–1030.

Bonica, J. J. (1980). Pain research and therapy: Past and current status and future needs. In L. Ng & J. J. Bonica (Eds.), *Pain, discomfort, and humanitarian care*. New York: Elsevier.

Bordin, E. S. (1959). Inside the therapeutic hour. In E. A. Rubinstein & M. B. Parloff (Eds.) *Research in psychotherapy*. Washington, DC: American Psychological Association.

Boring, E. G. (1929). *A history of experimental psychology*. New York: Appleton-Century.

Bower, G. H. (1981). Mood and memory. *American Psychologist, 36*, (2), 129–148.

Bower, G. H., & Hilgard, E. R. (1981). *Theories of learning* (5th ed.). Englewood Cliffs, NJ: Prentice-Hall.

Bown, O. H. (1954). *An investigation of therapeutic relationships in client-centered psychotherapy*. Unpublished doctoral dissertation, University of Chicago.

Brand, R. J., Rosenman, R. H., Sholtz, R. I., & Friedman, M. (1976). Multivariate prediction of coronary heart disease in the Western Collaborative Group Study compared to the findings of the Framingham Study. *Circulation, 53*, 348–355.

Breuer, J., & Freud, S. (1895). *Studies on hysteria*. London: Hogarth Press.

Bristow, A. P. (1971). *Police supervision readings*. Springfield, IL: Charles C Thomas.

Brooks, A. D. (1974). *Law, psychiatry and the mental health system*. Boston: Little, Brown.

Brown, E., Deffenbacher, K., & Sturgill, W. (1977). Memory for faces and the circumstances of encounter. *Journal of Applied Psychology, 62*, 311–318.

Brown, R. C., Jr. (1980). The "jock-trap": How the black athlete gets caught. In W. F. Straub (Ed.) *Sports psychology: An analysis of athlete behavior*. Ithaca, NY: Mouvement.

Browne, M. A., & Mahoney, M. J. (1984). Sport psychology. In M. R. Rosenzweig & L. W. Porter (Eds.), *Annual Review of Psychology, 35*, 605–625.

Brownell, K. D. (1982). Behavioral medicine. In C. M. Franks, G. T. Wilson, P. C. Kendall, & K. D. Brownell. *Annual review of behavior therapy: Vol. 8. Theory and practice*. New York: Guilford.

Brownell, K. D. (1984). Behavioral medicine. In G. T. Wilson, C. M. Franks, K. D. Brownell & P. C. Kendall. *Annual review of behavior therapy: Vol. 9. Theory and practice*. New York: Guilford.

Brownell, K. D., & Stunkard, A. J. (1980). Exercise in the development and control of obesity. In A. J. Stunkard (Ed.), *Obesity*. Philadelphia: Saunders.

Brownell, K. D., Stunkard, A. J., & Albaum, J. M. (1980). Evaluation and modification of exercise patterns in the natural environment. *American Journal of Psychiatry, 137,* 1540–1545.

Buchanan, P. C. (1969). Laboratory training and organizational development. *Administrative Science Quarterly, 14,* 466–480.

Buckhout, R. (1974). Eyewitness testimony. *Scientific American, 231* (6), 23–31.

Buckhout, R. (1975). Nearly 2,000 witnesses can be wrong. *Social Action and the Law, 2,* 7.

Buckhout, R., Alper, A., Chern, S., Silverberg, G., & Slomovits, M. (1974). Determinants of eyewitness performance on a line-up. *Bulletin of the Psychonomic Society, 4,* 191–192.

Buckley, K. W. (1982). The selling of a psychologist: John Broadus Watson and the application of behavior techniques to advertising. *Journal of the History of the Behavioral Sciences, 18,* 207–221.

Bunker, L. K. (1978). The effect of anxiety on performance: Psyching them up, not out. In L. Bunker & R. Rotella (Eds.), *Sports psychology: From theory to practice.* Richmond: University of Virginia.

Burt, C. (1925). *The young delinquent.* New York: Appleton.

Burtt, M. E. (1931). *Legal psychology.* Englewood Cliffs, NJ: Prentice-Hall.

Burwitz, L., & Newell, K. M. (1976). The effects of the mere presence of coactors on learning a motor skill. In A. C. Fisher (Ed.), *Psychology of sport: Issues & insights.* Palo Alto, CA: Mayfield.

Bush, D. V. (1922). *Applied psychology and scientific living.* Chicago, IL: D. V. Bush.

Butler, J. M. (1958). Client-centered counseling and psychotherapy. In D. Brower & L. E. Abt (Eds.), *Progress in clinical psychology: Vol 3. Changing conceptions in psychotherapy.* New York: Grune & Stratton.

Campbell, J. P. (1971). Personnel training and development. In P. H. Mussen & M. R. Rosenzweig (Eds.), *Annual Review of Psychology, 22,* 565–602.

Campbell, J. P., & Dunnette, M. D. (1968). Effectiveness of T-group experiences in managerial training and development. *Psychological Bulletin, 70,* 73–103.

Carlson, R. E. (1970). Effects of applicant sample on ratings of valid information in an employment setting. *Journal of Applied Psychology, 54,* 217–222.

Carron, A. V. (1980). *Social psychology of sport.* Ithaca, NY: Mouvement.

Carron, A. V., & Bennett, B. B. (1977). Compatability in the coach–athlete dyad. *Research Quarterly, 48,* 671–679.

Cascio, W. F. (1982). *Applied psychology in personnel management.* Englewood Cliffs, NJ: Prentice-Hall.

Catalano, R., & Dooley, D. (1980). Economic change in primary prevention. In R. H. Price, R. F. Ketter, B. C. Bader, & J. Monahan (Eds.), *Prevention in mental health: Research, policy and practice.* Beverly Hills, CA: Sage.

Cavan, R. S. (1955). *Criminology.* New York: Crowell.

Chance, E. (1959). *Families in treatment.* New York: Basic Books.

Chapman, A. J., & Foot, H. C. (Eds.) (1977). *It's a funny thing, humor,* Oxford: Pergamon.

Chelladurai, P., & Saleh, S. D. (1978). Preferred leadership in sport. *Canadian Journal of Applied Sport Sciences, 3,* 85–97.

Chenoweth, J. H. (1961). Situational tests: A new attempt at assessing police candidates. *The Journal of Criminal Law, Criminology, and Police Science, 52,* 232–241.

Chester, G. (1970). *The ninth juror.* New York: Random House.

Clinard, M. N., & Quinney, R. (1973). *Criminal behavior systems: A typology.* New York: Holt, Rinehart & Winston.

Cloward, R. A. & Ohlin, L. (1960). *Delinquency and opportunity: A theory of delinquent gangs.* New York: Macmillan.

Cohen, D. (1979). *J. B. Watson: The founder of behaviourism.* London: Routledge & Kegan Paul.

Cohen, H. L. (1968). Educational therapy: The design of learning environments. In J. M. Shlien (Ed.), *Research in psychotherapy, Vol. 3.* Washington, DC: American Psychological Association.

Colman, A. D. (1975). Environmental design: Realities and delusions. In T. Thompson & W. J. Dochens (Eds.), *Applications of behavior modification.* New York: Academic.

Comment (1979). Psychologist as expert witness: Science in the courtroom? *Maryland Law Review, 38,* 539–621.

Cooper, L. M., & London, P. (1973). Reactivation of memory by hypnosis and suggestion. *International Journal of Clinical and Experimental Hypnosis, 21,* 312–323.

Cottrell, N. B., Sekerak, A. J., Wack, D. L., & Rittle, R. H. (1968). Social facilitation of dominant responses by the presence of an audience and the mere presence of others. *Journal of Personality and Social Psychology, 9,* 245–250.

Covner, B. J. (1942). Studies in phonographic recordings of verbal material: I and II. *Journal of Consulting Psychology, 6,* 105–113, 149–153.

Craik, K. H. (1970). Environmental psychology. In R. Brown (Ed.), *New directions in psychology, Vol. 4.* New York: Holt, Rinehart & Winston.

Cratty, B. J. (1981). *Social psychology in athletics.* Englewood Cliffs, NJ: Prentice-Hall.

Cremin, L. A. (1961). *The transformation of the school.* New York: Knopf.

Cronbach, L. J. (1975). Five decades of public controversy over mental testing. *American Psychologist, 30,* 1–14.

Cronbach, L. J. (1977). *Educational psychology* (3rd ed.). New York: Harcourt Brace Jovanovich.

Cronbach, L. J., & Snow, R. E. (1977). *Aptitudes and instructional methods.* New York: Irvington.

Cuca, J. (1975, January). Clinicians compose 36 percent of APA. *APA Monitor,* 4.

Dane, F. C., & Wrightsman, L. S. (1982). Effects of defendants' and victims' characteristics on jurors' verdicts. In N. L. Kerr & R. M. Bray (Eds.), *The psychology of the courtroom.* New York: Academic.

Danet, B. (1980). Language in the legal process. *Law and Society Review, 14,* 445–564.

Davis, J. H., Kerr, H. L. Atkins, R., Holt, R., & Meek, D. (1975). The decision processes of 6- and 12-person mock juries assigned unanimous and 2/3 majority rules. *Journal of Personality and Social Psychology, 32,* 1–14.

Deitz, S. M., & Baer, D. M. (1982). *Is technology a dirty word?* Paper presented at the annual meeting of the Association for Behavior Analysis, Milwaukee, WI.

Dewey, J. (1896). The reflex arc concept in psychology. *The Psychological Review, 3,* 357–370.

Dewey, J. (1899). *The school and society.* Chicago, IL: The University of Chicago Press.

Dhanens, T. P., & Lundy, R. M. (1975). Hypnotic and waking suggestions and recall. *International Journal of Clinical and Experimental Hypnosis, 23,* 68–79.

Dipboye, R. L., Fromkin, H. L., & Wiback, K. (1975). Relative importance of applicant's sex, attractiveness, and scholastic standing in evaluation of job applicant resumes. *Journal of Applied Psychology, 60,* 39–43.

Dresser, H. W. (1924). *Psychology in theory and application.* New York: Crowell.

Drucker, P. F. (1972). School around the bend. *Psychology Today, 6,* 49–51, 86–89.

Dunbar, H. F. (1935). *Emotions and bodily changes: A survey of literature on psychosomatic interrelationships, 1910–1933.* New York: Columbia University Press.

Dunbar, H. F. (1947). *Mind and body: Psychosomatic medicine.* New York: Random.

Dunbar, H. F. (1954). *Emotions and bodily changes: A survey of literature on psychosomatic interrelationships, 1910–1953* (4th ed.). New York: Columbia University Press.

Dunnette, M. D. (1976). *Handbook of industrial and organizational psychology.* Chicago: Rand McNally.

Duquin, M. E. (1980). The dynamics of athletic persistence. In W. F. Straub (Ed.), *Sports psychology: An analysis of athletes' behavior.* Ithaca, NY: Mouvement.

D'Zurilla, T., & Goldfried, M. (1971). Problem solving and behavior modification. *Journal of Abnormal Psychology, 78,* 107–126.

Ebbinghaus, H. E. (1885). *Memory: A contribution to experimental psychology.* New York: Dover. (1964 reprint)

Ehrlich, N. J. (1972). *Psychology and contemporary affairs.* Monterey, CA: Brooks/Cole.

Ekman, P., & Friesen, W. (1974). Detecting deception from the body and face. *Journal of Personality and Social Psychology, 29,* 288–298.

Elder, J. P., Abrams, D. B., & Carleton, R. A. (1983). *Implications of a behavioral community perspective for behavior therapy: Utilizing community systems to effect clinical change.* Paper presented at the World Congress on Behavior Therapy, Washington, DC.

Ellis, A. (1977). The basic clinical theory of rational–emotive therapy. In A. Ellis & R. Grieger (Eds.), *Handbook of rational–emotive therapy.* New York: Springer.

Erdelyi, M. H., & Kleinbard, J. (1978). Has Ebbinghaus decayed with time? The growth of recall (hypermnesia) over days. *Journal of Experimental Psychology: Human Learning and Memory, 4,* 275–289.

Erikson, E. H. (1963). *Childhood and society* (2nd ed.). New York: Norton.

Evans, R. I., Rozelle, R. M., Mittlemark, M. B., Hansen, W. B., Bane, A. L., & Havis, J. (1978). Deterring the onset of smoking in children: Knowledge of immediate physiological effects and coping with peer pressure, media pressure and parent modeling. *Journal of Applied Social Psychology, 8,* 126–135.

Everett, P. B., Hayward, S. C., & Meyers, A. W. (1974). The effects of a token reinforcement procedure on bus ridership. *Journal of Applied Behavior Analysis, 7,* 1–9.

Eysenck, H. J. (1959). Learning theory and behavior therapy. *Journal of Mental Science, 195,* 61–75.

Eysenck, H. J., & Kamin, L. (1981). *The intelligence controversy.* New York: Wiley and Sons.

Fairweather, G. W. (1972). *Social change: The challenge to survival.* Morristown, NJ: General Learning Press.

Farquhar, J., Maccoby, N., Wood, P., Alexander, J., Breitrose, H., Brown, B., Haskell, W., McAlister, A., Meyer, A., Nash, J., & Stern, N. (June 4, 1977). Community education of cardiovascular health. *The Lancet,* 1192–1195.

Farquhar, J. W., Magnus, P. F., & Maccoby, N. (1981). The role of public information and education in cigarette smoking control. *Canadian Journal of Public Health, 72*, 412–420.

Farley, F. H., & Gordon, N. J. (Eds.). (1981). *Psychology and education: The state of the union.* Berkeley, CA: McCutchan.

Farrington, D. P., Hawkins, K., & Lloyd-Bostock, S. (1979). *Psychology, law and legal processes.* Atlantic Highlands, NJ: Humanities Press.

Featherstone, J. (1971). *Schools where children learn.* New York: Liveright.

Feimer, N. R., & Geller, E. S. (Eds.). (1983). *Environmental psychology: Directions and perspectives.* New York: Praeger.

Felner, R. D., Jason, L. A., Moritsugu, J. N., & Farber, S. S. (1983). *Preventive psychology: Theory, research and practice.* Elmsford, NY: Pergamon.

Ferdinand, T. C. (1966). *Typologies of delinquency: A critical analysis.* New York: Random House.

Ferguson, J. M., & Taylor, C. B. (Eds.). (1980). *The comprehensive handbook of behavioral medicine, Vols. 1–3.* Englewood Cliffs, NJ: Prentice-Hall.

Ferreira, A. E., & Rosen, M. (1982). Therapeutic relations in psychotherapy-psychoanalytic modality. In M. Lambert (Ed.), *A guide to psychotherapy and patient relationships.* Homewood, IL: Dow Jones-Irwin.

Ferster, C. B., & DeMyer, M. K. (1962). A method for the experimental analysis of the behavior of autistic children. *American Journal of Orthopsychiatry, 32*, 89–98.

Feuerstein, M., Labbé, E. E., & Kuczmierczyk, A. R. (1986). *Health psychology: A psycho-biological perspective.* New York: Plenum.

Fisher, J. D., Bell, P. A., & Baum, A. (1984). *Environmental psychology* (2nd Ed.). New York: Holt, Rinehart & Winston.

Fisher, A. C. (1976). *Psychology of sport: Issues & insights.* Palo Alto, CA: Mayfield.

Follick, M. J., Zitter, R. E., & Ahern, D. K. (1983). Failures in the operant treatment of chronic pain. In E. B. Foa, & P. Emmelkamp (Eds.), *Failure in behavior therapy.* New York: Wiley.

Fordyce, W. (1974). Treating chronic pain by contingency management. In J. Bonica (Ed.), *Advances in Neurology Vol. 4.* New York: Raven Press.

Fordyce, W. E., & Steger, J. C. (1979). Behavioral management of chronic pain. In J. Brady & O. Pomerleau (Eds.), *Behavioral medicine: Theory and practice.* Baltimore: Williams & Wilkins.

Foster, S., & Gurman, A. S. (1985). Family therapies. In S. J. Lynn & J. P. Garske (Eds.), *Contemporary psychotherapies.* Columbus, OH: Merrill.

Frank, J. D. (1961). *Persuasion and healing: A comparative study of psychotherapy.* Baltimore: Johns Hopkins Press.

Frank, J. D. (1978). *Psychotherapy and the human predicament.* New York: Schocken.

Franks, C. M. (1984a). Behavior therapy with children and adolescents. In G. T. Wilson, C. M. Franks, K. D. Brownell, & P. C. Kendall (Eds.), *Annual review of behavior therapy: Theory and practice. Vol. 9.* New York: Guilford.

Franks, C. M. (1984b). Behavior therapy with children and adolescents. In C. M. Franks, G. T. Wilson, P. C. Kendall, & K. D. Brownell (Eds.), *Annual review of behavior therapy: Theory and practice. Vol. 10.* New York: Guilford.

Franks, C. M., & Barbrack, C. R. (1983). Behavior therapy with adults. In M. Hersen, A. E. Kazdin, & A. S. Bellack (Eds.), *The clinical psychology handbook.* Elmsford, NY: Pergamon.

French, J. L. (1984). On the conception, birth, and early development of school psychology: With special reference to Pennsylvania. *American Psychologist, 39*, 976–987.

MAP—I

Freischlag, J., & Schmidke, C. (1980). Violence in sport: Its causes and some solutions. In W. F. Straub (Ed.), *Sports psychology: An analysis of athlete behavior*. Ithaca, NY: Mouvement.

Freud, S. (1950). Why war? In J. Strachey (Ed.), *Collected papers of Sigmund Freud* Vol. 5. London: Hogarth Press.

Friedlander, K. (1947). *The psychoanalytic approach to juvenile delinquency*. New York: International Universities Press.

Friedman, H. J. (1963). Patient expectancy and symptom reduction. *Archives of General Psychiatry, 8*, 61–65.

Friedman, M. (1977). Type A behavior: Some of its psychophysiological components. *Bulletin of the New York Academy of Medicine, 53*, 593–600.

Friedman, M., & Rosenman, R. H. (1974). *Type A behavior and your heart*. New York: Knopf.

Friedman, M., Thoresen, C. E., Gill, J. J., Powell, L. H., Ulmer, D., Thompson, L., Price, V. A., Rabin, D. D., Breall, W. S., Dixon, T., Levy, R., & Bourg, E. (1984). Alteration of Type A behavior and reduction in cardiac recurrences in postmyocardial infarction subjects. *American Heart Journal, 108*, 237–248.

Fryer, D. H., & Henry, E. R. (Eds.). (1950). *Handbook of applied psychology* (2 Vol). New York: Rinehart.

Fuhriman, A., & Barlow, S. H. (1982). Cohesion: Relationship in group therapy. In M. Lambert (Ed.), *A guide to psychotherapy and patient relationships*. Homewood, IL: Dow Jones-Irwin.

Gable, R. (1985). The resilient adolescent. In S. J. Apter, & A. P. Goldstein (Eds.), *Youth violence: Programs and prospects*. Elmsford, NY: Pergamon.

Gagné, R. M. (1977). *The conditions of learning* (3rd ed.). New York: Holt, Rinehart & Winston.

Gallway, W. T. (1974). *The inner game of tennis*. New York: Random House.

Gardner, W. I. (1969). Use of punishment with the severely retarded: A review. *American Journal of Mental Deficiency, 74*, 86–103.

Garfield, S. L., & Kurtz, R. (1976). A study of eclectic views. *Journal of Consulting and Clinical Psychology, 45*, 78–83.

Garske, J. P., & Lynn, S. J. (1984). Toward a general scheme for psychotherapy: Effectiveness, common factors, and integration. In S. J. Lynn & J. P. Garske (Eds.), *Contemporary psychotherapies*. Columbus, OH: Merrill.

Gelfand, D., & Hartman, D. (1978). Some detrimental effects of competitive sports on children's behavior. In R. Magil, M. Ash, & F. Small (Eds.), *Children in sport: A contemporary anthology*. Champaign, IL: Human Kinetics.

Geller, E. S. (1973). Prompting anti-litter behaviors [Abstract]. *Proceedings of the 81rst Annual Convention of the American Psychological Association, 8*, 901–902.

Geller, E. S. (1975). Increasing desired waste disposals with instruction. *Man–Environment Systems, 5*, 125–128.

Geller, E. S. (1980). Applications of behavior analysis for litter control. In D. Glenwick & L. Jason (Eds.), *Behavioral community psychology: Progress and prospects*. New York: Praeger.

Geller, E. S., Chaffee, J. L., & Ingram, R. E. (1976). Promoting paper recycling on a university campus. *Journal of Environmental Systems, 5*, 39–57.

Geller, E. S., Farris, J. C., & Post, D. S. (1973). Prompting a consumer behavior for pollution control. *Journal of Applied Behavior Analysis, 6*, 367–376.

Geller, E. S., Paterson, L., & Talbott, E. (1982). A behavioral analysis of incentive prompts for motivating seat belt usage. *Behavior Analysis, 15*, 403–415.

Geller, E. S., Winett, R. A., & Everett, P. B. (1982). *Preserving the environment: New strategies for behavior change.* Elmsford, NY: Pergamon.

Geller, E. S., Witmer, F., & Orebuth, A. L. (1976). Instructions as a determinant of paper disposal behaviors. *Environment and Behavior, 8*, 417–438.

Getzels, J. W., & Jackson, P. W. (1962). *Creativity and intelligence: Explorations with gifted students.* New York: Wiley.

Giaconia, R. M., & Hedges, L. V. (1982). Identifying features of effective open education. *Review of Educational Research, 52*, 579–602.

Gibbons, D. C. (1975). Offender typologies—two decades later. *British Journal of Criminology, 15*, 141–156.

Gill, D., & Martens, R. (1977). The role of task type and success-failure in group competition. *International Journal of Sports Psychology, 8*, 160–177.

Gill, J. J., Price, V. A., Friedman, M., Thoreson, C. E., Powell, L. H., Ulmer, D., Brown, B., & Drews, F. R. (1985). Reduction in Type A behavior in healthy middle-aged American military officers. *American Heart Journal, 110*, 503–514.

Gill, M. G., & Brennan, M. (1948). Research in psychotherapy. *American Journal of Orthopsychiatry, 18*, 100–110.

Glaser, D. (1972). *Adult crime and social policy.* Englewood Cliffs, NJ: Prentice-Hall.

Glasgow, R. E., & Rosen, G. M. (1978). Behavioral bibliotherapy: A review of self-help behavior therapy manuals. *Psychological Bulletin, 85*, 1–23.

Glass, D. C. (1977). *Behavior patterns, stress, and coronary disease.* Hillsdale, NJ: Erlbaum.

Glasser, W. (1965). *Reality therapy.* New York: Harper & Row.

Glenwick, D. (1982). Behavioral community psychology special interest group: Why we've changed our name. *Psychology Newsletter, 1*, 13–14.

Glueck, S., & Glueck, E. T. (1930). *Five hundred career criminals.* New York: Knopf.

Goldfried, M. (1982). *Converging themes in psychotherapy.* New York: Springer.

Goldiamond, I. (1974). Toward a constructional approach to social problems: Ethical and constitutional issues raised by applied behavior analysis. *Behaviorism, 2*, 1–84.

Goldschmid, M. L., Stein, D. D., Weismann, H. N. & Sorrels, J. (1969). A survey of the training and practices of clinical psychologists. *The Clinical Psychologist, 22*, 89–94.

Goldstein, A. G. (1977). The fallibility of the eyewitness: Psychological evidence. In B. D. Sales (Ed.), *Psychology in the legal process.* Englewood Cliffs, NY: Prentice-Hall.

Goldstein, A. P. (1959). *Therapist and client expectation of personality change and its relation to perceived change in psychotherapy.* Unpublished doctoral dissertation, Pennsylvania State University.

Goldstein, A. P. (1960). Therapist and client expectation of personality change in psychotherapy. *Journal of Counseling Psychology, 7*, 180–184.

Goldstein, A. P. (1962). *Therapist–patient expectancies in psychotherapy.* Elmsford, NY: Pergamon.

Goldstein, A. P. (1971). *Psychotherapeutic attraction.* Elmsford, NY: Pergamon.

Goldstein, A. P. (1973). *Structured learning therapy.* New York: Academic.

Goldstein, A. P. (1978). *Prescriptions for child mental health and education.* Elmsford, NY: Pergamon.

Goldstein, A. P. (1981). *Psychological skill training.* Elmsford, NY: Pergamon.

Goldstein, A. P. (1983). Behavior modification. In A. P. Goldstein (Ed.), *Prevention and control of aggression.* Elmsford, NY: Pergamon.

Goldstein, A. P., Apter, S. J., & Harootunian, B. (1983). School violence. Englewood Cliffs, NJ: Prentice-Hall.

Goldstein, A. P., & Heller, K. (1960). Role expectations, participant personality characteristics, and the client–counselor relationship. Unpublished manuscript.

Goldstein, A. P., & Kanfer, F. H. (1979). Maximizing treatment gains: Transfer enhancement in psychotherapy. New York: Academic.

Goldstein, A. P., Keller, H., & Erne, D. (1985). Changing the abusive parent. Champaign, IL: Research Press.

Goldstein, A. P., & Michaels, G. Y. (1985). Empathy: Development, training and consequences. Hillsdale, NJ: Erlbaum.

Goldstein, A. P., Monti, P. J., Sardino, T. J., & Green, D. J. (1979). Police crisis intervention. Elmsford, NY: Pergamon.

Goldstein, A. P. & Sorcher, M. (1974). Changing supervisor behavior. Elmsford, NY: Pergamon.

Goldstein, A. P., Sprafkin, R. P., & Gershaw, N. J. (1976). Skill training for community living. Elmsford, NY: Pergamon.

Goldstein, A. P., Sprafkin, R. P. Gershaw, N. J., & Klein, P. (1980). Skillstreaming the adolescent. Champaign, IL: Research Press.

Goldstein, A. P. & Stein, N. (1976). Prescriptive psychotherapies. Elmsford, NY: Pergamon.

Goldstein, J. H. (1983). Sports violence. New York: Springer-Verlag.

Goldstein, J. H., & Arms, R. L. (1971). Effects of observing athletic contests on hostility. Sociometry, 34, 83–90.

Goldstein, R. (1974). Brain research and behavior. Archives of Neurology, 1–18.

Goldston, S. E. (1981). Messages for preventionists. In G. W. Albee & J. M. Joffee (Eds.), Prevention through political action and social change. Hanover, NH: University Press of New England.

Golembiewski, R. T., & Blumberg, A. (1967). Confrontation as a training design in complex organizations. Journal of Applied Behavioral Science, 3, 525–547.

Goodall, K. (1972). Shapers at work. Psychology Today, 6, 53–63.

Goranson, R. E. (1970). Media violence and aggressive behavior: A review of experimental research. In L. Berkowitz (Ed.), Advances in experimental social psychology, Vol. 5. New York: Academic Press.

Gordon, R. (1968). A study in forensic psychology: Petit jury verdicts as a function of the number of jury members. Unpublished doctoral dissertation, University of Oklahoma.

Gottlieb, B. H. (1981). Social networks and social support. Beverly Hills, CA: Sage.

Gould, S. J. (1977). Ever since Darwin: Reflections in natural history. New York: Norton.

Gould, S. J. (1981). The mismeasure of man. New York: Norton.

Graubard, P., & Rosenberg, H. (1974). Classrooms that work: Prescriptions for change. New York: E. P. Dutton.

Gray, J. E. (Ed.). (1941). Psychology in use: A textbook in applied psychology. (2nd ed.). New York: American Book Co.

Green, E. (1961). Judicial attitudes in sentencing. New York: Macmillan.

Green, G. H. (1923). Some notes on smoking. International Journal of Psychoanalysis, 4, 323–324.

Greenberg, L. S. (1982). The relationship in Gestalt therapy. In M. Lambert (Ed.), A guide to psychotherapy and patient relationships. Homewood, IL: Dow Jones-Irwin.

Guerney, B. G., Jr. (1977). Relationship enhancement. San Francisco: Jossey-Bass.

Guthrie, E. R. (1944). Personality in terms of associative learning. In J. Mc V. Hunt (Ed.), *Personality and the behavior disorders*, Vol.1. New York: Ronald Press.

Guttmacher, M. S. (1960). *The mind of the murderer*. New York: Farrar.

Guttman, A. (1983). Roman sports violence. In J. H. Goldstein (Ed.), *Sports violence*. New York: Springer-Verlag.

Hagan, J. (1974). Extra-legal attributes and criminal sentencing: An assessment of a sociological viewpoint. *Law and Society Review*, *8*, 357–383.

Haigh, G. (1949). Defensive behavior in client-centered therapy. *Journal of Consulting Psychology*, *13*, 181–189.

Hakel, M. D., Ohnesorge, J. P., & Dunnette, M. D. (1970). Interviewer evaluations of job applicants resumes as a function of the qualifications of the immediately preceding applicant. An examination of contrast effects. *Journal of Applied Psychology*, *54*, 27–30.

Haley, J. (1973). *Uncommon therapy*. New York: Norton.

Halkides, G. (1958). *An experimental study of four conditions necessary for therapeutic change*. Unpublished doctoral dissertation, The University of Chicago.

Hall, E., & Purvis, G. (1980). The relationship of trait anxiety and state anxiety to competitive bowling. In W. F. Straub (Ed.), *Sport psychology: An analysis of athlete behavior*. Ithaca, NY: Mouvement.

Hall, G. S., Baird, J. W., & Geissler, L. R. (1917). Foreword. *Journal of Applied Psychology*, *1*, 5–7.

Hamburg, D. A. (1982). Health and behavior [editorial]. *Science*, *217*, 399.

Hannafin, M. J., & Witt, J. C. (1983). System intervention and the school psychologist: Maximizing interplay among roles and functions. *Professional Psychology*, *14*, 128–136.

Hawkins, C. (1962). Interaction rates of jurors aligned in factions. *American Sociological Review*, *27*, 689–691.

Hayes, S. C., & Cone, J. D. (1977). Reducing residential electrical energy use: Payments, information, and feedback. *Journal of Applied Behavior Analysis*, *10*, 425–435.

Heine, R. W., & Trosman, H. (1960). Initial expectations of the doctor–patient interaction as a factor in continuance in psychotherapy. *Psychiatry*, *23*, 275–278.

Heimstra, N. W., & McFarling, L. H. (1974). *Environmental psychology* (2nd ed.). Monterey, CA: Brooks/Cole.

Hellman, D., & Blackman, N. (1966). Enuresis, firesetting, and cruelty to animals: A triad predictive of adult crime. *American Journal of Psychiatry*, *122*, 1431–1435.

Hemphill, J. K., & Coons, A. E. (1957). Development of the Leader Behavior Description Questionnaire. In R. M. Stogdill & A. E. Coons (Eds.), *Leader behavior: Its description and measurement*. Columbus, OH: Ohio State University.

Henry, E. R. (1966). *Research conference on the use of autobiographical data as psychological predictors*. Greensboro, NC: The Creativity Research Institute.

Hersey, P., & Blanchard, K. H. (1969). Life cycle theory of leadership. *Training and Development Journal*, *28*, 26–34.

Hersey, P., & Blanchard, K. H. (1977). *Management of organizational behavior*. Englewood Cliffs, NJ: Prentice-Hall.

Herzberg, F., Mausner, B., & Snyderman, B. (1959). *The motivation to work*. New York: Wiley.

Highet, G. (1976). *The immortal profession: The joy of teaching and learning*. New York: Weybright and Talley.

Hilgard, E. R. (1948). *Theories of learning*. New York: Appleton-Century-Crofts.

Hilgard, E. R., & Bower, G. H. (1966). *Theories of learning*. New York: Appleton-Century-Crofts.

Hoehn-Saric, R., Frank, J. D., Imber, S. D., Nash, E. H., Stone, A. R., & Battle, C. C. (1964). Systematic preparation of patients for psychotherapy. I. Effects on therapy behavior and outcome. *Journal of Psychiatric Research, 2*, 267–281.

Hollien, H. (1980). Vocal indicators of psychological stress. In F. Wright, C. Bahn, & R. W. Rieber (Eds.), *Forensic psychology and psychiatry* (Annals of the New York Academy of Sciences, vol. 347). New York: New York Academy of Sciences.

Hollingworth, H. L. (1912). The influence of caffeine on mental and motor efficiency. *Psychological Bulletin, 9*, 78.

Hollon, S. D., & Beck, A. T. (1979). Cognitive therapy of depression. In P. Kendall & S. Hollon (Eds.), *Cognitive–behavioral interventions: Theory, research, and procedures*. New York: Academic.

Holzman, A. D., & Turk, D. C. (Eds.). (1985). *Pain management: A handbook of psychological treatment approaches*. Elmsford, NY: Pergamon.

Hornberger, R. H. (1959). The differential reduction of aggressive responses as a function of interpolated activities. *American Psychologist, 124*, 354.

Horsfall, J. S., Fisher, A. C., & Morris, H. H. (1980). Sports personality assessment: A methodological re-examination. In R. M. Suinn (Ed.) *Psychology in sports*. Minneapolis: Burgess.

Horvath, F. S. (1977). The effect of selected variables on interpretation of polygraph records. *Journal of Applied Psychology, 62*, 127–136.

Horwitz, R. A. (1979). Psychological effects of the "open classroom." *Review of Educational Research, 49*, 71–86.

Hudgins, B. B., Phye, G. D., Schau, C. G., Theisen, G. L., Ames, C., & Ames, R. (1983). *Educational psychology*. Itasca, IL: Peacock.

Hull, C. L. (1943). *Principles of behavior*. New York: Appleton.

Hunt, D. E. (1971). *Matching models in education: The coordination of teaching methods with student characteristics*. Toronto: Ontario Institute for Studies in Education.

Hunt, D. E., Greenwood, J., Brill, R., & Deineka, M. (1972). *From psychological theory to educational practice: Implementation of a matching model*. Paper presented at the meeting of the American Educational Research Association, Chicago.

Hunt, J. Mc.V., Ewing, T. N., LaForge, R., & Gilbert, W. M. (1959). An integrated approach to research on therapeutic counseling with samples of results. *Journal of Counseling Psychology, 6*, 46–54.

Hurd, G. S., Pattison, E. M., & Llamas, R. (1981). Models of social network intervention. *International Journal of Family Therapy, 3*, 246–257.

Husband, R. W. (1934). *Applied psychology*. New York: Harper.

Huxley, A. (1932). *Brave new world*. New York: Harper & Row.

Irwin, J. (1980). *Prisons in turmoil*. Boston: Little, Brown.

Iscoe, I. (1980). Foreword. In D. S. Blenwick & L. A. Jason (Eds.), *Behavioral community psychology: Progress and prospects*. New York: Praeger.

Ittelson, W. H., Proshansky, H. M., Rivlin, L. G., & Winkel, G. H. (1974). *An introduction to environmental psychology*. New York: Holt, Rinehart & Winston.

Jackson, P. W. (1968). *Life in classrooms*. New York: Holt, Rinehart & Winston.

Jacobson, N. S., & Bussod, N. (1983). Marital and family therapy. In M. Hersen, A. E. Kazdin, & A. S. Bellack (Eds.), *The clinical psychology handbook*. Elmsford, NY: Pergamon.

Jaffe, J. E. (1981). *Factors related to clinician's judgements of criminal responsibility*. Unpublished doctoral dissertation, Kent State University, Kent, OH.
James, R. (1959). Status and competence of jurors. *The American Journal of Sociology, 64,* 563–570.
Jeffrey, D. B., & Katz, R. C. (1977). *Take it off and keep it off: A behavioral program for weight loss and exercise.* Englewood Cliffs, NJ: Prentice-Hall.
Jeger, A. M., & Slotnick, R. S. (Eds.). (1981). *Community mental health: A behavioral–ecological perspective.* New York: Plenum.
Jenkins, R. L. (1943). Child relationships and delinquency and crime. In W. C. Ricklers (Ed.), The etiology of delinquent and criminal behavior [Special issue]. *Social Science Research Bulletin. 50.*
Jensen, A. R. (1972). *Genetics and education.* New York: Harper & Row.
Jensen, A. R. (1980). *Bias in mental testing.* New York: Free Press.
Joffe, J. M., & Albee, G. W. (Eds.) (1981). *Prevention through political action and social change.* Hanover, NH: University Press of New England.
Johnson, D. W., & Matross, R. P. (1977). Interpersonal influence in psychotherapy. In A. S. Gurman & A. M. Razin (Eds.), *Effective psychotherapy: A handbook of research.* Elmsford, NY: Pergamon.
Johnson, W. R. (1961). Body movement awareness in the nonhypnotic and hypnotic states. *Research Quarterly, 32,* 263–264.
Jones, R. A. (1977). *A modified basketball game: The effects of contingency management on competitive game behavior of girls attending a basketball camp.* Paper presented at the meeting of the Midwestern Association of Behavior Analysis, Chicago.
Kalven, H., & Zeisel, H. (1966). *The American jury.* Boston: Little, Brown.
Kanfer, F. H. (1965). Issues and ethics in behavior manipulation. *Psychological Reports, 16,* 187–196.
Karoly, P., & Steffan, J. (1980). *Improving the long-term effects of psychotherapy.* New York: Gardner Press.
Karpman, B. (1933). *Case studies in the psychopathology of crime.* New York: Mental Science Publishing.
Kazdin, A. E. (1977). *The token economy: A review and evaluation.* New York: Plenum.
Kazdin, A. E. (1978). *History of behavior modification: Experimental foundations of contemporary research.* Baltimore: University Park Press.
Kazdin, A. E. (1982). The token economy: A decade later. *Journal of Applied Behavior Analysis, 15,* 431–445.
Keefer, R., Goldstein, J. H., & Kasiary, D. (1983). In J. H. Goldstein (Ed.) *Sports violence.* New York: Springer-Verlag.
Keller, F. S. (1980). A vision of community development. In G. L. Martin & J. G. Osborne (Eds.), *Helping in the community: Behavioral applications.* New York: Plenum.
Kerr, N. L., & Bray, R. M. (1982). *The psychology of the courtroom.* New York: Academic.
Kirkley, B. G., Schneider, J. A., Agras, W. S., & Buchman, J. A. (1985). A comparison of two group treatments for bulimia. *Journal of Consulting and Clinical Psychology, 53,* 43–48.
Kirschenbaum, D. S., & Bale, R. M. (1980). Cognitive–behavioral skills in golf: Brain power golf. In R. M. Suinn (Ed.), *Psychology in sports.* Minneapolis, MN: Burgess.
Kistner, J. et al. (1982). Teacher popularity and contrast effects in a classroom token economy. *Journal of Applied Behavior Analysis, 15,* 85–96.

Klinger, E. (1969). Feedback effects and social facilitation of the vigilance performance: Mere coaction versus potential evaluation. *Psychonamic Science*, *14*, 161–162.

Knapp, M. L., Hart, R. P., & Dennis, H. S. (1974). An exploration of deception as a communication construct. *Human Communication Research*, *1*, 15–29.

Kolata, G. (1985). Obesity declared a disease. *Science*, *218*, 1019.

Komaki, J., & Barnett, F. T. (1983). A behavioral approach to coaching football. In G. L. Martin & D. Hrycaiko (Eds.), *Behavioral modification and coaching*. Springfield, IL: Charles C Thomas.

Korchin, S. J. (1976). *Modern clinical psychology*. New York: Basic Books.

Krasner, L. (1955). The use of generalized reinforcers in psychotherapy research. *Psychological Reports*, *1*, 19–25.

Krasner, L. (1962). The therapist as a social reinforcement machine. In H. H. Strupp & L. Luborsky (Eds.), *Research in psychotherapy*, Vol. 2. Washington, DC: American Psychological Association.

Krasner, L. (1965). The behavioral scientists and social responsibility: No place to hide. *Journal of Social Issues*, *21*, 9–30.

Krasner, L. (1971). Behavior therapy. In P. M. Mussen (Ed.), *Annual Review of Psychology*, Vol. 22, Palo Alto, CA: Annual Reviews.

Krasner, L. (1980). *Environmental design and human behavior: A psychology of the individual in society*. Elmsford, NY: Pergamon.

Krasner, L. (1983). The psychology of mystery. *American Psychologist*, *38*, 578–582.

Krasner, L. (1985). Learning theory applications in the environment. In B. L. Hammonds (Ed.), *Psychology and Learning: The master lecture series*, Vol. 4. Washington, DC: American Psychological Association.

Krasner, L., & Houts, A. A. (1984). A study of the "value" systems of behavioral scientists. *American Psychologist*, *39*, 840–350.

Krasner, L., & Ullmann, L. P. (Eds.). (1965). *Research in behavior modification: New developments and implications*. New York: Holt, Rinehart & Winston.

Krasner, L., & Ullmann, L. P. (1973). *Behavior influence and personality: The social matrix of human action*. New York: Holt, Rinehart & Winston.

Krasner, M. (1980). Environmental design in the classroom. In L. Krasner (Ed.), *Environmental design and human behavior*. Elmsford, NY: Pergamon.

Kretschmer, E. (1925). *Physique and character* (W. J. H. Sprott, Trans.). New York: Harcourt Brace Jovanovich.

Kristein, M. M. (1984). Variance and dissent: Forty years of U.S. cigarette smoking and disease and cancer mortality rates. *Journal of Chronic Disease*, *37*, 1–7.

Kristein, M., Arnold, C., & Wynder, E. (1977). Health economics and preventive care. *Science*, *195*, 457–462.

Kroes, W. H., Margolis, B., & Hurrell, J. J. (1974). Job stress in policemen. *Journal of Police Science & Administration*, *2*, 145–155.

Kroll, W. (1976). Current strategies and problems in personality assessment of athletes. In A. C. Fisher (Ed.), *Psychology of sport: Issues & insights*. Palo Alto, CA: Mayfield.

Kubis, J. (1973). *Comparison of voice analysis and polygraph as lie detection procedures*. Aberdeen Proving Ground, MD: U.S. Army Land Warfare Laboratory.

Kuhn, T. S. (1970). *The structure of scientific revolution* (2nd ed.). Chicago, IL: The University of Chicago Press.

Lahey, B. B., & Rubinoff, A. (1981). Behavior therapy in education. In L. Michelson, M. Hersen, & S. M. Turner (Eds.), *Future perspectives in behavior therapy*. New York: Plenum.

Lambert, M. J. (1982). *Psychotherapy and patient relationships*. Homewood, IL: Dow Jones-Irwin.

Landy, F. J. (1973). Another look at contrast effects in the employment interview. *Journal of Applied Psychology, 58*, 141–144.

Lane, J. F. (1980). Improving athletic performance through visuomotor behavior rehearsal. In R. M. Suinn (Ed.), *Psychology in sports*. Minneapolis, MN: Burgess.

Latane, B., & Darley, J. M. (1970). *The unresponsive bystander: Why doesn't he help?* New York: Appleton-Century-Crofts.

Lazarus, R. S., & Folkman, S. (1984). *Stress, appraisal, and coping*. New York: Springer.

Lefkowitz, J. (1977, May). Industrial-organizational psychology and the police. *American Psychologist*, 346–364.

Leifer, R. (1964). The psychiatrist and tests of criminal responsibility. *American Psychologist, 19*, 825–830.

Leippe, M. R., Wells, G. L., & Ostrom, T. M. (1978). Crime seriousness as a determinant of accuracy of eyewitness identification. *Journal of Applied Psychology, 63*, 345–351.

Lempert, R. D. (1975). Uncovering "nondiscernible" differences: Empirical research and the jury-size cases. *Michigan Law Review, 73*, 643–708.

Lennard, H. L., & Bernstein, A. (1960). *The anatomy of psychotherapy*. New York: Columbia University Press.

Lesieur, F. G. (1958). *The Scanlan Plan: A frontier in labor–management cooperation*. Cambridge, MA: MIT Industrial Relations Section.

Le Unes, A., & Nation, J. R. (1981). *Saturday's heroes: A psychological portrait of college football players*. Unpublished manuscript.

Levy, R. J. (1973). A method for identification of the high-risk police applicant. In J. R. Snibbe, & H. M. Snibbe (Eds.), *The urban policeman in transition*. Springfield, IL: Charles C Thomas.

Liberman, R. P., King, L. W., DeRisi, W. J., & McCann, M. (1975). *Personal effectiveness*. Champaign, IL: Research Press.

Lichtenstein, E., & Brown, R. A. (1982). Current trends in the modification of cigarette dependence. In A. S. Bellack, M. Hersen, & A. E. Kazdin (Eds.), *International handbook of behavior modification and therapy*. New York: Plenum.

Lind, E. A. (1982). The psychology of courtroom procedure. In N. L. Kerr & R. M. Bray (Eds.), *The psychology of the courtroom*. New York: Academic.

Lindesmith, A. R., & Dunham, H. W. (1941). Some principles of criminal typology. *Social Forces, 19*, 307–314.

Lindgren, H. C. (1980). *Education psychology in the classroom* (6th ed.). New York: Oxford University Press.

Lindner, R. M., & Selinger, R. V. (1947). *Handbook of correctional psychology*. New York: Philosophical Library.

Lindsley, O. R., Skinner, B. F., & Solomon, H. C. (1953). *Studies in behavior therapy* (Status report 1). Waltham, MA: Metropolitan State Hospital.

Lipkin, S. (1954). Clients' feelings and attitudes in relation to the outcome of client-centered therapy. *Psychological Monographs, 68*, No. 372.

Lipton, D., Martinson, R, & Wilks, J. (1975). *The effectiveness of correctional treatment*. New York: Praeger.

Locke, E. A. (1976). Nature and causes of job satisfaction. In M. D. Dunnette (Ed.), *Handbook of industrial and organizational psychology*. New York: Wiley Interscience.

Loew, C. A. (1967). Acquisition of a hostile attitude and its relationship to aggressive behavior. *Journal of Personality and Social Psychology, 5*, 335–337.

Loftus, E. F. (1975). Leading questions and the eyewitness report. *Cognitive Psychology*, 7, 560–572.

Loftus, E. F., & Palmer, J. C. (1974). Reconstruction of automobile destruction: An example of the interaction between language and memory. *Journal of Verbal Learning and Verbal Behavior*, 13, 585–589.

Logue, L. (1986). *The psychology of eating and drinking*. New York: Freeman.

Lorenz, K. (1966). *On aggression*. New York: Harcourt Brace Jovanovich.

Lorion, R. P. (1983). Evaluating preventive interventions: Guidelines for the serious social change agent. In R. D. Felner, L. A. Jason, J. N. Noritsugu, & S. S. Farber (Eds.), *Preventive psychology: Theory, research and practice*. Elmsford, NY: Pergamon.

Lovaas, O. I. (1968). Some studies on the treatment of childhood schizophrenia. In J. M. Schlien (Ed.), *Research in psychotherapy*. Washington, DC: American Psychological Association.

Luborsky, L., Singer, B., & Luborsky, L. (1975). Comparative studies in psychotherapy. *Archives of General Psychiatry*, 32, 995–1008.

Lutzker, J. R., & Martin, J. A. (1981). *Behavior change*. Monterey, CA: Brooks/Cole.

Luyben, P. D., & Bailey, J. F. (1976). Newspaper recycling: The effects of rewards and proximity of containers. *Environment and Behavior*, 11, 539–557.

Maccoby, N., Farquhar, J. W., Wood, P. D., & Alexander, J. (1977). Reducing the risk of cardiovascular disease: Effects of a community-based campaign on knowledge and behavior. *Journal of Community Health*, 3, 100–114.

Macgowan, K. (1928). Profiles: The adventure of the behaviorist. *The New Yorker*, 4, 30–32.

Magaro, P. A. (1969). A prescriptive treatment model based on social class and premorbid adjustment. *Psychotherapy: Theory, Research and Practice*, 6, 57–70.

Mahoney, M. J. (1976). *Scientist as subject: The psychological imperative*. Cambridge, MA: Ballinger.

Mahoney, M. J. (1984). Cognitive skills and athletic performance. In W. F. Straub, & J. M. Williams (Eds.), *Cognitive sports psychology*. Lansing, NY: Sports Science Associates.

Mahoney, M. J., & Mahoney, K. (1976). *Permanent weight control*. New York: Norton.

Mailer, N. (1984). *Tough guys don't dance*. New York: Random House.

Malpass, R. S., Devine, P. G. & Bergen, L. (1980). Realism and eyewitness identification research. *Law and Human Behavior*, 4, 347–357.

Mandler, G. (1980). Recognizing: The judgment of previous occurrence. *Psychological Review*, 87, 252–271.

Marcia, J., Rubin, B., & Effran, J. (1969). Systematic desensitization: Expectancy change or counter-conditioning. *Journal of Abnormal Psychology*, 74, 382–387.

Mark, M. M., Bryant, F. B., & Lehman, D. R. (1983). Perceived injustice and sports violence. In J. H. Goldstein (Ed.), *Sports violence*. New York: Springer-Verlag.

Marks, I. (1978). Behavioral psychotherapy of adult neurosis. In S. L. Garfield, & A. E. Bergin (Eds.), *Handbook of psychotherapy and behavior change*. New York: Wiley.

Marshall, J. (1968). *Intention in law and society*. New York: Minerva Press.

Martens, R. (1976). The paradigmatic crisis in American sport personology. In A. C. Fisher (Ed.), *Psychology of sport: Issues and insights*. Palo Alto, CA: Mayfield.

Martens, R., Landers, D. M., & Loy, J. (1980). *Sports cohesiveness questionnaire*. In A. V. Carron (Ed.), *Social psychology of sport*. Ithaca, NY: Mouvement.

Martens, R., & Peterson, J. A. (1976). Group cohesiveness as a determinant of success and member satisfaction in team performance. In A. C. Fisher (Ed.), *Psychology of sport: Issues & insights*. Palo Alto, CA: Mayfield.

Martin, G. L., & Hrycaiko, D. (1983). *Behavior modification and coaching*. Springfield, IL: Charles C Thomas.

Martin, G. L., LePage, R., & Koop, S. (1983). Applications of behavior modification for coaching age-group competitive swimmers. In G. L. Martin & D. Hrycaiko (Eds.), *Behavior modification and coaching*. Springfield, IL: Charles C Thomas.

Martin, G. L., & Osborne, J. G. (Eds.). (1980). *Helping in the community: Behavioral applications*. New York: Plenum.

Martin, J. E., & Dubbert, P. M. (1982). Exercise applications and promotion in behavioral medicine: Current status and future directions. *Journal of Consulting and Clinical Psychology*, 6, 1004–1017.

Maslow, A. H. (1954). *Motivation and personality*. New York: Harper & Row.

Maslow, A. H. (1970). *Motivation and personality* (2nd ed.). New York: Harper & Row.

Matarazzo, J. D. (1984). Behavioral health: A 1990 challenge for the health sciences professions. In J. D. Matarazzo, S. M. Weiss, J. S. Herd, & N. E. Miller (Eds.), *Behavioral health: A handbook of health enhancement and disease prevention*. New York: Wiley.

Matarazzo, J. D., Weiss, S. M., Herd, J. A., & Miller, N. E. (Eds.). (1984). *Behavioral health: A handbook of health enhancement and disease prevention*. New York: Wiley.

Matarazzo, J. M. (1980). Behavioral health and behavioral medicine: Frontiers for a new health psychology. *American Psychologist*, 35, 807–817.

Matarazzo, J. M. (1982). Behavioral health's challenge to academic, scientific, and professional psychology. *American Psychologist*, 37, 1–14.

Mayhew, K. C., & Edwards, A. C. (1936). *The Dewey school: The laboratory school of the University of Chicago*. New York: Appleton-Century.

Mayo, E. (1933). *The human problems of an industrial civilization*. New York: Harper & Row.

McCorkle, L., Elias, A., & Bixby, F. (1958). *The Highfields story: A unique experiment in the treatment of juvenile delinquency*. New York: Holt.

McGeoch, J. A. (1942). *The psychology of human learning*. New York: McKay.

McGuire, J., & Thomas, M. (1975). Effects of sex, competence and competition of sharing behavior in children. *Journal of Personality and Social Psychology*, 32, 490–494.

McKenzie, T. L., & Rushall, B. S. (1983). Effects of self-recording on attendance and performance in a competitive training environment. In G. L. Martin & D. Hyrcaiko (Eds.), *Behavior modification and coaching*. Springfield, IL: Charles C Thomas.

Megargee, E. I., & Bohn, M. J., Jr. (1979). *Classifying criminal offenders: A new system based on the MMPI*. Beverly Hills, CA: Sage.

Mehrabian, A. (1971). Nonverbal betrayal of feeling. *Journal of Experimental Research in Personality*, 5, 64–73.

Mehrabian, A., & Williams, M. (1969). Nonverbal concomitants of perceived and intended persuasiveness. *Journal of Personality and Social Psychology*, 13, 37–58.

Meichenbaum, D. (1985). Cognitive–behavioral therapies. In S. J. Lynn & J. P. Garske (Eds.), *Contemporary psychotherapies*. Columbus, OH: Merrill.

Meichenbaum, D., & Jaremko, M. E. (1983). *Stress reduction and prevention*. New York: Plenum.

Meichenbaum, D. H., & Turk, D. B. (1976). The cognitive-behavioral management of anxiety, anger, and pain. In P. O. Davidson (Ed.), *The behavioral management of anxiety, depression, and pain*. New York: Brunner/Mazel.

Meyer, A. J., & Henderson, J. B. (1974). Multiple risk factor reduction in the prevention of cardiovascular disease. *Prevention Medicine, 3*, 225–236.

Meyer, A. J., Nash, J. D., McAlister, A. L., Maccoby, N., & Farquhar, J. W. (1980). Skills training in a cardiovascular health education campaign. *Journal of Consulting & Clinical Psychology, 48*, 159–163.

Miller, L. K., & Miller, O. L. (1970). Reinforcing self-help group activities of welfare recipients. *Journal of Applied Behavior Analysis, 3*, 57–64.

Miller, N. E. (1979). Behavioral medicine. New opportunities but serious dangers. *Behavioral Medicine Update, 1*, 508.

Miller, N. E. (1984). Learning: Some facts and needed research relevant to maintaining health. In J. D. Matarazzo, S. M. Weiss, J. A. Herd, & N. E. Miller (Eds.), *Behavioral health: A handbook of health enhancement and disease prevention*. New York: Wiley.

Miller, R., & Berman, J. (1981). The efficacy of cognitive-behavior therapy: A quantitative review of the research evidence. Unpublished manuscript.

Miner, J. B. (1975). *The challenger of managing*. Philadelphia: Saunders.

Miner, J. B., & Brewer, J. F. (1976). Management of ineffective performance. In M. D. Dunnette (Ed.), *Handbook of industrial and organizational psychology*. New York: Wiley Interscience.

Mitchell, H. E. & Bryne, D. (1972). Minimizing the influence of irrelevant factors in the courtroom: The defendant's character, judge's instructions, and authoritarianism. Paper presented at the meeting of the Midwestern Psychological Association, Cleveland, OH.

Modgil, S., & Modgil, C. (Eds.). (1982). *Jean Piaget: Consensus and Controversy*. New York: Praeger.

Monahan, J. (1981). *The clinical prediction of violent behavior*. Rockville, MD: National Institute of Mental Health.

Monahan, J., & Loftus, E. F. (1982). The psychology of law. *Annual Review of Psychology, 33*, 441–475.

Moos, R. H. (1973). Conceptualizations of human environments. *American Psychologist, 28*, 652–665.

Moos, R. H., & Insel, P. (Eds.). (1974). *Issues in social ecology: Human milieus*. Palo Alto, CA: National Press Books.

Morawski, J. G. (1982). Assessing psychology's moral heritage through our neglected utopias. *American Psychologist, 37*, 1082–1095.

Morris, A. (1965). The comprehensive classification of adult offenders. *Journal of Clinical Law, Criminology, and Police Science, 56*, 197–202.

Morris, R. J., & Magrath, K. H. (1982). The therapeutic relationship in behavior therapy. In M. Lambert (Ed.), *A guide to psychotherapy and patient relationships*. Homewood, IL: Dow Jones-Irwin.

Morse, S. J. (1978). Law and mental health professionals: The limits of expertise. *Professional Psychology, 9*, 389–399.

Moses. J. (1980). Assessing the assessor. *Journal of Assessment Center Technology, 3*, 1–5.

Moskowitz, M. J. (1977). Hugo Munsterberg: A study in the history of applied psychology. *American Psychologist, 32*, 824–842.

Munsterberg, H. (1908). *On the witness stand: Essays on psychology and crime*. New York: Clark, Boardman.

Munsterberg, H. (1915). *Psychology: General and applied*. New York: Appleton.

National Advisory Committee on Criminal Justice Standards and Goals (1973). *Report on corrections*. Washington, DC: U.S. Department of Justice, Law Enforcement Assistance Administration.

Nideffer, R. M. (1976). The inner athlete: Mind plus muscle for winning. New York: Crowell.

Nideffer, R. M. (1980). The relationship of attention and anxiety to performance. In W. F. Straub (Ed.), *Sports psychology: An analysis of athlete behavior*. Ithaca, NY: Mouvement.

Nietzel, M. T., Winett, R. A., McDonald, M. L., & Davidson, W. S. (1977). *Behavioral approaches to community psychology*. Elmsford, NY: Pergamon.

Novaco, R. W. (1975). *Anger control*. Lexington, MA: Heath.

Nyquist, E. B., & Hawes, G. R. (Eds.). (1972). *Open education*. New York: Bantam.

O'Brien, R. M., Dickinson, A. M., & Rosow, M. F. (1982). *Industrial behavior modification*. Elmsford, NY: Pergamon.

O'Connor, W. A., & Lubin, G. (Eds.). (1984). *Community psychology comes of age: Distinctive theoretical frameworks*. New York: Wiley.

Ogilvie, B. C. (1976). Psychological consistencies within the personality of high-level competitors. In A. C. Fisher (Ed.), *Psychology of sport: Issues & insights*. Palo Alto, CA: Mayfield.

O'Leary, K. D., & Becker, W. C. (1968). The effects of a teacher's reprimands on children's behavior. *Journal of School Psychology, 1*, 3–11.

O'Leary, K. D., & Drabman, R. (1971). Token reinforcement programs in the classroom: A review. *Psychological Bulletin, 75*, 379–398.

O'Leary, K. D., & O'Leary, S. G. (1977). *Classroom management: The successful use of behavior modification* (2nd ed.). Elmsford, NY: Pergamon.

O'Leary, S. G., & O'Leary, K. D. (1976). Behavior modification in the school. In H. Leitenberg (Ed.), *Handbook of behavior modification and behavior therapy*. Englewood Cliffs, NJ: Prentice-Hall.

Orlick, T. (1978). *Winning through cooperation*. Washington, DC: Acropolis Books.

Orlick, T., & Botterill, C. (1975). *Every kid can win*. Chicago: Nelson-Hall.

Osborne, J. G., & Powers, R. B. (1980). Controlling the litter problem. In G. L. Martin & J. C. Osborne (Eds.), *Helping in the community: Behavioral applications*. New York: Plenum.

Ostrow, A. (1974). The aggressive tendencies of male intercollegiate tennis team players as measured by selected psychological tests. *New Zealand Journal of Health, Physical Education, and Recreation, 6*, 19–21.

Overall, B., & Aronson, H. (1962). Expectations of psychotherapy in lower socioeconomic class patients. *American Journal of Orthopsychiatry, 32*, 271–272.

Oxendine, J. B. (1980). Emotional arousal and motor performance. In R. M. Suinn (Ed.), *Psychology in sports*. Minneapolis, MN: Burgess.

Palazzoli-Selvini, M., Boscolo, L., Cecchin, & Prata, G. (1978). *Paradox and counterparadox: A new model in the therapy of the family in schizophrenic transactions*. New York: Aronson.

Palmer, M. H., Lloyd, M. E., & Lloyd, K. E. (1976). An experimental analysis of electricity conservation procedures. *Journal of Applied Behavior Analysis, 10*.

Palmer, T. (1978). Juvenile delinquency. In A. P. Goldstein (Ed.) *Prescriptions for child mental health and education*. Elmsford, NY: Pergamon.

Parloff, M. B. (1961). Therapist–patient relationship and outcome of psychotherapy. *Journal of Consulting Psychology*, 25, 29–38.

Parloff, M. B. (1976, February). Shopping for the right therapy. *Saturday Review*, pp. 14–16.

Parloff, M. B., Waskow, I. E., & Wolfe, B. E. (1978). Research on therapist variables in relation to process and outcome. In S. L. Garfield & A. E. Bergin (Eds.), *Handbook of psychotherapy and behavior change*. New York: Wiley.

Parsons, H. M. (July, 1979). Variables in human consequation/feedback. *Technical Report Number One*. Silver Springs, MD: Institute for Behavioral Research.

Patterson, A. (1974). Hostility catharsis: A naturalistic quasi-experiment. *Personality and Social Psychology Bulletin*, 1, 195–197.

Pavlov, I. P. (1928). *Lecture on conditioned reflexes*. (W. H. Gantt, trans.). New York: International Publishers.

Penrod, S., Loftus, E., & Winkler, J. (1982). The reliability of eyewitness testimony: A psychological perspective. In N. L. Kerr & R. M. Bray (Eds.), *The psychology of the courtroom*. New York: Academic Press.

Perloff, R. Craft, J. A., & Perloff, E. (1984). Testing and industrial applications. In G. Goldstein & M. Hersen (Eds.), *Handbook of psychological assessment*. Elmsford, NY: Pergamon.

Perry, M. A., & Furukawa, M. J. (1986). Modeling methods. In F. H. Kanfer & A. P. Goldstein (Eds.), *Helping people change* (3rd ed.). Elmsford, NY: Pergamon.

Pertschuk, M. (1982). *Revolt against regulation: The rise and pause of the consumer movement*. Berkeley, CA: University of California Press.

Phillips, E. L. (1982). *Stress, health and psychological problems in the major professions*. Washington, DC: University Press of America.

Piaget, J. (1926). *The language and thought of the child*. London: Routledge & Kegan Paul.

Piaget, J. (1981). *Intelligence and affectivity: Their relationship during child development*. Palo Alto, CA: Annual Reviews.

Piersel, W. C. & Gutkin, T. B. (1983). Resistance to school-based consultation: A behavioral analysis of the problem. *Psychology in the Schools*, 20, 311–320.

Plowden, L. (1967). *Children and their primary schools*. A report of the Central Advisory Council for Education (England), Vol. 1. New York: British Information Services.

Pomerleau, O. F. (1979). Behavioral medicine: The contribution of the experimental analysis of behavior to medical care. *American Psychologist*, 34, 654–663.

Pomerleau, O. F., & Brady, J. P. (1979). Introduction: The scope and promise of behavioral medicine. In O. F. Pomerleau & J. P. Brady (Eds.), *Behavioral medicine: Theory and practice*. Baltimore: Williams & Wilkins.

Pomerleau, O. F., & Pomerleau, C. S. (1984). Neuroregulators and the reinforcement of smoking. Towards a biobehavioral explanation. *Neuroscience and Biobehavioral Reviews*, 8, 503–513.

Pope, H. G., & Hudson, J. I. (1984). *New hope for binge eaters: Advances in the understanding and treatment of bulimia*. New York: Harper & Row.

Proctor, R. C., & Eckerd, W. M. (1976). "Toot-toot" or spectator sports: Psychological and therapeutic implications. *American Journal of Sports Medicine*, 4, 78–83.

Proshansky, H. M. (1976). Environmental psychology and the real world. *American Psychologist*, 31, 303–310.

Proshansky, H. M. (1980). Prospects and dilemmas of environmental psychology. In N. R. Feimer & E. S. Geller (Eds.), *Environmental psychology: Directions and perspectives*. New York: Praeger.

Proshansky, H. M., Ittelson, W. M., & Rivlin, L. G. (Eds.). (1970). *Environmental psychology: People and their physical settings.* New York: Holt, Rinehart & Winston.

Purcell, A. H. (February 1981). The world's trashiest people: Will they clean up their act or throw away their future? *The Futurist*, pp. 51–59.

Quay, H. C. (1964). Dimensions of personality of delinquent boys are inferred from factor analysis of case history data. *Child Development, 35*, 479–484.

Rachlin, H., & Logue, A. W. (1984). Learning. In M. Hersen, A. E. Kazdin, & A. S. Bellack (Eds.), *The clinical psychology handbook.* Elmsford, NY: Pergamon.

Rappaport, J. (1977). *Community psychology: Values, research and action.* New York: Holt, Rinehart & Winston.

Raskin, D. C., & Hare, R. D. (1978). Psychopathology and detection of deception in a prison population. *Psychophysiology, 15*, 126–136.

Raw, M. (1977). The psychological modification of smoking. In S. Rachman (Ed.), *Contributions to medical psychology. Vol. 12.* Elmsford, NY: Pergamon.

Reed, J. D. (1979). Rehearsal and recognition of human faces. *American Journal of Psychology, 92*, 71–85.

Reid, D. H., Luyben, P. L., Rawers, R. J., & Bailey, J. S. (1978). The effects of prompting and proximity of containers on newspaper recycling behavior. *Environment and Behavior, 8*, 471–483.

Reilly, R. R., Lewis, E. L., & Tanner, L. (1983). *Educational psychology.* New York: Macmillan.

Reis, H. T., & Jelsma, B. (1980). A social psychology of sex differences in sport. In W. F. Straub (Ed.), *Sport psychology: An analysis of athlete behavior.* Ithaca, NY: Mouvement.

Reynolds, D., & Sanders, M. (1973). *The effects of defendent attractiveness, age, and injury on severity of sentence given by simulated jurors.* Paper presented at the meeting of the Western Psychological Association, Anaheim, CA.

Rice, L. N. (1982). The relationship in client-centered therapy. In M. Lambert (Ed.), *A guide to psychotherapy and patient relationships.* Homewood, IL: Dow Jones-Irwin.

Rickel, A. V. (1984). Good beginnings have no end. President's Column, *Division of Community Psychology, 18*, 1–2.

Ricks, D. F. (1974). Supershrink: Methods of a therapist judged successful on the basis of adult outcomes of adolescent patients. In D. F. Ricks, M. Roff, & A. Thomas (Eds.), *Life history research in psychopathology.* Minneapolis: University of Minnesota.

Ritter, B. (1969). The use of contact desensitization, demonstrations plus participation, and demonstration alone in the treatment of acrophobia. *Behavior Research and Therapy, 7*, 157–164.

Roberts, T. B. (1975). *Four psychologies applied to education: Freudian, behavioral, humanistic, transpersonal.* New York: Wiley.

Roe, A. (1961). The psychology of the scientist, *Science, 134*, 456–459.

Roebuck, J. B. (1967). *Criminal typology: The legistic, physical-constitutional-hereditary, psychological-psychiatric and sociological approaches.* Springfield, IL: Charles C Thomas.

Roethlisberger, F. J., & Dickson, W. J. (1939). *Management and the worker: An account of a research program conducted by the Western Electric Company, Hawthorne Works, Chicago.* Cambridge, MA: Harvard University Press.

Rogers, C. R. (1942). *Counseling and psychotherapy.* Boston: Houghton Mifflin.

Rogers, C. R. (1951). *Client-centered therapy.* Boston: Houghton Mifflin.

Rogers, C. R. (1957). The necessary and sufficient conditions of therapeutic personality change. *Journal of Consulting Psychology, 21,* 95–103.

Rogers, C. R. (1969). *Freedom to learn.* Columbus, OH: Merrill.

Rogers, C. R., Gendlin, E. T., Kiesler, D. J., & Traux, C. B. (1967). *The therapeutic relationship and its impact.* Madison, WI: University of Wisconsin Press.

Rogers, R., & Cavanaugh, J. L. (1980). Differences in psychological variables between criminally responsible and insane patients: A preliminary study. *American Journal of Forensic Psychiatry, 1,* 29–37.

Rogers, R., & Cavanaugh, J. L. (1981). Rogers' criminal responsibility assessment scales. *Illinois Medical Journal, 160,* 164–169.

Rogers, R., Dolmetsch, R., & Cavanaugh, J. L. (1981). An empirical approach to insanity evaluations. *Journal of Clinical Psychology, 37,* 683–687.

Rogers, R., Seman, W., & Wasyliw, O. E. (1983). The RCRAS and legal insanity: A cross validation study. *Journal of Clinical Psychology, 39,* 554–559.

Rogers, R., Wasyliw, O. E., & Cavanaugh, J. L. (1984). Evaluating insanity: A study of construct validity. *Law and Human Behavior.*

Rogers, V. R. (1970). *Teaching in the British primary school.* New York: Macmillan.

Rohles, R. H. (1981). Thermal comfort and strategies for energy conservation. *Journal of Social Issues, 37,* 132–149.

Rose, T. L. (1981). The corporate punishment cycle: A behavioral analysis of the punishment in the schools. *Education and Treatment of Children, 4,* 157–169.

Rosen, H. (1985). *Piagetian dimensions of clinical relevance.* New York: Columbia University Press.

Rosenman, R. H. (1978). The interview method of assessment of the coronary-prone behavior pattern. In T. M. Dembroski, S. M. Weiss, J. L. Shields, S. C. Haynes, & M. Feinleib (Eds.), *Coronary-prone behavior.* New York: Springer-Verlag.

Rosenthal, R., & Jacobson, L. (1968). *Pygmalion in the classroom: Teacher expectation and pupils' intellectual development.* New York: Holt, Rinehart & Winston.

Rosenthal, D., & Frank, J. D. (1956). Psychotherapy and the placebo effect. *Psychological Bulletin, 53,* 294–302.

Roskies, E. (1980). Considerations in developing a treatment program for the coronary-prone (Type A) behavior patterns. In P. O. Davidson & S. M. Davidson (Eds.), *Behavioral medicine: Changing health life-styles.* New York: Brunner/Mazel.

Roskies, E., Spevack, M., Surkis, H., Cohen, C., & Gilman, S. (1978). Changing the coronary prone (Type A) behavior pattern in a nonclinical population. *Journal of Behavioral Medicine, 1,* 201–216.

Rothman, D. J. (1971). *The discovery of the asylum: Social order and disorder in the new republic.* Boston: Little, Brown.

Rowland, K. M., & Ferris, G. R. (1982). *Personnel management.* Boston: Allyn & Bacon.

Rubenfeld, J. B. (1965). *Family of outcasts: A new theory of delinquency.* New York: Macmillan.

Ruggles, T. R., & LeBlanc, J. M. (1982). Behavior analysis procedures in classroom teaching. In A. S. Bellack, M. Hersen, & A. E. Kazdin (Eds.), *International handbook of behavior modification and therapy.* New York: Plenum.

Rumsey, M. (1976). Effects of defendant background and remorse on sentencing judgments. *Journal of Applied Social Psychology, 6,* 64–68.

Rushall, B. S., & Siedentop, D. (1972). *The development and control of behavior in sport and physical education.* Philadelphia: Lea & Febiger.

Russell, G. W. (1981). Spectator moods at an aggressive sports event. *Journal of Sports Psychology, 3,* 217–227.

Russell, G. W. (1983). Crowd size and density in relation to athletic aggression and performance. *Social Behavior and Personality, 11,* 1.

Ryan, E. D. (1968). The cathartic effect of vigorous motor activity on aggressive behavior. *Research Quarterly, 41,* 542–551.

Ryan, E. D. (1976). Perceptual characteristics of vigorous people. In A. C. Fisher (Ed.), *Psychology of sport: Issues & insights.* Palo Alto, CA: Mayfield.

Rynes, S. L., Heneman, H. G., III, & Schwab, D. P. (1980). Individual reactions to organizational recruiting: A review. *Personnel Psychology, 33,* 529–542.

Saks, M. J. (1977). *Jury verdicts.* Lexington, MA: Lexington Books.

Saks, M. J. (1982). Innovation and change in the courtroom. In N. L. Kerr & R. M. Bray (Eds.), *The psychology of the courtroom.* New York: Academic.

Sandell, J. A. (1981). An empirical study of negative factors in brief psychotherapy. Unpublished doctoral dissertation, Vanderbilt University, Nashville, TN.

Sanford, R. N. (1947). A psychoanalytic study of three criminal types. *Journal of Criminal Psychopathology, 5,* 57–68.

Sarason, S. B. (1972). *The creation of setting and the future societies.* San Francisco: Jossey-Bass.

Sarason, S. (1981a). An asocial psychology and a misdirected psychology. *American Psychologist, 36,* 827–836.

Sarason, S. (1981b). *Psychology misdirected.* New York: Free Press.

Sarason, S. B. (1982). *The culture of the school and the problem of change* (2nd ed.) Boston: Allyn & Bacon.

Sarason, S. B. (1983). *Schooling in America: Scapegoat and salvation.* New York: Free Press.

Sarason, S. B. (1985). The school as a social situation. *Annual Review of Psychology, 36,* 115–140.

Savitsky, J., & Sim, M. (1974). Trading emotions: Equity theory of reward and punishment. *Journal of Communication, 24,* 140–147.

Schacter, S. (1977). Nicotine regulation in heavy and light smokers. *Journal of Experimental Psychology: General, 106,* 5–12.

Schacter, S. (1979). Regulation, withdrawal, and nicotine addiction. In N. A. Krasnegor (Ed.), *Cigarette smoking as a dependence process* (NIDA Research Monograph 23, DHEW Publication No. (ADM) 79–8000). Washington, DC: U.S. Government Printing Office.

Schofield, W. (1964). *Psychotherapy: The purchase of friendship.* Englewood Cliffs, NJ: Prentice-Hall.

Schofield, W. (1979). The role of psychology in the delivery of health services. *American Psychologist, 24,* 565–584.

Schutz, W. C. (1958). *FIRO: A three dimensional theory of interpersonal behavior.* New York: Holt, Rinehart & Winston.

Schwartz, G. E. (1982). Testing the biopsychosocial model: The ultimate challenge facing behavioral medicine. *Journal of Consulting and Clinical Psychology, 50,* 1040–1053.

Schwartz, G. E., & Weiss, S. M. (1978a). Yale Conference on behavioral medicine: A proposed definition and statement of goals. *Journal of Behavioral Medicine, 1,* 3–12.

Schwartz, G. E., & Weiss, S. M. (1978b). Behavioral medicine revisited: An amended definition. *Journal of Behavioral Medicine, 1,* 249–251.

Schwitzgebel, R. L., & Schwitzgebel, R. K. (1980). *Law and psychological practice.* New York: Wiley.

Scott, W. D. (1903). The theory of advertising: A simple exposition of the principles of psychology in their relation to successful advertising. Boston: Small, Maynard.

Scott, W. D. (1908). Psychology of advertising. Boston: Small, Maynard.

Selye, H. (1956). The stress of life. New York: McGraw-Hill.

Sheldon, W. H., Hartle, M., & McDermott, E. (1949). Varieties of delinquent youth. New York: Harper & Row.

Sherman, A. R. (1979). In vivo therapies for phobic reactions, instrumental behavior problems, and interpersonal and communications problems. In A. P. Goldstein & F. H. Kanfer (Eds.) Maximizing treatment gains: Transfer enhancement in psychotherapy. New York: Academic.

Sherman, J. A. (1965). Use of reinforcement and imitation to reinstate verbal behavior in mute psychotics. Journal of Abnormal Psychology, 70, 155–164.

Silberman, C. E. (1970). Crisis in the classroom. New York: Random House.

Singer, J. E., & Baum, A. (1980). Stress, environment, and environmental stress. In N. R. Feimer & E. S. Geller (Eds.), Environmental psychology: Directions and perspectives. New York: Praeger.

Singer, J. E., & Krantz, D. S. (1982). Perspectives on the interface between psychology and public health. American Psychologist, 37, 955–960.

Singer, R. N. (1972). Coaching, athletics, and psychology. New York: McGraw-Hill.

Sipes, R. G. (1973). War, sports and aggression: An empirical test of two rival theories. American Anthropologist, 75, 64–86.

Skinner, B. F. (1938). The behavior of organisms. New York: Appleton-Century-Crofts.

Skinner, B. F. (1948). Walden two. New York: Macmillan.

Skinner, B. F. (1953). Science and human behavior. New York: Macmillan.

Skinner, B. F. (1982). Why are we not acting to save the world? Invited Address, 90th Annual Convention, American Psychological Association, Washington, DC.

Skinner, B. F. (1983, September). A cure for American education. Psychology Today, pp. 22–33.

Slobogin, J. D., Melton, G. B. & Showalter, C. R. (1984). The feasibility of a brief evaluation of mental state at the time of the offense. Unpublished manuscript.

Smith, M. C. (1983). Hypnotic memory enhancement of witnesses: Does it work? Psychological Bulletin, 94, 387–407.

Smith, M. D. (1980). Hockey violence: Interring some myths. In W. F. Straub (Ed.), Sport psychology: An analysis of athlete behavior. Ithaca, NY: Mouvement.

Smith, M. D. (1983). What is sports violence? A sociological perspective. In J. H. Goldstein (Ed.), Sports violence. New York: Springer-Verlag.

Smith, M. L., Glass, G. V., & Miller, T. I. (1980). The benefits of psychotherapy. Baltimore: Johns Hopkins University Press.

Smith, S. M. (1979). Remembering in and out of context. Journal of Experimental Psychology: Human Learning and Memory, 5, 468–471.

Smykla, J. O. (1984). Probation and parole. New York: Macmillan.

Snyder, W. U. (1945). An investigation of the nature of nondirective psychotherapy. Journal of Genetic Psychology, 13, 193–223.

Socolow, R. H. (1978). Saving energy in the home. Cambridge: MA: Ballinger.

Sommer, R. (1969). Personal space: The behavioral bases for design. Englewood Cliffs, NJ: Prentice-Hall.

Staats, A. W., Minke, K. A., Finley, J. R., Wolf, M., & Brooks, L. O. (1964). A reinforcer system and experimental procedure for the laboratory study of reading acquisition. Child Development, 35, 209–231.

Staats, A. W., Staats, C. K., Schutz, R. E., & Wolf, M. M. (1962). The conditioning of textual responses using "extrinsic" reinforcers. *Journal of Experimental Analysis of Behavior, 5*, 33–40.

Stahmann, R. F., & Harper, J. M. (1982). Therapist–patient relationships in marital and family therapy. In M. Lambert (Ed.), *A guide to psychotherapy and patient relationships*. Homewood IL: Dow Jones-Irwin.

Stanton, M. D., & Todd, T. C. (1979). Structural family therapy with drug addicts. In E. Kaufman & P. Kaufman (Eds.), *The family therapy of drug and alcohol abuse*. New York: Gardner.

Stephens, T. M. (1976). *Directive teaching of children with learning and behavioral handicaps*. Columbus, OH: Merrill.

Stern, G. G. (1970). *People in context: Measuring person-environment congruence in business and industry*. New York: Wiley.

Stern, P. C., & Gardner, G. T. (1981). Psychological research and energy policy. *American Psychologist, 36*, 329-342.

Sternthal, B., & Craig, G. S. (1982). *Consumer behavior: An information-processing perspective*. Englewood Cliffs, NJ: Prentice-Hall.

Stokols, D., Novaco, R. W., Stokols, J., & Campbell, J. (1978). Traffic congestion, type A behavior, and stress. *Journal of Applied Psychology, 63*, 467–480.

Stone, G. C. (1979). A specialized doctoral program in health psychology: Considerations in its evolution. *Professional Psychology, 10*, 596–604.

Stone, G. C., Cohen, F., & Adler, N. E. (1979). *Health psychology: A handbook*. New York: Jossey Bass.

Stotland, E., & Berberich, J. (1979). The psychology of the police. In H. Toch (Ed.), *Psychology of crime and criminal justice*. New York: Holt, Rinehart & Winston.

Straub, W. F. (1980). *Sports psychology: An analysis of athlete behavior*. Ithaca, NY: Mouvement.

Straub, W. F., & Williams, J. M. (1984). *Cognitive sports psychology*. Lansing, NY: Sport Science Associates.

Strupp, H. H. (1977). A reformulation of the dynamics of the therapist's contribution. In A. S. Gurman & A. M. Razin (Eds.), *Effective psychotherapy: A handbook of research*. Elmsford, NY: Pergamon.

Strupp, H. H. (1982). Foreword. In M. R. Goldfried (Ed.), *Converging themes in psychotherapy*. New York: Springer.

Stuart, R. B. (1978). *Act thin, stay thin*. New York: Norton.

Stuart, R. B. (Ed.). (1982). *Adherence, compliance and generalization in behavioral medicine*. New York: Brunner/Mazel.

Suggs, D., & Sales, B. D. (1978). The art and science of conducting the voir dire. *Professional Psychology, 9*, 367–388.

Suinn, R. M. (1975). The cardiac stress management program for Type A patients. *Cardiac Rehabilitation, 5*, 13.

Suinn, R. M. (1976). Visuo-motor behavior rehearsal for adaptive behavior. In J. D. Krumbottz & C. E. Thoreson (Eds.), *Counseling methods*. New York: Holt, Rinehart & Winston.

Suinn, R. M. (1980a). Body thinking: Psychology for olympic champs. In R. M. Suinn (Ed.), *Psychology in sports*. Minneapolis: Burgess.

Suinn, R. M. (1980b). Psychology and sports performance: Principles and applications. In W. F. Straub (Ed.), *Sports psychology: An analysis of athlete behavior*. Ithaca, NY: Mouvement.

Sully, J. (1885). *Outline of psychology with special reference to the theory of education*. New York: Appleton.

Sulzer-Azaroff, B., & De Santamaria, M. C. (1980). Industrial safety hazard reduction through performance feedback. *Journal of Applied Behavior Analysis, 13,* 287–295.

Sulzer-Azaroff, G. (1982). Behavioral approaches to occupational health and safety. In L. W. Frederiksen (Ed.), *Handbook of organizational behavior management.* New York: Wiley.

Suppes, P. (1964). Modern learning theory and the elementary school curriculum. *American Educational Research Journal, 1,* 79–93.

Suppes, P. C. (Ed.). (1978). *Impact of research on education: Some case studies.* Washington, DC: National Academy of Education.

Sutherland, E. H. (1939). *Principles of criminology.* Philadelphia: Lippincott.

Sykes, G. M. (1958). *The society of captives.* Princeton, NJ: Princeton University Press.

Takanishi, R., DeLeon, P. H., & Pollak, M. S. (1983). Psychology and education: A continuing productive partnership. *American Psychologist, 38,* 996–1000.

Tapp, J. L. (1977). Psychology and law: A look at the interface. In D. B. Sales (Ed.), *Psychology in the legal process.* Englewood Cliffs, NJ: Prentice-Hall.

Tapp, J. L., & Kohlberg, L. (1977). Developing senses of law and legal justice. In J. L. Tapp & F. J. Levine (Eds.), *Law, justice and the individual in society.* New York: Holt, Rinehart & Winston.

Tapp, J. L., & Levine, F. J. (1977). *Law, justice, and the individual in society.* New York: Holt, Rinehart & Winston.

Telch, M. J., Killen, J. D., McAlister, A. L., Perry, C. L., & Maccoby, N. (1982). Long-term follow-up of a pilot project on smoking prevention with adolescents. *Journal of Behavioral Medicine, 5,* 1–8.

Thelen, M. H., & Fry, R. A. (1981). The effects of modeling and selective attention on pain tolerance. *Journal of Behavior Therapy and Experimental Psychiatry, 12* (3), 225–229.

Thomas, D. R., Becker, W. C., & Armstrong, M. (1968). Production and elimination of disruptive classroom behavior by systematically varying teachers' behavior. *Journal of Applied Behavior Analysis, 8,* 53–57.

Thoreson, C. E., Friedman, M., Gill, J. K., & Ulmer, D. K. (1982). The recurrent coronary prevention project: Some preliminary findings. *Acta Medica Scandinavia, 660,* 172–192.

Thorndike, E. L. (1906). *The principles of teaching based on psychology.* New York: Seiler.

Thorndike, E. L. (1903). *Educational psychology.* New York: Lemcke and Buechmen.

Thorndike, E. L. (1931). *Human learning.* New York: Century.

Titley, R. W. (1980). The loneliness of a long-distance kicker. In R. M. Suinn (Ed.), *Psychology in sports.* Minneapolis: Burgess.

Toch, H. (1979). *Psychology of crime and criminal justice.* New York: Holt, Rinehart & Winston.

Tollinton, H. J. (1973). Initial expectations and outcome. *British Journal of Medical Psychology, 46,* 251–257.

Tomkins, S. S. (1966). Psychological model for smoking behavior. *American Journal of Public Health, 12,* 17–20.

Triplett, N. (1898). The dynamogenic factors in pace-making and competition. *American Journal of Psychology, 9,* 507–533.

Turk, D. C., Meichenbaum, D. H., & Berman, W. H. (1979). Application of biofeedback for the regulation of pain: A critical review. *Psychological Bulletin, 86,* 1322–1338.

Turk, D. C., & Meichenbaum, D. (1984). A cognitive–behavioral approach to pain management. In P. D. Wall, & R. Melzack (Eds.), *Textbook of pain*. London: Churchill Livingstone.

Tutko, T. A., & Richards, J. W. (1971). *Psychology of coaching*. Boston: Allyn & Bacon.

Ullmann, L. P., & Krasner, L. (Eds.). (1965). *Case studies in behavior modification*. New York: Holt, Rinehart & Winston.

Vamplew, W. (1983). Unsporting behavior: The control of football and horse-racing crowds in England, 1875–1914. In J. H. Goldstein (Ed.), *Sports violence*. New York: Springer-Verlag.

Vander Veen F. (1965). Effects of the therapist and the patient on each other's therapeutic behavior. *Journal of Consulting Psychology*, 29, 19–26.

Vorrath, H. H. & Brendtro, L. K. (1974). *Positive peer culture*. Chicago: Aldine.

Wahba, M. A., & Birdwell, L. B. (1976). Maslow reconsidered: A review of research on the need hierarchy theory. *Organizational Behavior and Human Performance*, 15, 212–240.

Walker, J. W. (1980). *Human resource planning*. New York: McGraw–Hill.

Warren, M. Q. (1974). *Differential intervention with juvenile delinquents*. Paper presented at the meeting of the Juvenile Justice Standards Conference, American Bar Association, Berkeley, CA.

Warren, M. Q. (1976). Interventions with juvenile delinquents. In M. Rosenheim (Ed.), *Pursuing justice for the child*. Chicago: The University of Chicago Press.

Watson, J. B. (1919). *Psychology from the standpoint of a behaviorist*. Philadelphia: Lippincott.

Watson, J. B. (1929, June). Should a child have more than one mother? *Liberty*.

Webb, H. (1969). Professionalization of attitudes toward play among adolescents. In G. S. Kenyon (Ed.), *Sociology of sport*. Chicago: Athletic Institute.

Webster's new collegiate dictionary. (1977). Springfield, MA: G. & C. Merriam.

Weinberg, R. S., Seabourne, T. G., & Jackson, A. (1983). Effects of visuo-motor behavioral rehearsal, relaxation, and imagery on karate performance. In G. L. Martin & D. Hrycaiko (Ed.), *Behavior modification and coaching*. Springfield, IL: Charles C Thomas.

Weinberg, S. K. (1952). *Society and personality disorders*. Englewood Cliffs, NJ: Prentice-Hall.

Weiss, L., Katzman, M., & Wolchik, S. (1986). *Treating bulimia: A psychoeducational approach*. Elmsford, NY: Pergamon.

Weiss, S. M. (1981). Behavioral medicine in the U.S.: Research, clinical, and training opportunities. *International Journal of Mental Health*, 9, 182–195.

Wells, G. L., Leippe, M. R. & Ostrom, T. M. (1979). Guidelines for empirically assessing the fairness of a lineup. *Law and Human Behavior*, 3, 285–293.

Wenz, B. J., & Strong, D. J. (1980). An application of biofeedback and self-regulation procedures with superior athletes. In R. M. Suinn (Ed.), *Psychology in sports*. Minneapolis: Burgess.

Wexley, K. N., Sanders, R. E., & Yukl, G. A. (1973). Training interviewers to eliminate contrast effects in employment interview. *Journal of Applied Psychology*. 57, 233–236.

White, M. A. (1975). Natural rates of teacher approval and disapproval in the classroom. *Journal of Applied Behavior Analysis*, 8, 367–372.

Wicker, A. W. (1979). Ecological psychology: Some recent and prospective developments. *American Psychologist*, 34, 755–765.

Willems, E. P. (1974). Behavioral technology and behavioral ecology. *Journal of Applied Behavior Analysis*, 7, 151–165.

Wilson, G. T., & Evans, I. M. (1977). The therapist–client relationship in behavior therapy. In A. S. Gurman & A. M. Razin (Eds.), *Effective psychotherapy*. Elmsford, NY: Pergamon.

Winett, R. A. (1984). Echobehavioral assessment in health lifestyles. In P. Karoly (Ed.), *Measurement strategies in health psychology*. New York: Wiley.

Winett, R. A., Hatcher, J., Leckliter, I., Fort, T. R., Fishback, J. F., & Riley, A. (1981). Modifying perceptions of comfort and electricity used for heating by social learning strategies: Residential field experiments. *Ashrae Transactions*, *87*.

Winett, R. A., & Neale, M. S. (1979). Psychological framework for energy conservation in buildings: Strategies, outcomes and directions. *Energy and Buildings*, *2*, 101–116.

Winett, R. A., Neale, M. S., & Grier, A. C. (1981). The effects of self-monitoring and feedback on residential electricity consumption. *Journal of Applied Behavior Analysis*, *12*, 173–184.

Winett, R. A., & Winkler, R. C. (1972). Current behavior modification in the classroom: Be still, be quiet, be docile. *Journal of Applied Behavior Analysis*, *5*, 499–504.

Winick, C. (1979). The psychology of the courtroom. In H. Toch (Ed.), *Psychology of crime and criminal justice*. New York: Holt, Rinehart & Winston.

Winkler, R. C. (1971). Reinforcement schedules for individual patients in a token economy. *Behavioral Therapy*, *2*, 534–547.

Winkler, R. C., & Winett, R. A. (1982). Behavioral interventions in resource conservation: A systems approach based on behavioral economics. *American Psychologist*, *38*, 421–435.

Wohlwill, J. F. (1970). The emerging discipline of environmental psychology. *American Psychologist*, *25*, 303–312.

Wolfe, D. (1946). The reorganized American Psychological Association. *American Psychologist*, *1*, 3–6.

Wolpe, J. (1958). *Psychotherapy by reciprocal inhibition*. Stanford, CA: Stanford University Press.

Wysocki, T., Hall, G., Iwata, B., & Riordan, M. (1979). Behavioral management of exercise: Contracting for aerobic points. *Journal of Applied Behavior Analysis*, *12*, 55–64.

Yalom, I. D., & Lieberman, M. A. (1971). A study of encounter group casualties. *Archives of General Psychiatry*, *25*, 16–30.

Yarmey, A. D. (1979). *The psychology of eyewitness testimony*. New York: Free Press.

Youngblood, D., & Suinn, R. M. (1980). A behavioral assessment of motivation. In R. M. Suinn (Ed.), *Psychology in sports*. Minneapolis: Burgess.

Zajonc, R. B. (1976). Social facilitation. In A. C. Fisher (Ed.), *Psychology of sport: Issues & insight*. Palo Alto, CA: Mayfield.

Zikmund, W. G., Hitt, M. A., & Pickens, B. A. (1978). Influence of sex and scholastic performance on reactions to job applicant resumes. *Journal of Applied Psychology*, *63*, 252–254.

Zillmann, D., Bryant, J., & Sapolsky, B. S. (1979). The enjoyment of watching sport contests. In J. H. Goldstein (Ed.), *Sports, games, and play*. Hillsdale, NJ: Erlbaum.

PERMISSIONS

The following publishers have given permission for material quoted in this book:

Excerpts from: "Toward a General Scheme for Psychotherapy: Effectiveness, Common Factors, and Integration" by J. P. Garske and S. J. Lynn in *Contemporary Psychotherapies* (pp. 502–503, 505, 507) edited by S. J. Lynn and J. P. Garske, 1984, Columbus, OH: Merrill Publishing Company. Copyright 1984 by Merrill.

Excerpts from: *Classifying Criminal Offenders: A New System Based on the MMPI* (pp. 82–83) by E. I. Megargee and M. J. Bohn, Jr., 1979, Beverly Hills, CA: Sage Publications. Copyright 1979 by Sage.

Author Index

Subject Index

About the Authors

Arnold P. Goldstein, PhD (Pennsylvania State University, 1959) has spent his career as researcher and practitioner in a diversity of applied psychological settings—clinical, educational, industrial, and correctional. He joined the Clinical Psychology section of Syracuse University's Psychology Department in 1963, and taught there and directed its Psychotherapy Center until 1980. In 1981, he founded the Center for Research on Aggression, which he currently directs, and in 1985 moved to Syracuse University's Division of Special Education. Professor Goldstein has a career-long interest in difficult-to-reach clients. Since 1980, his main research and psychoeducational focus has been incarcerated juvenile offenders and child-abusing parents. He is the developer of Structured Learning, a psychoeducational program and curriculum designed to teach prosocial behaviors to chronically antisocial persons. Professor Goldstein's books include *Psychotherapy and the Psychology of Behavior Change*, *Psychotherapeutic Attraction*, *Changing Supervisor Behavior*, *Structured Learning Therapy: Toward a Psychotherapy for the Poor*, *Skill Training for Community Living*, *Skillstreaming the Adolescent*, *School Violence*, *Aggress-Less*, *Police Crisis Intervention*, *Hostage*, *Prevention and Control of Aggression*, *Aggression in Global Perspective*, *In Response to Aggression*, and *Aggression Replacement Training*.

Leonard Krasner is Clinical Professor of Psychiatry and Behavioral Sciences at Stanford University and Professor Emeritus at the State University of New York at Stony Brook. He received his PhD in Psychology from Columbia University. He has been, and continues to be, involved in a wide range of research in and applications of psychology, including behavior modification, behavior therapy, environmental design, token economy, "abnormal" behavior, health behavior, clinical psychology, and issues of values in science.

Pergamon General Psychology Series

Editors: Arnold P. Goldstein, Syracuse University
Leonard Krasner, SUNY at Stony Brook

*Out of print in original format. Available in custom reprint edition